BASIC SPEECH

BASIC
SPEECH

Second Edition

JON EISENSON

PROFESSOR OF SPEECH PATHOLOGY AND AUDIOLOGY
STANFORD UNIVERSITY

PAUL H. BOASE

PROFESSOR OF SPEECH
OHIO UNIVERSITY

The Macmillan Company, New York
Collier-Macmillan Limited, London

To
F. F. E. and M. B.

SIXTH PRINTING, 1967

Library of Congress catalog card number: 64-16047

THE MACMILLAN COMPANY, NEW YORK
COLLIER-MACMILLAN CANADA, LTD., TORONTO, ONTARIO

Printed in the United States of America

PREFACE

This second edition of *Basic Speech* is addressed to the college student with a firm belief that now, more than ever, he or she is likely to be an intelligent adult. We also believe that curiosity is a companion to intelligence and that the intellectually curious adult will want to find out something more about speech—the characteristic that sets man apart from all other living beings—than he is likely to have known before entering college. To be sure, the student may have taken his speaking for granted, perhaps not given the matter a second thought even if he had given it a first. If this is the case, we earnestly hope that his curiosity will be aroused and that he will begin to ask questions even though he may not too quickly be able to obtain all the answers.

THE OBJECTIVES OF THIS BOOK

Effective Communication as the Primary Objective

This book has several objectives. The primary objective is to help the motivated student to become proficient in oral communication—in speaking. An effective speaker is one who is able, with least difficulty, to convey his thoughts and feelings to another person or persons. He is one who is normally able, *when he so desires,* to get others to appreciate his feelings and to understand his thoughts. When necessary, he can secure action on the basis of these feelings and thoughts. An effective speaker is one who is able to modify the manner and content of his speech to the demands of the speaking situation. These modifications will vary according to the number of the listeners, as well as the time, the place, and the purpose of the speaking. In short, an effective speaker is a person who, within the limitations of the speaking situation,

[v]

can influence the behavior of his listeners in regard to feelings, thoughts, and actions. An effective speaker must at all times behave with awareness that communications is a two-way avenue. Somehow the speaker must make certain that what he is attempting to communicate is being received, understood, and appreciated. The speaker must be alert for responses from the individual listener and respond in turn on the basis of what he receives. Simply stated, a speaker must behave according to the principle that communication can take place only if there is a responding listener.

Knowledge of the Medium of Communication

Another objective of this book is to present a body of information about speech as a medium of communication and expression. We believe that intelligent adults can best act as such when they are well informed about what they are doing. Much of our life is spent in talking. Accordingly, basic information about the components of speech—language, action, and voice—will be presented. Throughout the book, pertinent applications of this information in everyday speaking situations will be made.

Improvement of Voice and Diction

Consistent with the primary objective of increasing the effectiveness of the individual as a speaker, is that of improving his voice and diction. The approach to such improvement will be made through a study of voice production, a rather detailed consideration of the sounds of American-English speech, and through the use of practice materials for both voice and speech sounds.

The ultimate objective of this book is to assist the student in becoming not only an adequate speaker but an adequate personality. With this in mind, the relationship between speech and personality will be considered. Further, the way in which a well-adjusted person deals with meanings and meaningful relationships will be studied. The adequate speaker and the well-adjusted person is one who manifests responsiveness through his speech to his own thoughts and feelings and to those who are listening and responding to him. Such responsiveness should go a long way in helping the speaker to communicate with maximum effectiveness.

This edition has been revised and expanded with the original basic organization maintained. As in the first edition, the organization of the book was determined by the objectives indicated above. Wherever possible, a body of information is presented to the reader to provide a basis of knowledge for a mode of communicative behavior. Thus, theory and practice can be correlated and the reader is able to learn the *what* and *why* as well as the *how* of the forms of communication with which this book is concerned.

We hope that the reader will find enough that is new and worthwhile to justify his studying the second edition of *Basic Speech*. In particular, we hope that the emphasis on the study of *intentional communication* and the multiple purposes of speech will justify the expanded condition of this content in the present edition. In addition, we hope that not too much of the traditional content of introductory texts in communicative speaking had to be sacrificed in order to make way for the new materials and the new emphasis of this book.

ACKNOWLEDGMENTS

The authors wish to acknowledge with thanks the assistance of several of their colleagues for their willingness to share their ideas in the preparation of the second edition of *Basic Speech*. Particularly, we are indebted to Mr. Ronald Williams for his perceptive criticism of the content and style of Chapters 11, 12, and 14 to 18; Dr. Ruth Lewis for her valuable suggestions in discussion and debate; Mr. Donald Finn for the line drawings of the symposium, round table and debate format; Mr. Robert J. Champion for his help in securing illustrations; and Dr. Joel Stark of Stanford University for the generous help and keen insight which he shared in his review of many of the chapters. Thanks are due, also, to the National Association of College Stores and to their photographer, Mr. Arthur A. Princehorn, for the use of illustrations from their files.

JON EISENSON
PAUL H. BOASE

CONTENTS

ILLUSTRATIONS

[xi]

CHAPTER 1

SPEECH: NATURE
AND FUNCTIONS

WHAT IS SPEECH?

Speech is a method of evoking meaningful responses from somebody. The somebody may include oneself or another person. The nature of the meaningful response may vary from the broad and crude to the precise and highly specific. To get meaningful responses through speech, words are usually employed. Spoken words may be *audible* or *visible*. Ordinarily, we have audible symbols in mind when we say that we speak. Audible words are produced by the actions of the lips, the tongue, the teeth, the palate, and the vocal mechanism. We also produce *visible symbols,* which are in many ways equivalent to words, through the actions of the face, hands, arms, shoulders, and occasionally other parts of the body. These actions, if readily identified, constitute visible symbols known as *gestures.*

To sum up, speech is a method of getting meaningful responses through the use of audible words and gestures produced by the activity of the human body. Words and gestures are known as *speech symbols.*

If we were to stop with this definition, our concept of speech would be limited. The significance of speech cannot be appreciated unless we know something about speakers and listeners *as persons.* If we have such understanding and appreciation, we can broaden our concept so that we may look upon speech as a complex function that is at once a manifestation of attitude, purpose, feelings, and thoughts. This manifestation is presented in a symbol (language) code and in a manner that is culturally determined yet individually formulated and expressed. Thus, we speak a variety of English, but the specific way we cast our thoughts, formulate our sentences, and utter our words are individualized so that we can often be identified by how we say what we think and feel. We do not have to be linguistic detectives to

[1]

recognize Winston Churchill or Dwight D. Eisenhower or Adlai Stevenson. Each speaks a variety of English, yet each speaks himself.

Speech is the way of life for man. What we are, what we do, and what we decide to do are accomplished through speech. Through the medium of speech we form and reveal our attitudes, our personalities, and our purposes in life; we learn how others feel and think and we indicate our own thoughts and feelings. Through speech, or indirectly through written language which records speech, we gain and give meaning to our existence. Through these devices we are able, in some measure, to modify and control our environment.

SPEECH SYMBOLS AND SPEECH PURPOSES

The symbols we use in speech and the manner in which we use them depends pretty much on the particular purpose we have in speaking. The purpose of our speaking may be determined by the response we seek. If we want an intellectual response, if we want to know how our listener is thinking, symbol use must be precise. We must then choose our words with care and make certain that our words not only convey our own thoughts, but are of the kind which are likely to induce and evoke thinking rather than feeling in others. By maner of speaking as well as by choice of words, thinking should be elicited. On the other hand, if we want a reaction of a nonintellectual nature, the precise choice of words may not be so important as the manner in which the words are presented. This point will become clear in our consideration of the various purposes of speech.

Expression

When speech is used merely as emotional expression, the words themselves have little significance. In fact, it is possible to get along without words and still be engaged in emotional expression. A sigh may be expressive beyond words, and crying requires only sobbed sounds. What matters in emotional expressions is the tone and manner in which the sounds are produced. Swearing, for example, isn't a matter of what you say but rather of how you say it. The tone is far more important than the words. Mark Twain was aware of this point; his wife, it seems, was not. Once, according to the story, the wife determined to cure her author-husband of his habit of swearing. The habit was firmly established and went back to the days when Mark Twain piloted a steamboat on the Mississippi. Mrs. Mark Twain, as an object lesson in the horrors of swearing, rebuked her husband with a selection of his favorite swear words. When she was finished, Mark Twain regarded his wife with sympathetic understanding, and then calmly informed her, "Woman, you know the words, but you don't know the music."

Expressive speech is not limited to emotional outbursts. Some of us talk for the sake of hearing ourselves make sounds. Small children talk to themselves even though other persons are near them. Adults sometimes talk to themselves when alone. A self-conscious adult may prefer talking to an animal pet who is incapable of responding to anything but the voice of the speaker. Mature women talk to stuffed dolls; full-grown men who think that talking to stuffed dolls or to animal pets is perfectly silly sometimes make queer sounds at uncomprehending infants. We speak to people who don't understand us, and we indulge in nonsense talk with those whose understanding of us includes tolerant acceptance of our shortcomings. Occasionally, we may even go on a talking jag and become almost intoxicated with the exhilarating effect of our verbal effusions. Because of social pressures, we usually pretend to be talking to somebody. Actually we are talking in the physical presence of somebody rather to somebody. In most of these situations we talk for the sheer pleasure of the activity. Making sounds can be fun. If the sounds are set to music, the pleasure may be heightened. How else can we account for many of the words and most of the refrains of our old English ballads and madrigals. For example, a madrigal by Thomas Nashe (1567–1601) called "Spring, the Sweet Spring" ends with:

> Cuckoo, jug-jug, pu-we, to-witta-woo!
> Spring, the sweet spring.

Shakespeare ends his *Twelfth Night* with a song that includes a once uttered and four times repeated line:

> With hey, ho, the wind and the rain.

Lewis Carroll used even fewer recognizable word forms for his "Jabberwocky" which opens with the telling lines:

> 'Twas brillig, and the slithy toves
> Did gyre and gimble in the wabe;
> All mimsy were the borogoves
> And the mome raths outgrabe.

However much some of us may disparage our contemporary writers of popular songs, we should appreciate that Shakespeare, the writers of sea chanties, and the writers of songs for adolescents may be kindred as to the motives for "creating" a line such as, "With a hey nonny-nonny and a ha-cha-cha."

Many alleged conversations fall into the category of expressive speech engaged in for the pleasure of talking. The tête-à-têtes of cocktail parties or tea parties are really monologues with one speaker waiting for an opportune moment to break in when a pause stops the verbal flow of the other.

The pause may have been necessary because of the need to stop for breath or to quench thirst with a sip of cocktail or tea. Whatever the cause, the second speaker seizes upon the opportunity and begins another monologue. In time, an arising need may permit the tables to be turned and the first of the interrupted monologues may again be resumed or a new one undertaken.

Social Gesture

When speech is used for the purpose of social gesture, individual words are not greatly significant. In fact, it is not even important that all the words we use should be precisely understood. It is only important that in a given social situation we say something which sounds right for the situation. Occasionally, the words may be quite inappropriate, except that there is little likelihood that anyone will pay much attention to them. The wag who went through a long receiving line and who mumbled at each of the notables to whom he was introduced, "I've just murdered my wife, and I'm glad to meet you," created no stir. It was assumed that he said something appropriate, something along the lines of, "How do you do, I'm very happy to know you." That something very different was said went entirely unnoticed because the manner of speaking, if not the actual speech content, was approriate to the social situation.

Most greetings between persons who are acquainted with one another fall into the category of social-gesture speech. Here, for example, we have an item of conversation between two men who have known one another for many years.

BILL   Hi, Joe, where have you been hiding?
JOE   Bill, you son of a sea-cook, it's sure good to see you.
BILL   You too, you old horse thief, what do you know?
JOE   Not too much. How about you?
BILL   The usual. Wife and kids O.K.?
JOE   Just fine, how's your family? Mary, the kids?
BILL   No complaints.
JOE   Good, Bill, good. Fellah, I've got to be getting along.
BILL   Sure enough. Take care but don't take any wooden nickels.
JOE   So long, you old stick-in-the-mud and give my regards at home.

Now, what does such talk mean? Certainly not what any literal interpretation of the interchange might imply. It is safe to assume that Bill does not expect Joe to tell him where, if any place, he has been in hiding. Joe may be bright, or limited in intelligence or wordly knowledge, but there is little likelihood that Bill has the time in a casual meeting to listen to Joe relate what he knows. Joe, it may be noted, seemed to ignore Bill's question and Bill wasn't ruffled that he was ignored. Instead of pouring forth his body of knowledge, Joe literally "accused" Bill of illegal activities in horse flesh. Then, in an apparently unrelated way, Joe shifted the conversation to inquiries about his companion's family and its state of health. Bill answered with advice about a nonexistent coin of the realm.

We would continue the analysis of the remaining portion of the conversation, but that would be laboring the point. In speech used as social gesture, the individual words and even isolated sentences have little specific intellectual significance. Taken together, the words and the sentences assume a vague significance. In the conversation cited above, the speakers felt that the situation required more than a simple "Hello," or a smile, or a nod of the head. The elaboration of the greeting was an indication that something more needed to be said. Beyond the significance of "Hello," all the rest was talk. But it is the kind of talk out of which the amenities of civilized society are made. Social-gesture speech may be meaningless if we expect that each spoken word be weighted with significance. But social speech seldom makes such demands. What is demanded is a pattern of words accompanied by a voice which sounds amiable. If the reaction to the pattern is friendly, the purpose of social-gesture speech is served. People who know one another expect to converse when they meet. What is said, in terms of the literal significance of words, is of little or no importance.

Speech To Allay Fear

We often talk when we feel afraid in the hope that we can talk ourselves out of being afraid. Such talk may be referred to as "whistling in the dark." The superstition of whistling as one goes by a graveyard at night probably has its origin in the unconscious hope that the graveyard spirits will interpret whistling as unconcern and not molest the whistler who, by the very act of his whistling, is supposedly presenting audible evidence of his bravery. Some of us pretend to be talking to someone else when entering a dark house or a dark room of the house. Such talk has a dual function. It is expressive in that it is a manifestation of fear. At the same time the talk is supposed to impress a possible lurker in the dark with the idea that the speaker is not alone and that more than one person will have to be contended with in the event of trouble.

We sometimes use speech in a social situation in order to prevent or allay hostility. This is exemplified in our behavior when we approach or are approached by an ominous-looking stranger. We talk to him—what we say is of little moment—"to show him that we are not afraid." The stranger may answer us for the very same reason. Speech may be very useful in talking ourselves out of fear.

Specific Responses

Speech reaches its highest level of capability when we use it to convey a specific idea in order to get a specific response. The ability to differentiate his ideas and to distinguish between concepts of objects nearly alike belongs to man alone. This ability is employed usually for obtaining satisfaction of wants and needs, for getting what we like, and putting off what we don't like or don't want. We may use this ability for immediate situations or for remote or anticipated situations. We may use the ability to convey our thoughts or to conceal them by communicating ideas we wish the listener to have even though we may not hold them ourselves.

Our thoughts as well as our tastes can be presented through carefully chosen words. Most of us, however, are not nearly so certain about what we think as we are about what we want in the way of indulging our tastes. That is why we are much more expert in ordering our meals than we are in putting our thoughts in order. How to do something about making our ideas specific and clear will be considered in a later chapter.

Speech Responses

When we speak we get responses from one or more persons. One of these persons is always the speaker himself. We listen to our own words as we talk. If they sound satisfactory, we continue in our intended way. If we find ourselves not saying what we had in mind, we change our words and our thoughts, or expand them, or present the same words with a different emphasis. Usually, the responses we obtain from our listener or listeners, give us added information as to the adequacy of our speech.

Audience Responses

When we address a group of persons who constitute an audience we do not usually get the same kind of response as when we talk to a few people or to one person in a conversation. In a conversation we get an almost immediate reaction, even if it is only a dead silence. By what is said or not said, we are able to judge the effectiveness of our speech. If we try to convince someone to a way of thinking, we try to get some response which tells us how successful we are in our purpose. When we talk to a large group, no such immediate verbal judgment is possible. Except when the group escapes our control, or when its members become unsocial enough to boo or walk out, it takes some time to get a verbal reaction to a speech. In fact, unless individual persons of the group can be questioned, the speaker may never know precisely how his listeners reacted.

There are, of course, other significant responses a speaker gets from his listeners. Failure to elicit anticipated smiles or laughter and physical movements indicating tension, boredom, or annoyance are evidences of unfavorable response when these are not desired by the speaker. On the other hand, activity such as laughter or applause in the "proper places" and postures and facial expressions reflective of attentive listening give the speaker important information about how the listeners are going along with him.

Thinking

Much, probably most, of our speaking takes place with only ourselves as significant reactors. Such a situation exists whenever we talk for the pleasure of talking. More important, however, is the talking that goes on with ourselves when we engage in thinking. We think in symbols, and often in verbal or word symbols. Usually, thinking is inner speech. When we are alone we may think by speaking aloud. Even those of us who think in silent speech may not be so silent as is usually supposed. Even for the "silent" thinker, thinking is frequently accompanied by lip movements which fall just short of being suppressed. In fact, a sensitive electrical instrument attached to the throat just below the "Adam's apple" reveals that sounds often are made which are not quite aloud enough to be heard. Frequently, thinking, is accompanied by subvocal speaking.

SOME BARRIERS TO COMMUNICATION

Although communication is one of the most important of speech purposes, we are not always in a position to be able to communicate the thoughts or feelings in our minds. There are many instances in which it becomes socially necessary to avoid presenting the content of our minds and to offer instead some socially acceptable content.

Social Appropriateness

The bachelor by choice who is asked by a fond mother, "Now, what do you think of my baby?" may be forgiven if he answers, with appropriate tone and inflection, "Well, this is a baby." Husbands by the score have learned that it takes courage bordering on foolhardiness to answer with truth the wives' question, "Tell me, what do you *really* think of my new hat?"

There is another kind of situation, more serious in its implications, in which it becomes difficult to communicate what we are actually thinking or feeling. The situation might be typified by the scene of the irate mother confronting her small son with the pieces of a broken picture frame and demanding to know, "Why did you break Aunt Susan's picture?" It would do the small boy little good to explain that he doesn't like Aunt Susan because she's mean and crotchety and a little bit on the ugly side and that he was tired of seeing Aunt Susan leer at him every time he entered the living room. Such an explanation, despite its close adherence to the truth, is less likely to be accepted than another the small boy may offer. The boy may have learned that it is socially more acceptable to explain, "I'm sorry; it was an accident. I promise I won't do it again."

Truth, if it is painful to offer and painful to accept, may become a barrier to the communication of our thoughts. As children we learn that frequently our listeners do not want to know how we really think or feel. We learn that it is sometimes socially desirable to reveal only that part of the content of our minds which our listeners are willing to accept. We learn that there are barriers to communication, and that sometimes the desire for communicative speech must give way to social-gesture speech.

Personal Objectives

There is another barrier to communication less innocent than the desire to be safe rather than courageous or socially proper rather than completely truthful. The barrier is the desire a speaker may have to persuade his listeners that he believes something which he really does not believe. Political speakers may make inconsistent statements, directly or by implication, to different groups of listeners. A political speaker may wish one audience to be left with the impression that he favors continued high prices for farm products. The same speaker may wish to give another group of listeners the impression that he advocates a sharp cut in the cost of living. Another political speaker may favor a high tariff or a low tariff or have no opinion on the question of the tariff. He may, however, speak as if he had a definite opinion and appear to have a different opinion according to his particular group of listeners.

Personal and ulterior objectives may become barriers to the communication of our thoughts. Political speakers, however, are not the only ones who, because of personal objectives, encourage listeners to think as they may not themselves really think. Political speakers possibly do so in public situations more often than other speakers. All of us, however, may do so both in our private conversations and in our public pronouncements.

Meaning

There is still another barrier to communication for which the speaker has less responsibility. It is the barrier of meaning. Our communication conventionally takes place through word symbols. Unfortunately, the symbols do not have precisely the same meanings for all speakers and for all listeners. Differences in meanings result in misunderstanding, and constitute what is probably the most important unintentional barrier to communication. How to overcome this barrier will be considered in Chapter 8.

Defective Speech

Speech, if defective, may disturb or interfere with communication. The speech sounds we produce and the way we produce them, the voice and the gestures which accompany the speech sounds, may get in the way of our meanings. Sounds of speech which are difficult to identify or which are produced in an atypical manner attract attention to themselves and so away from what they are intended to mean. A deficient voice, one which is either not loud enough or too loud, a voice of such quality that it fails to reflect changes in feelings or thought, is likely to become a barrier to communication.

Other Barriers

This discussion of barriers to communication is intended to be suggestive rather than conclusive. Other barriers may exist which may deserve no less or even more attention than those which have been briefly mentioned in this limited space. For example, the personal prejudices and special interests of listeners may cause them to read so much of their biases into what the speaker is telling them that they cannot really understand what is being said. It is also possible that a speaker, becoming aware of the listeners' personal prejudices and interests, may not say what he would really like to say.

Although we cannot control all factors which interfere with communication, some are definitely subject to modification. These will be considered in greater detail in other parts of this book.

SUMMARY

Speech is a distinctly human accomplishment. Man was able to achieve speech because of his possession of (1) a set of organs capable of being modified and adapted for the function of speech, and (2) a nervous mechanism including a highly developed brain. Through the nervous mechanism man is able to integrate and translate his sensory impressions and experiences into spoken words. Speech may be defined as a method of getting meaningful responses from one or more persons through the use of audible and visible symbols. Spoken words and gestures are speech symbols.

Speech is used effectively when the speaker is readily able to convey his thoughts and his feelings to another person or persons. The effective speaker is one who knows how to modify the manner and content of his speech in keeping with the needs of the speech situation.

The use we make of speech symbols depends upon the purpose of our speech according to the individual speaking situation. Speech may be used for the following general purposes: (1) to express feelings and emotions; (2) as social gestures; (3) to prevent or allay hostility; (4) to convey or communicate specific ideas in order to get specific responses. Speech responses come from the speaker himself as well as from the person or persons addressed. When we speak to a single person or a small group of persons in informal situations, responses are almost immediate. Through the responses we are able to evaluate the success of our purpose in speaking. When speaking to large groups in formal situations, verbalized responses are usually delayed, and an evaluation of our success of speech purpose is not immediately possible.

Thinking often is a modified form of speaking in which the speaker and responder is the same person. Thinking is usually accompanied by inner, silent speaking.

We are not always able to communicate the thoughts and feelings we entertain. Barriers to communication include (1) social appropriateness (or inappropriateness), (2) personal and ulterior objectives, (3) failure of words to have the same meaning for speaker and listener, (4) defective speech or voice, and (5) listener prejudices and special interests.

Much of this book will be concerned with the improvement of speech so that (1) barriers to communication of meanings will be minimized and (2) maximum responsiveness consistent with our legitimate purposes as speakers may be achieved.

QUESTIONS AND EXERCISES

1. (a) What is speech? (b) What is meant by the statement: "Speech is behavior reduced to symbols"? (c) What is a speech symbol?

2. (a) Can you think of any purposes of speech not indicated in the text? (b) What is the relationship between our speech purpose and the way in which we use speech symbols?

3. Analyze two or three brief social conversations. How much of the speech employed was for the purpose of communicating or obtaining specific information? How much of the speech content was essentially self-expressive?

4. Does speech serve the same purposes for a three-year-old child as it does for a child of thirteen?

5. Are there any significant differences between adult men and women in their use of speech?

6. Analyze your speech activities for a full day. What speech purposes did you satisfy? How much of the time were you interested in communicating specific ideas?

7. (a) How do we determine the effectiveness of our speaking? (b) How does the situation differ when we are talking to one person and when talking to a large group of listeners?

8. In what way may thinking be considered talking? How does it differ from talking to another person?

9. Listen to a speech over the radio. Record your impressions as soon as the speech is concluded. Read the same speech, or a different speech, as reported in a newspaper. What are the differences in your reactions? Why?

10. What are the barriers to communication? Are all of them surmountable? Why?

11. What are the minimum essentials for adequate speech? When is speech better than just adequate?

12. Would our civilization be possible without speech? Explain your point of view.

13. Conjecture what our civilization might be like if the tape recorder had been invented before the printing press.

14. Do you speak as you think and think as you speak? If not, what are the differences?

RECOMMENDED READINGS

Black, J. W., and Moore, W. E. *Speech: Code, Meaning, and Communication.* New York: McGraw-Hill, 1955, Chap. 1.

Eisenson, J., Auer, J. J., and Irwin, J. I. *The Psychology of Communication.* New York: Appleton-Century-Crofts, 1963, Chap. 1.

Hayakawa, S. I. *Language and Thought in Action.* New York: Harcourt, Brace, 1949, Chaps. 1 and 2.

Pei, M. *The Story of Language.* New York: Lippincott, 1949, Chaps. 1–4.

Whatmough, J. *Language.* New York: St. Martin's Press, 1956.

CHAPTER 2

THE SPEECH
MECHANISM

ESSENTIALS FOR SOUND PRODUCTION

For the production of sound, three requisites must be satisfied. The first requisite is a body capable of vibration (the vibrator), the second is a force which may be applied to the vibrator, and the third is a medium for transmitting the results of vibration. These requisites are contained in the breathing, or respiratory, mechanism of the human body. The first two will be considered in some detail. Normally, the medium for transmission of sound is air.

The Vibrator (Vocal Bands)

The vibrators which satisfy the first essential are the vocal bands.[1] These are two very small bands, or folds, of connective tendinous tissue situated in the larynx, or voice box. The larynx is located in the neck between the root of the tongue and the trachea, or windpipe. The outer and largest part of the larynx is the shieldlike cartilage known as the thyroid cartilage. (Actually, the thyroid cartilage consists of two cartilaginous shields fused together along an anterior line.) We can locate the thyroid cartilage, and so the larynx, by feeling for the "Adam's apple." The "Adam's apple" is at the front apex of the larynx. After locating the "Adam's apple," we can determine the location of the vocal folds by running the index finger and thumb down toward the chest on a straight line from the "Adam's apple" while vocalizing a long *ah*. Vibration should be felt all along the line, but should be greatest about halfway down the line of the thyroid cartilage. That is the place of attachment of the vocal bands to the thyroid

---

[1] The terms *vocal bands, vocal folds,* and *vocal cords* will be used synonymously.

[12]

cartilage within the larynx. This fact will become clear after an examination of the diagram of the larynx.

The vocal bands are attached to the curved walls of the thyroid cartilage at either side. In the midline, they are attached to the angle formed by the fusion of the two halves (shields) of the thyroid cartilage. At the back of the larynx, each of the vocal bands is attached to a pyramidal-shaped

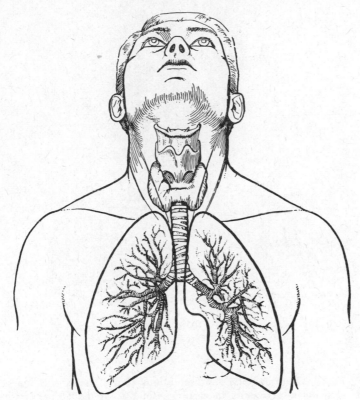

Figure 1.   The larynx, trachea, and lungs.

cartilage known as the arytenoid. The arytenoids, because of their shape and muscular connections, can be made to move in several ways. They can pivot or rotate, tilt backward, and slide backward and sidewise. Through these movements of the arytenoids, the vocal bands can be brought together or pulled apart. When the vocal bands are brought together, vocalization becomes possible. When the vocal bands are separated, the wide opening between them permits ordinary quiet breathing rather than vocalization. It might be pointed out that for normal vocalization the vocal bands are brought together (approximated or adducted) so that they are close and parallel (see Figures 2 and 3).

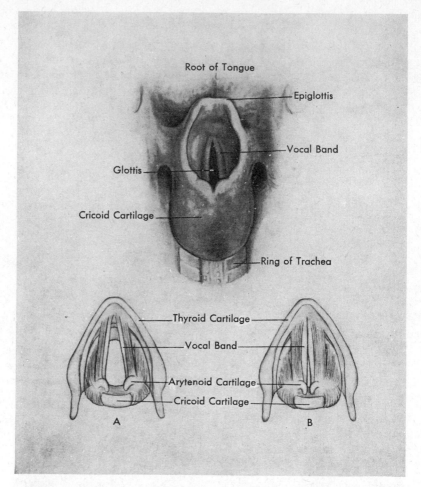

Figure 2. Diagrammatic representations of the larynx and the vocal bands showing attachments to cartilages of the larynx. *Upper diagram:* The larynx seen from above and behind; posterior (dorsal) aspect. *A:* Vocal bands in position for quiet breathing. *B:* Vocal bands in position for vocalizaton.

Voice Production

Normal vocalization (phonation) results when the stream of breath under pressure meets the approximated vocal bands and forces them to be "blown" apart. As a consequence, the stream of air flowing with relatively high velocity escapes through the glottis (the opening between the vocal bands). The vocal bands, of course, continue to be held together (approximated) at both ends. Vocalization is maintained as a result of a combina-

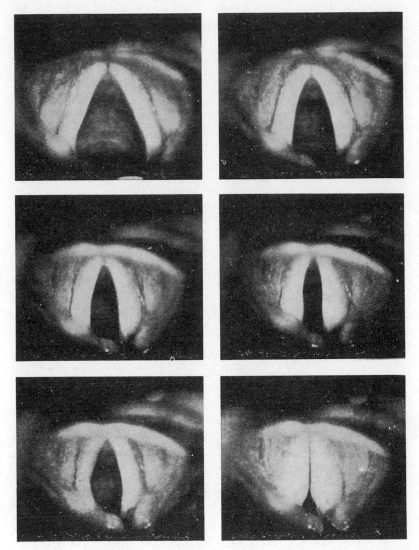

Figure 3. High-speed photos showing changes in position of the vocal bands from quiet breathing to voicing. [Courtesy Bell Telephone Co. Laboratories, N. Y.]

tion of several factors: (1) reduction of pressure beneath the bands, (2) reduction of pressure along the sides of the high velocity air stream, (3) the action of the bands themselves in terms of their elasticity. Together, these factors bring about recurrent closures after successive outward movements of the bands. The effect is maintained vocalization. When the activity

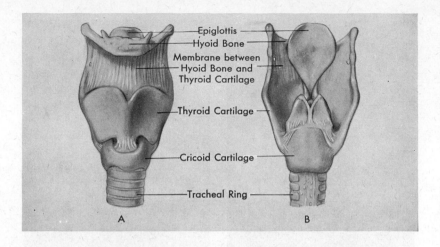

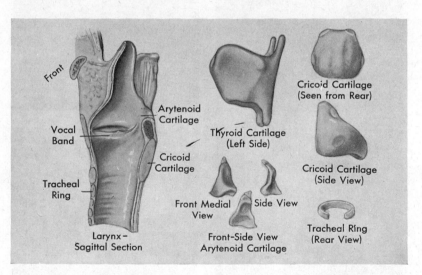

Figure 4. *Upper diagram:* **The larynx and trachea.** *A:* **Anterior view.** *B:* **Posterior view.** *Lower diagram:* **The cartilages of the larynx.**

or the position of the vocal bands fails to produce a "complete" though momentary interruption in the flow of air, we get a quality of voice that is identified as breathy or hoarse.

The *vocal bands,* as we have indicated, are comparatively small, tough strips of connective tissue,[2] continuous with folds of muscle tissue. As seen

---

[2] *The larynx* is lined by *mucous membrane.* On each side of the larynx, the mucous membrane is thrown into two transverse folds that constitute the vocal bands. The upper pair of transverse folds form the false vocal bands. The lower pair form the true vocal bands.

from above, the vocal bands appear to be flat folds of muscle which have inner edges of connective tisue. In adult males the vocal bands range from about ⅞ inch to 1¼ inches in length. In adult females the length ranges from less than ½ inch to about ⅞ inch. (See page 22 for the relationship between length of vocal fold and pitch of voice.)

It might be pointed out that the vocal bands assist in a very vital function not related to speech. This function is to keep foreign matter out

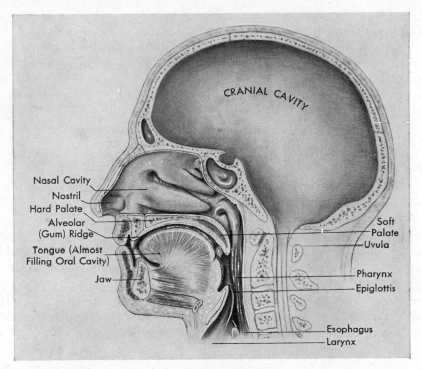

CRANIAL CAVITY

Nasal Cavity
Nostril
Hard Palate
Alveolar (Gum) Ridge
Tongue (Almost Filling Oral Cavity)
Jaw

Soft Palate
Uvula
Pharynx
Epiglottis
Esophagus
Larynx

Figure 5.   Section of head showing articulatory organs and principal resonators.

of the breathing mechanism. This becomes clear when we recall the coughing which takes place when saliva or a bit of food is "inhaled" when we try to talk and swallow at the same time. The vocal folds are sensitive to the presence of foreign matter. If any foreign matter touches the vocal folds, reflexive activity will occur. This activity produces the sudden expulsion of air that we recognize as coughing. The action serves to clear the foreign matter from the trachea.

Loudness and Reinforcement

The loudness of vocal tones is determined mostly by the vigor with which air is forced from the lungs through the larynx. Fortunately, however, we are able to "build up," or reinforce, vocal tones without resorting to constant energetic use of air pressure. This reinforcement takes place in the resonating cavities of the human speech mechanism. These important resonators are the cavities of (1) the larynx itself, (2) the throat (pharynx, (3) the mouth (oral cavity), and (4) the nose (the cavity above the roof of the mouth). To a lesser degree, the trachea—the part of the windpipe below the larynx—also acts as a resonator.

The Chest Cavity (Motor Mechanism)

The thoracic, or chest, cavity consists of a framework of bones and cartilages which include the collar bone, the shoulder blades, the ribs, the sternum, and the backbone. The *diaphragm* is the floor of the thoracic cavity as well as the roof of the abdominal cavity. Above the diaphragm are, among other organs, the lungs and trachea. Below in the abdominal cavity are the digestive organs including the stomach, the intestines, and the liver.

The Lungs

The lungs consist of a mass of tiny air sacs supplied by a multitude of air tubes and blood vessels. The lungs contain much elastic tissue. They play a passive role in respiration. They expand or contract only because of differences in pressure brought about as a result of the activity of the rib and abdominal muscles that expand and contract the thoracic cavity. The lungs, having no muscle tissue, can neither expand nor contract directly. Air is forced into the lungs as a result of outside air pressure when the expanded chest cavity provides increased space for the air. Air is forced out of the lungs when, as will soon be described, the chest cavity decreases in size and the pressure of the enclosed air is increased.

Diaphragmatic Action

Air enters the lungs by way of the mouth or nose, the throat, and the trachea when the volume of the chest cavity is increased. Such an increase may be produced by the downward movement of the diaphragm, by the outward movement of the lower ribs, or by a combination of both activities. In inhalation, the contraction of the diaphragm is an active process. In exhalation, the diaphragm merely relaxes. The diaphragm returns to its former position because of the pressure of the abdominal contents upon it. In controlled muscular activity necessary for speech, the muscles of the front and sides of the abdominal wall contract and press inward on the liver, stomach, and intestines. These organs exert an upward pressure on the undersurface of the diaphragm, which in turn exerts pressure against the lungs and so causes air to be expelled. Throughout the respiratory cycle the diaphragm remains roughly dome-shaped (actually, double dome-shaped), but the height of the dome is greater after exhalation than after inhalation (see Figure 7).

Although the diaphragm is muscularly active only in the process of inhalation, it nevertheless serves a highly important function in exhalation.

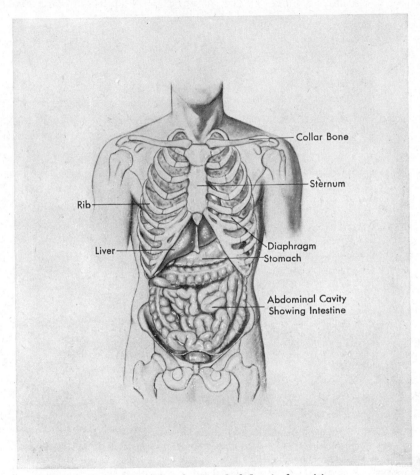

Figure 6.   The chest and abdominal cavities.

The diaphragm maintains some degree of muscle tension at all times. In relaxing as a result of pressures of the abdominal contents upon it, it does so slowly and gradually as the breath is expired. If the diaphragm were to lose all muscle tone at once and to relax suddenly and completely, the air from the lungs would be expelled with a sudden rush. Such an expulsion of air would be useless for speech purposes. By maintaining some degree of muscle tonus, a steady stream of breath is provided which can be used for speech purposes.

The Respiratory Cycle

In *normal breathing* which does not involve speech, only a small part of the air in our lungs is moved or exchanged. Each respiratory cycle probably

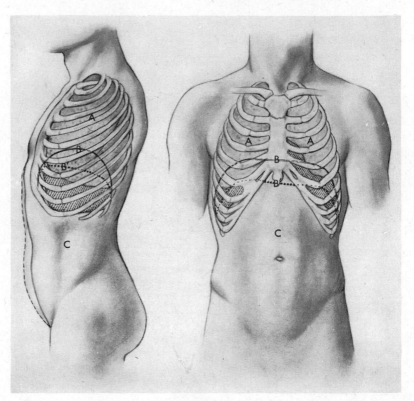

Figure 7. Diaphragmatic and abdominal action in breathing. *A:* The thorax or chest cavity. *B:* The diaphragm "relaxed" as at the completion of exhalation. *B′:* The diaphragm contracted as in deep inhalation. *C:* The abdominal cavity. Note the forward displacement of the abdominal wall which accompanies the downward movement of the diaphragm during inhalation. The cross-hatched portion of the lung represents the additional volume of the expanded lung as in deep inhalation.

involves no more, on the average, than an interchange of about a pint (500 cc.) of air. Vigorous speaking or shouting may require more air. Many persons, however, use no more breath for speaking loudly than they do for conversational speech. In any event, we seldom use more than a small amount, perhaps 10 to 20 per cent of the volume of air we are capable of holding in our lungs. The amount of air we are capable of inhaling has little significance for voice production. Of greater significance is the control of the breath and the use of the resonators to reinforce vocal tones.

The contraction and relaxation of the diaphragm and the abdominal muscles produce the cycles of inhalation and exhalation in the process of breathing. Under normal circumstances, when vocalization and speech are not involved, changes in the physiological conditions of the parts of the breathing mechanism determine the manner of our breathing. Usually, these changes take place without conscious effort and with little or no awareness of what is going on. It is only when something unusual happens that we become aware that we are breathing. Running up several flights of stairs, for example, is generally enough to make us conscious that we are breathing more rapidly than normally. After running, we need to breathe more rapidly to restore the oxygen supply that has been used up because of our energetic action.

Breathing for speech usually calls for a modification of the respiratory cycle. In silent (nonspeech) breathing, the periods of inhalation and exhalation are about equal. In speech, the period of exhalation exceeds the length of the period of inhalation. That means that normally, in speaking, we inhale quickly and, while speaking, exhale slowly. The necessary modification of the respiratory cycle creates the need for voluntary, or conscious, control which is not required for automatic breathing.

Articulated Sound

Voice, as we know, is but one component of speech. Combinations of articulated sounds presented in conventional patterns constitute spoken words. Speech sounds are produced when the stream of breath coming up from the lungs by way of the windpipe and larynx is modified in the mouth before it (the breath) is permitted to leave the body. The breath is modified in the mouth by the action of the tongue, the teeth, the lips, and the parts of the roof of the mouth (the palate). Most sounds in English speech are emitted through the mouth. The exceptions are the sounds *m* and *n* and the consonant sound usually represented by the letters *ng*. These three are nasal sounds—that is, they are routed through the nose before they are emitted.

Flexibility of Human Voice

The human sound-producing mechanism has a wide range of variability and can produce different kinds of sounds because it is so highly modifiable. Voice can be varied in pitch by changes in the tension of the vocal bands. At will, we can stop or continue the flow of breath which produces sound. The shape and to some extent the size of our resonators can be modified through muscular contraction and relaxation. Within limits, the openings of our sound mechanisms can be small or large and of various shapes according to what we do with our jaws and lips. Through these modifications, both pitch and tone quality can be changed.

A mechanism so highly modifiable must necessarily be fairly complex in its functioning. And the human speech mechanism is a most complicated apparatus! Fortunately, the superior nervous system man possesses makes it possible for him to modify and control the delicate mechanisms involved in the production of speech. The nature of this control will be considered later in the chapter.

VOICE AND THE PHYSICS OF SOUND

In this section we shall consider briefly the production of voice from the point of view of the science of physics. Although voice is not produced directly as a result of vibratory action, the determinants of vocal pitch nevertheless pertain to human vocal production.

Breathing

If a cavity having a single opening is increased in size, the pressure of the surrounding atmosphere will cause air to come in by way of the opening. When, on the other hand, the size of the cavity is decreased, air will be forced out. As we have noticed, air enters the lungs (we inhale) when the size of the chest cavity is increased, and air is forced out of the lungs (we exhale) when the chest cavity is reduced in size. In controlled exhalation, air is forced out gradually so that it may serve the function of speech.

Pitch

The pitch of a sound is determined by three characteristics of the vibrating body. These are length, mass or thickness, and tension. Short vibrators produce higher pitched sounds than long ones; thin vibrators (small mass) produce higher pitched sounds than thick vibrating bodies of equal length; vibrators which are taut or tense produce higher pitched sounds than less taut vibrators of equal length and mass. In brief, the pitch of a sound-producing body varies directly with the degree of tension and inversely as the length and mass of the body.

The basic reason for the higher pitched voices of women is apparent. Both the length and mass of women's vocal folds are less than those of men's. We have considerable control over the degree of tension of our vocal folds and so can voluntarily control the pitch of our voices. Involuntary pitch changes, however, do take place when muscle tensions change. The tension of the vocal folds tends to vary as other muscles voluntarily or involuntarily become tense. We might test this point by producing the sound *ah* continuously while gradually clenching our fists. It will be noted that as our fists become tightly closed, the pitch of the voice becomes higher. It is likely also that the voice will become somewhat louder as our fists become tighter. Our voices under states of heightened emotion become higher in pitch because heightened emotion brings with it increased muscle tension.

Cavity Resonance and Quality

The reinforcing or resonating function of the larynx, throat, mouth, and nose may be explained in terms of cavity resonance. We know that sounds are "built up" when a hollow form or cavity is close to the source of the sound. The body of a musical instrument serves this function. In the violin, for example, the sounds produced by the vibrating strings are reinforced by the hollow shape of the form below the strings. In a wind instrument, the hollow horn reinforces the sounds resulting from the vibration of the reed in the mouthpiece. A given sound may be reinforced by a number of possible resonating cavities, but of the number, one cavity will produce better results (reinforce the sound) than the others. When a cavity is especially built to reinforce a particular sound or range of sounds, optimum reinforcement is obtained. We might test this through a very simple experiment. Arrange five or six glass tumblers in a row and fill each tumbler with a different amount of water. Strike a metal bar or a fork (if available, use a tuning fork) and hold it over each tumbler. The unfilled parts of the tumblers are resonating cavities. Each cavity, being different in size and shape from the others, will reinforce the sound produced differently. One tumbler cavity will do the job better than the others.

In the human sound mechanism, the resonating cavities of the head and throat (speech mechanism) reinforce the sounds produced in the larynx. Because we can modify the size and shape of our resonating cavities,[3] we can get different qualities of sound. We can also reinforce sounds more widely than a musician can who is handling a musical instrument. For example, the vowels we produce in our speech are essentially different qualities of sound resulting from the variations in the size and shape of the mouth. A little vowel exercise in front of a mirror will make this point visibly apparent. Try producing the vowel in the words *he, hit, hay, hen, hat, who, ho, ha, her,* and *hum.* Note the position of the jaw and the shape of the lips, and that the tongue position will vary somewhat for each of the vowels.

We attain optimum resonance in speaking when, as a result of adjustments of our resonating cavities, we are able to produce easily audible sounds with the least expenditure of effort. We characterize vocal sounds by the resonating cavity most concerned in their production. Thus, we talk of a throaty tone or a nasal tone. An important difference between a trained

---

[3] The mouth is the most modifiable of our resonating cavities; the nasal cavity the least.

singer and someone who just sings is that the trained singer uses his resonating cavities to optimum advantage. He does not use a "bull fiddle"-shaped mouth for a violin-string tone. The same point might be made in comparing trained speakers with persons who just talk. Most of us learn to make resonator adjustments unconsciously. Those of us who have never learned to do the job well enough to talk without strain or to talk with fairly pleasant voice need help in making the proper adjustment for attaining optimum resonance. (See page 93 for suggested exercises for this purpose.)

HEARING AND SPEAKING

Hearing

Without hearing, few of us could learn to speak. Speaking, for most persons,[4] is learned through seeing and hearing. As children we learn to speak by unconsciously imitating the sounds and voice patterns we hear. Through seeing we learn how speech sounds look. Through hearing we are able to check on our speech so that we know whether the sounds we produce are like those we are trying to imitate. Listening to ourselves enables us to check on our voices as well as on our articulation.[5] In short, through hearing we discover whether we are using the appropriate sounds to form the words we mean to say.

The process of hearing involves three integrated functions: (1) the reception of sounds; (2) the transmission of sounds and the transformation into nerve impulses; and (3) the interpretation or translation of sounds for their meaning. Sound reception and transmission are made possible by the structure known as the ear. Interpretation or translation of sound into meaning is achieved through the operation of special nerve fibers and the cortex of the brain. (See pages 27–30 for a discussion of the functions of the brain cortex.)

The Ear

There are three parts to the ear (see Figure 8): (1) the outer ear, (2) the middle ear, and (3) the inner ear. *The outer ear* consists of a shell-like structure known as the *pinna,* and a short canal or auditory *meatus* which carries sounds to the eardrum, or *tympanic membrane.* The auditory

---

[4] Children with severe hearing losses can be taught to speak orally through the use of other combinations of sensory avenues, such as seeing and feeling. Usually, the speech of such persons is not of as good a quality as the speech of persons without hearing loss.

[5] It is known that persons who develop hearing losses after they have learned to speak tend to have faulty articulation and poorly modulated voices.

meatus is approximately one inch in length. The eardrum consists of a somewhat dome-shaped and taut connective tissue membrane.

The middle ear begins on the inner side of the eardrum. In its cavity are three very small connecting bones which extend from the eardrum to the inner ear. Functionally, the middle ear transmits sound (vibrations) from the outer ear to the inner ear. A short passageway, the *Eustachian tube,* connects the middle ear cavity with the upper part of the throat cavity. The Eustachian tube plays no part in assisting us to hear. Frequently, in fact, the Eustachian tube interferes with hearing because of infections which begin there and spread to the middle ear.

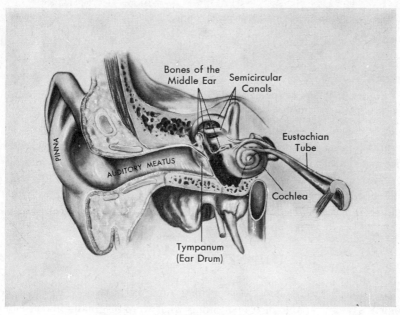

Figure 8.   A sectional view of the ear.

The inner ear is a complicated structure. It consists of a series of passage-ways, or canals, which extend from the middle ear deep into the temporal bone. Part of the inner ear—the *semicircular canals*—is concerned with the function of balance rather than of hearing.

The passageways of the inner ear are filled with fluid. The vibrations of the middle-ear bones are transmitted to the fluid of the inner ear. Part of the inner ear, the *cochlea,* contains tiny cells with hairlike projections that are sensitive to these vibrations. These hair cells are connected to the fibers of the auditory nerve which relay the translated sound waves to the brain.

In brief, we hear in the following way: Sound vibrations stimulate the eardrum. The vibrations are transmitted by the bones of the middle ear to

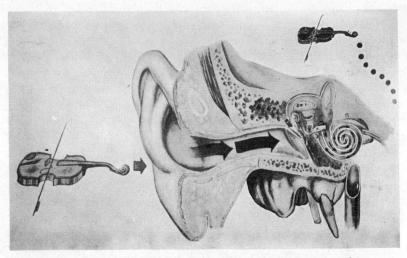

Figure 9.   View of the ear, indicating schematically how sound is transmitted to and interpreted by the brain.

the fluid lying within the inner ear. The inner ear contains nerve endings
which transmit to the brain the nerve impulses produced by the vibrator. In
the cortex of the brain, the nerve impulses are interpreted for their symbolic
significance. To appreciate how the transmission and interpretation by nerve
impulses is accomplished, we now turn to a study of the nervous mechanism.

THE NERVOUS SYSTEM

The speech mechanism exists in man alone because only he has a neu-
rological system capable of transforming what were originally unconsciously
produced grunts and wheezes into articulated sounds and voice. The sounds
of speech are produced, as we have learned, by organs concerned for the
most part with the vital processes of breathing and eating. Many animals
have mechanisms capable of producing vocal sounds. The ape comes closest
to producing sounds in an almost human way. But only man can start with
a sneeze and end with an articulated apology for having sneezed. Man's
capacity to talk lies in his ability to integrate organs of respiration and digestion for an additional purpose. In this special integration there is also an
ability to inhibit the actions of the organs in their original biological purpose.
But even beyond this, man's capacity to talk must be explained by his *ability
to learn and to remember what he has learned*. Vocal occurrences which
happen to the child as incidents of play can be recalled and used again as
words. Human beings can take greater advantage of "accidental" experi-

ences than can any other form of life. With superior insight, the human being can seize upon an incidental occurrence and have it stand out and acquire a new significance. This essentially explains the how and the why of our learning language and speech.

To understand the "unregulated miracle" of speech, we must learn something about the nervous system. More especially, we must learn something about the brain of man, because therein lies man's superiority over animals.

The division of the nervous system which is especially concerned with speech is part of the so-called *central nervous system* (CNS). This division includes the brain itself and the spinal cord. Associated with the central nervous system are a series of nerves which extend from the lower part of the brain and the spinal column to the muscles of the body that are under conscious or voluntary control.

Except for the cerebrum of the brain (the cerebral hemispheres), the nervous system of a man is pretty much like that of a dog and almost identical with that of an ape. The cerebrum, however, is significantly different. To begin with, there is a lot more of it than even the ape possesses. We can see the difference in the high expanse of the forehead which covers the frontal bulge of the brain. In man, this brain area pushes farther forward and is considerably larger than is the case with any other animal. Though our scientific knowledge of the brain is still limited, this much we know: injury to this part of the nervous mechanism brings about important changes in the personality, in the thinking, and in the speaking of the person.

The nerves are the message carriers. Nerve fibers much like telephone wires carry messages from the skin, the hands, the eyes, the ears, the tongue, the lips, and the other organs of the body to the brain. In addition, they carry the impulses the brain initiates to the muscles and glands. These impulses induce the movements of muscles involved in speaking, writing, and reading.

The Brain Cortex

The brain itself is a great coordinator and integrator of activity. In the brain, impulses set up by sounds and movements received through the ear and eye and other sense organs are translated into words and images which have significance and meaning.

"Brain power" may best be considered as a form of chemicoelectrical energy. All the impulses that course throughout our nervous systems and carry and convey the messages that result in thoughts and actions are, in effect, minute bursts of electrical energy. These bursts of energy are produced within the ten billion or more individual nerve cells that comprise each of our nervous systems.

The brain is divided into areas according to a division-of-labor arrangement. Most of this can be seen in the diagram of the cortex (outer covering of gray matter) of the brain (see Figure 11). We may notice that

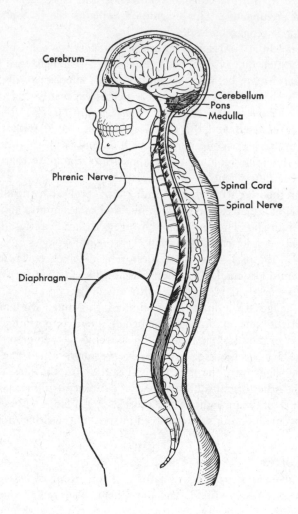

Figure 10.   The central nervous system in relation to speech. The Cerebrum: normal meaningful speech is dependent upon the integrative activity of the parts of the cerebrum. The Cerebellum "sorts and arranges" muscular impulses that come to it from higher brain centers. Impulses are here correlated so that precise muscular activity such as is needed for speech becomes possible. The Pons is a bridge of nerve fibers between the cerebral cortex and the medulla. The Medulla contains the respiratory and other reflex centers. The Spinal Cord and its nerves control the respiratory muscles. The Phrenic Nerve emerges from the spinal cord in the neck region and extends to the diaphragm. It supplies the impulses which cause the diaphragm to contract in breathing.

among the marked areas are those for "hearing," "seeing," "movement," and "motor speech." The significance of these areas lies in their capacity to analyze and synthesize, to evaluate specialized experience for the brain as a whole. For example, the region in the back part (occipital lobe) of the cortex functions especially in the evaluation and interpretation of impulses coming from the eyes. Without that area we might see an object such as a tree, but fail to understand that the combinations of brown trunk, branches, and leaves together constitute a tree, or that a particular combination of

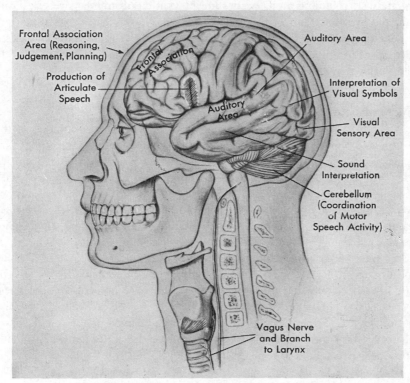

Frontal Association Area (Reasoning, Judgement, Planning)

Production of Articulate Speech

Frontal Association

Auditory Area

Auditory Area

Interpretation of Visual Symbols

Visual Sensory Area

Sound Interpretation

Cerebellum (Coordination of Motor Speech Activity)

Vagus Nerve and Branch to Larynx

Figure 11.   Localization of brain function in relation to speech.

glass and brick and wood means a house. In fact, even color or shape or size could not be appreciated without the visual brain area. Similarly, the auditory area interprets and evaluates experiences brought to it by way of the ear.

Most of what we know becomes known to us through more than one sensory avenue. A peach is something we taste and smell, see and feel. It is juicy and sweet and round and fuzzy and smells "peachy." The combination means a peach. As perceived merely by the sense of taste, a peach or a steak, soup or coffee, mean little. Take away the nose and the eyes and you have merely one-dimensional objects. Smell and see, as well as taste, and you have full-bodied dishes. The added meaning is a result of interinterpretations of sensory values which is made possible for us by the many billions of cells in our brain cortex. The interconnections among these cells make it almost literally possible to "see sounds" and "feel noises" and "taste" the cold and the warmth. In this way the ocean gets meanings, and winter and summer mean more than changes in the time of the year.

From the point of view of speaking rather than of understanding, the motor speech area of the brain is of especial interest. In this and the immediately surrounding areas occurs an integration of impulses received and evaluated by other parts of the brain. In addition, impulses originating here are sent eventually to the tongue and the lips and the other parts of the so-called speech mechanism, enabling us to articulate sounds and give voice to them in the activity called speech.

Effects of Brain Damage

It is fairly evident that unless the brain is intact, we cannot get the most meaning out of our experiences. We cannot, because meanings are impaired if the brain is damaged. That is why children born with brain injuries are slow in beginning to talk and often seem retarded compared with most children born without such handicaps. Damage to the brain after we have learned what things mean results frequently in a disturbance of their meanings, as shown by defective understanding and speaking, and sometimes in impairments in the parallel functions of reading and writing.

We may suffer a permanent injury to the brain as a result of a blow, exposure to explosives, or because of disease. Temporary injury may be caused by shock, excessive fatigue, or overindulgence in alcohol. The effects on speech and language, except for the matter of time, are similar. Strong emotion such as fear and anger may also serve to make us behave as if we had no cerebral integration and control and render us temporarily unable to produce speech on a normal, voluntary level.

THE ENDOCRINE SYSTEM

The endocrine system is another part of the bodily mechanism which enables us to correlate activities and make adjustments to the environment.[6] The important difference between the two systems—nervous and endocrine —is to be found in the kind of correlation of activity which each helps to accomplish. Through the functioning of the nervous mechanism, and es-

---

[6] The nervous mechanism has its own endocrine system which makes it possible for impulses to be mediated through its circuits.

pecially of the central nervous system, immediate, rapid, and specific responses to situations are made. For example, we look at an object and call it by its name ; we engage in conversation and respond with particular words to what is said to us.

The endocrine system exerts influence over the manner of responding rather than over the content of the response. The endocrine system exerts an influence over general and long-term reaction patterns toward situational changes in the environment. For instance, the sitting hen's urge to "sit" is largely determined by endocrine changes within her. Having the urge, the hen looks for something on which to sit. If she has no eggs of her own, the hen will use another chicken's eggs. If no eggs are available, she may sit on objects resembling eggs. The point is that when a hen is so inclined, she appears bound and determined to "sit" on something. The human being having a "set," or attitude, is more discriminating and is not likely to confuse golf balls with eggs. But the internal condition of the organism makes one kind of behavior—behavior consistent with the set—more likely to take place than another in regard to general or cyclic changes in the environment.

The products of the endocrine system are known as *hormones*. Hormones go directly from the glands which produce them into the blood stream. By means of the circulating blood, hormones are quickly diffused throughout the entire body. This ready diffusion makes it possible for an over-all bodily response to take place as a result of endocrine system action.

Our consideration of the endocrine system will be necessarily brief and limited to those glands and their products which have some close or direct relationship to voice and speech production. The location of each of the glands can readily be seen by referring to Figure 12.

The pituitary gland is located in a small, bony pocket in the center of the skull directly underneath the brain. Through the several hormones produced by the pituitary, the gland serves many and diverse functions. It has a master function of serving as a regulator or controller of most of the other endocrine glands. The growth-promoting hormone of the pituitary has a definite influence on voice and speech. This influence can best be observed when the gland fails to function normally in regard to its hormone production. Overactivity results in an abnormal enlargement of the muscles, bones, and cartilages of the head and throat. Specifically, the tongue, the vocal folds, the larynx, and the lower jaw become enlarged. The effects on speech frequently include a hoarse and husky voice and blurred, thick articulation. In the event of underactivity of the growth-promoting hormone, voice and articulation are likely to be weak and to sound "infantile."

The pituitary exercises an indirect effect over voice and speech by way of its regulatory action on the sex glands. The changes in speech, and more especially in voice pitch, associated with adolescence and physical maturity, are under the indirect influence of the pituitary.

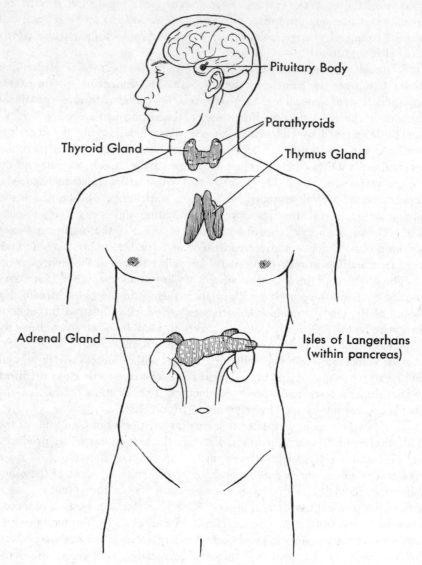

Figure 12.   The endocrine glands.

The thyroid gland is located at the base of the neck lying in front of the windpipe. In its functioning, the thyroid gland is intimately associated with the pituitary. The hormone *thyroxin* is produced by the thyroid. The effect of thyroxin hormone is to speed up metabolic activity of the body cells and to increase *tonus* to the muscles of the body. An overactive thyroid gland tends to make the individual highstrung, irritable, and restless. This condition may reflect itself in speech by a rapid rate of articulation or a high-pitched, unpleasant voice. An underactive thyroid gland is likely to have opposite effects. These include general muscular sluggishness, slow and indistinct articulation, and a hoarse, poorly modulated voice. Intellectual sluggishness to a degree of mental deficiency may accompany underactive thyroid gland activity. This is especially significant in small children, where insufficient thyroxin may result in a failure of physical and mental development. In extreme form, this developmental failure is called *cretinism*. The speech of a cretin is consistent with his mental and physical deficiencies. Not much is spoken by the cretin because he entertains few ideas. What he does say is spoken slowly, articulated poorly, and accompanied by a colorless and immature voice.

The parathyroids are tiny glands which may be found lying close to the thyroid gland. The hormone of the parathyroids regulates the concentration of calcium in the blood stream. The responsiveness of the nervous and muscular system is determined by the calcium content of the blood. Persons with parathyroid hormone deficiency tend to be high-strung, irritable, and "nervous." The speech of such persons will frequently be rapid and arhythmic, closely resembling the kind of speech usually associated with stuttering.

The adrenal glands are found in the abdominal cavity just above the kidney. Different hormones are produced by the inner and outer portions of the adrenal glands. The inner portion of the adrenals produces the hormone known as adrenalin. The effect of adrenalin is to prepare the individual for quick and energetic emergency action. The entire body becomes toned up and ready for physical struggle. Adrenalin brings about a more rapid heart beat so that the blood circulates more quickly, the blood pressure is raised, and added sugar is released from the liver into the blood. The bodily changes we recognize as part of the picture of violent emotional states such as fear and anger and rage are brought about by the action of adrenalin in the blood stream. The speaker who is excited and the speaker suffering from stage fright may attribute many of the physical changes which take place within him to the effects of adrenalin.

The sex glands, in addition to producing sex cells necessary for reproduction, are also producers of hormones. The hormones of the sex glands help to bring about the physiological and behavioral changes which are necessary in reproduction. In addition, secondary sex characteristics such as bodily contour, hair distribution, and vocal changes are effected. The latter, especially noticeable in the adolescent male, result from the rather sudden enlargement of the larynx which takes place at puberty.

There are several other endocrine glands which we need not consider here because no intimate relationship to voice or speech can be demonstrated. These include the adrenal cortex, the pancreas, the thymus, and the pineal gland.

The endocrine system is intra- and interrelated—with respect to the activities of the individual glands and in the correlated functioning of the system as a whole with the nervous system. Probably the best way to think of both systems is as coordinators of behavior. The more complex the behavior, the finer the coordination required. There is little question that speech represents the most complex act of all human behavior.

SUMMARY

Speech production is accomplished through the adapted use of organs of respiration and digestion.

In producing vocal tones, the vocal folds act as pulsators. They are set into action by air coming from the lungs. The voiced sound is reinforced by the resonating cavities of the body. The chief resonators are the cavities of the larynx, pharynx, mouth, and nose.

Articulated (speech) sounds result from a modification of the breath by the organs of articulation. The articulators include the lips, teeth, gum ridge, tongue, and palate.

The essentials for sound and speech production are summarized in the table below.

SOUND PRODUCTION

Requisites for Sound	Musical Instruments	Human Sound (Voice)-Producing Mechanism
1. Body capable of vibration	Reeds, plates, skins, strings, air column	Paired vocal bands and pulsations of air
2. Energy applied to body (1)	Air, percussion, friction	Air (breath)
3. Medium for transmission	Air, wires, water, solid masses, etc.	Air
4. Reinforcers of sound (an aid but not a requisite)	Resonating cavities, sounding boards, pipes, etc.	Cavities of the larynx (voice box), pharynx (throat), mouth, and nose

Hearing enables most persons to learn to speak. The process of hearing includes three highly integrated functions: (1) sound reception, (2) sound transmission, and (3) sound interpretation. Sound reception takes place in the outer and the middle ear. Transmission of sound in the form of nerve impulses is the function of special parts of the inner ear and the auditory nerve. Interpretation of sound is accomplished in the cortex of the brain.

The high degree of complexity of nervous mechanism of man has made it possible for him to achieve speech. The presence of a well-developed cerebral cortex most clearly distinguishes man's nervous system and speech mechanism from those of "higher animals" such as the ape.

The endocrine system supplements the functioning of the nervous mechanism. The glands of the endocrine system produce hormones. These are chemical products which affect the over-all activity of the living individual. The thyroid and pituitary glands have the most direct influence over speech activities.

QUESTIONS AND EXERCISES

1. Compare a wind instrument with the human voice-producing mechanism as to (a) the vibrators, (b) the force applied to the vibrators, (c) the manner in which pitch changes are brought about.

2. Why do most women have higher pitched voices than most men? Do you identify the sex of a speaker by attributes other than pitch?

3. Why is the pitch range of a cello lower than that of a violin?

4. What is the relationship between sound quality and resonance?

5. Why is accurate speech difficult to produce when one is tired?

6. Why is the pitch of the voice raised in excitement?

7. Why are persons with defective hearing likely to have some defect in speech? Can you suggest how normal voice quality may be retained despite defective hearing?

8. Indicate briefly the function of each part of the hearing mechanism.

9. Why does brain damage often result in impaired speech?

10. Recent findings suggest that the long-accepted explanation of vocal fold activity may explain only part of phonation. Consult the literature on phonation and summarize the changing points of view.

RECOMMENDED READINGS

Anderson, V. A. *Training The Speaking Voice*. New York: Oxford University Press, 1961, Chaps. 2–4.

Curry, R. *The Mechanism of the Human Voice*. New York: Longmans Green, 1940.

Eisenson, J. *Improvement of Voice and Diction*. New York: Macmillan, 1958, Chap. 2.

Fairbanks, G. *Voice and Articulation Drillbook,* Rev. ed. New York: Harper and Row, 1960, Chap. 2.

Gray, G., and Wise, C. M. *Bases of Speech,* Rev. ed. New York: Harper and Row, 1959, Chap. 3.

Kaplan, H. *Anatomy and Physiology of Speech*. New York: McGraw Hill, 1960.

Thomas, C. K. *An Introduction to the Phonetics of American English,* Rev. ed. New York: Ronald, 1958, Chap. 2.

Van Riper, C., and Irwin, J. V. *Voice and Articulation*. Englewood Cliffs, N.J.: Prentice-Hall, 1958, Chaps. 7–10 and 13.

CHAPTER 3

THE COMPONENTS

OF SPEECH

(WORDS, VOICE, AND ACTION)

Almost all audible speech, including most emotional expression, may be thought of as words set to impromptu music with some accompanying action. We are more likely to be aware of the words we speak than we are of our vocal tones or of our actions. Words usually inform the listener about our thoughts. Voice, though capable of communicating intellectual content,[1] is more frequently used to express how we feel about our thoughts. Actions (gestures) help us to get our ideas across. This effect is accomplished in two ways. Directly, actions help us to underscore and to reinforce ideas. Occasionally, actions may succeed in communicating our thoughts when words are not found or are not wholly adequate for our purpose. Indirectly, actions are helpful because their use frees us from or reduces physical tension and so makes thinking and communicating easier. Most of us use gestures almost as much to help ourselves in speaking as we do to make our speech intelligible to others. That is why we gesticulate even when our listeners cannot see us, as we do when talking over the telephone, making a recording, or talking into a microphone.

The three components of speech—words, voice, and action—usually tell a consistent story. When the musical underscoring provided by the voice is not too strong, we are likely, as listeners, to accept the words for their intellectual significance. When the vocal tones predominate, what we feel rather than what we think becomes emphasized. At such times the music drowns out the words, and we react to the essential feelings expressed rather than to the words which assume only an incidental significance.

---

[1] This will be considered in some detail later in this chapter.

We could, of course, express feelings without using words. We could regularly make vocal noises, as infants and animals do, and so express our feelings. Training and the pressures of convention, however, work against our using a mere snarl to express anger or distaste, or a purr to express satisfaction. Convention permits laughter, and on special occasions weeping, as emotional expression.

VOICE AND STATES OF FEELING

Voice, when not consciously controlled, reflects our feelings readily and involuntarily because the production of voice is a muscular activity, and muscle tonicity is tied up with the emotional state of the organism. The role of the adrenal glands on muscular action was explained in the discussion of the endocrine system. Under strong emotion the entire body becomes tense. The vocal bands, because of their tension, produce tones of a higher pitch. The added sugar in the blood stream permits more energetic

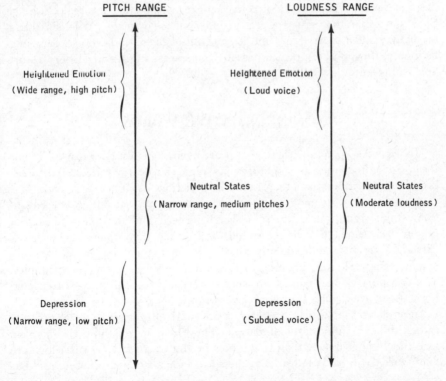

Figure 13.   The relationship between changes in pitch, loudness, and states of feeling.

activity. As a result, voice becomes louder. Because of these involuntary muscular changes, heightened emotion in a speaker is reflected in a louder, higher pitched voice than is characteristic of relatively unemotional speech.

Depressed states are associated with muscular relaxation. When we feel "let down," our muscles tend to go flabby. Technically, our muscles lack adequate tone. Vocal bands which are relatively overrelaxed, or hypotonic, produce low-pitched tones of comparatively weak intensity. When we are depressed, our voices are on the dull, soft, low-pitched end of the scale.

When we speak with relatively neutral feeling, our voices tend to be moderate in pitch and loudness. That is, the vocal tones will fall somewhere within the middle part of our pitch range. Changes in pitch and loudness occur, but they are not of the marked variety associated with the extremes of emotion. The diagram on page 37 presents graphically the relationship between voice and emotional states.

Our use of words to accompany the voice gives us a definite advantage over animals. We can express shades of feeling and subtleties of meaning. By a vocal tone we can make a single oral word express a paragraph's equivalent in writing. We can make words say what they don't ordinarily mean or reveal feelings without being held responsible for any real meaning. So a young man may say of a pretty girl about his own age, "Yes, sir, that's my baby," and not have anyone demand proof of his fatherhood. A young lady may, through her vocal tones, invite a caress by turning to her escort and asking him, "Isn't this a heavenly night?"

NONINFORMATIVE WORDS

It becomes apparent, then, that words may not always be used to inform. Sometimes they are no more than vehicles to carry tones, used to express feeling rather than to provide information.

Almost any word may be uttered in such a way that only the vocalization retains significance. But some English words, notably those of Anglo-Saxon derivation, seem better suited for snarling than others.[2] The names of some animals are frequently snarled when applied by one to another human being. Skunks, hounds, curs, snakes, and rats are a few examples. We also purr animal names for very different effects. Bunny, kitten, and honey bear are among the more favored animals.

It is clear that words used for their vocal effects serve an expressive rather than an informative function. They help to tell how the speaker feels much more clearly than to tell how he thinks. In fact, words which are "not words" probably tell us that the speaker has stopped thinking and has

---

[2] It may, of course, be possible that we are just better able to snarl the short Anglo-Saxon words because we have practiced on them more frequently and regularly than on others.

given way almost entirely to feeling. Probably only the residual influences of social pressure and the desire to hold on to some degree of human dignity prevent the person from going completely animalistic under the stress of emotion. If we were not concerned with what our friends and neighbors might say, it is possible that some of us, like the animal, might use nonverbal vocalizations to indicate our strong feelings about others, or to express our own internal disturbances associated with hunger, love, or fear.

INFLECTIONAL CHANGES

Although changes in vocal tones normally are produced involuntarily as a by-product of muscular change, we are capable of voluntary control of vocal tones. Intentionally produced changes in vocal tone are revealed in the inflections of our speech. Because these changes are intentional and voluntarily produced, they are associated essentially with the intellectual rather than the emotional aspects of speech.

Vocal variation is inherent in almost all spoken languages. In some languages the changes in vocal tones are relatively slight. In English speech, vocal tone changes, and especially those of pitch, are outstanding characteristics of the spoken language. Through changes in pitch, emphasis and intellectual significance are given to particular words within groups of words. In some instances the literal, or denotative, meanings of words are modified by pitch changes so that a group of words is given an interpretation which would not obtain from an understanding of any one of the words, or the usual meaning of the words taken together. (Examples of this situation will be given later.)

Through pitch change, or intonation, the speaker reveals his attitude about what he is saying or toward the person to whom he is speaking. Through pitch change, temporary modifications or additions are made to the basic or stable meanings of the word or words which are derived from a particular combination of sounds. The basic meanings of written language can be found in a dictionary.[3] The meanings of spoken words go considerably beyond these denotative meanings, or definitions. The infinity of shades and subtleties to which we respond when we hear spoken language goes beyond the recording possibility of any dictionary.

INTONATION

A change in pitch on an individual sound is technically known as *inflection*. A combination, or pattern, of pitch changes on a meaningfully

---

[3] The meaning of any statement is, of course, determined by context and the relationship of the words within the linguistic situation.

related group of sounds is known as *intonation*. Each spoken language has its own intonation pattern. We speak with a *foreign intonation* when a pattern native to one language is carried over to another language. In essence, a foreign intonation means that we are mixing the words of one language with the tune or melody native to another language. It is something the English-speaking person may do when he learns the words, but not the melody pattern, of French. The Frenchman is using a foreign intonation when he intones English words with his native French melody.

American-English intonation patterns are characterized by the use of downward inflections to indicate complete or emphatic statements and upward inflections to indicate doubt or uncertainty.[4] For example, a representative intonation pattern demonstrating the use of the falling inflection at the conclusion of a unit of thought would be:

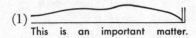
(1) This is an important matter.

This pattern may be contrasted with one in which the (first phrase) of the thought unit includes the use of a rising inflection:

(2) I don't know whether this is an important matter.

Other more or less representative intonation patterns are illustrated in the following sentences:

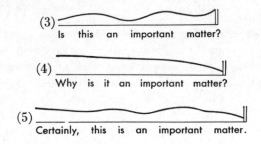
(3) Is this an important matter?

(4) Why is it an important matter?

(5) Certainly, this is an important matter.

It must be emphasized that there are pattern types. They do not actually present the speech of any one person. Each speaker varies in his pitch pattern according to the occasion and specific intent of his speech. An actual graphic representation will not be nearly so smooth as the curves

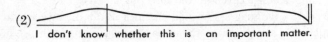

---

[4] This is admittedly a simplification—perhaps an oversimplification—of the complex subject of American intonation. For a detailed and advanced consideration of the subject, see Kenneth Pike's *The Intonation of American English*, Ann Arbor, Michigan: University of Michigan Press, 1946.

here illustrated. For example, the statement "This is an important matter" might specifically be spoken as

This   is   an   important   matter.

rather than as in example (1) above.

The following graphic representation is that of a somewhat more complex sentence than most of those above.

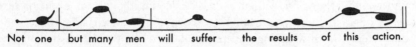

Not   one   but many   men   will   suffer   the   results   of   this   action.

With these reservations in mind, we might arrive at the following generalizations relative to the use of pitch changes and intonation patterns in American speech:

(a) *A falling inflection* is used when we make positive assertions (5) and when we wish to indicate the completion of a thought (1). A falling inflection is also used on the final word of questions which begin with an interrogative word (4).

(b) *A rising inflection* is used to indicate incomplete, or dependent, thoughts and to express doubt or uncertainty (2). The rising inflection is also used in questions which may logically be answered by the word "Yes" or "No" (3).

(c) *The pitch level* of the most important word within a thought unit is likely to be higher than the other words of the phrase.

(d) *The stressed syllable* of a word is usually spoken on a higher pitch level than the unstressed syllable or syllables of the word.

(e) *A circumflex inflection* is used when the speaker's intended meaning is not consistent with the literal meaning of the word or thought unit.

Pitch in Speaking and Singing

In speaking, pitch changes are continuous within a spoken phrase, or unit of thought. This contrasts with the pitch changes in singing, which are generally characterized by the holding of each note (sung syllable) on a relatively constant level. Changes in pitch while singing usually occur in relatively distinct steps between syllables of the words of the song.

Another important distinction between pitch changes in speech and in song is related to the matter of meaning. In spoken utterance, the general tendency is for the more important words to be on a higher pitch level than the less important words. In singing, however, changes in pitch are related to the over-all melody of the song, often without regard to the intellectual significance of the particular word or syllable on which the pitch change occurs. These differences may be brought out by first singing and then speaking the words of a familiar song.

Pitch Changes in Other Languages

All spoken languages do not employ pitch changes as we do in English. The Chinese use inflectional variation to give one sound combination several very different meanings. We can see how different the word meanings can be from the single example of the Mandarin (North Chinese) sound combination *shih*. When *shih* is pronounced with an even, or level, tone, it has a dictionary meaning of "corpse"; with a rising inflection, it means "ten"; with a falling inflection, it becomes the English equivalent of "scholar"; and with a falling-rising inflection, it means "arrow."

It is apparent, then, that pitch changes in Chinese are an integral rather than an incidental aspect of the spoken language. It is more closely associated with the intellectual content of speech than is pitch as used in English. Whereas we use pitch to reveal our subjective reaction to what we are thinking and saying, the Chinese use pitch to distinguish different meanings for what is essentially a basic sound combination. In Chinese, pitch changes are as much a part of a word as are the vowels and consonants of the word.[5]

We recognize, of course, that there are differences among the dialects of Chinese. Spoken Mandarin employs four different tones. Other spoken Chinese dialects use as many as thirteen different tonal patterns.

The use of pitch change to give words intellectual significance is not restricted to the Chinese. The African Sudan languages make a comparable use of pitch. In fact, in African Sudan different vowel-consonant combinations with the same pitch tones may constitute words having the same dictionary, or denotative, meaning. Persons speaking different dialects of African Sudanese will understand one another if the same pitch levels are used in speaking even though they are intoned on otherwise different sound combinations.

We need not go to China or to the African Sudan to find languages in which the melody is an integral part and intellectual aspect of the spoken language. Norwegian, Swedish, and Lithuanian, to name but a few, are languages which, compared with English, have relatively fixed intonation. English pitch variation is relatively free.[6] There is melody in English speech, but it is a melody determined in part by the mood of the speaker and in part by the conventions of sentence formation. In Chinese and in

---

[5] The Chinese speaker *must* use the proper tone in order to identify all but a very small number of relatively unimportant words such as the negative particle "bu." In Chinese, intonation is denotative; in English, intonation is normally connotative.

[6] German and Dutch share this characteristic with English.

many other languages, pitch melody is more closely related to the semantic or intellectual significance of the particular words within the sentence.

FORCE

Another type of vocal change, that of variation of energy, or *force* (stress), is a strong feature of English speech. Syllable stress in English is used to distinguish words which are otherwise the same. Its value therefore is intellectual rather than emotional. For example, *digest* has two basic meanings. If the first syllable is stressed, we have a noun; if the second syllable is stressed, we have a verb. We may also notice that the shift in stress results in a change in the pronunciation of the vowels of both syllables of the word. Other examples of this type of vocal change include *re*bel and re*bel;* *con*duct and con*duct.*

Along this line of vocal change, a syllable which is ordinarily unstressed may occasionally be stressed to clarify the meaning of a sentence. For example, the word *undo* is ordinarily spoken with a second-syllable stress. If, however, the sentence, "I want you to undo it," were to be spoken in answer to the question, "Shall I do it?" the word *undo* would receive a first-syllable stress and so be pronounced *un*do.

Whole-word or even whole-phrase stress is used in English for the purpose of emphasis. In general, words spoken with greater force are made more prominent in relationship to the total speech context. Prominence and emphasis go together. Because of this, increased energy of vocalization is essentially an intellectual rather than an emotional aspect of speech. Stress is usually used to clarify the speaker's meanings rather than to reveal the speaker's feelings about what he is saying.

DURATION

Duration is another aspect through which vocalization is given variety and meaning. Changes in duration, as in pitch, may be used for communicating either intellectual or emotional implications of speech content.

Duration and Significance

On the emotional side, a slow rate of utterance is associated with depressed states; a rapid rate with happier states. We behave slowly when depressed, in speaking as well as in our general conduct. Our behavior when happy is characterized by more rapid movement, and in speech by relatively rapid articulation. When in a high state of elation our articulatory activity may become so rapid as to be indistinct.

On the intellectual side, speech content articulated at a slow rate is considered more important than content spoken at a rapid rate. The reason for this can be readily explained on a psychological basis. If we are listening to what is spoken, we necessarily listen longer to content which is spoken slowly. Having given the content more time and more attention, we assume it to be more important. The assumption of importance is usually not consciously formed. We cannot help but remember better that which we have attended to longer. Other things being equal, words spoken slowly become more significant than words spoken quickly.

Changes in duration are achieved either through variations in rate of articulation or through the use of pauses between groups of articulated sounds. Either device may be used to make a word or a phrase stand out and so become important. Frequently lengthened duration is accompanied by increased intensity so that two factors make for the added intellectual significance given the stressed word or phrase.

Vowels and vowel-like consonants such as *l, r, m,* and *n* lend themselves by nature of their manner of production to modifications in rate of articulation. Words having many vowels and vowel-like sounds take longer to be articulated than do words with a smaller proportion of vowels and a larger proportion of consonants. We would have to make a special effort to say lines such as:

> Alone, alone, all, all alone,
> Alone on a wide, wide sea!

in anything but a slow manner. On the other hand, lines such as:

> Come, and trip it as you go,
> On the light fantastic toe

lend themselves to a rapid rate of articulation.

A comparison of the two verses above bring out the differences in emotional value between slowly articulated and rapidly articulated utterance. The effect of the first two lines of verse from Coleridge's *The Rhyme of the Ancient Mariner* is a depressing one. The second verse, from Milton's *L'Allegro,* is obviously in a gayer mood.

SUMMARY

The components of speech are words, action, and voice. Generally, words reveal what we think, and voice reveals how we feel about what we think. Gestures usually reinforce thoughts. Gestures are also used in place of words which are not adequate to convey our thoughts. Words are sometimes used to reveal nonintellectual content. Voice, on the other hand, may be used to convey subtleties of intellectual content.

Some vocal variation is inherent in the pattern of almost all spoken languages. In English speech, pitch changes are especially important. Through pitch changes, English-speaking persons give emphasis and intellectual significance to words within phrases.

Inflection is a pitch change which occurs in the production of a sound. Patterns of inflectional changes constitute *intonation*. A foreign intonation is a pattern of pitch change which is native to one spoken language and applied to another language.

American-English speech uses three basic kinds of inflectional changes. (1) The falling inflection generally indicates emphasis or finality. (2) The rising inflection implies indefiniteness, uncertainty, or incompletion. (3) The circumflex inflection is used when the literal meanings of the speaker's words are inconsistent with his intended meaning.

In Chinese, inflectional changes are an integral rather than an incidental aspect of the spoken language. The Chinese use pitch changes to distinguish different meanings for a particular combination of sounds constituting a word.

Besides pitch variation, American-English speech employs changes in *force* and *duration*. Syllable stress obtained through changes in force usually has intellectual significance. Changes in duration may be used for either intellectual or emotional significance. When used in an intentional, controlled manner, changes in duration are associated with intellectual content. When the rate of speech is not intentionally controlled, duration becomes associated with feelings and emotions. As such, a slow rate is related to a depressed state of mind, and a fast rate is associated with heightened feelings and emotions.

QUESTIONS AND EXERCISES

1. (a) What are the components of speech? (b) What function does each serve in conveying meaning? (c) When a speaker's voice and words are in apparent conflict, which do you accept and respond to as revealing the speaker's true state of thinking and feeling? (d) What is meant by the statement "Actions speak louder than words"? (e) Under what circumstances may a speaker use voice without words to convey meaning?

2. What is the general relationship between: (a) pitch changes and feeling? (b) pitch changes and meaning?

3. Words are not always used to inform. (a) How else may words be used? (b) Under what circumstances? (c) What are "purr words" and "snarl words"? Give examples of each.

4. (a) What are the three basic types of pitch change? (b) What is the intellectual significance of each? (c) What is the relationship between irony, sarcasm, and innuendo to pitch?

5. (a) What is intonation? (b) When does a speaker use a foreign intonation? (c) Compare two foreign born speakers of different national origin in their American-English speech. What differences do you note?

6. (a) What is the relationship between force and meaning? (b) In the sentence "I want to go away" what different meanings are indicated by changing the stressed word from *I* to *want* to *away*?

7. (a) What is the relationship between duration and meaning? (b) How are changes in duration achieved? (c) How is the use of *pause* related to meaning?

8. Determine which form of emphasis (pitch, force, or duration) or which combination you would use for the italicized word in the following sentences.

    (a) Come here *immediately*!

    (b) I feel just plain *tired*.

    (c) Well, *that* idea *never* occurred to me.

    (d) It's *no* use asking *again*. The *answer* is still *no*.

    (e) What *you* have to say interests me *very* little.

Recommended Readings

Anderson, V. A. *Training The Speaking Voice*, 2nd ed. New York: Oxford University Press, 1958, Chap. 5.

Goldberg, Isaac. *The Wonder of Words*. New York: Appleton-Century-Crofts, 1938, pp. 62–66.

Graff, W. L. *Language and Languages*. New York: Appleton-Century-Crofts, Chap. 4.

Pike, K. *The Intonation of American English*. Ann Arbor, Michigan: University of Michigan Press, 1946.

CHAPTER 4

GESTURE

(VISIBLE ACTION AND COMMUNICATION)

When we communicate we are engaged in an activity, and so we are, of necessity, beings in action. Some of our actions are formalized; most are culturally determined and consciously employed. A few of our actions may be highly individualized and not readily discerned as an integral part of a communicative system. Yet every movement serves some function and says something about the person in action, even though what is said may not be immediately clear. Our discussion in this chapter will be concerned mostly with relatively formalized gestures and their implications for communicative efforts. We shall, however, consider briefly some individualized, expressive movements and their significance for the speaker and the listener.

WHAT IS GESTURE?

The words and the melody of speech would not be possible without action. A considerable amount of the action is not readily seen, but the results are heard in the production of voice and articulated sounds. It is thought possible that conventionalized actions—gestures—formed the basis for human speech. The essence of the theory might be summed up as follows: Human speech arose out of unconsciously produced actions, or gestures, made initially by the hands, arms, and the body as a whole as well as the tongue and lips. When the hands were occupied with tools, the gesture movements were confined to the tongue and the lips and resulted in the production of conventionalized sound symbols or words. Sound symbols were recognized by the hearer because he unconsciously reproduced the original gesture which accompanied the production of the sound patterns (words).[1] The linguist Mario Pei, states his position and that of many students who are concerned with the origin of language with the observation: ". . . gestural language is commonly conceded to have preceded oral speech, some say by at least one million years. It is further estimated that some seven hundred thousand distinct elementary gestures can be produced by facial expressions, postures, movements of the arms, wrists, fingers, etc., and their combinations. This imposing array of gestural symbols would be sufficient to provide the equivalent of a full-blown modern language."[2]

In our discussion of language it was pointed out that language is capable of being specific and intellectual, but that language is not always used for such purposes. A similar point might be made for gestures. On their highest level of capability, gestures may be used to enhance or clarify the meanings of the sound symbols with which they are usually accompanied in speech. Gestures may even be used a step beyond this. When words fail us, we may resort to gesturing in a final attempt to communicate our meanings. If we fail in our attempts at communication, but persist in our efforts to try to say something, thought is likely to give way to feeling, and feeling to emotion. Gestures, like words, may lose their intellectual significance and become movements expressive of emotion. Comprehension of such gesticulation is possible because the actions excite sympathetic movements in the observer, who then begins to respond approximately as he himself feels when the movements are self-initiated.

TYPES OF GESTURES

If we wish then, we may classify gestures into two broad types. The first would be *articulatory gestures,* which have symbolic, or intellectual, value. Articulatory gestures are oral sound equivalents. A second type would be *expressive,* or nonsymbolic, which call forth feelings or arouse emotions, but do not have significant intellectual value. Postures which reveal emotional states and facial grimaces such as sneering and smiling are examples of expressive nonsymbolic gestures.

Articulatory gestures may be subclassified along functional lines. *Graphic gestures* are those which, through suggestion of an outline, suggest a meaning or stand for an object. For example, if we turn our hand, index finger extended, in a continuous series of loops, we are using a gesture to describe a spiral-shaped object. *Plastic gestures* are those in which we suggest the shape of an object or a person through executing molding movements of

---

[1] This is one brief theoretic explanation of the origin of speech. Many other explanations have been offered. Some of these are reviewed in G. W. Gray and C. M. Wise, *The Bases of Speech,* 3rd ed., New York: Harper and Row, 1959, Chap. 8.

[2] M. Pei, *The Story of Language,* New York: Lippincott, 1949, p. 13.

the hands. The shape of a box or an "hour-glass figure" can readily be suggested with such a gesture.

On a higher symbolic level, we may use *denotative gestures*. This type of gesture involves the selection and suggestion of a striking characteristic of an object to stand for the object. For example, the sign language used by many deaf-mute persons employs a gesture suggesting the removal of a hat to stand for the idea of a man. On a still higher level of abstraction, we have the *symbolic gesture*. This type of gesture is probably closest to abstract language usage. The meaning is dependent upon an association of idea and symbol. In the sign language of the American Indian, for example, cupped hands stand for *drinking* rather than for an object for drinking. If cupped hands were to stand for an object, we should have an example of a *plastic* gesture. But when cupped hands stand for an act rather than an object, a higher level of abstraction is attained, and we have a *symbolic* gesture.

Articulatory gestures probably began as involved and elaborate movements. In time, both the complexity and amount of movement were reduced. With the reduction in the nature and amount of movement came an increase in the intellectual significance of the movements. As we think of articulatory gestures today, we may characterize them as intentionally produced, meaningful acts which have gradually been reduced to a few relatively simple movements for convenience in presenting ideas and in obtaining intellectual responses.

GESTURE AS AN INTERNATIONAL LANGUAGE

Articulatory gestures are as close as we have ever come to an international language. Men who have no common audible language and who must communicate with one another are likely to resort to the use of gesture. Usually a modicum of communication is possible even for those who have made no special study of the language of gesture. For those who have made this study, a considerable amount of communication is possible.

The American Indian was aware of the advantages of gesture language. The intelligent American Indian spoke in two ways. One was the audible language of his tribe or nation, in which oral words were reinforced by gestures; the second was the use of a gesture language for purposes of intertribal communication.

Probably the most completely standardized international gesture language is that which has been evolved by deaf-mute persons. In many of the signs employed, the gesture language of the deaf-mute bears a striking resemblance to the intertribal sign language of the American Indian. The Trappist monks, whose members take a vow of perpetual silence, have evolved a system of gestures which also strikingly resembles that used by deaf-mutes. The reason for the resemblances among gesture languages, regardless of place of origin, should be fairly apparent. Gesture words are for the most part limited to the immediate experiences of the speaker which frequently include the observer. When not so limited, the many descriptive "words" of gesture language recall concretely the basic element for idea association. The vocabulary of gesture language consists mostly of concepts which have objective attributes, or states of being.

DIFFERENCES AMONG GESTURE LANGUAGES

Though gesture languages are characteristically more striking for their similarities than for their differences in meanings, differences do exist. For example, in Western cultures hand clapping means approval or applause; in Eastern cultures hand clapping is usually used to summon an inferior or menial person. In some European countries, military personnel may, upon ceremonial occasions, bestow kisses on one another's cheeks. American military persons being honored by their European counterparts, accept this gesture. They do not, however, include the kiss-on-cheek as part of their own awarding of military honors. The embrace and the kiss of greeting among women have their counterpart in a handshake or slap on the back among men. Specific gestures occasionally assume a local significance which may constitute a source of danger among the uninformed or unwary. Thumbs in ears and waving fingers may be silly or amusing as a gesture among Americans in most parts of the United States; the use of the same gesture may be foolhardy or dangerous in some parts of the United States inhabited by recent immigrants or first-generation Americans.

CONVENTIONS OF GESTURE LANGUAGES

Organized gesture languages, such as are used by deaf-mute persons, have conventions of sentence structure and syntax. For example, in the sign language of deaf-mutes, the subject of the sentence comes first, and the object of the sentence generally precedes the verb; adjectives precede the modified noun. A fundamental rule of gesture language is to present signs or words in the same order as we are likely to see and respond to them visually.

The language of gesture is devoid of prepositions, conjunctions, and abstract words. The convention of order of presentation makes it possible for the gesture speaker to dispense with prepositions and conjunctions. Abstract verbs are replaced by specific concepts which permit the essential meaning to be communicated.

The gesture languages we have been considering are ones which deal in signs which stand for ideas. Another type of language gesture, now in comparative disuse, is the sign-language alphabet once widely employed by deaf-mute persons. This system is slow because it requires the spelling out of words. Both one-handed and two-handed manual alphabets are in existence.

GESTURES AS USED BY PERSONS WITH AUDIBLE SPEECH

Those who can hear and have learned to use oral speech, have little or no opportunity for using highly organized gesture language. In ordinary circumstances, we use gestures to reinforce, or emphasize, our audible part. We use gestures unconsciously and become aware of their use only when, for some reason, we are physically or socially restrained from gesturing. What would happen if we agreed to eliminate gestures completely from our speech? This was done in an experiment, with highly significant results. In the first place, there was a considerable reduction in the fluency of the oral speech. Second, the speaker's articulation was not as clean-cut and precise as was usually the case. Finally, the size of the speaker's effective vocabulary was appreciably reduced. In brief, the speaker who is accustomed to using gestures but who is restrained from doing so has difficulty in speaking and in being understood. It would appear, then, that in conversational situations we not only depend upon gestures to make ourselves understood, but also are accustomed to respond to gestures in order to comprehend the speech of others.

EXPRESSIVE AND SELF-DIRECTED GESTURES

Many of us have had an experience in which we found that our manner of speaking somehow failed to support the assertions we wanted others to accept. We did not succeed in sounding persuasive. Our vocal tones, even if they were not quivering, did not suggest security and self-conviction. In such situations it is highly likely that our actions, as well as our voices, betrayed us. The "betrayal" was a result of a lack of control of our visible movements as well as those that produce words and voice.

THE GESTURES OF EMOTION

Earlier we saw what happens to oral language when the controls are relaxed or broken down. Comparable changes take place in gestures—the

Figure 14. Through facial expression and the unconscious use of gesture, Senator McClellan displays his feelings as he pursues his thoughts during a session of a congressional investigating committee.

visible aspect of speech. When our hands tremble, when we feel uncomfortable standing and fidget when sitting, when our muscles twitch and our knees "turn to water," we are revealing through unconscious but expressive movements that we are no longer in complete control of the intellectual situation and are giving way to emotion. Some of us have seen the wild and disorganized activity of a hysterical person. A few of us may recognize that among insane persons actions as well as words are queer. In one form of insanity, bizarre postures, which a mentally normal person could not maintain for more than a few moments, are assumed and maintained by the hour. A morbidly depressed individual scarcely moves. An emotionally excited individual is likely to engage in disorganized and exaggerated movement.

The gestures of emotion in which we are most interested are those most of us produce without awareness and without apparent cause. Such gestures include licking our lips when they are not dry, closing our eyes when we are not sleepy, adjusting our clothes when they are in perfectly good order, and smothing our hair when it is in no need of further attention. These are examples of movements or gestures which are not intended for the response of another person. They are self-directed gestures which represent instead an unconscious aspect of the response of the performer.

Support for the unconscious aspect of these self-expressive movements comes from Wolff, who found that under experimental conditions subjects failed to recognize movements of their hands and face and their own gait.[3]

According to the findings of one investigator,[4] self-directed gestures are supposed to have a definite relationship to personality type. The clothes-adjuster may be an insecure individual; the hair-smoother, a vain but not altogether adequate personality; the pouter, a dependent, infantile person.

Self-directed gestures may arise as a result of inner conflict and may be indicative of personal frustration, or unresolved conflict. The frustration may be momentary, as may the feeling of tension which accompanies unresolved conflict. Tension may be lessened by the execution of such a gesture as snapping the fingers or scratching the head. We recognize that when we get into a "tight spot" most of us engage in self-directed gestures. We may suddenly feel an itchy nose, or find that our ears require scratching. Sometimes these acts might actually create an element of danger. The ear-scratching or eye-blinking which begins to take place while we drive a car under difficult road conditions would increase the difficulty of driving except that the gestures serve to reduce physical tension.

Some self-directed gestures occur often enough in different persons to have acquired symbolic significance. For example, a sudden tightening of the jaw may very well stand for aggression. The gesture of passing the

---

[3] W. Wolff, "Involuntary Self-Expression in Gait and Other Movements," *Character and Personality*, **3**, 327–344 (1935).

[4] M. H. Krout, "Autistic Gestures: An Experimental Study in Symbolic Movement," *Psychological Monographs*, **46**, No. 208 (1935).

hand over the face, eyes shut, may stand for a wish to evade or get rid of an unpleasant situation. According to one student of unconscious gesture movements, this gesture constitutes an escape from the world of reality, an escape in which the actor momentarily, at least, removes himself from a situation which he cannot physically leave.

GESTURE IN ART AND RELIGION

Although gesture is possibly the basis of human speech and continues as an element of spoken language, the language of gesture continues to have an independent existence. It has an almost completely intellectual function in organized sign languages. Gesture, however, has an artistic as well as an intellectual inclination. In the drama, gesture is seen in pantomime, a play employing action without words. Interpretative dancing is gesture which suggests artistic mood as well as meaning.

Gesture has also been incorporated into religious behavior. Worshipers in churches perform certain movements which have significance only as the actions pertain to the ceremony of religion. In some churches, priests perform elaborate ritualistic gestures as part of the religious ceremony. Ritualistic gesture is part of the religion of ancient as well as contemporary cultures. It was and is employed in Oriental as well as Western civilization. The American Indian appealed to his tribal gods through pantomime and the dance. The North American white man does not appeal to God through the dance, but he has not given up pantomime.

INDIVIDUAL DIFFERENCES IN USE OF GESTURES

The frequency and kind of gesture used depend upon the particular speaker and the circumstances of the speaking. There are individual differences as well as cultural and possible racial differences. Persons with large vocabularies and relatively fluent speech would have less need for gesture than persons with more limited vocabularies and less fluent speech. Voluble persons usually talk with an abundance of gesture as well as an abundance of audible words. Gestures appropriate to some public speakers may be most inappropriate to others. A medium-sized man on a public platform might emphasize a point by banging his fist on the speaker's stand. The same gesture by a short person might seem ludicrous. For a tall, heavy-set person to bang on a speaker's stand might constitute a threat.

Cultural differences become apparent when we contrast the frequent and generous use of gestures by the Southern Europeans with the more restrained use of gestures by the Northern Europeans. The French, the

Italians, and the Spanish people as a group are much freer in their use of gesture than are the inhabitants of the Scandinavian countries. The differences are more likely cultural than racial. This is suggested by the results of a study among American immigrants. It was found that first- and second-generation Americans tend to use gestures in keeping with the prevalent custom of their new environment rather than with the custom of their racial group. For example, the Italian immigrants who lived among other Italians continued to use gestures much as they did in their native land. The children of Italian immigrants, on the contrary, were less disposed to the gestures of Italy and more inclined to the use of those prevalent among Americans in their part of the United States. It is reasonable to assume that persons of Nordic origin living in South Europe or among persons of Latin derivation anywhere might begin to take their hands out of their pockets and become more mobile in their speech. Whatever the initial reason for cultural variations in use of gesture, there is no good reason for believing the variations to be biologically inherited. We learn to use visible movements much as we learn to use oral vocabulary. If gestures are a customary part of the manner of speech, gestures will be incorporated into our speaking. If immobility and physical restraint characterize the speakers of our community, most of us will learn to speak with a minimum use of gesture. Gestures, like oral words, are learned through imitation of persons in our environment. The imitation, however, still permits considerable room for individual variability. Our actions, as well as our words, continue to be our own because of the manner in which we use them.

SUMMARY

Gestures—the "words" of action—are an integral part of speech. Like oral language, gestures have levels of significance. As used by the individual, gestures may signify specific thoughts, imply attitudes or moods, or be expressive of thoughts or feelings. Gestures tend to be alike the world over. Because of their similarity of meaning, the language of gesture comes close to being an international medium of comunication. Gesture has independent art forms and plays an important role in the rituals of religion. Properly employed and controlled, gestures may be adequate substitutes for oral words. When not controlled, gestures are equivalent to the use of voice without words. Unconsciously produced, self-directed gestures may reveal conflicts of personality.

RECOMMENDED READINGS

Critchley, M. *The Language of Gesture*. London: Edwin Arnold, 1939.
Eisenson, J., Auer, J. J., and Irwin, J. V. *The Psychology of Communication*. New York: Appleton-Century-Crofts, 1963, Chap. 2.

CHAPTER 5

AN INTRODUCTION
TO PHONETICS

(THE STUDY OF AMERICAN-ENGLISH SPEECH SOUNDS)

If an individual produces a speech sound, or a combination of sounds, in an atypical manner, he gets in the way of the purpose of his speaking. An atypical manner is one which varies significantly from the accepted manner of most members of the speaker's community. Speech which sounds different attracts attention to itself rather than to the meanings of the speech symbols. Whenever the person attracts attention directly to his manner of speaking, he detracts from his meaning. Such detraction may result from the use of an unusual speech melody (see pages 39–42) or from unusual or unacceptable ways of producing particular sounds or combinations of sounds.

Our interest in studying the sounds of American speech is twofold. The first purpose is in keeping with the general thesis of this text. It is to present a body of knowledge which will make us better informed and therefore more intelligent about the tools of speaking. Oral speech is sound production. It is important that we know not only how sounds are produced, but something about the character of the sounds which we intend to produce.

The second purpose in studying phonetics develops from the first. Sound production which falls within acceptable standards will enhance the communication of meaning. If listeners must divide their efforts between trying to determine the symbols and trying to interpret them, understanding is impaired. Speech which falls within acceptable standards is easy to listen to and easy to understand.

[56]

SOUND REPRESENTATION

English Spelling Unphonetic

There is only a rough correspondence between the sounds of English speech and the 26 letters of our alphabet which are used to represent the sounds. As small children we learned that the frequently occurring combinations of the letters *ough* had many different pronunciations. Some of these are represented in the words *bough, enough, through, thorough* and *cough*. We also learned that the same sounds were frequently represented by different alphabetic letters, and that this was true for both consonants and vowels. Spelling became something of a chore when we had to remember that the sound usually spelled *sh* in some words had spelling as variable as: *ci, delicious; ch, machine; ss, assure; s, sugar; ti, patience*. The vowel sound usually represented by the double *e* as in *see* could also be represented, we had to learn, by such different spellings as *ea, mean; eo, people; i, machine; ei, receive; ie, believe*.

When we grew up, some of us had an opportunity to learn that there usually was a reason for the inconsistency between English spelling and pronunciation. We may have been informed that the spelling of most of our words represented their pronunciation at *some former* period in English history. This knowledge may have consoled us for the difficulties we had, and may still have, in spelling and pronunciation. In any event, our spelling today is highly unphonetic. That is, there is little consistency between words as pronounced and the manner in which the words are spelled. An approach other than spelling is needed for the study of pronunciation. This approach is provided for in the study of phonetics.

QUESTIONS AND EXERCISES

1. (a) How many different pronunciations do you know for the letters *ough?* (b) for the letter *c?* (c) for the letters *th?* (d) for the letter *s?* (e) for the letter *z?*

2. (a) How many different pronunciations do you know for the letter *a?* (b) for the letters *ea?* (c) for the combination *oo?*

3. Do all educated speakers pronounce words the same way in your community? If not, what are some differences?

4. List ten words which have two or more acceptable but different pronunciations.

THE SOUNDS OF AMERICAN ENGLISH

The Phoneme

Our study of phonetics will be aproached through a consideration of the basic sound unit, or the *phoneme*. Phonemes are distinctive phonetic elements of a word. Distinctive sounds are those which enable us to distinguish between words. For example, the words *hip* and *hid* are distinguished by their last sounds; the words *dime* and *time* are differentiated by their first sounds; *bag* and *bug* are phonetically different because of their second sounds. *Distinctive significance* is one aspect of the phoneme concept.

A second aspect of the phoneme concept is the recognition of variation. Speech sounds vary in production according to context. The vowel in *hit* is somewhat different from the "same" vowel in the word *ink*. The vowel in *cat* is essentially the same but not identical with the vowel of *cad*. The production of the *t* in *lets* differs somewhat from the *t* of *tin* and the *t* of *later*. The first sound of *can* is not identical with the first sound of *car*. The *r* in *tree* differs from the *r* in *very* and the *r* in *run*. All of these variations are relatively minor. They do not represent distinctive differences in the basic sound unit.

There is also considerable variation from person to person relative to the production of speech sounds. Nationwide, we are not as one in the way we pronounce the vowel of the word *hat*. Rarely, however, despite possible modifications in the length or quality of the vowel, is the variation so significant that we fail to recognize what word was intended. Individually, we may even consider the other person's pronunciation a bit unusual and be aware that it is unlike our own. If, despite differences, there is no question in the mind of the listener as to what is meant, if meaning is not disturbed, then we are dealing with a nondistinctive variation of the sound.[1]

A phoneme, then, may be defined as the smallest distinctive group or class of sounds in a language. Each phoneme includes a variety of closely related sounds (*allophones*) which differ somewhat in production and in acoustic result because of context or conditions of speech. In American speech there are approximately forty-four distinctive groups of sounds or phonemes.

The International Phonetic Alphabet

Our approach to the study of pronunciation will be simplified through the use of a system of sound symbols free of the historical whimsies of our spelling. We shall use the symbols of the International Phonetic Alphabet (the IPA). In general, we may accept the principle that in the IPA system

---

[1] In another sense, we might consider that there is a phonetic and phonemic difference whenever "an individual becomes aware of a variation in the production of a given speech sound that is divergent enough to make him feel that the speaker has used a different sound from the one he, himself would have used." (See C. E. Kantner and R. West, *Phonetics,* Rev. ed., New York: Harper and Row, 1960, p. 24.)

only one symbol is used for each distinctively different sound or phoneme. The same phoneme, including all its variants, is always represented by the same symbol. Sounds and the symbols which represent them are consistent.

The different sounds of American-English speech and their phonetic symbols are listed in the following table.

CONSONANT AND VOWEL SOUNDS

Key Word	Phonetic Symbol for Italicized Letter or Letters	Key Word	Phonetic Symbol for Italicized Letter or Letters
1. *p*et	/p/	23. *h*e	/h/
2. *b*e	/b/	24. *w*e	/w/
3. *t*en	/t/	25. *wh*at [a]	/ʍ/ or /hw/
4. *d*ime	/d/	26. fr*ee*	/i/
5. *c*ake	/k/	27. *i*t	/ɪ/
6. *g*ot	/g/	28. c*a*ke	/e/
7. *f*un	/f/	29. l*e*t	/ɛ/
8. *v*ote	/v/	30. h*a*t	/æ/
9. *th*ing	/θ/	31. *a*sk [b]	/a/
10. *th*an	/ð/	32. c*a*lm	/ɑ/
11. *s*ee	/s/	33. h*o*t [c]	/ɒ/
12. *z*ero	/z/	34. s*a*w	/ɔ/
13. *sh*all	/ʃ/	35. el*o*pe	/o/
14. mea*s*ure	/ʒ/	36. f*u*ll	/ʊ/
15. *ch*urch	/tʃ/	37. s*oo*n	/u/
16. ju*dg*e	/dʒ/	38. c*u*t	/ʌ/
17. *m*ay	/m/	39. *a*bove [d]	/ə/
18. know*n*	/n/	40. supp*er* [d]	/ɚ/
19. ri*ng*	/ŋ/	(General American Pro-	
20. *l*ay	/l/	nunciation)	
21. *r*an	/r/	41. b*ir*d [e]	/ɜ/ or /ɝ/
22. *y*es	/j/		

[a] Many Americans do not distinguish between the /hw/in *what* and the /w/ in *watt*, but pronounce both as *watt*.

[b] Most Americans do not use this sound except as part of the diphthong sound in the words *I, aisle, mine*. The vowel of *ask* is most frequently pronounced with the vowel of *hat* and occasionally with the vowel of *calm*.

[c] Most Americans use the same vowel in *hot* as they do in *calm*.

[d] This sound, as a pure vowel, is used only in unstressed syllables.

[e] Persons who habitually pronounce their *r*'s whenever the letter appears in the spelling of a word are likely to use the vowel /ɝ/ which has definite *r* coloring in words such as *bird, heard, girl*, and *spurn*.

DIPHTHONGS^f

by	/aɪ/	go	/ou/
poise	/ɔɪ/	fuse	/ɪu/
how	/ɑʊ/ or /aʊ/	using	/ju/
may	/eɪ/		

OTHER SYMBOLS USED IN PHONETIC TRANSCRIPTION

ı   Placed below a symbol, a syllabic sign
~   Indicates nasalization
:   Lengthening sign
ı   Placed above and before the beginning of a syllable to indicate primary stress
ı   Placed below and before the beginning of a syllable to indicate secondary stress
/ʔ/ Indicates a glottal or laryngeal "stop."

f It should be noted that not all vowels in immediate sequence are diphthongs. For example, the words *drawing* and *sawing* have the sequence of vowels /ɔ/ and /ɪ/ rather than the diphthong /ɔɪ/.

The diphthongs /aɪ/, /ɔɪ/ and /au/ are phonemic. The others are not. /eɪ/ and /ou/ are nondistinctive diphthong variants of /e/ and /o/.

In learning the phonetic symbols, it may be of some help to know that sixteen of them are taken from the orthographic alphabet. These sixteen are: /p/, /b/, /t/, /d/, /k/, /g/, /f/, /v/, /s/, /z/, /m/, /n/, /l/, /r/, /h/, and /w/.

STANDARDS OF PRONUNCIATION

A person doing much traveling in the United States and who is inclined to believe that those who are unlike him are queer, might soon come to the conclusion that many, perhaps most, people are queer. A more tolerant traveler might form another opinion. He might, even if he were only a moderately good listener, conclude that people spoke somewhat differently in various sections of the United States. For the most part, however, though he might note shades of differences, he would have little or no difficulty in understanding American speech wherever he might be. If the American traveler had the additional advantage of having been in England, the thought might also occur to him that despite the geographic smallness of England proper, the variations in speech in England are much greater than those in his own larger country.

Speech Areas

Any attempt to divide the United States into speech areas must necessarily be in terms of broad approximations. We shall follow the approximations of C. K. Thomas who recognizes ten speech areas in the United States.[2] These comprise: (1) Eastern New England; (2) the Middle Atlantic area: (3) the South; (4) New York City, a rather anomalous region in its resemblances to both the Middle Atlantic and Southern speech areas; (5) the North Central area; (6) Western Pennsylvania; (7) the Southern

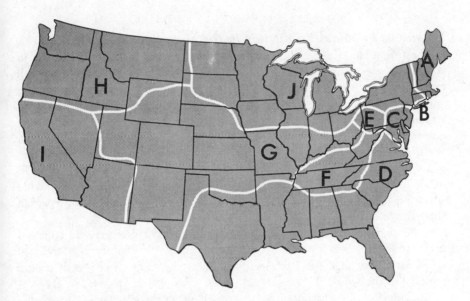

Figure 15. Map showing the major regional speech areas: *A:* **Eastern New England;** *B:* **New York City;** *C:* **Middle Atlantic;** *D:* **Southern;** *E:* **Western Pennsylvania;** *F:* **Southern Mountain;** *G:* **Central Midland;** *H:* **Northwest;** *I:* **Southwest;** *J:* **North Central.**

Mountain Area (most of the mounatin settlements of the southern states); (8) the Central Midland; (9) the Northwest; and (10) the Southwest Coastal area.

The geographic distribution of these major speech areas is indicated in the map on this page.

It is important to remember that no hard and fast lines divide the speech regions, and that all the regions are much more alike than they are different in their speech. Even the special characteristics of a given

---

[2] C. K. Thomas. *An Introduction to the Phonetics of American English,* 2nd ed. Copyright © 1958 by The Ronald Press Company.

region are shared, in part, by other regions. For example, New York City speech shows some characteristics of Southern speech and many of the Middle Atlantic areas. It must above all be emphasized that no educated person of any speech region would have any difficulty in understanding the normal speech of an educated person in any other of the American speech regions. It might also be noted that, by and large, differences in speech among better educated persons are not usually as wide as among persons who have had fewer educational advantages. Geographically and numerically, the General American dialect (Central Midland) is most widely represented throughout the country.

Variations in Sound Production in the Main Speech Areas

Consonants. Except for the sound /r/, there is little difference in consonant production on a purely regional basis. All the major speech areas follow the same practice for the articulation of words beginning with the letter *r* (*right, run, real,* etc.) and in words in which the letter *r* is preceded by a consonant and followed by a vowel (*great, proud, three,* etc.). Except for parts of the South, the /r/ is also regularly articulated when it is preceded as well as followed by a vowel as in *very*. Practices differ, however, relative to words such as *carpet, sharp,* and *sword,* in which there is a medial *r* followed by a consonant. There is also wide variation of practice in words such as *bar, star, fear,* and *door* in which the letter *r* is final.

The regional tendencies for the articulation of the *r* may be summed up as follows:

1. In all regions, the letter *r* is pronounced as /r/ whenever it occurs initially in the word.

2. In general, *r* is pronounced as /r/ whenever the letter *r* is immediately followed by a vowel in the same word. Exception to this will be found in some parts of the South.

3. In the South, eastern New England, and usually in New York City the /r/ is likely to be omitted in the pronunciation of words in which:

(a) the letter *r* is followed by a consonant as in *sharp, fearful,* and *carpet,* and

(b) whenever the letter *r* is final in the spelling of a word as in *fear, door, bear,* and *lower* and is *not* immediately followed by another word beginning with a vowel in the same phrase.

4. When the letter *r* occurs at the end of the word and is followed by a word beginning with a vowel in the same phrase (*far along, pour out, roar of a lion*) the /r/ sound or a vowel with /r/ coloring /ɚ/ is pronounced by most speakers in eastern New England and New York City.

5. In General American speech, the /r/ sound or a close equivalent

is usually pronounced whenever the spelling of the word includes the letter *r*.

Vowels. Differences in practice relative to the pronunciation of vowels are fairly wide among the major speech regions. Space limitations of this text will not permit detailed discussion of the varied and acceptable pronunciations of the vowel sounds. Brief mention will be made of the differences in the pronunciation of the vowel in words such as *class, path, laugh, last, branch,* and *dance.* In eastern New England, many speakers regularly use the vowel /a/ or /ɑ/ in these words, though /æ/ may also be heard. In New York City, most speakers are likely to use the vowel /æ/, but the vowels /a/ and /ɑ/ are also heard. Throughout the remainder of the United States, including the General American area, the vowel /æ/ as in *hat* is likely to be heard fairly uniformly and consistently.

In our later consideration of the vowel sounds, individual variations will be taken up in somewhat greater detail.

Dictionaries and Pronunciation

Many of us regard dictionaries as authorities for the pronunciation of the words we speak. We may fail to appreciate that if a particular dictionary has any authority, it is authority democratically arrived at through the process of recording the most frequent pronunciations of the listed words. A dictionary does not determine word pronunciation or word usage. The editors of dictionaries record the current pronunciation and usage of words. If a given dictionary is revised so that it continues to be current, if the indicated pronunciations (and definitions) are revised periodically so that contemporary speech is reflected, the dictionary may be considered authoritative. An outdated, unrevised dictionary becomes a historical document rather than a guide for determining how speakers should pronounce words in current use.

Most dictionaries indicate more than one pronunciation for many of their listed words. The order of listing is usually decided on the basis of frequency of usage.[3] The authority of a dictionary, in respect to meaning (and grammar) as well as pronunciations, is clearly summed up by Harrison Platt, Jr., in the preface to *The American College Dictionary.*[4]

What, . . . is the role of a dictionary in settling questions of pronunciation or meaning or grammar? It is *not* a legislating authority on good English. It at-

---

[3] Some specialized dictionaries such as Daniel Jones's *An English Pronouncing Dictionary* record the pronunciations of a selected group of persons in a given area. In the case of the Jones dictionary it is the speech of the South of England. The dictionary of John S. Kenyon and Thomas A. Knott, *A Pronouncing Dictionary of American English,* G. and C. Merriam Co., Springfield, Mass., 1944, represents a recording of the pronunciations most current in the United States.

[4] *The American College Dictionary,* New York: Harper and Row, and Random House, 1948, p. XXXI.

tempts to record what usage at any time actually is. Insofar as possible, it points out divided usage. It indicates regional variations of pronunciation or meaning wherever practical. It points out meanings and uses peculiar to a trade, profession, or special activity. It suggests the levels on which certain words or usages are appropriate. A dictionary . . . based on a realistic sampling of usage, furnishes the information necessary for a sound judgment of what is good English in a given situation. To this extent the dictionary is an authority, and beyond this authority should not go.

STYLES OF SPEECH

Informal and Formal Speech

Our speech-minded traveler pondering the question, "Which is the correct way to say a word?" would arrive at no adequate answer unless he modified his question. If his modified question were to take the form of "Under a given set of circumstances, and for a specific occasion, how should a particular word in context be pronounced?" an attempt at an adequate explanation might be made.

Speech—in manner as well as in content—is appropriate or inappropriate, "correct" or "incorrect," according to circumstances and occasion. Whether the speaker be educated or uneducated, his manner of speaking will vary according to time, place, and speech situation. The minister at home, speaking to members of his family, is not likely to address them as he would members of his church when delivering a sermon. The lecturer speaking to a large audience on a formal occasion will use more "elevated" language than the same lecturer talking to his friend on a fishing trip.

Speech may be "correct" and highly informal if it is appropriate to the occasion. In general, when we speak informally we use more contractions than on formal occasions. (This, incidentally, though to a lesser degree, is also true of informal writing.) When we speak conversationally to intimate friends, *he's, won't, don't,* and *I'm* are likely to be used instead of the more formal *he is, will not,* etc. In conversations held with persons who are in some relationship superior to us, we are not so likely to make use of contractions.

Public addresses, in general, are likely to be delivered in a more formal style than most conversations. Important exceptions are the humorous after-dinner speeches and broadcasts of athletic events. Sports announcers do not hesitate to use contractions and unusual grammatical constructions in their description of sports events. In fact, American audiences would consider it strange if an announcer at a boxing match were to tell his listeners, "Joe has just been knocked down. I do not think he will be able to get up. No, I am wrong. He is up on his feet. Gentlemen, I wish to tell you that this is surely a good fight." The listeners would be more likely to hear,

"Joe's down. I don't think he'll get up. No. I'm wrong, he's up again. Boy—I wanna tell you, this sure is a good fight."

Substandard Speech

Speech, in brief, depends upon the audience, the speaker, and the occasion. Pronunciations are appropriate if they are consistent with the objective of the speaker in his role of communicating meanings. Within these limits, speech is "standard." Speech becomes substandard if the pronunciations of words are such that they violate the judgments and tastes of the listeners. We are likely to feel such violation if a lecturer on nuclear physics were to speak like a sports announcer. We would probably get the same feeling if we thought that a speaker was careless rather than informal in his speech.

Pronunciations become distinctly substandard if they are not currently used by any persons whose backgrounds as speakers make their speech judgments worthy of respect. For example, the word *ask* is *not* pronounced *ast* [æst] by most mature and careful speakers, regardless of the speech area in which they may live, and regardless of the degree of informality of the speech occasion. Neither should *picture* be pronounced [pɪtʃ ə (r)], *ten* as [tein], or *escape* as [ɛkskep].

Pronunciations which reveal foreign language influence, such as the substitution of a sound which approximates the appropriate one in English, would also constitute substandard speech. The substitution of a /v/ for a /w/ in words such as *water* and *wind;* /f/ for /v/ in words such as *love* and *leave;* and /d/ for *th* /ð/ as in *that, these,* and *them* are examples of substandard sound substitutions usually resulting from foreign language influence.

QUESTIONS AND EXERCISES

1. What is a phoneme? What factors determine phonemic differences in sounds?

2. How does the International Phonetic Alphabet differ from the alphabet used in the spelling of American-English words?

3. Which word in each of these groups (reading across) has a vowel sound distinctly different from the vowels of the other words of the group?

hack	hat	harm	hang
rail	cake	pain	aisle
rule	should	through	sue
arms	alms	scalp	heart

4. What is the practice relative to the pronunciation of the letter *r* of persons living in your speech area?

5. In what major speech region do you live? Are you aware of whether your own speech pattern conforms to the general characteristics of most speakers in

your region? Is there any way in which your own speech appears to be different? Can you account for the difference?

6. Indicate phonetically the vowel you would use in the stressed syllable of each of the following words: *drama, hand, ask, class, path, market.*

7. List five words which might be pronounced differently by speakers in the eastern New England region and persons in the General American region. What is your own practice in regard to the pronunciation of these words?

8. Listen to your local radio announcer. Compare his speech on a local program with that of an announcer on a nation-wide hookup. What basic differences in pronunciation do you hear?

9. Read the discussions on standards of pronunciation in *Webster's New International Dictionary*, 2nd ed. (G. and C. Merriam Company, 1939) and *The American College Dictionary* (Random House or Harper and Row, 1948). Is a single standard of pronunciation recommended in either of these dictionaries? What is your own point of view?

10. When is the pronunciation of a word substandard? Indicate phonetically substandard pronunciations you may have heard for any of the following words: *ask, burst, column, February, chimney.*

11. You know many words with more than one acceptable pronunciation. Such words might include the following: *abdomen, caisson, catchup, guard, length, penalize, roof, Tuesday, neither,* and *aunt.* What would determine your own choice of pronunciation of these words?

12. How can the choice of the pronunciation of a word affect ready understanding of speech?

13. *Webster's Third New International Dictionary* (G. & C. Merriam Co., 1961) has been subject to considerable criticism because of its listings of words, usages, and pronunciations previously considered substandard. What is your position relative to the criticism and controversy?

ANALYSIS OF SOUND PRODUCTION

The physical basis for the production of speech sounds was discussed in the chapter on speech production (Chapter 2). Articulated speech (speech sounds) we learned are produced when the organs of articulation —the lips, gum ridge, teeth, tongue, and palate—modify the stream of breath coming from the lungs. In the present section we shall analyze the movements and contacts made by the organs of articulation in the production of the various speech sounds.

Sounds of speech are generally classified into three groups: consonants, vowels, and diphthongs. Each of these will be defined.

Consonants are speech sounds produced with some degree of obstruction of or interference with the breath stream by the organs of articulation.

Vowels are produced by a modification in the size and shape of the mouth and position of the tongue *without* obstruction of or interference with the breath stream.

Diphthongs are voice glides uttered in a single breath impulse. Some diphthongs are blends of two vowels. Most, however, represent an instability or "breakdown" of what was originally one vowel.

Voiced and Voiceless Sounds

Consonants may be produced with or without accompanying vocalization. Those produced with vocalization are known as *voiced consonants*. Those produced without accompanying vocalization are *voiceless*. All vowels and diphthongs are voiced except when speech is intentionally whispered.

Consonant Classifications

If we produce the following pairs of words slowly and carefully, paying especial attention to the initial sounds, we will be able to arrive at the bases for the classification of consonant sounds.

car	and	*tar*
sue	and	*zoo*
me	and	*be*
sum	and	*gum*

The acoustic difference between *car* and *tar* is a result of the different place of contact made by the tongue and the palate in the production of the initial sounds. The /k/ sound of *car* is produced by contact between the back of the tongue and the soft palate; the /t/ of *tar* is produced by contact between the tip of the tongue and the upper gum ridge. For both /k/ and /t/ the stream of breath is completely obstructed and then suddenly released with a puff or "explosion."

In the words *sue* and *zoo,* the distinguishing element in the production of the first sounds is that of voice rather than place or manner of articulation.

The initial sounds of the words *me* and *be* are different because of their manner rather than place of articulation. Both the /m/ and the /b/ are produced by action of the lips. The /b/ is emitted through the mouth when the lips are suddenly separated. The /m/ sound is emitted through the nose while the lips are closed.

In the words *sun* and *gum,* three kinds of differences characterize the production of the initial sounds. The /s/ is produced with the tip of the tongue close to but not quite touching the upper gum ridge. The sound emerges "fricatively" through a narrow opening between the teeth. It is unvoiced. The /g/ is produced with the middle or back of the tongue in contact with the soft palate. The stream of air is, as with the /t/ and /d/, completely cut off and then suddenly released. The sound /g/ is voiced.

Other differences would be found if we were to compare words such as *lame* and *dame, yet* and *when, chum* and *from,* and *three* and *thee.* If we were to analyze carefully what is done for the production of each of these consonants, we might arrive at a conventional phonetic classification. Consonants may be classified as to (1) *place* of articulation, (2) *manner* of articulation, and (3) the element of *vocalization.* The chart on page 69 is based on this threefold classification.

The chart gives us considerable descriptive information as to the production of each of the consonants. With practice, we should be able to produce each of the sounds in isolation on the basis of the directions implied in the descriptions. This should be relatively easy after some of the more specialized terms are explained.

Plosives are produced by a stopping and sudden releasing of the stream of breath. The plosive sounds are /p/, /b/, /t/, /d/, /k/, /g/. When a voiceless plosive is the first sound of a stressed syllable and is immediately followed by a vowel, the release of air is accompanied by a puff of breath (aspiration). This may be observed in the pronunciation of words such as *pen, atone,* and *comely.*

Fricatives are produced by a partial closure of the articulators. This partial closure results in the creation of a constricted passage through which the stream of breath must be "forced." This may take place as a result of a grooving of the tongue, or by having other organs of articulation come close together. In the production of the /s/ *and* /z/, both may take place. The fricative sounds of American speech are /f/, /v/, /θ/, /ð/, /s/, /z/, /ʃ/, /ʒ/, and /h/. The /r/, as in *tree,* may also be included as a fricative consonant.

Nasal sounds are reinforced and emitted through the nose rather than the mouth. All three nasal sounds, /m/, /n/, /ŋ/, are produced with accompanying vocalization.

Affricates are blends of two sounds, one a fricative and the other a plosive. Of the affricates in American speech, /tʃ/, as in *chum* is produced without vocalization; /dʒ/ as in *jam* is produced with accompanying vocalization.

There is one *lateral consonant* /l/ in American speech. The /l/ is produced by having air emitted at both sides of the tongue while the tip of the tongue is in contact with the gum ridge.

A *glide* consonant is characterized by continuous movement of an articulator or articulators while the sound is being produced. The glide consonants include /w/, /j/, and /r/ in some contexts. The sound /w/ results from simultaneous activity of the lips and the back of the tongue. (Note its double placement on the consonant chart.)

The /r/ sound results from either the activity of the tongue tip or mid-

PRODUCTION OF CONSONANTS IN AMERICAN-ENGLISH SPEECH

MANNER OF ARTICULATION	ARTICULATORS USED					
	Lips (Bilabial)	Lip-Teeth (Labio-dental)	Tongue-Teeth (Lingua-dental)	Tongue Point Gum (Lingua-alveolar)	Tongue and Hard or Soft Palate (Palatal)	Vocal Folds (Glottal)
Voiceless stops	p			t	k	
Voiced stops	b			d	g	
Voiceless fricatives	hw /ʍ/	f	θ (th)	s, ʃ (sh)		h
Voiced fricatives		v	ð (ŧħ)†	z, /ʒ/ (zh)†		
Nasals (all voiced)	m			n	ŋ (ng)	
Glides (vowel-like consonants)	w			r*	j (y), r‡	
Lateral				l		

* The tongue tip in many instances is curled away from the gum ridge toward the center of the hard palate.
† Two additional consonant blends should be noted. These are the affricates /tʃ/ and /dʒ/, the first a voiceless and the second a voiced blend. Because of the second component, they are actually produced with the tongue in a post-alveolar position.
‡ In combinations such as k or g followed by r, the r sound may be produced in this position.
Source: From Eisenson and Ogilvie, *Speech Correction in the Schools*, 2nd ed. (New York: Macmillan, 1963).

tongue. When /r/ is immediately preceded by the sounds /t/, /d/, or /θ/ in the same syllable, it is likely to be produced as a fricative sound.

The sound /hw/ is sometimes produced as a fricative-glide and so may also be included among the glide consonants. It is more frequently produced as a pure fricative, as indicated by its position on the consonant chart.

The sound /j/ is produced by activity of the front of the tongue raised towards the hard palate.

The glides, as may be noted from the consonant chart, are included among the *semivowels*. The articulation of consonants is characterized by contact or narrowing of the organs of articulation. Vowels are characterized by changes in resonance associated with modification in the shape of the oral cavity. The glides share some of the characteristics of the consonants as well as the resonant quality of the vowels. For this reason they are included among the semivowels.

At this point it should not be difficult to figure out why the consonant /b/ is described as a voiced bilabial plosive or why /s/ is described as a voiceless, lingua-alveolar fricative. The student can test his ability to follow directions as well as his knowledge of the specialized vocabulary of phonetics by producing the sounds according to each of the following prescriptive descriptions, in this fashion: *The labio-dental voiced fricative.* (Lower lip in contact with upper teeth; breath forced through constricted passage between lip and teeth; vocal folds in vibration. The sound /v/ is produced.)

By way of practice, the following might be tried:
1. bilabial nasal
2. lingua-dental voiceless fricative
3. lingua-velar voiced plosive
4. lingua-alveolar voiceless plosive
5. labio-dental voiceless fricative
6. bilabial voiced glide.

AMERICAN VOWELS AND DIPHTHONGS

Vowels

Production. When we studied the production of consonants we were able to conclude that these sounds differed from one another according to (1) place of articulation, (2) manner of articulation, (3) the element of voice. If we produce a few of the vowels of American speech listed in our phonetic alphabet (page 59) we will see that the criteria for differentiation among consonants do not hold for vowels. Vowels, we will notice, have these characteristics in common: (1) All are voiced sounds; (2) all are articulated in essentially the same manner; that is, all vowels are continuant sounds produced without interruption and without restriction of the stream of breath; (3) though lip activity is involved, tongue activity characterizes the production of all vowels.

Vowel Classification.   Vowels may be conveniently classified according to the *part of the tongue*[5] most actively involved in the production of the sound.

If we concentrate on the vowel sound of the words *sea* and *soon*—/i/ and /u/—we should be able to note that the blade of the tongue moves forward towards the hard palate for *sea*. In the word *soon,* the back of the tongue moves towards the soft palate for the articulation of the vowel. Now, let us contrast the vowels in *set* and *saw*—/ɛ/ and /ɔ/. In *set* as in *see,* the vowel sound is produced with the blade of the tongue most active in front of the mouth. The tongue, however, is not so high up for /ɛ/ as it is for /i/. (Compare *see* and *set.*) For the vowel of *saw,* the back of the tongue is most active in the back of the mouth, but the tongue is lower for /ɔ/ than it is for /u/. (Compare *soon* and *saw.*) On the basis of the production of the four vowels considered above, a twofold classification is possible.

1. Vowels differ in production as to place of articulation. They may be produced either in the front or in the back of the mouth with the blade or back of the tongue most active. If we attend to the production of the vowel sounds in the words *burn, butter* (second vowel), and *sun,* we will note that the *midtongue* is most actively involved.

2. Vowels differ as to the height of the tongue position. Some vowels such as /i/ and /u/ are produced with a high-tongue position. The vowels /ɛ/ and /ɔ/ have a lower tongue position. The vowels of the words *hat* /æ/ and *calm* /ɑ/ are still lower in respect to tongue position.

Muscle tension provides a third basis for the classification of vowels. If we compare the vowel of *peek* with that of *pick,* we should be able to feel that the tongue is tense for the vowel of *peek* and relaxed for the vowel of *pick.* Similarly, the vowel of *shoot* is produced with a tense tongue in contrast with the vowel of *should,* which is produced with a lax tongue. Differences in tension are not confined to the muscles of the tongue. The muscles under the chin also show characteristic differences. In addition, the apex of the larynx—the "Adam's apple"—rises more for the tense vowels than it does for the lax vowels. These distinctions in muscle tension may be observed if you look at the mirror while producing the vowels of *peek* and *pick* or *shoot* and *should.* You should be able to note the following: (1) For the vowels of *peek* and *shoot,* a tense tongue, upward movement of the apex of the larynx, and bunching of the muscles under the chin; (2) for vowels of *pick* and *should,* a relaxed tongue, no muscle bulge under the chin, and little or no upward movement of the apex of the larynx.

---

[5] It is clear of course, that the entire tongue takes part in the production of all vowel sounds.

The Vowel Chart. If we trace the tongue position for the vowels in the words *be, bit, bath, bet, bat,* it will be noted that the blade of the tongue and the lower jaw are lowered from a relatively high position in *be* to a low position in *bat.* Those of us who use a different vowel for *bath* /a/ than for *bat* /æ/ should be able to notice an even lower tongue position for the vowel /a/. In terms of tongue position, we might outline the tongue roof of mouth relationship for the front vowels as shown in Figure 16.

It might be noted that the tip of the tongue is placed behind the lower gum ridge in the production of all the front vowels. This tip-of-tongue posi-

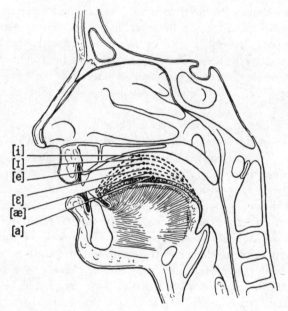

Figure 16.   Representative tongue positions for front vowels.

tion holds for the articulation of all vowels, whether front, mid, or back. For back vowels, however, the tongue tip is pulled back a little along the floor of the mouth.

If we continue this analysis for midvowels, our outline of tongue position changes would now approximate those shown in Figure 17.

Similarly, the back vowel outline might be presented as in Figure 18.

Now, if we combine all three vowel diagrams into one figure and re-place the tongue outlines by dots to indicate the *high point* of the tongue, our diagram would approximate Figure 19.

Lip- Rounding.   If we produce all the vowels as isolated sounds accord-ing to their position on the vowel diagram, a fourth basis for vowel classi-fication becomes apparent. The back vowels, especially the high back vowels

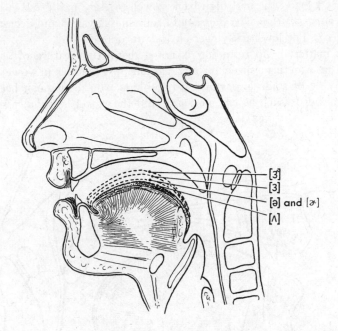

Figure 17.   Representative tongue positions for central vowels.

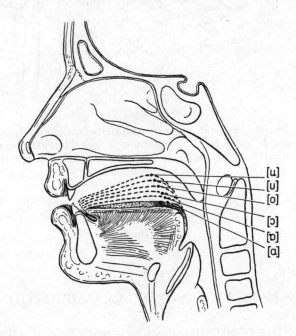

Figure 18.   Representative tongue positions for back vowels.

/u/ *and* /ʊ/ and the mid high back vowel /o/, are produced with the lips in a *rounded position*. The degree of "roundness" varies and decreases from /u/ to /ɒ/. The low back vowel /ɑ/ is "unrounded."

The matter of lip rounding is not a distinctive feature of vowel production in American speech. Emphasis on lip rounding in vowel articulation may be of some importance to speakers who distinguish between the vowel in words such as *cot, hot, doll* and the vowel in *palm, farm, harm.*

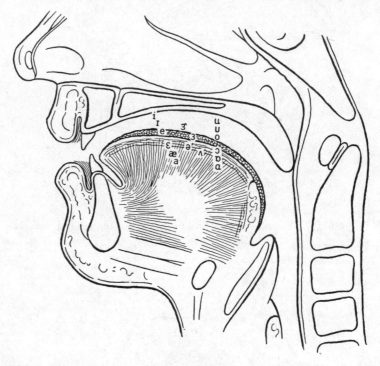

Figure 19. Representative tongue positions for the vowels of American English speech. In actual speech there is considerable variation from these positions from person to person, and according to speech context, for each person.

For speakers interested in making the distinction, one way of doing so is to make a point of rounding the lips for the vowel in *cot, hot,* and *doll* as we would for the vowel in *pall,* while assuming the lowered tongue position as we would for the vowel in *alms.*

SUMMARY OF VOWEL CLASSIFICATION

Now, by way of summary, we may list the fourfold bases for vowel classification. Vowels differ in articulation according to:

1. Place of articulation (front, mid, or back of the mouth in relationship to the palate).

2. Height of the tongue. (Tongue is arched high, midway, or low.)

3. Degree of muscle tension.

4. Lip-rounding. (Back vowels with the exception of /ɑ/ may be rounded. Front vowels and central vowels are not rounded. Lip-rounding, however, is not a distinctive feature of vowel articulation.)

SOUNDS IN CONNECTED SPEECH

Strong and Weak Forms

If we say the words *butter, mother, brother* while concentrating on the articulation of the vowels we should be able to observe the difference between *strong* and *weak* vowels. Two vowels are used in each of the words *butter, mother,* and *brother* /ʌ/ and /ə/ or /ɚ/. The vowels sound very much alike. On the basis of their articulation, they are very much alike. The significant difference between them is that in each word the first vowel is *stressed* and *strong* while the second vowel is *unstressed* and therefore *weak*.

Weak Vowels

As mentioned earlier, an outstanding characteristic of American-English speech is the general use of weak vowels in unstressed syllables of polysyllabic words. This may readily be noted in such words as *about, woman, today, conclude*. In each of these words, the vowel of the unstressed syllable is approximately the same as the unstressed vowel /ə/ in the word *about*.

The vowel /ə/, though the most frequently used vowel in unstressed syllables, is not the only vowel so used. Perhaps next in frequency is the vowel /ɪ/ which we find in the unstressed syllables of the words *added, noses, hurting* and as alternatives for /ə/ in such words as *obligate, exist, certain,* and *satisfy*. It may be of some interest to note that though the vowel /ə/ as a pure vowel is used only in unstressed syllables, the vowel /ɪ/ may be used in either stressed or unstressed syllables. In the words *sinful, tin, filter,* the vowel /ɪ/ is stressed. In the words *purify, beautiful, infer,* the vowel /ɪ/ is unstressed. It should be noted, however, that /ə/ might also be used as the unstressed vowel instead of /ɪ/ In the words *singing, vindicate, instill,* the vowel /ɪ/ appears in both the stressed and unstressed syllables.

Weakening of vowels is a frequent occurrence in so-called "connecting words" of English. Pronouns, prepositions, auxiliaries, articles, and conjunctions, unless they are stressed for a special reason, are generally used in their weak forms. For example, the most frequent pronunciation of the article *the* is /ðə/. Ordinarily, a sentence such as "The book is green" would be transcribed "[ðə bʊk ɪz grin]." If, however, a particular book were being talked about, which had special significance for both speaker and listener, the sentence might then become "[ði bʊk ɪz grin]." A study of the words listed below will reveal some of the differences in vowel usage in stressed and unstressed syllables.

Vowel when *stressed*	Vowel when *unstressed*
/ɛ/ rebel (noun)	/ɪ/ or /ə/ rebel (verb)
['rɛbɪl] *or* ['rɛbəl][6]	[rɪ'bɛl]
	[rə'bɛl]

/ʊ/	full [fʊl]	/ə/ pitiful	['pɪtifəl]
/æ/	man [mæn]	/ɪ/ or /ə/ woman	['wʊmɪn] or [wʊmən]
/i/	scene [sin]	/ɪ/ or /ə/ scenario	[sɪ'næriou]
			[sə'næriou]

The following list presents some of the more common words which are usually spoken in their weak forms.

Written Word	*Strong Form or Forms*	*Weak Form or Forms*
a	[eɪ] (rarely used)	[ə]
an	[æn] (before a vowel)	[ən], [n]
and	[ænd], [æn]	[ənd], [ən], [nd], [n]
at	[æt]	[ət]
could	[kʊd]	[kəd]
do	[du]	[də]
for	[fɔ], [fɔr]	[fə], [fər]
from	[frɑm], [frɒm]	[frəm]
have	[hæv]	[həv], [v]
he	[hi]	[hɪ], [ɪ]
her	[hɜ] or [hɜ˞]	[hə], [hə˞], [ə]
must	[mʌst]	[məst], [məs]
of	[ɑv], [ɒv]	[əv]
shall	[ʃæl]	[ʃəl], [l]
she	[ʃi]	[ʃɪ]
that	[ðæt]	[ðət]
the	[ði]	[ðə], [ðɪ] before a vowel)
them	[ðɛm]	[ðəm], [əm], [m]
to	[tu]	[tə], [tʊ] (before a vowel)

---

[6] The stress mark (') in phonetic transcription appears *before* the stressed syllable.

Written Word	Strong Form or Forms	Weak Form or Forms
was	[wɑz], [wɒz]	[wəz]
were	[wɜ], [wɝ]	[wə], [wɚ]
will	[wɪl]	[wəl], [l] (as a contraction)
you	[ju]	[jə]
your	[joə], [joər]	[jʊ], [jə]
	[jɔə], [jɔr]	[jʊr], [jər]

ASSIMILATION

The person who indicates his intention to buy some new clothes for the winter by telling us [aɪm ɡɔnə baɪ səm nu klouz ðɪs wɪnə] may be thought of as a careless speaker. A phonetician or student of language, however, might view with greater understanding such pronunciations of [ɡɔnə] for *going to* and [wɪnə] for *winter*. These pronunciations might well be viewed as illustrations of economy of effort in speech. They would exemplify the general tendency to simplify the movements of the articulatory mechanism in producing speech sounds. To the student of language these pronunciations, though they would be characterized as substandard, would nevertheless represent the same kind of changes which have produced the accepted pronunciations of [hæŋkətʃɪf] for *handkerchief* and [tɪʃu] for *tissue*. The name given to this kind of phonetic change is *assimilation*.

Assimilation in speech refers to the phonetic changes which take place when one sound is modified as a result of the influence of a neighboring sound. A detailed analysis of assimilation is beyond the scope of this book.[7] We might, however, briefly consider a few types of assimilative changes.

Anticipatory Changes

Most assimilations reveal the influence of anticipatory changes. That is, the articulators, in anticipation of a sound which is to follow, modify a preceding sound. The change will be such as to simplify or facilitate articulation. For example, in *congress* the letter *n* is sounded as /ŋ/ in anticipation of the sound /ɡ/ which follows. It is easier to articulate the combination /ŋɡ/ than /nɡ/ simply because both the /ŋ/ and the /ɡ/ are produced with the same parts of the tongue and palate. Similarly, it is easier to say

---

[7] The reader interested in such an analysis might consult C. K. Thomas, *An Introduction to the Phonetics of American English,* New York: Ronald, 1958, Chap. 22, or J. S. Kenyon, *American Pronunciation,* Ann Arbor, Michigan: George Wahr, 1940, or A. J. Bronstein, *The Pronunciation of American English,* New York: Appleton-Century-Crofts, 1960, Chap. 11.

[hɔ(r)ʃʃu] than [hɔ(r)sʃu] for *horseshoe;* [ðɪʃʃou] for *this show;* and [ɪŋkəm tæks] for *income tax.*

Voicing

This type of assimilative change is perhaps best exemplified in the matter of voicing or unvoicing of final *d* or *s*. In words such as *aped, leaped, raked, guessed,* and *hoped* the next to the last sound is a voiceless consonant. (The letter *e*, in each case, is silent.) As a result, the final sound is /t/ despite the spelling of *d*. Similarly, the letter *s* is sounded as /s/ in words such as *ropes, lifts,* and *takes.*

In words such as *passes, wishes, ledges,* and *stitches,* the final *s* is pronounced as /z/ under the influence of the preceding sound. (The letter *e* is sounded as a weak vowel.) In words such as *tags, kegs, teams,* and *reams,* the final *s* is pronounced /z/ because of the influence of the preceding voiced consonant.

Other Assimilations

Some assimilations result in the complete loss of one or more sounds replaced by a third sound. This happens in the assimilated pronunciations of *nature, lecture,* and *feature*. An extreme form of such assimilation is exemplified by the pronunciation of the English proper name of Cholomondeley as [tʃʌmli].

In the pronunciation of [klouz] for *clothes,* the *th* /ð/ is dropped because of the difficulty in pronouncing this sound before a /z/.

Assimilation, it should be noted, frequently takes place within a phrase because of the influence of sounds in adjacent words. For example, *miss you* and *meet you* may be assimilated in conversational speech to [mɪʃu] and [mitʃu]. The individual words *miss, meet,* and *you,* if spoken in isolation, would not show any such phonetic modification.

Assimilations and Speech Standards

Although it is easy to understand the general nature of assimilation and the influence of the process in speech, not all assimilative changes are acceptable. Persons who would use the word *lazy* where we use the phrase *economy of effort in articulation* would be inclined to resist recognized changes in speech sounds. Such persons might, for example, object to the pronunciation of *income* as [ɪŋkʌm] and insist that the prefix *in* maintain its identity in the more careful pronunciation of [ɪnkʌm]. A similar argument might be presented for the maintenance of the pronunciation of *congress* as [kɑngrɪs] rather than [kɑŋgrɪs].

Some assimilative influences are not considered desirable because quality of tone is affected. For example, if the words *nice, nail,* and *my* are produced with no effort to raise the soft palate after the articulation of the nasal consonant, in each instance the entire word tends to become nasalized.

In any event, regardless of influence or counterinfluence at work, not all assimilations are acceptable as standard. The word *gas,* for example, is pronounced [gæs] and not [gæz] in American standard speech regardless of region; [opəm] or [opm] is not acceptable for *open.*

QUESTIONS AND EXERCISES

1. Define assimilation. What is the basis for assimilative change?

2. Give examples of assimilative pronunciations which are not considered standard in your community.

3. May the nasalization of the vowel or diphthong in words such as *on, aim, answer,* and *wrong* be accounted for on the basis of assimilation? Explain.

4. What is your pronunciation for the words *educate, don't you, won't you,* and *culture?* Do they reveal assimilative influence?

RECOMMENDED READINGS

Bronstein, A. J. *The Pronunciation of American English.* New York: Appleton-Century-Crofts, 1960.

Carrell, J., and Tiffany, W. R. *Phonetics.* New York: McGraw-Hill, 1960.

Kantner, C. E., and West, R. *Phonetics,* Rev. ed. New York: Harper and Row, 1960.

Thomas, C. K. *An Introduction to the Phonetics of American-English,* Rev. ed. New York: Ronald, 1958.

CHAPTER 6

IMPROVING
YOUR VOICE

OBJECTIVES

In earlier chapters (Chapters 2 and 3) we learned how voice is produced and the role of voice as a component of speech. We shall apply that information in the present chapter. In addition, we shall arrive at practical answers to three key questions:
1. What is an effective voice?
2. How can I voluntarily control my voice?
3. How can I improve my voice to make it an instrument to reveal my thinking and feeling—to secure the responses I want my listeners to make to my speaking?

WHAT IS AN EFFECTIVE VOICE?

An effective voice is one which attracts no attention to itself either because of the manner in which it is produced or because of the acoustic product. An effective voice must necessarily be appropriate to the age, sex, and physical make-up of the speaker. An effective voice is a responsive voice. It must be able to reflect the responses that the individual makes to persons with whom he is speaking. It must also be capable of reflecting the individual's responses to his own inner reactions. An effective voice, by being responsive, is able to communicate meanings of intellect and of feeling.

Appropriateness

An immature voice is appropriate—if it comes from a child. If thin, high pitches are produced by a person old enough to be an adult, we are struck by incongruity and distracted from meaning.

If we listen to a three-year-old, we cannot always tell whether the child is a boy or a girl. With increasing age, vocal differences of the sexes become clearer. Voice becomes appropriate according to the sex as well as the age of the speaker.

Pleasantness

From the viewpoint of the listener, an effective voice is one which can be heard without conscious effort or strain. It is a voice which is consonant with the speaker's content and which helps to make the content readily intelligible. The voice should be pleasant to hear. The feeling of pleasure, however, should not so dominate the listener's reactions that he responds to the speaking voice as he might to the singing voice. When the speaker becomes consciously aware of his enjoyment of a voice, he is likely to lose sight of the meanings which, fundamentally, the voice should be helping to convey. In short, the enjoyment of listening to a speaker's voice should be passive and unconscious. An effective speaking voice should neither interfere with nor distract from meaning. It should be easy to listen to and help the speaker to maintain attention to the content rather than the manner of his speech. In brief, an effective voice is one that helps the speaker to convey his message—his thoughts and feelings—to his listeners.

OBJECTIVE CHARACTERISTICS

The qualities of an effective voice discussed above are essentially subjective. Objectively, we may consider several characteristics for effective voices:

1. Adequate and Controlled Loudness.   An effective voice should be as loud as the speaking occasion demands. It should be heard with ease by all persons in the audience and yet not disturb any listener because of its loudness. The voice should be well controlled, changing in volume according to the significance of the content. Though the voice may become subdued when the content is not significant, it should never be so subdued as to be difficult to hear. If the speaker is engaged in conversation, there should be no need to ask him to repeat because of a failure to hear him. Neither should we wish to withdraw because our eardrums are assaulted.

2. Variety of Pitch.   Whether in conversation or in a public speaking situation, the speaker's voice should have variety of pitch. The pitch, of course, should vary with the intellectual and emotional significance of what is being said.

The extent of the pitch range should not be forced so that unpleasant, poorly sustained tones are produced. Whether the pitch be relatively high or low, the voice should have the support of an adequate supply of breath. The extent of the pitch range varies considerably from person to person. Most of us, however, can increase our range considerably with comparatively little effort. How to accomplish this will be considered later.

3. Good Tone Quality.   An effective voice should be clear. Clarity is achieved when a voice has no fuzziness, harshness, breathiness, or rasp. The voice has good tone when it does not sound throaty, husky, raspy, or in any way forced. On the positive side, good tone quality is resonant, alive, and vibrant. It reflects and conveys the changes in mood and in feeling which accompany the nuances of thought the speaker wishes to convey to his listeners.

4. Rate and Timing.   The well-controlled voice must reveal a sense of timing. If what is spoken is not timed to the speech content, the audience, and the situation, the significance of the content will be impaired.

It sometimes becomes necessary for a speaker to control his rate of utterance—the presentation of his thought products—in a way inconsistent with his personality. Some of us tend naturatlly to move, think, and in general to behave slowly. Others behave at a faster pace. Our external speech must, however, vary according to the needs of our listeners rather than the inclinations of our personalities. (Applications of this point are made in the discussions on reading and public speaking.)

5. Responsiveness.   An effective voice not only should reflect the feelings and meanings the speaker wishes to communicate, but also should reveal that the speaker is observing and responding to the reactions of his listener or listeners. If the speaker observes signs of boredom or of restlessness, it may be that his lack of vocal variety has induced such effects. Evidence of listener strain that suggests difficulty in hearing should be met with an increase in loudness, providing, of course, that the listener's hearing is not so poor as to impose abnormal demands on a speaker's vocal efforts.

Tonal variety—changes in loudness, pitch, rate, and quality that are consonant and adjustable to the changes in a speaking situation—characterizes a responsive speaker. A flexible, adjustable voice should be able to reflect feelings of sympathy, deference, respect, and appreciation as well as the more negative feelings of irritation, annoyance, or rejection, if indeed these feelings are called for by the situation. We hope that no speaker makes a specialty of being proficient in expressing unpleasant reactions without developing at least equal aptitude for the more pleasant vocal responses.

IMPROVING YOUR VOICE

Hearing Your Voice and Analyzing It

You are too close to your own voice to know how it really sounds to others. The surprised look of the person who hears his recorded voice played back for him, the look which says, "It this really my voice?" attests to this unfamiliarity. It also provides mute evidence for the need most of us have to hear ourselves as others hear us so that we may learn how to improve our voices.

There are several mechanical devices which can help us listen to our voices as we listen to others. Tape and disc recordings are now easily available at professional offices, commercial studios, and speech clinics as well as in many homes. It is important that the recording instrument and the playback have sufficiently high fidelity so that the reproduced voice is a "reasonable facsimile" of the original.

The voice should be recorded in situations which include or simulate conversation, reading aloud, and public address. The speaker turned self-listener should then analyze his voice as a basis for asking himself a number of questions. The speaker might ask himself:

1. Does the voice reflect the personality picture that I have of myself? Am I pleased with this portrait?
2. Is the voice easy to listen to? Is it pleasant?
3. Does the voice reflect what I feel and think?
4. Is the voice adequately loud, controlled, and varied in its volume? Is there any evidence of strain in its production?
5. Is the pitch range wide enough?
6. Are the tones clear and well sustained?

Supplied with answers to these questions, the speaker-listener might be sufficiently motivated to change some of the answers. The discussion which follows should help him to bring about some of the desired changes.

Voice and Personality

In a later chapter (see Chapter 9) the relationship between speech and personality will be considered. We shall see that our evaluation and judgments of personalities is considerably influenced by what the voices tell us. Sometimes we have only the voice of the individual as the basis for our opinion. For most of us, radio personalities are their voices. We like some announcers and commentators; others leave us cold; we are indifferent to some of them, and may actually dislike a few. Whatever our reaction, it is usually based on how the voice affects us.

The way a voice affects us is not entirely a hit-or miss affair. Radio performers present themselves as *kinds of personalities* by their voices. We have stereotypes of personalities which are associated with kinds of voices. Radio writers and directors, especially those concerned with "soap operas," take advantage of these stereotypes in their productions. They can count on pre-established reactions in their selection of the voices which communicate themselves almost immediately as personalities to be liked or disliked, to be responded to pleasantly or unpleasantly. We can be expected to recognize the average villain or hero the moment we hear him. The sweetness of the heroine comes to us through her voice. So does the staunchness, dependability, and unselfishness of the ever-available, good, but somewhat past-middle-aged friend.

We recognize, of course, that many times the stereotypes are wrong. Some very fine persons have very poor voices. And some very bad characters have excellent and deceptive voices. The fact remains, however, that our initial responses tend to be consistent with the stereotypes. If we, as speakers, have no opportunity to modify the initial responses of the listeners, then the stereotyped response, whatever it may be, will remain.

In responding to our own voices, we should determine whether we are revealing the personality we want revealed. Is there a suggestion of a whine when no whine is intended? Does the voice reveal aggresion when agression is not meant? Does the voice suggest irritability, indifference, annoyance, fatigue, boredom? Are the suggestions consistent with the actual situation? If they are not, their recognition may be enough for the speaker to eliminate them. If, howeevr, they reveal traits of personality which are truly those of the speaker's, recognition alone will not be sufficient. An approach which emphasizes psychotherapy will then be needed.

It is important to recognize at this point that habits of voice and speech may persist and tell us of a personality that used to be rather than the one currently that of the speaker. The maladjustments of yesteryear may linger in the voice. This is understandable when we realize that voice production is a motor act. The adjustment may have taken place without an accompanying change in vocal behavior. A conscious effort must then be made to modify vocal habits so that the adjusted personality may be reflected.

LOUDNESS CONTROL

An effective voice as we indicated earlier must be adequately loud. That means that the volume of the voice must be under the voluntary control of the speaker so that, as the occasion demands, the voice may be appropriately soft as well as appropriately loud.

Control of loudness is established through control of breathing. Specifically, it is a matter of learning how to release air so that the expiratory part of the breathing cycle is coordinated with the act of vocalization. That is, air is forced between the vocal folds which have approximated so that voice may be produced (see pages 14–15 and Figure 2). Air intake (inspiration), except for persons having a pathology of the respiratory mechanism, is usually accomplished with ease. The establishment of exhalation which is gradual and subordinated to the needs of vocalization sometimes requires instruction.

Controlled breathing is best established through voluntary action of the muscles constituting the front and sides of the abdominal wall. See pages 14–21 for a review of the breathing process.) We may become readily aware of abdominal breathing by observing a sleeping or thoroughly relaxed person. Observation will reveal that in inhalation the abdominal area moves forward; in exhalation the abdominal area recedes. In terms of muscular activity this means that the abdominal muscles relax in inhalation and contract in exhalation. When the contraction of the abdominal muscles is brought under voluntary control, we can, through an act of will and responsive abdominal muscles, determine how long and how much contraction is to take place. Breathing is then under control. (Such control, of course, is useful only for purposes of speech. For ordinary life purposes not related to speaking it would become a nuisance to have to think about breathing.)

To become aware of abdominal activity the following exercises are suggested:

1. Lie on a couch or bed. Place your hands gently on the abdominal area immediately below the ribs. Inhale as for normal breathing. Your hands should rise during inhalation and fall during exhalation. If this does not happen—if there is a tendency for the abdominal area to pull in and fall during inhalation—then the abdominal activity is incorrect and should be changed.

Repeat the first exercise from a sitting position and then from a standing position. Make certain that the abdominal wall expands—pushes out—on inhalation, and contracts—pulls in—on exhalation.

3. Inhale fully and then breathe out slowly, hands still on the abdominal muscles. Repeat by sustaining the sound *ah!* while exhaling. (Do not force the exhalation to a point of discomfort, but become aware of when the discomfort-point is reached. This is important because it will help you to anticipate breath needs while talking.)

4. Inhale fully and then count out evenly and slowly without noticeable pause between numbers. Maintain even pitch and loudness. Stop before you feel any need to force your breath. Note the extent of the count. Did any breath escape during the brief pause? If so, repeat the exercise, and this time avoid wasting breath. At the rate of two numbers per second, it should

be possible for almost all adults to count at least to fifteen and for most adults to count to twenty on one sustained breath. Practice this exercise until at least a count of fifteen is achieved.

5. Repeat the exercise *whispering* while counting. What number did you reach? It should be lower than for vocalized counting because more air is expelled for whispered speech than for voiced speech. Practice this exercise until the initial count is extended by 20 per cent.

6. Repeat exercises 4 and 5, reciting the alphabet rather than counting. Make certain that no breath is wasted *between the enunciation* of the letters.

7. Breathe in fully and count out in groups of three, pausing the equivalent of a number after each group. Do not exhale during pauses. If no breath is wasted, it should be possible to reach the same number as in straight counting. Repeat, pausing after each four numbers.

8. Follow the instructions for exercise 7, but substitute the recitation of the alphabet for counting.

9. Count in groups of three, but this time exert pressure on the abdominal muscles with the hands on each third number. The exertion of pressure should produce increased loudness. Extra breath is used, and the count should be less than in exercises 4 and 7.

10. Remove the hands from the abdomen and repeat exercises 4, 6, 7, and 8.

11. Repeat exercise 9, without the hands at the abdomen. Pull in the abdominal muscles directly to force out the additional air necessary for increasing the loudness on the third numbers.

12. Count out from one to ten, beginning with a voice barely audible (but *not* whispered) and ending in a voice just below a shout.

13. Reverse the sequence of exercise 12 from a very loud voice to one that is barely audible but not whispered.

14. Say each of the following sentences on a single breath:

    (a) Let us do what must be done.
    (b) It's a long road that has no turning.
    (c) Together now, let's haul away.
    (d) All aboard! Everybody aboard!
    (e) No! You can't make me do it.

15. Read the following couplets in one breath.

    (a) My name is Ozymandias, king of kings;
        Look on my works, ye Mighty, and despair!
            SHELLEY—*Ozymandias*
    (b) I hope to see my Pilot face to face
        When I have crost the bar.
            TENNYSON—*Crossing the Bar*

    (c) The day is cold, and dark, and dreary;
          It rains, and the wind is never weary.
             LONGFELLOW—*The Rainy Day*

16. Read the following selections, if possible on a single full breath. Do not force the breath. In any event, try not to renew the breath supply until after the third line.

    (a) Please to listen, my fair lady,
          There's a lyric in my soul;
          There's a lilting lovely lyric
          That I'd like to tell you whole.

    (b) Sere leaves are a token
          Of a spirit that's broken
            And a life that is spent,
          That weeps for the living
          Spent life that is giving
            Its final lament

    (c) The cataract strong
          Then plunges along,
          Striking and raging
          As if a war waging
          Its caverns and rocks among—
             SOUTHEY—*The Cataract of Lodore*

    (d) Mastiff, greyhound, mongrel grim,
          Hound or spaniel, brach or lym;
          Or bobtail tike or trundle-tail.
             SHAKESPEARE—*King Lear*

The exercises suggested above are intended to assist in establishing voluntary control of the loudness of voice through breathing. Adequate loudness, however, should not be a matter of breath use alone. Proper resonance and ease of voice production should make it unnecessary, in conversation at least, for energetic breathing to be used. Energetic breath usage is a worthwhile achievement, but it should not replace, for most speech purposes, the less effortful reinforcement of tone through resonance. In fact, with public address systems so widely available, a speaker is rarely required to use anything but a conversational voice regardless of where he may be speaking. The voice that rings the rafters need no longer be an objective for either private or public speakers. Reinforcement of tone through resonance will be discussed later in the chapter.

THE PRODUCTION OF CLEAR TONES

Voice or tone, we know, is a result of the activity of the vocal folds. Earlier we learned that the vocal folds are set into action to produce voice as a result of the integrated activity of muscles of the larynx. When the vocal folds are brought together to set up resistance to the column of air being forced up from the lungs, voice is produced. When the vocal folds are apart, so that the column of air is free to flow through them, quiet, unvocalized breathing takes place. For the present we shall be concerned with the vocalization of good tones, easily initiated.

A good tone is clear and free from the interference of tension or strain. It is produced with ease, sustained with ease, and appropriately reinforced. Tonal impurities result from tensions of the muscles of the neck and throat which interfere with the free action of the laryngeal muscles. This, in turn, prevents proper action of the vocal folds. Tonal impurities may also result from inappropriate resonance, for the most part related to the nasal cavities. The problem of nasality will be considered later. Our immediate concern will be with the initiation and maintenance of tone.

Initiation of Tone

To initiate a good tone, the vocal mechanism must be ready for vocalization. That means that the vocal folds must be brought together a moment before the column of air is forced up to set them into action. The vocal folds must be tense enough to set up resistance to the flow of air, but not so tense that the resistance is too great to permit breath to blow them apart. The speaker can determine his own *readiness for vocalization* by trying the exercises which follow:

1. Contract the throat muscles as if to swallow. Note the sensation of the contracted muscles. Open the mouth as if to produce the sound *ah*. Do the throat muscles still feel as they did in swallowing? If they do, they are too tense for the initiation of good tone. Note the sensation of contracted throat muscles so that you will know what to avoid.

2. Yawn *gently* with mouth half open. Then breathe in and out through the mouth. Note the feeling of air in the back of the throat. Contrast this sensation with that of swallowing. If the yawning is gentle the throat should be relaxed. This is the state of muscle tonus you wish to achieve while talking. If the throat still does not feel relaxed, then try the next two exercises.

3. Sit back in a chair and let your head drop to your chest. Permit your head to hang from the neck as a dead weight. Yawn gently and then take three or four breaths through the mouth. Note the sensation. Swallow and contrast the tonus of the throat muscles in swallowing with that of gentle yawning. Repeat the yawning and mouth breathing. Fix these sensations in your mind.

4. Stand erect, but not rigid. Repeat exercise 3 in the standing position.

5. In a standing position, with throat muscles relaxed, say the vowel /ɑ/. Then try /ɔ/, /æ/, /u/ and /i/. Go from one vowel to the other without pausing. Throat tension will necessarily increase for the vowels /u/ and /i/ if the proper vowel values are to be produced. Try, however, to avoid undue tension.

6. Open your mouth as if to yawn gently, but instead of yawning say *ha, how, ho, ha, haw, ho.* Then try the sentence *Who am I?* (The purpose of opening the mouth *as if to yawn* is to make certain that the vocal mechanism is ready for vocalization before an attempt is made to imitate the tone. In addition, the act of *almost yawning* requires a relaxed, open throat which is essential for a good tone.)

7. With a relaxed throat, count from one to ten, accentuating the activity of the lips and tongue. Become aware of oral activity in the *front of the mouth.* Now count from one to twenty. If there is any tendency for the throat muscles to tighten, stop, recapture the "yawning sensation," and begin again.

8. Repeat exercise 7, reciting the letters of the alphabet rather than counting. Continue to accentuate lip-tongue activity. If such activity has not been habitual, it is likely that your lips will feel tired. This is an excellent indication that you are following directions. With practice, the feeling of lip fatigue will disappear.

9. Read the following selections aloud, maintaining a relaxed throat. Make certain that you are *ready for vocalization* before you begin to speak. If at any time your throat muscles begin to tighten, stop reading and go back to exercises 3, 4, 5, and 6.

    (a) Martha and Maud walked about the garden.

    (b) Lawrence enjoyed talking but avoided all argument.

    (c) Audred and Alfred won honors for their abstract drawings.

    (d) Niagara Falls produces an endless flow of water for energy and power.

    (e) An ohm is a unit of electrical resistance.

    (f) The ring is on my hand
        And the wreath is on my brow;
    Satins and jewels grand
    Are all at my command
        And I am happy now.

    And my lord he loves me well;
        But, when first he breathed his vow,
    I felt my bosom swell—
    For the words rang as a knell,

And the voice seemed *his* who fell
In the battle down the dell,
    And who is happy now.
        POE—*Bridal Ballad*

(g) Then hate me when thou wilt; if ever, now;
Now, while the world is bent my deeds to cross,
Join with the spite of fortune, make me bow,
And do not drop in for an after-loss.
        SHAKESPEARE—*Sonnets*

(h) Is this the face that launched a thousand ships
And burnt the topless towers of Ilium?
        MARLOWE—*Dr. Faustus*

(i) Double, double, toil and trouble
Fire burn and cauldron bubble.
        SHAKESPEARE—*Macbeth, I, 1*

(j) Sweet day, so cool, so calm, so bright,
    The bridal of the earth and sky!
The dew shall weep thy fall tonight;
    For thou must die.

Sweet rose, whose hue, angry and brave,
    Bids the rash gazer wipe his eye,
Thy root is ever in its grave,
    And thou must die.

Sweet spring, full of sweet days and roses,
    A box where sweets compacted lie,
My music shows you have your closes,
    And all must die.

Only a sweet and virtuous soul,
    Like seasoned timber, never gives;
But though the whole world turn to coal,
    Then chiefly lives.
        HERBERT—*Virtue*

Breathiness (*The Fuzzy Voice*)

There is an element of danger that a relaxed throat and easy initiation of tone may result in a breathy voice quality because of associated partial relaxation of the vocal folds. This will happen, of course, only if the vocal folds are not brought close enough together to prevent "leakage" of air when vocalization takes place.

To be able to overcome breathiness, it is first necessary to become aware of a breathy voice quality. Speech which is intentionally whispered employs breath which is not used for vocalization. Fricative and stop-plosive consonants, especially those which are voiceless, are breathy sounds. You can feel the breath by placing your hand in front of your mouth while saying sentences such as:

1. She threw the pots and pans out of the house through the open window.
2. Harry, the hatless hero, caught cold while playing ball.
3. The foghorn sounded as the ship slipped down the bay.
4. Peter and Paul both liked pumpkin pie.

Voiced consonants and all vowels, unless intentionally whispered, should be produced without any of the breathy or aspirate quality which characterizes the fricative and voiceless stop-plosive consonants. The following sentences should be spoken so that a minimum of breath is felt if your hand is held before your mouth.

1. The runner ran a mile.
2. There are more widows than widowers.
3. As the day began there was a roaring blizzard.
4. Our man will win the relay.

Breathiness may result from carrying over the aspirate quality of a fricative or plosive consonant to the vowel which follows. To prevent this kind of assimilative influence, care should be taken not to prolong the aspirate consonants, and to produce them only with as much aspiration as is needed to identify the sound. The sound /h/ is particularly wasteful of breath, especially if prolonged.

The following pairs of words should be spoken so that there is no more aspiration on the vowel or diphthong of the second than there is on the first. (There should be *no aspiration on the first*.)

eel	heel	eye	tie
ill	hill	ell	tell
am	ham	at	cat
ooze	whose	ear	fear
old	hold	are	far
ire	hire	out	pout
awl	haul	eat	sheet
awe	paw	air	chair

The following sentences should be spoken with emphasis on the vowels and care not to carry over the aspirate quality of the consonants to the vowels.

1. Come home, Henry. All is forgiven.
2. Hate can kill men—the haters as well as the hated.
3. A hobo's life is not always happy.
4. A harried husband is not a happily married man.
5. The horn honked as the car sped around the corner.
6. He came to scoff and so he did though none found cause for scoffing.

Reinforcement of Tone-Resonance[1]

If we depended upon the energetic use of breath to produce audible voice, speech would be fatiguing. Fortunately, as has already been pointed out, except for public addresses before a large audience, energetic use of breath is only occasionally necessary. Vocal tones are reinforced by the resonating cavities which are part of the speech mechanism. The chief resonators are the cavities of the larynx, pharynx, mouth, and nose. If these cavities are not obstructed by organic growths such as enlarged tonsils or adenoids, or by muscular tensions created by the speaker, reinforcement of tone is easy to achieve.

There is little we can or need do about the *larynx as a resonator*. In the absence of any organic pathology the larynx will function automatically to reinforce the tones produced within it by the action of the vocal folds. Laryngitis will interfere with laryngeal resonance. A person suffering from laryngitis will do well not to talk. If the condition is persistent or recurrent, a visit to a physician is recommended.

The *pharynx* functions best as a resonator when it is relatively open and relaxed. When the walls of the pharynx become tense, the voice tends to lose mellowness, and becomes metallic. Higher-pitched sounds are reinforced at the expense of low-pitched sounds. The over-all result is an unpleasant voice with poor carrying power. How to achieve a relaxed pharynx (throat) was discussed earlier (see pages 88–89) and might be reviewed at this point.

The mouth is the most modifiable of the resonators and is readily subject to voluntary control. The different vowels are produced as a result of changes in the size and shape of the oral cavity plus some modification in the tensions and shape of the upper part of the pharynx. Variations in the shape of the mouth are brought about by changes in the positions of the lower jaw, lips, tongue, and soft palate.

Oral resonance is generally improved if the speaker makes a conscious effort to emphasize lip and tongue activity. This is what is generally meant when singing teachers direct their students to "place the tone forward in the

---

[1] For a review of the physics of resonance, see pages 23–24.

mouth." Though front-of-the-mouth activity should be emphasized, it should not be so exaggerated as to attract attention to itself rather than to the resultant speech content.

The exercises which follow are intended to help create an awareness of tongue and lip activity in oral resonance.

EXERCISES TO CREATE AWARENESS OF ORAL RESONANCE

1. Observe your mouth in a mirror as you produce these vowels in pairs:

/u/ and /ɪ/
/o/ and /e/
/ɔ/ *and* /ɛ/
/ɑ/ and /æ/

2. Produce all the front and back vowels in sequence, without stopping between vowels. Note the change in lip, tongue, and jaw position.

3. Say *tic, tac, toe, we will go* several times with awareness of oral activity.

4. Combine the sounds /t/, /p/, and /w/ with each of the front and back vowels.

5. Practice the following sentences and verses which emphasize front-of-the-mouth sounds. Make certain that the breath is controlled and the voice well sustained.

(a) Who is there? It is I.

(b) Bing, bang, beat the drum!

(c) Heigh, ho, away we go!

(d) The wind whistled through the trees.

(e) We wish you were well.

(f) She was a phantom of delight
When first she gleam'd upon my sight.
WORDSWORTH—*She Was a Phantom of Delight*

(g) Here once, through an alley Titanic,
of Cypress, I roamed with my Soul.
POE—*Ulalume*

(h) With ruin upon ruin, rout on rout,
Confusion worse confounded.
MILTON—*Paradise Lost*

(i) A dwarf sees farther than the
giant when he has the giant's shoulder
to mount on.
COLERIDGE—*The Friend*

(j) Carson in *The Sea Around Us* talks of the growth of huge
submarine volcanoes which build up large lava cones on the floor
of the ocean.

(k) Weep on! and, as thy sorrows flow,
I'll taste the luxury of woe.
THOMAS MOORE—*Anacreontic*

Nasal Resonance

Just how important the nasal cavities are for the reinforcement of sound
still remains to be determined. That the nasal resonators are important
cannot be denied. The sounds /m/, /n/, and /ŋ/, though articulated orally,
are resonated in the nasal cavities and emitted through the nose. That is,
the soft palate *is lowered* for the production of these sounds. In connected
speech, sounds in close proximity to nasals, like the vowels in *men* and
name, are at least partly reinforced through nasal resonance. This type of
assimilated nasality, if excessive, is considered undesirable in American-
English speech. How to avoid excessive nasality will be considered later.

Appropriate nasal resonance lends considerable roundness and carrying
power to the voice. We may become aware of nasal reinforcement through
sustained humming. Make certain that the throat muscles and the tongue
and the soft palate are relaxed, and the jaws almost but not quite together.
Close the lips so that they barely touch. Initiate a humming sound on a sustained breath. Place the thumb and forefinger lightly on the sides of the
nostrils. The hum should be both felt as well as heard.

The vibratory effect and fullness resulting from appropriate nasal reinforcement of tone can be appreciated by comparing a sentence such as
Many merry men may marry with a sentence containing no nasal sounds
such as *Do you wish six fish?*

To establish nasal reinforcement, the following exercises are suggested.

EXERCISES TO ESTABLISH NASAL RESONANCE

Begin each exercise with a relaxed throat, tongue, and soft palate. Sustain an even tone through controlled, gradual, abdominal contraction.

1. Hum gently on a sustained breath. Repeat three or four times.

2. Blend a hum with the vowel /ɑ/, making certain that the soft palate is raised for the vowel.

3. Produce the sound /n/ and blend with the vowels /ɑ/ and /ɔ/. Hold the /n/ at least twice as long as in normal conversational speech.

4. Repeat exercise 3, beginning with the /ŋ/. Try /ŋɑ/, /ŋɔ/, /ŋoʊ/, /ŋu/.

5. Chant: Mabel and Mary want a man to marry,
    They do not mind a Tom or a Harry,
    They merely mind that he might tarry.

6. Recite the following slowly, doubling the length of each nasal sound.

(a) And now, as the night was senescent
    And star-dials pointed to morn—
    As the sun-dials hinted of morn—
    At the ends of our path a liquescent
    And nebulous lustre was born,
            POE—*Ulalume*

(b) Sunset and evening star,
    And one clear call for me!
    And may there be no moaning of the bar,
    When I put out to sea.
            TENNYSON—*Crossing the Bar*

(c) In Xanadu did Kubla Khan
    A stately pleasure dome decree:
    Where Alph, the sacred river, ran
    Through caverns measureless to man
    Down to a sunless sea.
            COLERIDGE—*Kubla Khan*

(d) "Inconsistencies of opinion, arising from changes of circumstances, are often justifiable."
            DANIEL WEBSTER—*Speech, July 25, 1846*

Insufficient nasal resonance or denasality may usually be attributed to obstructions to or within the nasal passages. Adenoidal tissue, if enlarged, will prevent sound from getting to the nasal cavities for reinforcement. Growths or restrictions within the nasal cavities prevent proper reinforcement or emission of nasal sounds. Extreme tension in the region of the nasopharynx may produce an effect comparable to an actual obstruction. The most frequent obstruction results from the common cold when nasal catarrh clogs the passages. Regardless of the cause, insufficient nasal reinforcement of tone results in a flat, lifeless voice. Unless there is severe organic pathology requiring medical attention, the exercises described above for the establishment of nasal resonance should help in overcoming denasality.

Excessive nasality is a defect opposite to that of denasality. It results usually from an overrelaxed soft palate which fails to rise when necessary in order to block off the stream of breath for nonnasal sounds. In some instances, excessive and inappropriate nasality is associated with a general muscular sluggishness and an "I don't care" attitude on the part of the speaker. If attention is directed to speech activity, it will be found that the jaw, lips, and tongue as well as the soft palate are sluggish.

If the muscular sluggishness has a physical basis, medical attention is indicated. If the basis is in an attitude, speech exercises alone will not help greatly to overcome the nasality. If, however, excessive and inappropriate nasality has been learned unconsciously, and the will to change is present, the following exercises should be of help.

EXERCISES TO OVERCOME EXCESSIVE NASALITY

1. *Raising the soft palate.* Stand before a mirror and yawn with a wide open mouth. Note that the soft palate is raised while the yawn is maintained. Repeat and become aware of the feeling when the soft palate is elevated.

2. With mouth closed, try to elevate the soft palate. Then open the mouth to produce the vowel /ɑ/. Permit the soft palate to drop and intentionally produce a nasalized /ɑ/. Then raise the soft palate to produce a nonnasal /ɑ/. Capture the sensation of the elevated soft palate when the vowel sound is produced. Repeat for the vowels /ɔ/ and /u/

3. Close your nostrils by pinching them. Say /ɑ/. Repeat with open nostrils. There should be little or no difference in the sound either way. Repeat for all the back vowels.

4. Say /ŋ/ while observing and feeling the action of the soft palate. Then say /ɑ/. The soft palate should be lowered and relaxed for /ŋ/ and raised for /ɑ/. Alternate between the two sounds until there is immediate awareness of the difference in palatal position.

5. Place a cold hand-mirror under your nostrils and produce a prolonged /ɑ/. If the soft palate is raised, there should be no clouding of the mirror. Practice until there is *no clouding*. Then repeat for all the back vowels.

6. Repeat exercise 5, for the front vowels. Avoiding clouding will be somewhat more difficult, but should soon be established. The vowels /ɛ/ and /æ/ may require special attention.

7. Pinch your nostrils closed and say each of the following sentences. If there is a feeling of stuffiness in the nose, or pressure in the ears, then the

soft palate is not blocking off the passage of air to the nasal cavity. Make a conscious effort to raise the palate.

(a) This is where I wish to stay.
(b) All aboard! The boat is about to leave.
(c) The expected reply arrived too late.
(d) The sky was red, the clouds ablaze.

8. Say the following pairs of words with attention to the activity of the soft palate. The soft palate should be raised throughout the articulation of the second member of the pair.

moo	boo	nail	sail
me	be	no	go
my	die	me	tea

9. Practice the following words, making certain that the soft palate is elevated as soon as the nasal consonant is completed.

meek	moose
may	now
my	nerve
mat	nuts
neighbor	kneel
more	news

Associated Nasality

The only sounds in American and English speech which require intentional nasalization are /m/, /n/, and /ŋ/. In connected speech, however, sounds in close proximity to the nasal consonants are almost always slightly nasalized. The nasalization is an assimilative effect resulting from the manner of articulation of /m/, /n/, and /ŋ/. Specifically, one of three things may happen: (1) The lowered soft palate may not be raised soon enough to prevent the following vowel from being somewhat nasalized. This would account for nasalization of the vowels, and occasionally consonants, in words such as *me, mail, not,* and *news.* (2) The soft palate may be lowered while the sound preceding the nasal is articulated as in words such as *am, sing, and,* and *own.* (3) The soft palate may not be completely elevated because of the influence of preceding as well as following nasal consonants as in *man, known, mountain,* and *mangle.*

There is little point in trying to avoid all traces of assimilative nasality. This feat could probably be achieved, but the required effort would be great, and the manner of articulation so self-conscious and precise as to be undesirable. It is important, however, that the amount of assimilative influence be kept to a minimum so that the articulation as a whole does not become characterized by nasality.

The exercises recommended earlier to gain control of the soft palate are directly applicable for overcoming excessive associated nasality. Emphasis on front-of-the-mouth activity for vowel production is also important. In addition, the following suggestions should be of help.

1. Where the nasal consonant precedes the vowel, lengthen the nasal consonant. This will afford the added moment of time needed to elevate the soft palate. The result should be a reduction of assimilated nasality on the sound which follows.

> (a) Practice on the following sound combinations. At first exaggerate the duration of the nasal to a marked degree. Then reduce the degree of exaggeration, but maintain the nasal consonant for a time you consider about twice as long as normal.

$$/m/ : /\alpha/ \qquad /m/ : /\varepsilon/$$
$$/m/ : /\mathcal{o}/ \qquad /m/ : /æ/$$
$$/m/ : /u/ \qquad /m/ : /eɪ/$$
$$/m/ : /i/ \qquad /m/ : /aʊ/$$

> (b) Repeat the foregoing exercise, prefixing the sound /n/ and then /ŋ/.
>
> (c) Practice saying the following words, exaggerating the length of the nasal consonants.

may	more	not	never
mar	mood	gnaw	knee
mug	map	know	new

> (d) Practice saying the following sentences, taking care to increase the length of the nasal consonants

We may move to a new city.
Mary may marry Ned next May.
The mouse gnawed at the new rope.
Mabel mailed the note to mother.

2. Where the nasal consonant follows the vowel, emphasize oral activity for the production of the vowel. This is especially important for front vowels and for the diphthong /aʊ/, which tend most often to be nasalized.

(a) Practice on the following sound combinations.

[æ m]	[æ n]	[æ ŋ]
[ɛ m]	[ɛ n]	[ɛ ŋ]
[eɪ m]	[eɪ n]	[eɪ ŋ]
[i m]	[i n]	
[ɑʊ m]	[ɑʊ n]	

(b) Practice careful enunciation of the following words:

amber	can't	angle
emerald	another	length
I'm	kind	single
ohm	own	sung

(c) Incorporate the words of the foregoing exercise into sentences
     such as the following:

Amy dislikes wearing emeralds.
The deer's antlers were two feet in length.
We sang a single song.
Amber is a kind of yellow-brown.

3. Where nasal consonants precede and follow the vowel, lengthen the
first nasal and emphasize oral activity for the vowel.

(a) Practice on words such as the following:

mean	moan	meandering
minnow	unknown	remembering
main	number	drowning
many	namely	cringing
meant	mingle	crowning
moon	banging	grinding
mine	numbing	frowning

(b) Practice careful enunciation of the following:

Men manifest their personalities by their conduct.
For months on end the snow showed no signs of melting.
The moon spread a silvery blanket over the meadow.
Men sometimes sing mournful songs without living mournful lives.

(c) Practice items 5 and 6 of the EXERCISES TO ESTABLISH NASAL
     RESONANCE (see page 95).

WIDENING THE PITCH RANGE

In the chapter on the components of speech (Chapter 3), we discussed the significance of pitch changes for communicating thoughts and feelings. The point was emphasized that though pitch changes tend naturally to follow emotional changes, pitch modifications in American speech are used to give intellectual significance to our words. It follows, therefore, that a voice which is narrow in pitch range tends to limit its user in communicating speech content. In addition, of course, the pitch-monotonous voice is not likely to attract attention or to maintain whatever initial attention the speaker may have.

Optimum Pitch

In the absence of any pathology, there is a natural level about which the pitch of the voice can vary with greatest ease and effectiveness. Unfortunately, there is considerable evidence to indicate that many persons use a habitual level which is not the natural or best one for them. The result is that both pitch variety and voice quality suffer.

To determine the natural or optimum pitch level the following instructions should be followed.

1. Relax the throat muscles. Take a moderately deep breath and produce a well-controlled *ah* at whatever pitch level seems normal for you. Note the pitch of the sound.

2. Repeat, but this time produce a sound a step lower in pitch.

3. Continue, going down a step at a time, until you have produced the lowest pitched tone you can. Do not strain for an abnormally low pitch.

4. Go back to the initial pitch. Now produce tones on an upward scale.

It should be possible for you to go up in pitch from the initial tone about twice the number of pitch levels you moved down. If this is the case, you are using your natural or optimum pitch level. (The optimum pitch level, for most persons, is *approximately one-third up from the lowest tone* the individual can comfortably produce.)

An alternate method of determining optimum pitch is to match tones with the notes of a piano. Produce tones down to as low a level as feels comfortable. Match each tone with a note on the piano. Then go up the scale as high as you can. Select a tone approximately a third of the way up from the bottom as the optimum pitch level for you.

Make a mental note of the optimum pitch level. Learn to recognize how it feels to produce this pitch and how it sounds. Most exercises to widen pitch range will be based on the *optimum or natural pitch level as the point of departure*.

If the pitch level at which you habitually initiate a tone and the determined optimum pitch level deviate significantly (by more than two tones), then work to bring the two levels closer together. There is no need for exact correspondence between habitual pitch level and optimum level. It has been found, however, that superior speakers tend to use their optimum pitch as their most habitual, or frequently used, pitch level. For this reason it is recommended for persons interested in voice improvement.

Habitual Pitch

Although even a monotonous speaker does not have a voice limited to a single pitch, most of us tend to initiate and speak at a level and speak within a range which includes a recurrent or habitual pitch. If this pitch happens to be the optimum one, or no more than a level higher or lower than the optimum pitch, then the speaker has no need to be concerned about exercises for maintaining vocalization at or near the optimum pitch. If, however, the optimum and habitual pitch are more than two full steps apart as equated on a musical scale, then the exercises for optimum pitch are very strongly recommended.

Habitual pitch may be determined by a relaxed (but not overrelaxed) reading of a 50 to 75 word paragraph of material with relatively neutral content. Choose a simple passage, with words easy to pronounce and free of great challenge to the mind or to the feeling. Read the passage three or four times in an intentionally monotonous manner, but avoid dropping the voice to the extreme lower end of the pitch range. Instead, let the voice come and be sustained as it will, and note the level at which it is sustained. This is probably your habitual pitch. Record the reading, play it back, and compare it with a recorded reading of the same passage in which you emphasize vocalizing at optimum pitch. A passage such as the following may be of help.

Considered as a chemical compound, water is an oxide of hydrogen and oxygen. Ordinary water is represented by the chemical formula H_2O. Seldom, however, is water so pure as to contain only hydrogen and oxygen. Though every schoolchild now knows that water is a compound, it was once regarded as a single chemical element. The English chemist Cavendish proved that water was not an element but a compound.

How wide should one's pitch range be? In general terms, the answer is "As wide as necessary to give adequate expression to your thoughts and feelings." A practical and experimentally observed answer is that most good speakers employ a range of an octave or more. Poor speakers, more frequently than not, have a narrow pitch range. Most persons use a range narrower than they are capable of employing, tending to concentrate on the lower parts of the pitch range.

Because the normal pitch range is about two-thirds up and one-third down from the optimum pitch, there is more room for variety if the upper pitch levels are developed. By no means, however, should low pitch levels be ignored. Nor should we strain for higher pitches that cannot be easily reached or supported.

Pitch Change in Singing vs. Speaking

Before leaving our general discussion of pitch changes in speaking, a reminder is in order. Though singing is an excellent medium for establishing and extending pitch range, the method of employing pitch changes in singing is different from that of speaking. In the first place, almost all pitch changes in singing are discrete. The singing voice moves in separate steps from note to note with each sound held longer than it is likely to be in speaking. Syllables within a sung word are spoken on distinctively different tonal levels. This is not usually the case in speaking. Most vocal changes in speaking are subtle. Except where a word is to be made conspicuous for the purpose of emphasis, a distinctive change in level is not likely to take place in conversational speech or in nonmelodramatic public speech. If we compare the pitch changes in the spoken and sung first line of the song *America,* the differences should become clear.

A second difference between pitch changes in speech and in singing should be noted. In singing, a pattern of pitch changes is established and then repeated with occasional modification. The repetition of pattern in singing constitutes melody. Such repetition is to be avoided in speaking where it constitutes monotony rather than melody. The pitch changes in speaking must be correlated with variations in thought and feeling. In English and American speech, subtleties of ideational content are conveyed through such changes. Patterned changes tend, therefore, to interfere with meaning and to impair effective communication. (For a review of the relationship of pitch to meaning see pages 39–42.)

Flexibility and Responsiveness

It is axiomatic that a flexible, responsive voice requires voluntary control for production and an awareness of what is produced. The speaker must learn to appreciate his own vocal limitations and to evaluate what he hears in the voices of others. A widened pitch range can be achieved only after the speaker realizes fully the extent of his present habitual range. This requires sensitive and discriminating listening. Unless differences can be heard, practice and exercises cannot be put to fruitful use. Training in hearing differences is essential for any aspect of voice improvement, whether it be for breath control, tone initiation, or a widened pitch range.

EXERCISES FOR WIDENING PITCH RANGE

1. Determine your natural or optimum pitch by one of the methods described above. Then say the sentence *I am John Jones,* initiating it on your optimum pitch level. Practice saying the same sentence, initiating the first word on succeeding lower levels until you reach the lowest comfortable pitch level. Begin again, going to the highest comfortable level.

2. Check your optimum pitch on a piano. Repeat exercise 1. Work for a range of at least one octave.

3. Beginning at your optimum pitch level, count down a tone at a time, as low as you can with comfort. Begin again, this time counting up. Do you go about twice as high up as you can down? Work to accomplish this.

4. Repeat exercise 3 using the syllables [la], [na], [da], [mi], [meɪ], and [deɪ].

5. Review the discussion on kinds of pitch changes (pages 39–41). Then answer the following questions.

    (a) How many kinds of inflectional changes are there? How is each used in English-American speech?

    (b) What is a step? How does it differ from a slide?

6. Count from one to fifteen, using an upward inflection on the numbers five and ten, and a downward inflection on fifteen.

7. Recite the alphabet, using a falling inflection on each third letter.

8. Say the word *yes* to indicate (a) decision, (b) doubt, (c) irony or sarcasm.

9. Say the word *no* so that, by means of pitch change, you indicate the following:

    (a) Emphatic negation,

    (b) Uncertainty or doubt,

    (c) Interest,

    (d) Surprise,

    (e) Annoyance.

10. Repeat exercise 9, using the sound /m/.

11. Say the sentence *I will do it* so that the following meanings are suggested:

    (a) Determination,

    (b) Surprise,

    (c) Pleasant agreement,

    (d) Annoyance and doubt.

✔ 12. Say the sentence *You're a fine fellow* in ways which will bring out the following meanings:

    (a) Admiration for the person addressed.
    (b) Encouragement,
    (c) Dislike,
    (d) Surprise at the discovery of the person's qualities.

✔ 13. Pronounce the words *Please, come here* so that they will constitute:

    (a) A polite request,
    (b) An entreaty,
    (c) A polite command,
    (d) An abrupt command.

✔ 14. Pronounce the sentence *I like him* to bring out the following meanings:

    (a) A direct statement of fact,
    (b) A contradiction of the literal meaning of the words,
    (c) Irritation and surprise that anyone could conceivably accuse you of liking *the likes of him,*
    (d) Indecision as to your feelings about *him,*
    (e) Indication that your liking is for *him* and not for anyone else,
    (f) An answer to the question "Who likes him?"
    (g) An aggressive answer to the question "Who could possibly like someone like him?"

15. Read the following selections using pitch variations to emphasize changes in thought and in feeling.

    (a) "—Is life so dear, or peace so sweet, as to be purchased at the price of chains and slavery? Forbid it, Almighty God! I know not what course others may take; but as for me, give me liberty, or give me death!"
           PATRICK HENRY—*Speech in Virginia Convention, 1775*

    (b) There is nothing we receive with so much reluctance as advice. We look upon the man who gives it as offering an affront to our understanding, and treating us like children or idiots.
           ADDISON—*Spectator*

    (c) There are two ways of being happy: we may either diminish our wants or augment our means. Either will do, the result is the same. And it is for each man to decide for himself, and do that which happens to be the easiest. . . .
           BENJAMIN FRANKLIN

(d) "What shall I say to you? Should I not say, Hath a dog
money? Is it possible a cur can lend three thousand ducats?"
SHAKESPEARE—*Merchant of Venice*

(e) Gather ye rose-buds while ye may,
　　Old Time is still a-flying:
And this same flower that smiles today,
　　Tomorrow will be dying.
　　　　HERRICK—*To the Virgins, to Make Much of Time*

(f) Home they brought her warrior dead;
　　She nor swooned, nor uttered cry:
All her maidens, watching said,
　　"She must weep or she will die."
　　　　TENNYSON—*Home They Brought Her Warrior Dead*

(g) Fear death?—to feel the fog in my throat,
　　The mist in my face,
When the snows begin, and the blasts denote
　　I am nearing the place,
The power of the night, the press of the storm,
　　The post of the foe;
Where he stands, the Arch Fear in a visible form,
　　Yet the strong man must go:
For the journey is done and the summit attained;
　　And the barriers fall.
Though a battle's to fight ere the guerdon be gained,
　　The reward of it all.
I was ever a fighter, so—one fight more
　　The best and the last!
I would hate that death bandaged my eyes, and forbore,
　　And bade me creep past.
No! let me taste the whole of it, fare like my peers,
　　The heroes of old,
Bear the brunt, in a minute pay life's glad arrears,
　　Of pain, darkness and cold.
For sudden, the worst turns the best to the brave,
　　The black minute's at end,
And the elements' rage, the fiend voices that rave,
　　Shall dwindle, shall blend,
Shall change, shall become first a peace out of pain,
　　Then a light, then thy breast,

O thou soul of my soul! I shall clasp thee again,
And with God be the rest!

BROWNING—*Prospice*

QUALITY

Most of our discussion of voice quality has been from the negative side. We have considered undesirable qualities such as breathiness and excessive nasality. There is a positive side to voice quality which is associated with the mood, feelings, and emotions of the speaker. Because voice quality is related to the nonintellectual aspects of behavior, it is not a subject which can be directly taught. The person who *feels what he says* need not be told what voice quality to use to reveal his feelings. The changes in muscle tone which naturally accompany changes in feeling will help to produce the appropriate voice quality. The overrestrained, inhibited person who tries to use an intellectual approach to quality will only succeed in conveying the idea that he does not really feel the way he would like the listener to think he feels. The responsive speaker who initiates tone properly and who uses an appropriate and flexible pitch range and rate of utterance need not concern himself about what voice quality to use. In the absence of any mental or physical disturbance, it is likely to come naturally and spontaneously.

Although we believe that quality of voice is generally a by-product of a state of being, there is always a possibility that in a given instance it may reflect a past rather than a present state. On occasion vocal habits may become reinforced and "fixed" and may suggest an attitude or a feeling no longer entertained by the speaker. The best way to make certain that this is not so, or to determine to modify the situation if it is so, is to have a recording made and to listen to the playback as objectively as if the voice were not your own. If the voice does not reflect the state you feel, or at least the feelings or attitude you intended to convey, compare your voice with that of another speaker who is successful in the expression of his states of affect, and try to do with your voice what you admire in the other speaker. Do not, however, violate your own personality by trying to speak like another speaker. Be yourself, but be certain that your voice reflects the self you wish to be, and at any given moment, the aspect or state-of-being of yourself you wish to reveal.

EXERCISES

Determine the underlying mood of each of the selections which follow, and then read them aloud to reveal the mood.

1. During the whole of a dull, dark, and resoundless day in the autumn of the year, when the clouds hung oppressively low in the heavens, I had been passing alone, on horseback, through a singularly dreary tract of country, and at length found myself, as the shades of evening drew on, within view of the melancholy House of Usher. I know not how it was—but, with the first glimpse of the building, a sense of insufferable gloom pervaded my spirit.

   POE—*The Fall of the House of Usher*

2. A poor Relation—is the most irrelevant thing in nature,—a piece of impertinent correspondency,—an odious approximation,—a haunting conscience—a preposterous shadow, lengthening in the noontide of our prosperity,—an unwelcome remembrance,—a perpetually recurring mortification,—a drain on your purse,—a more intolerable dun upon your pride,—a drawback upon success, —a rebuke to your rising,—a stain in your blood,—a blot in your 'scutcheon,—a rent in your garment,—a death's head at your banquet,—Agathocles' plot,—a Mordecai in your gate,—a Lazarus at your door,—a lion in your path,—a frog in your chamber,—a fly in your ointment,—a mote in your eye,—a triumph to your enemy, and apology to your friends,—the one thing not needful,— the hail in the harvest,—the ounce of sour in a pound of sweet.

   CHARLES LAMB—*Poor Relations*

3. "And the earth was without form, and void; and darkness was upon the face of the deep."

   —GENESIS

4. ". . . For the sea lies all about us. The commerce of all lands must cross it. The very winds that move over the lands have been cradled on its broad expanse and seek ever to return to it. The continents themselves dissolve and pass to the sea, in grain after grain of eroded land. So the rains which rose from it return again in rivers. In its mysterious past it encompasses all the dim origins of life and receives in the end, . . . the dead husks of that same life. For all at last return to the sea—the ever-flowing stream—."

   RACHEL L. CARSON—*The Sea Around Us.* (New York: Oxford University Press, 1951, p. 216.)

5. Why do our joys depart
   For cares to seize the heart?
   I know not. Nature says,
   Obey: and man obeys.

I see, and know not why,
Thorns live and roses die.
LANDOR—Why Do Our Joys Depart

6. I strove with none, for none was worth my strife,
   Nature I loved, and next to Nature, Art;
   I warmed both hands before the fire of life,
   It sinks, and I am ready to depart.
LANDOR—On His Seventy-fifth Birthday

7. Jenny kissed me when we met,
   Jumping from the chair she sat in;
   Time, you thief, who loves to get
   Sweets into your list, put that in:

   Say I'm weary, say I'm sad,
   Say that health and wealth have missed me,
   Say I'm growing old, but add
   Jenny kissed me.
LEIGH HUNT—Rondeau

8. Sunset and evening star,
   And one clear call for me!
   And may there be no moaning of the bar,
   When I put out to sea,

   But such a tide as moving seems asleep,
   Too full for sound and foam,
   When that which drew from out the boundless deep
   Turns again home.

   Twilight and evening bell,
   And after that the dark!
   And may there be no sadness of farewell,
   When I embark;

   For though from out our bourne of Time and Place
   The flood may bear me far,
   I hope to see my Pilot face to face
   When I have crost the bar.
TENNYSON—Crossing the Bar

9. St. Agnes Eve—Ah, bitter chill it was!
   The owl, for all his feathers, was a-cold;
   The hare limped trembling through the frozen grass,

And silent was the flock, in wooly fold:
Numb were the Beadsman's fingers, while he told
His rosary, and while his frosted breath
Like pious incense from a censer old,
Seemed taking flight for heaven, without a death,
Past the sweet Virgin's picture, while his prayer he saith.
KEATS—*The Eve of St. Agnes*

10. I must go down to the seas again,
   to the lonely sea and the sky,
And all I ask is a tall ship,
   and a star to steer her by,
And the wheel's kick and the wind's song
   and the white sail's shaking,
And a gray mist on the sea's face
   and a gray dawn breaking.
MASEFIELD—*Sea Fever*[2]

11. Here, where the world is quiet,
   Here, where all trouble seems
Dead winds' and spent waves' riot
   In doubtful dreams of dreams,
I watch the green field growing
   For reaping folk and sowing,
For harvest time and mowing,
   A sleepy world of streams.

I am tired of tears and laughter,
   And men that laugh and weep,
Of what may come hereafter
   For men that sow to reap.
I am weary of days and hours,
   Blown buds of barren flowers,
Desires and dreams and powers,
   And everything but sleep.
SWINBURNE—*The Garden of Proserpine*

12. Rough wind, that moanest loud
   Grief too sad for song;
Wild wind, when sullen cloud
   Knells all the night long;

---

[2] From *Poems* by John Masefield. Copyright 1912 by The Macmillan Company, renewed 1940 by John Masefield, and reprinted by permission of the publisher.

Sad storm, whose tears are vain,
 Bare woods, whose branches strain,
Deep caves and dreary main,—
 Wail, for the world's wrong!
    SHELLEY—*Dirge*

13. Is the night chilly and dark?
 The night is chilly, but not dark.
 The thin gray cloud is spread on high,
 It covers but not hides the sky.
 The moon is behind, and at the full;
 And yet she looks both small and dull.
 The night is chill, the cloud is gray:
 'Tis a month before the month of May,
 And the spring comes slowly up this way.
    COLERIDGE—*Christabel*

SUMMARY

In the absence of any organic pathology or abnormality of personality, it should be possible for each of us to develop an effective voice.

An effective voice is appropriate to the age, sex, and physical make-up of the individual. It reflects the person's inner responses and enhances the communication of thoughts and feelings.

Objective characteristics of an effective voice include: (1) adequate and controlled loudness (2) variety of pitch, (3) good tone quality and (4) appropriate rate and timing.

Voice improvement begins with an awareness of the sound of one's own voice and an appreciation of its limitations. Voice and personality are closely related. If you recognize the reactions others have to your voice, you can estimate the personality picture your listeners have of you because of your voice.

Control of loudness is established through controlled abdominal breathing. Energetic breathing should not replace proper reinforcement of tone through resonance.

The production of clear, easily produced, pleasant tones requires integrated activity of the muscles of the larynx and the pharynx. A tone free from tension and strain can be produced if the throat is relatively relaxed and the vocal folds *ready for vocalization* when voice is initiated.

Breathiness and excessve nasality are common defects of voice quality. Both can be avoided through the establishment of proper attitude and good muscle tone. *Appropriate nasal resonance* lends fullness and carrying power to the voice. A lack of nasal resonance is associated with obstruction to or within the nasal passages.

A flexible pitch range is best established about the *optimum or natural* pitch level of the voice. The optimum pitch is approximately one-third the distance above the lowest tone within the pitch range that can normally be produced. Superior speakers, as a group, use a pitch range of at least one octave.

Voice quality helps in the communications of feelings and emotions. If vocal tones are properly initiated, and feelings not overly restrained, appropriate quality will usually be a spontaneous and natural accompaniment of speech content.

Voice improvement can take place only with the active and intelligent cooperation of the person who feels the need for such improvement. The speaker must become aware of his limitations and learn what to do to overcome them. This is so whether the limitation is one of pitch, loudness, quality, or an underlying defect of personality which is manifest in a deficient voice.

REVIEW SELECTIONS FOR VOICE IMPROVEMENT

The selections which follow are intended for practice in all the aspects of voice improvement considered in this chapter.

1. *An Elegy on the Death of a Mad Dog*

   Good people all of every sort,
       Give ear unto my song,
   And if you find it wondrous short,
       It cannot hold you long.

   In Islington there was a man,
       Of whom the world might say,
   That still a godly race he ran,
       Whene'er he went to pray.

   A kind and gentle heart he had,
       To comfort friends and foes;
   The naked every day he clad,
       When he put on his clothes.

   And in that town a dog was found,
       As many dogs there be,

Both mongrel, puppy, whelp, and hound,
   And curs of low degree.

This dog and man at first were friends;
   But when a pique began,
The dog, to gain some private ends,
   Went mad, and bit the man.

Around from all the neighbouring streets,
   The wondering neighbours ran,
And swore the dog had lost his wits,
   To bite so good a man.

The wound it seem'd both sore and sad
   To every Christian eye;
And while they swore the dog was mad,
   They swore the man would die.

But soon a wonder came to light,
   That showed the rogues they lied—
The man recovered of the bite,
   The dog it was that died.
            OLIVER GOLDSMITH

2. *La Belle Dame Sans Merci*

"Ah, what can ail thee, knight-at-arms,
   Alone and palely loitering!
The sedge has wither'd from the lake,
   And no birds sing.

"Ah, what can ail thee, knight-at-arms!
   So haggard and so woe-begone?
The squirrel's granary is full,
   And the harvest's done.

"I see a lily on thy brow
   With anguish moist and fever dew,
And on thy cheeks a fading rose
   Fast withereth too.

"I met a lady in the meads,
   Full beautiful—a faery's child,

Her hair was long, her foot was light,
   And her eyes were wild.

"I made a garland for her head,
   And bracelets too, and fragrant zone;
She look'd at me as she did love,
   And made sweet moan,

"I set her on my pacing steed,
   And nothing else saw all day long.
For sidelong would she bend, and sing
   A faery's song.

"She found me roots of relish sweet,
   And honey wild, and manna dew,
And sure in language strange she said—
   'I love thee true.'

"She took me to her elfin grot,
   And there she wept, and sigh'd full sore,
And there I shut her wild wild eyes
   With kisses four.

"And there she lulled me asleep,
   And there I dream'd—Ah! Woe betide!
The latest dream I ever dream'd
   On the cold hill's side.

"I saw pale kings and princes too,
   Pale warriors, death-pale were they all;
They cried—'La belle Dame sans Merci
   Hath thee in thrall!'

"I saw their starv'd lips in the gloam
   With horrid warning gapèd wide,
And I awoke and found me here
   On the cold hill's side.

"And this is why I sojourn here,
   Alone and palely loitering.
Though the sedge is wither'd from the lake,
   And no birds sing."
        JOHN KEATS

3. *The Erl King*

O, who rides by night thro' the woodland so wild?
It is the fond father embracing his child;
And close the boy nestles within his loved arm,
To hold himself fast and to keep himself warm.

"O father, my father, see yonder," he says;
"My boy, upon what dost thou fearfully gaze?"
"O, 'tis the Erl-King with his crown and his shroud."
"No, my son, it is but a dark wreath of the cloud."

"O, come and go with me, thou loveliest child;
By many a gay sport shall thy time be beguiled;
My mother keeps for thee full many a fair toy,
And many a fine flower shall she pluck for my boy."

"O, father, my father, and did you not hear
The Erl-King whisper so low in my ear?"
"Be still, my heart's darling—my child, be at ease;
It was but the wild blast as it sung thro' the trees."

"Oh, wilt thou go with me, thou loveliest boy?
My daughter shall tend thee with care and with joy;
She shall bear thee so lightly thro' wet and thro' wild,
And press thee, and kiss thee and sing to my child."

"O father, my father, and saw you not plain,
The Erl-King's pale daughter glide past through the rain?"
"O yes, my loved treasure, I knew it full soon;
It was the gray willow that danced to the moon."

"O, come and go with me, no longer delay,
Or else, silly child, I will drag thee away."
"O father! O father! now, now keep your hold,
The Erl-King has seized me—his grasp is so cold!"

Sore trembled the father; he spurred thro' the wild,
Clasping close to his bosom his shuddering child;
He reaches his dwelling in doubt and in dread,
But, clasped to his bosom, the infant was dead!
                    Translated by SIR WALTER SCOTT

RECOMMENDED READINGS

Anderson, V. A. *Training the Speaking Voice,* 2nd ed. New York: Oxford University Press, 1961, Chaps. 1–6.

Brodnitz, F. S. *Keep Your Voice Healthy.* New York: Harper and Row, 1953.

Curry, R. *The Mechanism of The Human Voice.* New York: Longmans Green, 1940.

Eisenson, J. *Improvement of Voice and Diction.* New York: Macmillan, 1958, Chaps. 2–9.

Fairbanks, G. *Voice and Articulation Drillbook,* Rev. ed. New York: Harper and Row, 1960, Chaps. X–XV.

Greene, M. *The Voice and Its Disorders.* New York: Macmillan, 1957.

Hahn, E., Lomas, C. W., Hargis, D. E., and Vandraegen, D. *Basic Voice Training for Speech.* New York: McGraw-Hill, 1957.

Van Dusen, C. R. *Training the Voice for Speech.* New York: McGraw-Hill, 1953.

CHAPTER 7

IMPROVING

YOUR DICTION

OBJECTIVES

Ease of Comprehension

The objective of our discussion of the improvement of speech sounds (diction)[1] is the enhancement of meanings in speaking. As pointed out earlier, atypical speech attracts attention to itself and away from the meaning and purpose of speaking. Speech production which falls within acceptable standards permits the listener to concentrate on the content of speech without distraction by the manner in which the content is produced.

For varied and numerous reasons, many adults who speak the English language do so in a way which serves to direct attention to the manner rather than the content of speaking. The listener may, after a short time, adjust himself to the differences in the speaker's manner and have little or no difficulty in following what is being said. Sometimes, however, the adjustment may be difficult. Occasionally, the speaker may even be through with what he has to say before the listener has made the required adjustments. As a result, comprehension will at best be partial. At worst, there is impaired communication and limited comprehension.

CAUSES OF FAULTY DICTION

Foreign-Language Influence

The speaker for whom English is a second language and who produces English speech sounds in a manner closer to the sounds of his native tongue

---

[1] The term *diction* is here being used to refer to the degree of distinctness with which speech sounds are uttered in context.

[116]

than to those of our speech is likely to have some difficulty in communicating his meanings. He may, of course, have something so decidedly worthwhile to say that the listener will make the necessary effort to understand him. Even such a speaker loses something of his effectiveness because of the special effort required for comprehension.

Many native-born speakers may have learned English from someone for whom it was a foreign language. For persons exposed to foreign-language influence, their spoken English may sound as if it were a second language learned as adults. Our difficulty in comprehending such speakers is occasionally as great as if they were actually foreign born.

Mechanical Faults

Sometimes the difficulty with the production of speech sounds is on a mechanical basis. There may have been some difficulty in childhood with one or more of the organs of articulation which made conventional sound production difficult. A substitute sound or an alternate manner of producing a particular sound may have been learned. A tongue-tie, for example, may have required that a *d* or a *t* be produced behind the lower teeth rather than behind the upper teeth; the *s* may have been learned as a laterally emitted sound because of malformations of dental structure. In any event, if the acoustic end result is significantly different from that heard when the articulators execute conventional movements for the production of American-English sounds, diction is to be considered faulty.

Imitation

Occasionally, the reason for the faulty diction is purely imitative. As a child the speaker may have imitated an adult who, for one reason or another, spoke with faulty diction. Having no basis for exercising discriminative judgments, the child unwittingly may form the habit of faulty sound production. These habits, unless corrected, tend to persist into adult life.

Substandard Speech

Another reason for faulty diction is the influence of substandard speech in the environment of the speaker. As children, we have little choice as to the speech we learn. We learn what we hear. If it is substandard speech, that is what we hear and learn.

Whatever the reason for faulty diction, the material in this chapter is intended to help the interested speaker overcome his speech faults. The sounds to be studied are those which have been found to cause most difficulty for native as well as foreign-born persons. Descriptions of the sounds, word lists, and other exercise materials will be provided.

THE PHONETIC APPROACH TO SPEECH IMPROVEMENT

The Most Frequent Place of Articulation

If we examine the consonant chart on page 69, we may readily note that many of the sounds of American-English speech are produced at or near the upper gum ridge. At this point, by contact with the tongue tip, the sounds /t/, /d/, /l/, and /n/ are produced. A fraction of an inch behind the gum ridge, articulatory contacts are made for the sounds /s/, /z/, /ʃ/,

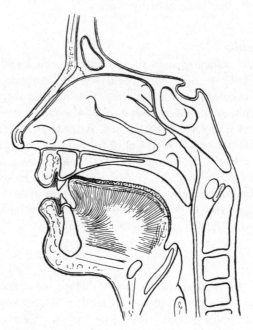

Figure 20.   Diagram of the mouth showing contact point for /t/, /d/, and /l/. Essentially the same tongue tip and gum ridge contact is made for the /n/. The /n/, however, is produced with a relaxed and lowered soft palate.

/ʒ/, /tʃ/, /dʒ/, and /r/. It becomes important therefore, to become acquainted with the apparently favored place of articulation for American-English speech.

For speakers who have been exposed to foreign-language influence, it may be of some help to know that most spoken languages seem to have favored places of articulation. In French, Spanish, and Italian, many sounds are produced by contact between the tongue-tip and the upper teeth. In German, the point of contact is a bit lower. Because many of the sounds produced at these contact points correspond to the sounds of American-English speech, the tendency to carry over foreign-language articulatory habits becomes readily understandable. The need for a considerable amount of practice to overcome this carry-over should also be clear. A study of the diagram of the mouth should provide a visual aid for becoming acquainted with the alveolar (upper gum) ridge area (see Figure 20).

INDIVIDUAL STUDY OF TROUBLESOME SOUNDS IN AMERICAN-ENGLISH SPEECH

/t/ as in *ten*

We shall begin our study with the consonant /t/. It has been our experience that if the contact point and manner of articulation for /t/ is mastered, it becomes an excellent point of reference for the articulation of other American-English speech sounds.

To produce the /t/ as in *ten* or as an isolated sound, the tongue is extended so that the tongue tip comes into contact with the upper gum ridge. The sides of the tongue near the tip are in contact with the upper gum. Farther back, the sides of the tongue are in contact with the upper molars. The tense, extended tongue is held in this position for a fraction of a second. Then, as suddenly and completely as possible, the tongue is retracted with a resultant slight "explosion" at the tongue tip. This should be felt as a puff of breath if the hand is held in front of the mouth.

The /t/ sound as just described occurs whenever the /t/ is in a stressed syllable and is immediately followed by a vowel as in *ten, ton, atone, attend,* and *intact.* /t/ as in *ten* may be described as a lingua-alveolar, voiceless, stop-plosive consonant.

In producing the /t/ sound as just described the following cautions should be observed:

1. Make certain that the tongue tip is in contact with the gum ridge and *not the upper teeth.* The contact, when broken, should be quick and complete.

2. Do not permit the tongue to slide so that contact is made between the front surface of the tongue and the gums. If this happens, the /ts/ blend is likely to be produced.

/t/ in a stressed position followed by a vowel. Practice the following:

tea	tap	ton	tome
tip	tuck	taught	tall
test	ton	terse	tight

attain	rotate	pertain	return
attach	untie	hotel	portend
retell	contest	fortell	potato

/t/ as in *plenty*

The sound /t/ in an unstressed syllable followed by a vowel is produced in a less vigorous manner than when in a stressed syllable. The contact between tongue tip and gum ridge is not held as long as for a stressed /t/ and there is less breath puff following the breaking of the tongue contact. Care should be exercised that the tongue contact is not so weakened that a variety of /d/ is produced or that the unstressed /t/ is entirely omitted. The following words should provide practice for the unstressed /t/.

city	item	later
plenty	utter	pater
better	flatter	pointed
latter	fifty	reality
faulty	tempted	motor
meaty	witty	beauty

Practice discriminating between the unstressed /t/ and /d/ in the following pairs of words:

latter	ladder
betted	bedded
heated	heeded
bitter	bidder
rating	raiding
wetting	wedding
written	ridden
butting	budding
tenting	tending
contented	contended

Other varieties of /t/

According to context, the consonant /t/ varies somewhat as to manner of production and acoustic end result. Some of the more frequent variations will now be considered.

1. /t/ followed by /θ/ or /ð/ as in *light things* and *at the*

In combinations such as *at the, hit that,* and *light things,* it is permissible to produce the /t/ by contact between the tongue tip and upper teeth rather than at the alveolar ridge. The dentalized /t/ in these combinations is produced as a result of the assimilative influence of the next sound /ð/ or /θ/ which is articulated dentally.

For persons whose English speech is influenced by French, Spanish, Italian, or German, this variety of /t/ is likely to be the one habitually used. It is least likely to be defectively produced when foreign-born persons speak English.

2. /t/ followed by /l/ or /n/ as in *little* and *button*

When the /t/ sound is immediately followed by an /l/ or /n/ it is not necessary to remove the tongue tip from the gum ridge to complete the sound. Instead, the sides of the front part of the tongue break contact with the teeth to permit a *lateral* explosion. When /t/ is followed by /l/ as in *little, bottle, settle, cattle, fettle,* and *mortal* the explosion is emitted orally.

In words in which the /t/ is followed by an /n/, as in *bitten, button, cotton,* and *mutton,* the tongue position is maintained in going from the /t/ to the /n/. In effect, a nasal explosion takes place. If the hand is placed in front of the nostrils, a nasally emitted puff of air may be felt.

There is a marked tendency to substitute a laryngeal click (glottal catch) for the /t/ when followed by /l/ or /n/. This substitution, in American speech, is generally considered substandard. The speaker may check on this tendency by placing his hand at the larynx while pronouncing the list of words and sentences which follow. If a "click" is felt, it is likely that a glottal catch is being submitted for the /t/. To avoid this tendency, special attention should be paid to the prescribed manner of articulation for /t/ in [tl] and [tn] contexts.

little	bitten
battle	button
kettle	cotton
bottle	mountain
metal	eaten
mortal	rotten
glottal	batten
brittle	written
scuttle	fatten
fettle	gotten

Little by little the content of the bottle was drained.

The cattle men were sometimes mortal enemies of those who raised mutton.

The cotton dress had a row of bright buttons.

Batten down the hatches or we will have to scuttle the ship.

3. /t/ followed by /s/ as in *posts*

In contexts in which /t/ is immediately followed by an /s/, the tip of the tongue is permitted to slide forward a bit in anticipation of the /s/. Care should be taken not to omit the /t/ sound entirely, especially in combinations where the /t/ is preceded as well as followed by an /s/. The fine articulatory movements required for the [sts] combination increase the tendency for the omission of the /t/.

Practice on the following contexts should help to focus attention on precise articulation required for [ts] and [sts].

its	lots	insists
eats	facts	posts
meats	pots	rests
heats	flights	pests
feats	paints	ghosts

The ghosts of fallen men parade on military posts.

The last acts of plays should be best.

The hard facts of life frequently prevent the attainment of the heart's desire.

Here rest ten fallen hosts.

ADDITIONAL PRACTICE MATERIAL

1. Practice the following lists of words:

tell	ate	between	tighten
ten	boat	return	tentative
till	waste	continue	titillate
time	last	atone	protested
told	quite	fateful	temptress
tab	after	inter	tempestuous
tangle	comet	contain	tainted
taut	emit	dialectic	totter
terse	incite	potent	torment
toll	lout	rotary	touting

2. Practice the following sentences, paying special attention to the /t/ sounds:

(a) Tea for two tends to be pleasant.

(b) Tell Tom to wait until tomorrow.

(c) Put the cat and the light out at ten-twenty.

(d) The tidings of the times indicated a monetary tendency.

(e) Some atone for their cruelties; others take refuge in dialectics.

(f) Take heed! Are you certain it is not for you for whom the bell tolls?

(g) By turns, the Westerner was terse or taciturn.

(h) It is easy to incite. It takes more thought to know when to palliate.

(i) Tucker was better at twitting and taunting than at constructive thinking.

(j) Thomas anticipated a trying time.

3. The following selections might be practiced for sound production with meaning a secondary factor:

(a)   The candle lit at both ends
      Still burned a bit too slow;
      It's lit now at the middle—
      I've no time to watch it go.

(b)   I told my heart that all was bright,
      That time alone would turn things right,
      I told my heart love had not died,
      My rude heart answered that I lied.

(c)   "The next time you stand on a beach at night, watching the moon's bright path across the water, and conscious of the moon-drawn tides, remember that the moon itself may have been born of a great tidal wave of earthly substance, torn off into space."

                    RACHEL CARSON—*The Sea Around Us* (New York: Oxford University Press, 1951), pp. 4–5.

(d)   "Let your study
      Be to content your love, who hath
            received you
      At fortune's alms. You have
            obedience scanted,
      And well are worth the want that
            you have wanted."

                    SHAKESPEARE—*King Lear,* I, 1

/d/ as in *done*

The consonant /d/ as in *done* is articulated in essentially the same manner as the /t/ in *ten* except that /d/ is voiced. The /d/, like /t/, is a variable consonant. The varieties of /d/ parallel those of /t/. Faults in articulation also parallel those for /t/, the chief being the tendency toward dentalization. A second tendency to be avoided is the substitution of /t/ for /d/ in words in which the /d/ is final and voiced. This fault may be especially noted in German-born persons or in the speech of persons who had had German as an early influence. The reason for this is that the final /d/ does not occur in German.

The following lists of words and sentences will provide practice material for the /d/ sound.

dance	diet	add	pallid	admit	eddy
dare	doleful	crowd	trend	garden	bedlam
delight	drape	fade	shod	hidden	prudent
dress	dross	old	hoard	crowded	girder
debit	dupe	amid	greed	fading	candor

Distinguish between final /t/ and /d/:

fate	fade	not	nod
eight	aid	sot	sod
late	laid	sent	send
set	said	grant	grand
but	bud	want	wand
bat	bad	plant	planned
boat	bode	stunt	stunned
hurt	heard	lent	lend

PRACTICE MATERIALS FOR /d/ AND /t/:

1. Dieting makes ladies by the dozen feel doleful.
2. Candor is a frequent excuse for rudeness.
3. The mermaid was confused by the dikes of Holland.
4. It is difficult to detect a trend if one is doing his part to create it.
5. In Bedlam there is generally much ado about nothing.
6. At eight o'clock the ship's captain called for aid.
7. The poet Yeats asked, "How can we tell the dancer from the dance?"

8. The day was dismal and suited only to be dreamt or wished away.

9. At seventeen years, many their fortunes seek,
   But at fourscore it is too late a week.
   Yet fortune cannot recompense me better
   Than to die well, and not my master's debtor.
                    SHAKESPEARE—*As You Like It,* II, 2

10.   "Then let wrath remove;
    Love will do the deed,
       For with love
    Stony hearts will bleed."
                    GEORGE HERBERT—*Discipline*

11. O attic shape! Fair attitude! with brede
       Of marble men and maidens overwrought,
    With forest branches and the trodden weed;
       Those, silent form, dost tease us out of thought
    As doth eternity: Cold Pastoral.
                    JOHN KEATS—*Ode on a Grecian Urn*

12. "I want a hero: an uncommon want,
       When every year and month sends forth a new one,
    Till, after cloying the gazettes with cane,
       The age discovers he is not the true one:
    Of such as these I should not care to vaunt,
       I'll therefore take our ancient friend Don Juan—
    We all have seen him, in the pantomime,
       Sent to the Devil somewhat ere his time . . . "
                    LORD BYRON—*Don Juan,* Canto the First

13. The day is done—and darkness
       Falls from the wings of night
    As a feather is wafted downward
       From an eagle in its flight.

    And the night shall be filled with music
       And the cares that infest the day
    Shall fold their tents like the Arabs
       And as silently steal away.
                    LONGFELLOW—*The Day Is Done*

/s/ as in *see*

The consonant /s/ is a high-pitched, voiceless, lingua-alveolar fricative which requires careful and precise articulatory action for its production. The adjustments involve the following:

1. The entire tongue is raised so that the sides of the tongue are pressed firmly against the inner surfaces of the upper molars.

2. The tongue must be slightly grooved along the mid-line. Air is forced down along this groove.

3. The tip of the tongue is placed about a quarter of an inch behind the upper teeth. The tongue tip is almost in position for a /t/. (Persons not able to attain this adjustment will probably find it easier to place the tongue tip against the lower gums.)

4. The teeth are brought in line, with a very narrow space between upper and lower teeth.

5. The breath is directed along the groove of the tongue toward the cutting edges of the lower teeth.

6. The velum is raised to prevent nasal emission of the sound.

The use of a mirror is recommended for the practice of the consonant /s/. The recommended articulatory position is represented in Figure 21.

In producing the /s/, special care should be exercised to avoid having the tip of the tongue touch either the upper teeth or the gum ridge. Neither should the tongue tip be permitted to slide down to protrude between the rows of teeth. The first articulatory error will result in the production of a /ts/ blend or a lateral sound resembling a voiceless /l/. The second articulatory error will result in an infantile, lingual, protrusion lisp resembling a /θ/.

Persons who habitually produce /t/ and /d/ sounds with dental rather than gum ridge contacts are likely to lower the tongue-tip for the production of /s/. The result, in most cases, is the production of a dull, low-pitched sound.

In some instances the articulatory adjustments just described do not help to produce the desired result—a high-pitched, sibilant sound. Occasionally, the person, possibly because of an unusual mouth structure, must make individual adjustments to arrive at the same acoustic end result. With some articulatory adjustments, a low-pitched sound may be the best that the individual can hope to produce. Most persons, however, regardless of articulatory mechanism, can learn to produce an /s/ which acoustically resembles the high-pitched fricative described above.

Apart from the matter of articulation, the sound /s/ in American-English speech presents difficulty to the foreign-born because of the many ways the sound is spelled. The most frequent representation is the alphabet letter *s*; other representations include *ss* as in *lass, sc* as in *scene, c* as in *pace,* and *x* as in *hoax.* The foreign-born speaker of English can be forgiven his failure to know when to produce the sound /s/if we realize the many ways the letter **s** can be sounded. In addition to the /s/ we have /ʒ/ as in *treasure,* /ʃ/ as in *sure,* and /z/ as in *was.* To add to the foreign-born speaker's consternation we have the "silent" *s* as in *aisle* and *island.*

Practice Material

Because of the frequency of the /s/ sound in English speech, it is recommended that after the sound is produced in isolation, nonsense combinations be practiced. The advantage of nonsense syllable practice lies in the avoidance of the carry-over of habitual but faulty habits of articulation. Suggested nonsense syllable combinations follow.

[sif]	[sav]
[sig]	[sʌt]
[sɛk]	[sɜt]
[sæf]	[saɪp]
[suk]	[saʊk]
[sʊb]	[seɪg]
[sɔp]	[soʊm]

Vowel sounds may be prefixed and blended with these combinations to produce new ones such as: [sɪf], [æsɪg], [asɛk], etc.

If the /s/ sound cannot be mastered directly, it may help to begin with a /t/ and to work for a /ts/ blend. This is especially helpful for persons who have mastered the /t/ sound but who still have difficulty with the /s/.

Words such as *eats, its, hats, lets, wets, hoots, ruts, forts, pots, notes, coats* are recommended for practice.

Additional Practice Material For /s/:

sing	salt	stroll	miss
city	satire	serene	puts
sea	scoff	helps	tense
scene	senior	grace	yachts
divots	most	unceasing	seacoast
terse	aspect	wistful	signpost
coax	explain	sightless	statesman

emergence	jurist	sinister	stylistic
asleep	mystic	senescent	soundless
beast	professor	seamstress	sunset

The combinations /sts/ and /sks/ are somewhat difficult because of the quick and precise tongue movements needed in their production. The following words lists and sentences provide practice material for these and other troublesome combinations:

fists	ghosts	hosts
lists	pests	tastes
wrists	posts	frosts
twists	asks	tracks
mists	sneaks	crisps
trysts	snakes	asps

1. The eastern coast was covered with seaweed.
2. A sleeping beast is a peaceful animal.
3. There seldom is a sanctuary from satire.
4. The ghosts walked serenely across the grass to the desolate house.
5. The mystic bent his wrists and foresaw six trysts.
6. Genius plus unceasing work is about as useful as good sense.
7. The moon spread its silver light over the sea.
8. The signposts warned of steep grades unsafe for speeding young-sters.
9. The golfer with scruples replaces all divots.
10. An objective jurist considers the issues in all possible aspects.
11. As I would not be a slave, so I would not be a master. This expresses my idea of democracy. Whatever differs from this, to the extent of the difference, is no democracy.
   ABRAHAM LINCOLN—*Letter, 1858*

/z/ as in *zoo*

The sound /z/ is produced like the /s/, except that there is accompanying vocalization for /z/. The spellings for /z/ are many and varied. The more frequent orthographic representations include *z* as in *zoo, zz* as in *buzz,* and *s* as in *nose.*

Persons who have difficulty with the articulation of the /s/ are also likely to find the /z/ troublesome. The element of vocalization, however, may make the acoustic defects less apparent than in the case of the /s/.

Practice Material

zeal	because	busy
zebra	choose	easy
zoo	these	music
zenith	avows	season
zephyr	eaves	used
zinc	goads	blizzard
zest	snores	frenzy
zodiac	transpose	nozzle
Zeus	yearns	rosin
zone	symbols	stanza

1. Zoological specimens are not confined to the zoo.
2. Zestful living is one of man's objectives.
3. Bronze is one of our most frequently used alloys.
4. His sleep rather than his snores transposed him to pleasant surroundings.
5. Because he learned to deal with symbols, man learned to speak with words.
6. The architect's clever designs transformed the eaves into things of beauty.
7. The intense blizzard caused the travelers to pause in their journey.
8. Aries is one of the signs of the zodiac.
9. Zelde was not afraid of buzzing bees.
10. The zany business man was from Missouri.

There is a marked tendency among persons of Spanish and German background to substitute voiceless /s/ for /z/. This tendency, shared by many American speakers in the production of final /z/, breaks down the phonetic distinction between words such as *pays* and *pace, as* and *ass, prize,* and *price*. Practice on these pairs and the following exercises should help to maintain the phonetic differences between /z/ and /s/:

bays	base	pods	pots	zinc	sink
raise	race	cents	sends	lazy	lacy
maize	mace	bids	bits	raising	racing
lose	loose	codes	coats	seizing	ceasing
hers	hearse	zoo	sue	prizing	pricing
rise	rice	zeal	seal	razor	racer

1. Spies and secret agents practice secretive smiles.
2. The sink was lined with zinc.
3. The maize was pounded with a mace.

4. For the adolescent male a little fuzz on the cheek is worth much fuss.
5. A rise in the price of rice threatens the welfare of the Chinese.
6. Sue enjoyed her visit to the zoo.

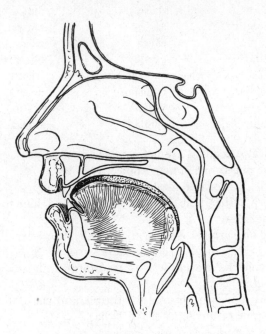

Figure 21.   Representative tongue position for /s/ and /z/.

ADDITIONAL PRACTICE MATERIAL FOR /S/ AND /Z/

1. "Now, blessings light on him that first invented this same sleep!
   . . . There is only one thing, which somebody once put into my head,
   that I dislike in sleep; it is that it resembles death; there is very
   little difference between a man in his first sleep, and a man in his
   last sleep."

   CERVANTES—*Don Quixote*

2. In one of his insightful writings, Harry Stack Sullivan advised:
   "When the satisfaction or the security of another person becomes as
   significant to one as is one's own satisfaction or security, then the
   state of love exists. So far as I know, under no other circumstances
   is a state of love present, regardless of the popular usage of the
   word."

3. John Adams, the second president of the United States observed
   and advised that: "Know thyself is as useful a precept to nations as
   to men." President Adams' position was consistent with that of

Goethe who wisely suggested that persons can possess what is beyond their understanding.

/ʃ/ as in *she*

With the consonant /s/ as a basis for articulation, the /ʃ/ sound should be easy to master. Compared with /s/, the /ʃ/ is produced with the entire tongue drawn back slightly and broadened. The stream of breath is forced over a broad surface rather than through a narrow groove as for the /s/. In addition, the /ʃ/ is usually produced with slight lip-rounding. Acoustically, /ʃ/ is a lower-pitched sound than /s/. Phonetically, /ʃ/ may be described as a *voiceless, blade-tongue, fricative sound.*

The sound /ʃ/ is represented by many spellings. The most common is the combination *sh* as in *she.* Other frequent combinations include *ti* as in *ration, si* as in *tension, ci* as in *delicious, ch* as in *machine,* and *s* as in *sugar.*

The similarities in orthographic representations for the /s/ and /ʃ/ as well as the similarity in manner of articulation may cause foreign born speakers some confusion. Practice before a mirror provides a visual aid to distinguish between the /s/ and the /ʃ/. Try the following pairs:

shy	sigh	she	sea
shell	sell	ship	sip
shay	say	shine	sign

Practice Material

she	bush	machine
ship	dish	passion
shell	mesh	notion
shall	wash	ocean
shade	finish	pension
shoe	punish	fissure
sugar	crush	pressure
sure	push	delicious
should	flush	conscience
shrine	harsh	anxious

1. Charlotte had a passion for precious stones.
2. The fishing boat was far out on the ocean.
3. Crushed berries sprinkled with sugar are a delicious dish.
4. A passion for peace is a proper aspiration for a great nation.

5. Many wives unblushingly prefer husbands to machines for washing dishes.
6. Ship-to-shore telephone service is available for most of this nation.
7. Lucretia shook potions for men who had notions!

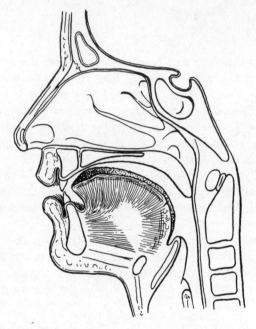

Figure 22.   Tongue position for /ʃ/ and /ʒ/

8. Shellie waited patiently for the wind to shift so that she could set sail.
9. Shakespeare's Falstaff complained that hostess Quickly was neither fish nor flesh.
10. Sheila had great affection for a shy shepherd.
11. Petruchio is a leading character is Shakespeare's *Taming of the Shrew*.

/ʒ/ as in *pleasure*

The sound /ʒ/ is produced like /ʃ/ with accompanying vocalization. /ʒ/ usually occurs medially in English words. The sound may occasionally be heard at the end as in *rouge* and *mirage*. It does not occur initially in any English word. The most frequent spellings for /ʒ/ are *s* and *z*.

PRACTICE MATERIAL

azure	intrusion	treasure
casual	measure	vision
confusion	pleasure	garage
conclusion	seizure	mirage
decision	usual	prestige
division	usurious	rouge
explosion	derision	camouflage

1. An azure sky is usually a pleasurable sight.
2. The seizure of the payroll was prevented by the intrusion of the police.
3. Rouge, properly applied, creates an illusion of good health.
4. The explosion was followed by confusion.
5. A mirage is a visual delusion.
6. Evasion and indecision seldom help in reaching conclusions.

/tʃ/ as in *chest*

The sound /tʃ/ is a blend of /t/ followed immediately by /ʃ/. It presents no special difficulty to native American or English speakers. The sound may be troublesome, however, for speakers for whom English is not a first language and in whose native language the /tʃ/ does not occur. For example, /tʃ/ may be troublesome to native French speakers because it does not occur in the French language. For such persons the expected tendency is to substitute the sound /ʃ/ for the affricate /tʃ/. For speakers who show this tendency, the following exercises should be helpful in creating an awareness of the difference between /tʃ/ and /ʃ/.

/tʃ/	/ʃ/	/tʃ/	/ʃ/
chin	shin	catch	cash
chip	ship	ditch	dish
cheer	sheer	hatch	hash
chew	shoe	latch	lash
choose	shoes	match	mash
chair	share	much	mush
chore	shore	witch	wish

1. It is sometimes pleasant to share a chair.
2. It does not take long to have too much of mush.
3. Macbeth went to the witch to realize his wish.

4. The hash was flung down the hatch.
5. Charles bruised his shin and skinned his chin.
6. Choose the correct pair of shoes.

/dʒ/ as in *judge*

/dʒ/ is the voiced counterpart of /tʃ/. This voiced affricate may occur initially, medially, or finally. In *judge* and *George* it occurs both initially and finally. In *agent* and *engine* the voiced consonant blend /dʒ/ occurs medially.

The most frequent spellings for /dʒ/ are *g, j,* and *dge,* as in *age, jump,* and *fudge.*

French, Spanish, and German speakers may have difficulty with /dʒ/ because the sound does not occur in their native languages. There is a marked tendency for German speakers to unvoice /dʒ/ so that it becomes /tʃ/. Many American speakers tend to unvoice /dʒ/ when it occurs finally.

PRACTICE MATERIAL

general	merge	adjust
generous	bridge	agent
gin	carriage	changed
jaw	edge	imagine
job	manage	soldier
join	purge	stranger

Distinguish between /dʒ/ and /tʃ/:

/dʒ/	/tʃ/
gin	chin
jar	char
jeer	cheer
jump	chump
jigger	chigger
jug	chug
bridges	britches
ridge	rich
badge	batch

The following materials should be practiced with a view to avoiding the unvoicing of the final /dʒ/.

1. George is the son of a judge.

2. Madge attends college.
3. We stood at the edge of the ridge.
4. Jones ate a large orange.
5. By two years of age, most children can speak their language.
6. The engineers constructed a large suspension bridge.
7. Jennie shared her jam and jelly recipes with Jane.
8. Joe met Jill at the lodge on Lake George.
9. Jones joined the junket against his judgment.
10. James had the courage and the energy for his jaunt.
11. George avoided jail by keeping his pledge.
12. In the judgment of the historian Commanger, it was not just by chance that revolutionary Virginia gave us George Washington, John Marshall, James Madison, and George Wythe; genius, Commanger holds, may spread by contingency.

/l/ as in *lily*

The /l/ is a lingua-alveolar, voiced, lateral sound. It is produced with the tongue tip in contact with the upper gum ridge. The portion of the tongue just behind the tip (the blade) is lowered to permit the air to escape over the sides. The middle part of the tongue is raised and spread so that the sides are in contact with the side teeth.

The /l/ sound may occur initially as in *law, let, lad;* medially as in *alone, also, elbow;* and finally as in *ball, well, mail.* The spellings are either the single *l* or the double *ll.*

In articulating the sound /l/ make certain that the tip and not the blade of the tongue is in contact with the gum ridge. Avoid contact with the teeth.

Practice Material

lake	ball	allow	labial
laugh	girl	yellow	locale
like	mile	ballad	lawful
lower	ale	clan	lentil
lapse	eel	eloquent	labile
lucid	vigil	elicit	listless
linger	guile	dilute	lonely
loan	cabal	pallid	landlord
lyric	artful	blunder	Leslie
labor	cannibal	fluent	linoleum

1. Lucid lyrics make pleasant listening.
2. The electric eel seldom employs guile.
3. The yellow-petaled flower held the scent of fall.
4. Two glasses of ale loosened the tongue and unleashed eloquence.
5. The wages of labor usually lag behind prices.
6. Defective *l*'s make adults sound infantile.
7. Preelection eloquence is rarely characterized by logic.
8. Lyman Beecher held that eloquence is logic on fire.

9. A tale is told of a New England farmer who owned a large apple orchard. In the fall he would pick the apples and place them in large barrels in the cellar of his house. Frequently he would go to the cellar to get some apples for his family. He would look the apples over carefully and select a few speckled ones. His principle was to have his family eat the speckled apples before those that were clean and completely unspoiled. Somehow, and this is the sorry part of the tale, there were always some speckled apples left and the family, despite complaints, never ate one that was completely unspoiled.

10. Lonely and waste is the land they inhabit,
     Wolf-cliffs wild and windy hindlands,
   Ledges of mist, where mountain torrents
     Downward plunge to dark abysses
   And flow unseen.
       —*Beowulf*

11. Daniel Bell, a sociologist, holds that ideology is the translation or conversion of ideas or beliefs into social levers.

12. The word *lounge* is used by the upper class in Britain to refer to rooms in hotels and clubs; the middle class Briton uses the term *lounge* to refer to the equivalent of the American living room. For the middle class, the *lounge* is the room that is likely to be fully carpeted, to have a large screen television set, and to include a three piece Chesterfield suite.

13. The lemming is an oversized field mouse with an inclination that appears suicidal. Periodically lemmings clog the fiords of the Scandinavian Peninsula. An old belief for this inclination was that the lemmings were looking for their place of origin, the lost Atlantis below the North Sea.

/r/ as in *rose*

There is considerable variation, as has already been indicated (see page 62) as to the production and pronunciation of the /r/ sound according to context. In this section the /r/ as in *rose, ready, around, derive* will be considered.

Two ways of producing the /r/ when the sound is immediately followed by a vowel in a stressed syllable will be described. The first method is to raise the tongue tip toward the roof of the mouth. The tongue tip may be brought close to the gum ridge, but actual contact with the gum ridge is avoided (see Figure 23). The tongue tip may also be flexed slightly toward the back of the mouth. Compare this position with those for the /t/ and /l/ sounds.

The second method of articulating an /r/ before a vowel in a stressed syllable approximates the production of a vowel sound. The tip of the tongue is lowered and the central portion of the tongue is raised toward the roof of the mouth where the hard palate ends and the soft palate begins. This is illustrated in Figure 24.

For both methods of articulation, the /r/ sound is produced with accompanying vocalization.

PRACTICE MATERIAL

race	racial	grass
rest	routine	aroma
roof	rotate	brig
rabies	three	criminal
rally	dress	frugal
random	broken	nitrogen
realist	breeze	grain

1. The report on the riot was presented to the press.
2. The aroma of fresh-cut grass is fragrant.
3. The criminal was apprehended and placed in the brig.
4. Some proponents of racial theories are more likely to induce than to contract rabies.
5. The air we breathe contains approximately four parts of nitrogen to one part of oxygen.
6. Byron stressed the point that easy writing makes for hard reading.
7. Plato averred that what is honored in a country will be cultivated there.
8. The unscrupulous realty broker appropriated the widow's property.
9. The red leaves rustled in the crisp fall breeze.

Words beginning with p and b (*proud, brown*) may be troublesome. Because of the lip activity involved, the /r/ may be produced with excessive lip movement. The result is an infantile sound resembling a /w/.

Other difficult combinations are /gr/ and /kr/ as in *green* and *crumb*.

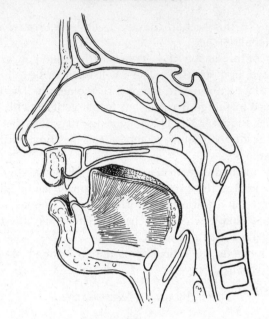

Figure 23.   Tongue position for retroflex /r/

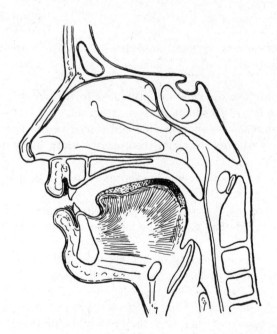

Figure 24.   Tongue position for velar /r/.

The practice words which follow emphasize the more difficult combinations.

preen	breathe	cream	green
prince	brig	crib	grin
pray	bray	crayon	grime
prattle	bride	cry	gray
prove	bring	crumb	grub
press	bread	crew	grew
proud	brought	crawl	groan
price	brown	cross	grotto

/r/ as in *true, through, dry*

Another variety of /r/ approximates a fricative sound in manner of articulation. It is produced by placing the tip of the tongue close to but not quite touching the gum ridge. When air is forced over the tongue tip, a fricative /r/ sound is produced (see Figure 25). When this variety of

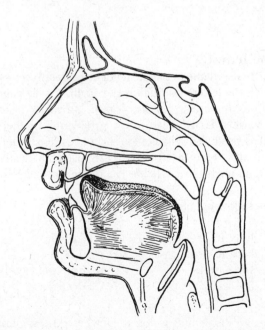

Figure 25.   Tongue position for fricative /r/.

/r/ occurs in the initial position, the sound is vocalized. When it occurs after a voiceless sound as in three and tree, the /r/ may be completely or partly unvoiced. The sound is described as a *postdental fricative*. It is most likely to be heard after tongue-tip consonant sounds such as /t/, /d/, and /θ/.

PRACTICE MATERIAL

trip	thrill	drown
trick	through	draw
tripe	three	dream
trump	throw	dry
train	tray	drain
tree	thrift	drop

1. The pitcher prayed before each throw.
2. The pressed flower made the book fragrant.
3. The tree was three years old.
4. The train sped swiftly through the night.
5. Trent was thrilled on his first train trip.

Linking /r/ and Intrusive /r/

Earlier we discussed the regional tendencies relative to the use of /r/ in words in which the letter *r* is final in the spelling (see page 62). The /r/ in contexts such as *far away, for us, fear it* is usually heard as a *linking sound* between vowels. If we listen to the production of the linking /r/ we may note that it is produced with less vigor and is of shorter duration than the initial /r/ or the /r/ in a stressed position. Acoustically, the sound is much like the /r/ in unstressed syllables, as in the words *berry, merry, carry,* and *ferry.*

Practice the following phrases:

hear it	dare I
bore in	dire act
for a time	bear under
fire away	dear aunt

Occasionally, an /r/ sound is intruded where the spelling of the word does not include the letter *r*. The /r/ may be intruded in combinations such as *law and order, idea of it, banana ice cream, vanilla* and *orange*. The use of the intrusive *r* is generally considered substandard and so this practice is not recommended.

By way of practice, the following sentences should be spoken slowly, and intrusive *r*'s avoided.

1. Law and order must be maintained.
2. The basic idea of the selection should be clear.
3. Are you fond of vanilla ice cream?
4. Banana is my favorite fruit.

ADDITIONAL PRACTICE MATERIAL FOR /r/

1. Americans who are accustomed to a degree of impartiality in the report of sports stories are likely to be surprised at the fierce and outright partiality of Russian reporting. For example, sports writers for *Pravda,* or any other Russian newspaper for that matter, are likely to report a two-runner race between Ivan Russ and Joe American as follows: "Ivan Russ ran second; Joe American ran next to last."

2. Briefly stated, Parkinson's Law asserts that the more persons there are to do less work, the more time will be required for the work to be done. The "law" was formulated and promulgated by the British teacher and writer, Professor C. Northcote Parkinson. The underlying principle for the "law" was probably the result of a report of the British Royal Navy published after World War I. The report presented figures that revealed that after the demobilization of the World War I British Navy, the over-all personnel was as large or larger than it had been at any prior time, including the period when the war with Germany was at its height.

3. Bryson was free with his promises. Usually Bryson's promises were no better than pie crust, made to be broken.

/θ/ as in *thin*

/θ/ is a voiceless fricative sound. It is produced by placing the tip of the tongue either against the back of the upper front teeth or against the cutting edge of the upper teeth.[2] Air is forced through the place of contact to produce the characteristic fricative quality.

/θ/ is represented by the letters *th* in the spelling of a word. The sound may occur initially as in *thin* and *through;* medially as in *athlete* and *mathematics;* or finally as in *bath* and *mirth*.

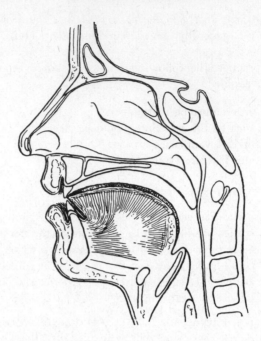

Figure 26.   Representative tongue position for /θ/ (the postdental /θ/).

Some Americans who have been exposed to substandard speech influences tend to substitute a /t/ for the /θ/, especially in initial positions. Foreign-born persons who do not have the /θ/ sound in their first language tend to substitute an approximate sound for it. South German and Swiss speakers, for example, are inclined to substitute a dental /s/ for the initial /θ/. North German speakers are more likely to substitute a dental /t/.

PRACTICE MATERIAL

thank	both	anything
thick	cloth	author
thin	death	bathtub
third	earth	strengthen
thought	fourth	everything
thaw	length	ruthless
theory	moth	orthodox
threat	myth	atheist
thyroid	uncouth	enthusiasm
therapy	zenith	slothful

[2] Some persons produce /θ/ by placing the tongue tip between the upper and lower front teeth.

Distinguish between /θ/ and /t/ :

thank	tank
thin	tin
thought	taught
forth	fort
bath	bat
oath	oat
ruthless	rootless

1. Thelma's story had neither theme nor thesis.
2. Thackeray held that threats make poor therapy.
3. The thermometer was at zero on the third and fourth days of the month.
4. Ethel kept her troth on her thirteenth birthday.
5. Youthful thoughts are frequently unorthodox.
6. The sheet of tin was thin enough to be rolled.
7. Emotions, it is thought, are more easily caught than taught.
8. The fort was captured on the fourth.
9. Theodore would rather bat a ball than take a bath.
10. Horace Smith, a nineteenth century author wrote:
    "Thinking is but an idle waste of thought,
    And nought is everything, and everything is nought."

/ð/ as in *that*

/ð/ is the voiced counterpart of /θ/. It is represented by the letter *th* and may occur initially, medially, or finally in the pronunciation of a word.

There is no certain way of knowing whether a particular word should be pronounced with /θ/ or/ð/. There is a tendency, in initial positions at least, for words which are meaningfully significant and stressed in a sentence—nouns, verbs, and adjectives—to be pronounced with the voiceless /θ/. Pronouns, articles, and conjunctions—words which are likely to be weak in a sentence—are more likely to be pronounced with the voiced /ð/. The words *thumb, think, throw, thick, them, the, than* exemplify these tendencies. Words ending in silent *e* preceded by a *th* as in *bathe* and *soothe* are usually pronounced with a /ð/.

Foreign-born persons who are inclined to substitute a /t/ for a /θ/ are likely to substitute a /d/ for /ð/. This kind of substitution may also be heard in substandard American speech.

PRACTICE MATERIAL

them	bathe	although
that	breathe	another
there	clothe	brother
these	with	either
those	blithe	father
though	loathe	northern
they'll	scythe	smother
they've	teethe	logarithm

Distinguish between /ð/ and /d/:

they	day	then	den	lather	ladder
thine	dine	there	dare	loathe	load
though	dough	thy	dye	tithe	tide

1. The Northerner found the times difficult.
2. This farmer maintained a blithe spirit while wielding his scythe.
3. Neither the father nor the mother was able to smother the fire.
4. They saved time by using logarithms.
5. Though Thurston and Durston were brothers, they loathed one another.

ADDITIONAL PRACTICE MATERIAL FOR /ð/ AND /d/

1. ". . . they breathe truth that breathe their words in pain."
   SHAKESPEARE—*King Richard the Second*, II, 1
2. Throw away thy rod,
   Throw away thy wrath,
     O my God,
   Take the gentle path.
   GEORGE HERBERT—*Discipline*
3. In *The Two Gentlemen of Verona*, Valentine maintains that:
   That man that hath a tongue, I say,
     is no man,
   If with his tongue he cannot
     win a woman
4. Nothing to do but work,
     Nothing to eat but food,
   Nothing to wear but clothes
     To keep one from going nude.
   BENJAMIN F. KING—*The Pessimist*

/ŋ/ as in *ring*

/ŋ/ is a velar nasal sound. It is produced by having the back of the tongue in contact with a lowered soft palate while the vocal folds are in vibration. /ŋ/ is a continuant sound which is emitted through the nose.

Except for possible confusion between the /n/ and the /ŋ/, there is seldom any difficulty in the actual articulation of the velar nasal consonant. There is some tendency, however, to add either a /g/ or a /k/[3] following the /ŋ/ so that all words containing /ŋ/ are pronounced with either /ŋg/ or /ŋk/. For the most part, this tendency may be traced to the influence of a foreign dialect. A second influence may be attributed to the speaker's

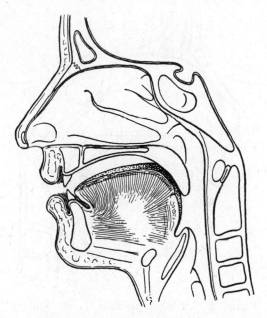

Figure 27. Tongue position for /ŋ/.

inability to remember just how the particular word should be pronounced. A third influence is a direct result of the manner of articulating the /ŋ/. If the soft palate is raised before the tongue contact is broken, a /k/ or /g/ sound is produced. To avoid adding a /k/ or /g/ when only the velar nasal consonant is desired, the speaker must watch his articulatory timing. Specifically, he must make certain that the back of his tongue is moved away from his soft palate before the soft palate is raised to block off the nasal passage.

Practice with phrases such as the following should be of help in estab-

---

[3] German speakers, however, tend to omit the /g/ and /k/ and use only the /ŋ/.

lishing timing and control of the velar nasal consonant: *long ago, going away, Long Island, coming and going, running on, bringing it up, ring a bell, spring is here, King of England, swing along.*

The /ŋ/ is represented by the letter *n* or the letters *ng*. It occurs usually in words in which the letter *n* is followed either by a *k* or a *g* in the same syllable as in *sink, tinkle, sing*, and *single*. /ŋ/ is generally not heard in standard speech in combinations where the *n* and the *g* which follows are in different syllables as in *ingrate* and *congratulate*.

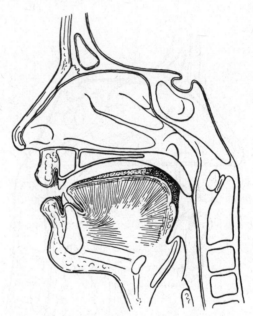

Figure 28.   Tongue position for /k/ and /g/.

To know how to produce an /ŋ/ is not enough. We must also know whether the velar nasal is to be followed by a velar plosive /k/or /g/, or by some other sound. There is, of course, only one certain way to learn the pro-nunciation of a word with velar nasal consonants. The certain way is to learn each word individually, using a large, up-to-date dictionary as a guide. A second approach is to learn the so-called "rules" for the use of the velar consonants in English speech. These follow:

1. When the word ends with the letters *ng* or *ngue*, the pronunciation calls for the /ŋ/. Examples include *thing, rang, tongue,* and *harangue.*

2. Usually, when a suffix is added to a root word which is pronounced with the /ŋ/, the pronunciation calls for the /ŋ/. Examples include *things, rings, singer, longing,* and *ringing.*

The exceptions to this general tendency include the comparative and superlative of the adjectives *long, young,* and *strong,* e.g., *longer, longest; younger, youngest; stronger, strongest.* These have the /ŋ/ followed by /g/.

3. Where the letters *ng* are medial in a root word, as in *finger, tingle, hunger, tangle, extinguish,* and *single,* standard pronunciation calls for the use of /ŋg/. An exception is the pronunciation of *gingham* as [gɪŋəm].

4. In combinations in which the letter *n* is immediately followed by *k, c,* or *x* in the same syllable, the /ŋk/ is used. Examples include *ink, yank, distinct, anxious,* and *larynx.*

It should be noted that not all words which include the letters *ng* in their spelling call for a /ŋ/ in their pronunciation. For example, words such as *range, singe,* and *longevity* are pronounced with the combination /ndʒ/ rather than with either the /ŋ/ or the /ŋg/.

Apply these "rules" to the list of words which follow:

/ŋ/	/ŋg/	/ŋk/
wing	tingle	link
rang	spangle	anchor
young	younger	wink
meringue	elongate	sank
evening	anger	bunk
ringing	bungalow	trinket
longing	longest	lynx
springs	jangle	strength[4]
strong	stronger	length[4]
banging	Congo	tanker

Additional Practice Material for /ŋ/ and /ŋg/

The following sentences and selections are intended for general practice and review.

1. Bringing up one's parents is a problem for growing children.

2. Many young husbands have a longing for their mother's meringue pies.

3. The swinging of the pendulum was marking the running out of time.

4. Speeding along the tracks, the Long Island Express raced to Blarings Landing.

5. For Browning man's yearnings and strivings were never vain doings.

6. The road was widened and lengthened for increasing traffic.

7. The angler was no stranger to these fishing waters.

8. He worked with singular purpose where others no longer tried.

---

[4] The words *strength* and *length* are acceptably pronounced as either [strɛŋkθ] or [strɛŋθ] and [lɛŋkθ] or [lɛŋθ].

9. Long ago Fielding learned that counting and recounting his shillings did nothing to increase their total.

10. She wrung her hands in anguish while her gangster husband swung on the gallows.

11. The linguist spoke seven languages.

12. The younger brother was stronger than the older, but the youngest was strongest.

13. While the singer was suffering from laryngitis, his neighbors were enjoying the strange quiet.

14. Ring out, wild bells, to the wild sky,
    The flying cloud, the frosty light:
The year is dying in the night;
    Ring out, wild bells, and let him die.
          TENNYSON—*In Memoriam*

15. Sherrington, the eminent English neurologist, described an awakened brain as, "an enchanted loom where millions of flashing shuttles weave a dissolving pattern, always a meaningful pattern though never an abiding one."

16. The humming bird
Taking to wing
Hovering over a new grown
    thing,
The humming bird
Quivering,
Pulsating,
Fixing time,
Encompassing motion,
Quick sipping a potion
From its nectared thing
Brings wordless word
    of spring.
        J.E.

17. A man—I let the truth out—
Who's had almost every tooth out,
Cannot sing as once he sung,
When he was young as you are young,
When he was young and lutes were strung,
And love-lamps in the casement hung.
      WILLIAM M. THACKERAY—*Mrs. Katherine's Lantern*

THE VOWELS OF AMERICAN-ENGLISH SPEECH
CONSIDERED INDIVIDUALLY

/i/ as in *free*

A glance at the vowel diagram (Figure 19 on page 74) will reveal to us that /i/ is a high front vowel. It is produced with a considerable degree of tension of the tongue and less degree of tension of the lips. The blade of the tongue is raised high so that it is almost in contact with the anterior part of the hard palate. The lip position approximates a tight-lipped grin.

The sound /i/ has many orthographic representations. The most frequent spellings include *e, ea, ee, ei, i,* and *ie.* These are indicated in the following transcriptions:

be	[bi]
tease	[tiz]
see	[si]
receipt	[rɪsit]
machine	[məʃin]
yield	[jild]

PRACTICE MATERIAL FOR /i/.

each	alleviate	agree
eager	conceivable	appeal
ease	displeasing	believe
east	illegal	Dixie
eel	intriguing	discreet
eerie	machinery	esteem
ether	precedence	esprit
even	subpoena	police
green	unceasing	receive
meager	unseasonable	species

1. Pass the green peas, please.
2. Did Adam or Eve rule in the Garden of Eden?
3. The wild geese beat their wings against a bleak sky.
4. An effective team possesses *esprit de corps.*
5. A queen bee has other bees eager to follow.
6. Even an eel may be intriguing.
7. He was served a subpoena when he indiscreetly refused to answer the policeman's appeal.
8. Beans are likely to be eaten at evening meals.
9. Socrates said he was not an Athenian or a Greek, but a citizen of the world.

/ɪ/ as in *hit*

One of the differences in manner of production between /i/ as in *free* and /ɪ/ as in *hit* is in the degree of articulatory tension for the two vowels. The sound /ɪ/ is produced with a relatively lax tongue. In addition, as may be observed from Figure 16, the tongue position is slightly lower for /ɪ/ than for /i/. The lip position for /ɪ/ is approximately a relaxed smile contrasted with the tight-lipped grin for /i/.

The most frequent spelling for /ɪ/ is the letter *i*, as in *bit, sit, lit, inn.* Less frequent spellings include *u, ui,* and *e* as in *business, build,* and *English.*

Some speakers use the vowel /ɪ/ for the final *y* in words such as *pretty, very,* and *city*. For most speakers, however, final *y* is likely to be pronounced with a vowel closer to that of *free* rather than the vowel /ɪ/ of *hit*. The reader might determine for himself which vowel he approximates for words ending in the letter *y*. The following list of words should be of some help:

key	catty	kit
sea	city	sit
pea	petty	pit
lea	leggy	lit
knee	knotty	knit

PRACTICE MATERIAL FOR /ɪ/

ill	business	addict
imply	differ	admit
Indian	fill	agile
infer	hymn	begin
indicate	pick	cryptic
ink	quilt	eclipse
inn	sieve	instill
it	trip	mystic
ingot	women	respite
Italy	wishes	until

inch by inch	little intake
kindred spirit	bitter pill
spin inside	dig in
silver tip	six slips

1. We stopped at an inn during our trip to Italy.
2. It was done as quickly as a flick of the eyelid.
3. The Indian mystic made his few cryptic remarks as if he were intoning a hymn.

4. Intelligent action is adaptive and well directed.

5. Truth is not infrequently sacrificed for the sake of wit.

6. Pitt paid his bills with his winnings.

7. Bill Wilson, for fifty years a bachelor, had a ditty he repeated to himself six times whenever he felt in imminent danger of changing his singular state. Bill's ditty was:

Needles and pins, needles and pins.

If I marry Jill my trouble begins.

8. That he is mad, 'tis true: 'tis true
     'tis pity
And pity 'tis 'tis true.
          SHAKESPEARE—*Hamlet, Act II*

9. To ridicule philosophy is really to philosophize.
          PASCAL—*Pensées*

10. We were to do more business after dinner; but after dinner is after dinner—an old saying and a true, "much drinking, little thinking."
          SWIFT—*Journal to Stella*

/e/ as in *state*

The vowel /e/ is infrequently used as a pure vowel. More often, the sound becomes a diphthong and might be more precisely represented as /eɪ/ in words such as *way, say,* and *blame.* /e/ as a pure vowel is produced with somewhat less articulatory tension than /i/ but more than for the vowel /ɪ/. As indicated on the vowel diagram, it is front and midhigh. When used, /e/ is likely to appear either in an unstressed syllable as in *chaotic* or in a syllable in which the sound is immediately followed by a voiceless, stop-plosive consonant /p/, /t/, /k/ as in *cape, plate,* and *cake.*

The difference between /e/ and /eɪ/ is not phonemic. That is, there are no words in our language which would be distinguished in meaning from one another on the basis of the use of the pure vowel /e/ or the diphthong variant /eɪ/. The same word may have /e/ in one context and become /eɪ/ in another.

In the sentence, "She wore the cape all day," it is likely that the word *cape* would be pronounced [kep] and *day* as [deɪ]. In another context such as "She wore a long cape" the word *cape* might very well be pronounced with the diphthong /eɪ/ rather than the vowel /e/.

The words which follow include examples of the most frequent orthographic representations for /e/ or /eɪ/. The letter *a* is probably the most frequent spelling; *ay, ai, ea, ey,* and *ei* are also represented as in *date, rate, sale, make, stain, paint, ray, steak, vein, they.*

PRACTICE MATERIAL FOR /e/ OR /eɪ/

ace	caged	acquaint
age	fading	byplay
ague	failure	delay
ail	feinted	dismay
aim	hasten	enrage
angel	haven	entree
bail	lazy	gainsay
bait	reigning	persuade
dame	strafed	portray
deign	zany	repay

1. Angel food cake, well made, is good date bait.
2. The caged animal was enraged by the zany tactics of the keeper.
3. The portrait was of a quaint dame who reigned in ancient days.
4. It is hard to gainsay an aged male.
5. Maine is a New England state.
6. The weary lover could not say whether his lady love was pale or his love had become stale.
7. Clayton Cain was fond of saying:
   "They who get themselves in jail
   May not taste of cakes and ale."

8. There is something in a face,
   An air, and a peculiar grace,
   Which boldest painters cannot trace.
   SOMERVILLE—*The Lucky Hit*

9. The wasting moth ne'er spoil'd my best array;
   The cause was this, I wore it every day.
   ALEXANDER POPE—*Paraphrases from Chaucer*

/ɛ/ as in *met*

The vowel /ɛ/ differs from /e/ in that it is produced with less articulatory tension and with a slightly lowered front tongue position.

/ɛ/ is usually represented by the letter *e* in word spelling. Less frequent spelling are *a* as in *any, ay* as in *says, ai* as in *said,* and *ea* as in *head.*

Additional specimen words which contain the vowel /ɛ/ when spoken according to acceptable standards include: *beg, best, bend, elk, enter, elm, said,* and *breast.*

A nondistinctive variant of the vowel /ɛ/ is heard in words such as *their, fare, bare,* and *dare.* These words are also pronounced with the diphthong /ɛə/ and the omission of the final /r/ by many New York City, Southern, and eastern New England speakers. In General American speech the words are more likely to be pronounced with the vowel /ɛ/ followed by /r/ or by the vowel blend /ɛɚ/.

PRACTICE MATERIAL FOR /ɛ/

ebb	beckon	attest
echo	check	behead
edge	deaf	detest
egg	feather	fret
elder	gesture	inept
elevate	guess	instead
elfin	meant	intend
ends	pleasant	invest
energy	ready	regret
enter	settle	request

1. Many men are not meant for marriage.
2. Ted and Ed elected to settle their bets on Wednesday.
3. The men of finance were ready to settle their debts.
4. The deaf men gestured to beckon their friends.
5. Pent-up energy can be spent for pleasant ends.
6. Not many men admit that they aspire to be among the ten best-dressed.
7. An investment is characterized by careful investigation and the expectation of a small but steady increase in capital; speculation is characterized by more guessing, greater hopes, and frequent regrets.

8.   The bell invites me.
   Hear it not, Duncan: for it is a knell
   That summons thee to heaven or to hell.
            SHAKESPEARE—*Macbeth, Act II*

9. Life that dares send
   A challenge to his end,
   And when it comes, say,
      Welcome, friend!
            CRASHAW—*Wishes to His Supposed Mistress*

/æ/ as in *hat*

/æ/ is a low front vowel. It is heard rather regularly throughout the United States in the standard pronunciations of the words *rat, mash, rack, angle,* and *gather.*

In some parts of the United States there is a tendency for speakers to substitute the vowel blend /ɛə/ for the sound /æ/. In the General American speech area many speakers use a vowel that belongs to the phoneme /ɛ/ rather than /æ/ in words such as *marry, Harry,* and *parry* in which the vowel is followed by the sound /r/.

The vowel /æ/ is usually produced with a lax tongue, though a tense variety of /æ/ is produced by some speakers. A tendency which should be avoided is the production of the vowel /æ/ with excessive tension and accompanying nasality.

The reader may use the following word list and sentences to determine his own practice for words which have the vowel /æ/ in acceptable pronunciation.

Practice Material for /æ/

cat	shall	carry	parrot	drank
band	fact	marriage	sand	family
back	fad	carriage	land	fancy

sad sack	atomic blast
rag bag	mad dash
pact for action	random facts
dank camp	Yankee band

1. The groom lifted his bride out of the carriage and carried her into the house.

2. The angry members of the family banded together to prevent the marriage.

3. Random thoughts may include both facts and fancy.

4. Parrots can repeat, but cannot establish, facts.

5. Harris planned to make concessions, but he began with several demands.

6. Barrett did not understand Calvin's complaint about being asked to carry coals to Newcastle.

7. Provided a man is not mad, he can be cured of every folly but vanity.
JEAN JACQUES ROUSSEAU—*Émile*

/a/ as in *ask*

As a pure vowel, /a/ is rarely used by most Americans. It is more often used as part of the diphthong /aɪ/[5] as in *I, my,* and *ice.*

/a/ in both sound and manner of articulation is a "compromise" somewhere between /æ/ as in *gather* and /ɑ/ in *calm.* Some speakers, principally from the eastern New England area, use the vowel /a/ in the words *path, bath, ask, park,* and *laugh.* Other speakers may use either /æ/ or /ɑ/ for these words.

Review Material

Front Vowels

1. It is when we try to grapple with another man's intimate need that we perceive how incomprehensible, wavering, and misty are the beings that share with us the sight and the warmth of the sun.

    joseph conrad—*Lord Jim*

2. "Yes", I answered you last night;
    "No", this morning, sir, I say:
    Colors seen by candle light
    Will not look the same by day.

    elizabeth barrett browning—*The Lady's "Yes"*

3. In skating over thin ice our safety is on speed.

    ralph waldo emerson—*Prudence*

4. Battles, in these ages, are transacted by mechanism; with the slightest possible development of human individuality or spontaneity, men now even die, and kill one another, in an artificial manner.

    thomas carlyle—*The French Revolution*

5. No sadder proof can be given by a man of his own littleness than disbelief in great men.

    thomas carlyle—*Sartor Resartus*

6. The very hair on my head
    Stands up for dread.

    sophocles—*Oedipus Coloneus*

7. Experience is the name everyone gives to his mistakes.

    oscar wilde—*Lady Windermere's Fan*

8. I can resist everything except temptation.

    oscar wilde—*Lady Windermere's Fan*

---

[5] See page 168 for a discussion of the diphthong /aɪ/.

/ɑ/ as in *calm*

/ɑ/ is produced with the tongue in about as low a position as it is likely to get without using direct external pressure. Such pressure is applied when a physician uses a tongue depressor and asks the patient to say "ah." The patient is asked to say "ah" because in the production of the sound he relaxes and flattens his tongue and so permits the doctor to see the back of his throat. /ɑ/ is a low, back, lax vowel. The mouth is "open wide" and the lips are unrounded.

The vowel /ɑ/ is most frequently represented in spelling by the letter *a* or *o*. Other individual spellings include *e* (sergeant) and *ea* (heart and hearth). In words such as *ah, alms, barn, farm, psalm,* and *balm* the sound /ɑ/ is consistently heard throughout the United States.

In the words *not, hot, cog, fog,* and *grog* the vowel is represented by the letter *o*. These words, however, are also frequently pronounced with the vowel /ɒ/ and occasionally with /ɔ/.

The vowel /ɑ/ is also heard occasionally in the words *office, coffee, long,* and *song. The vowels /ɔ/* and /ɒ/ are, however, more frequently used in these words.

PRACTICE MATERIAL FOR /ɑ/

ah	Antarctic	afar
alms	archives	alarm
artist	armory	bazaar
barber	balmy	becalm
cargo	bombardment	disarm
dart	departed	discharge
farthing	dishearten	disembark
father	guardian	shah
hearth	pardon	spa
harbor	remarkable	unharmed
qualm	swamped	unscarred
sergeant	unqualified	vanguard

ardent farmer	large barn
calm harbor	army sergeant
honest art	harsh marshal
far star	doll cart

1. Fathers are not all guardian angels.
2. Calm waters are well charted.
3. The harbor was bombarded but no person was harmed.
4. The alarm was heard from afar.

5. Bargains can be had at a bazaar.

6. A coat of varnish may prevent tarnish.

7. The Bard of Avon wrote many sonnets.

8. Tom, who was a hod carrier, also shod horses when he had the time.

9. All Hollywood stars do not enjoy their parts.

10. Charles thought that Marcus was balmy for sending cargo to the arctic.

/ɒ/ as in *clog*

In manner of articulation and in acoustic impression, /ɒ/ is somewhere between /ɔ/ as in *fall* and /ɑ/ as in *calm*. The vowel /ɒ/ is produced with the tongue in a low and relatively lax position. The lips usually are slightly rounded.

No list can be given or words for which the vowel /ɒ/ is consistently used throughout the United States or even in any major speech region. The sound is more likely to be heard in eastern New England than elsewhere, but its use is by no means confined to this area.

The vowel /ɒ/, as we noted, may be heard in words such as *not, hot, cog, fog,* and *grog*. The use of the vowel /ɑ/, however, is more frequent in these words.

The vowel /ɒ/ may also be heard in words in which the spelling includes the letter *o* followed by a voiceless fricative or a nasal consonant. Such words include *off, lost, cost, loft, long,* and *song*. The vowels /ɔ/ and /ɑ/ may also be heard for these words.

Other words in which the vowel /ɒ/ may be heard, but probably less frequently than either /ɔ/ or /ɑ/ include *horrid, foreign, orange, porridge,* and *florid*. It may be noted that in each of these words the letter *o* is followed by a single or double letter *r*.

/ɔ/ as in *call*

/ɔ/ is a mid-, low, back vowel produced with slight tongue and lip tension and lip rounding. The most frequent spellings for /ɔ/ include *a* as in *call, aw* as in *awful, au* as in *taught* or *taut, ou* as in *sought,* and the single letter *o* as in *horse*.

In many words, including some of those just presented, the vowels /ɒ/ or /ɑ/ may be heard instead of /ɔ/.

The interested reader may test his own practice in regard to the use of /ɔ/, /ɒ/, or /ɑ/ by pronouncing the following lists of words and sentences. The first column is of words which are most likely to have the vowel /ɔ/ consistently used. The words of the other columns may also be pronounced with the vowels /ɒ/ or /ɑ/.

PRACTICE MATERIAL FOR /ɔ/ AND /ɒ/

hawk	doll	collar
call	song	foreign
bought	long	borrow
calked	wrong	horrible
ought	soft	sorrow
taught	coffin	torrid
wall	cost	forest
August	lost	orange
auto	off	porridge
maul	mock	dollar

1. Calmly the frog sat on a log at the edge of the water.
2. He lay on a cot in the jungle to escape the torrid heat.
3. For long he had considered it wrong to be confined to his office.
4. He became taut as he came close to the object he sought.
5. Laura was taught that to borrow even a dollar was to invite sorrow.
6. In *The Course of Empire* De Voto warned that the dawn of knowledge is usually the false dawn.
7. Men must be taught as if you taught them not.
   POPE—*Essay on Criticism*
8. The horn, the horn, the lusty horn
   Is not a thing to laugh to scorn.
   SHAKESPEARE—*As You Like It,* Act III

/u/ as in *ooze*

/u/ is characterized by a greater amount of lip-rounding than any of the other vowels in American speech. The back of the tongue is arched, tense, and high.

The most frequent spelling for /u/ is *oo* as in *school, too, fool,* and *ooze;*

other spellings include the single letter *o* as in *do* and *to; u* as in *dupe;* and *ou* as in *coup* and *soup.*

If prolonged, /u/ may change to the diphthongal variant /ʊu/. This modification of /u/ is similar to the changes of the vowels /i/, /e/, and /o/ to the nondistinctive diphthongal variants /ɪi/, /eɪ/, and /oʊ/.

PRACTICE MATERIAL FOR /u/

boon	blooming	accrue
coop	druid	ado
doom	lampoon	afternoon
food	prudent	brew
group	ruler	buffoon
move	spoofing	grew
rude	toothsome	recluse
rumor	troopers	shrew
swoon	truant	threw
troupe	truthful	zoo

1. It takes more than two afternoons to tame a shrew.
2. Fools as well as flowers bloom in the afternoon.
3. The rumor grew as the time flew.
4. A truant from thought needs a rude awakening.
5. Truth makes no demand that the truthful be ruthless.
6. They who carve on tombstones are uncouth if they insist on telling the truth.

/ʊ/ as in *pull*

/ʊ/ is a high, back, lip-rounded vowel. The tongue is relaxed and in a slightly lower position than for the vowel /u/. Though the vowel /u/ may occur either initially, medially, or finally, /ʊ/ occurs only medially. The spellings include *u* as in *pull, full,* and *bull; oo* as in *book, took, wood,* and *look.* Other spellings include *ou* as in *could* and *should* and *o* as in *wolf.*

In many words of native English origin, especially those spelled with *oo,* practice varies as to the use of /u/ or /ʊ/. The reader may test his own inclination by pronouncing the words *root, roof, broom, hoof,* and *soot* and attending to whether the tongue feels tense or relaxed when the vowel is articulated. If it is tense and the lips are very rounded, the sound /u/ is probably being produced. If the tongue feels relaxed and the lips are less rounded, the vowel sound is probably /ʊ/.

The distinction between /u/ and /ʊ/ may be brought out by comparing the pronunciations of the following pairs of words:

pool	pull
shoe	shook
boo	book
fool	full
too	took

The vowel /ʊ/ is also heard in the unstressed syllables of the words *casual* and *gradual* and for *to* when it is followed by a word beginning with a vowel or diphthong as in *to England* and *to Iowa*.

PRACTICE MATERIAL FOR /ʊ/

bush	bullet	forsook
could	bosom	Lynbrook
foot	butcher	mistook
good	cooking	neighborhood
put	crooked	overlook
shook	pudding	partook
stood	pulley	pulpit
took	should	retook
wolf	wooden	sugar
would	woolen	understood

1. The cook made the pudding in such haste that she forgot to add sugar.
2. The crooks used a wooden pulley to lift their loot.
3. It was understood that the debate was to allow for refutation.
4. A spook needs no rubber heels to be unheard on foot.
5. Goods once woolen are now made of materials once wooden.
6. After a hail of bullets, the soldiers retook the fort in Old Brooklyn.

/o/ as in *boat*

/o/ is a tense vowel made with the raised portion of the tongue in a mid-back position and the lips rounded. /o/ is infrequently used as a pure vowel. It is most likely to be used as a pure vowel in words in which a stop-plosive sound follows the vowel as in *goat, oat, oak,* and *open.* In words where the sound is final, /o/ is likely to be lengthened and blended with /ʊ/ to become /oʊ/ as in *go, sew, toe, bone, owe, soul,* and *home.* (See page 171 for further discussion of /oʊ/.) In general, a lengthened /o/ is likely to become the diphthong /oʊ/.

The most frequent spelling for /o/, as may be noted in the key words, are *o, oe,* and *ou.*

PRACTICE MATERIAL FOR /o/ OR /ou/

oaf	boulder	below
ocean	coma	bestow
ode	comely	crow
oh	folder	dough
ohm	frozen	explode
only	growing	flow
own	loaded	foe
boast	moaning	hollow
beau	poser	sorrow
bones	precocious	tomorrow
nose	slowly	untold
roam	soldier	woe

1. Joe Stoke holds that though sticks and stones may break your bones, names can also harm you.
2. The grouse were hunted with loaded guns.
3. Tomorrow is time enough for sorrow.
4. The beau grew bolder as his love grew older.
5. The boasting gave way to moaning as the foe approached.

REVIEW MATERIAL

Back Vowels

1. To sorrow,
   I bade good-morrow,
And thought to leave her far away behind;
   But cheerly, cheerly,
   She loves me dearly;
She is so constant to me, and so kind.
   JOHN KEATS—*Endymion*

2. Last night we saw the stars arise,
   But clouds soon dimmed the ether blue:
And when we saw each other's eyes
   Tears dimmed them too!
   GEORGE DARBY—*Last Night*

3. Slight not what's near through aiming at what's far.
   EURIPIDES—*Rhesus*

4. Time stoops to no man's lure;
    And love, grown faint and fretful,
    With lips but half regretful
    Sighs, and with eyes forgetful
Weeps that no loves endure.
              ALGERNON CHARLES SWINBURNE—*The Garden of Proserpine*

5. Those who in quarrels interpose
    Must often wipe a bloody nose.
              JOHN GAY—*The Mastiffs* (*Fables*)

/ɜ/ or /ɝ/ as in *curl*

/ɜ/ and /ɝ/ are mid-central vowels. In their production the middle of the tongue is arched towards the roof of the mouth. The two vowels are essentially the same in their manner of production and acoustic end result. The sound /ɜ/ acoustically suggests the sound /r/. The vowel /ɝ/ contains more than a mere suggestion of the /r/ sound. It is, in effect, a vowel /ɜ/ blended with the sound /r/.

Whether the speaker uses /ɜ/ or /ɝ/ usually depends upon his practice relative to the pronunciation of words spelled with a medial *r*. Those speakers who are inclined to pronounce the sound /r/ whenever the letter *r* appears in the spelling are likely to use the vowel /ɝ/ or the combination /ɜr/. Those speakers who are likely to pronounce /r/ only when the spelling includes the letter *r* immediately followed by a vowel, are also likely to use the vowel /ɜ/.[6] In eastern New England and in Southern speech, /ɜ/ is usually heard in words such as *curl, hurl, word, fir, girl, burn, whirl, earn,* and *kernel.* In General American speech the same words are likely to be pronounced with the vowel /ɝ/.

The spelling of words in which /ɜ/ or /ɝ/ is used usually includes the letters *ur, or, ir,* or *ear.* An interesting exception is the word *colonel.*

Some speakers substitute the sound blend /ɜɪ/ for the vowel /ɜ/. The acceptance of this substitution depends upon the practices of the speech area in which the speaker lives. Persons who wish to avoid the substitution of /ɜɪ/ for /ɜ/ might practice the regular inclusion of the /r/ sound following the vowel to produce either a distinct /ɜr/ combination or the sound /ɝ/.

Differences in speaker usage may be determined by an analysis of the pronunciation of the following words:

---

[6] See page 62 for a discussion of practice in the use of /r/.

cur	cursive
heard	hurting
burr	burden
mirth	murmur
occur	occurring

PRACTICE MATERIAL FOR /ɜ/ or /ɝ/

certain	ascertain	avert	inter
curl	bestirred	demur	refer
earn	concerning	deter	aver
err	determine	observe	stir
first	discursive	occur	purr
guerdon	disturbing	preserve	swerve
hurt	excursion	rehearse	stern
mirth	impersonal	reverse	surf
sermon	indeterminate	taciturn	spur
terse	uncertain	unfurl	third

1. Gertrude considered Thurston to be a person of sterling worth.
2. Merton determined to be stern as he worked.
3. A good merchant is seldom taciturn.
4. A pretty curl may make up for a lack of learning.
5. The pilot of the excursion boat averted an accident.
6. A stirring sermon may produce a rebirth of religious fervor.
7. To earn her keep, the farm girl churned the butter.

8. Burton told a story of a girl named Myrtle and her friend Earl. Myrtle complained that even in the summer Earl was stern and cool and lacking in affection. When asked about her plans, Myrtle replied, "I'm not certain, but I think that when spring returns I'll just have to change my Earl."

9. Cursed be the verse, how
        well so e'er it flow,
    That tends to make one worthy
        man my foe.
            ALEXANDER POPE—*Epistle to Dr. Arbuthnot*

10. He too serves a certain purpose who
        only stands and cheers.
            HENRY B. ADAMS—*The Education of Henry Adams*

/ʌ/ as in *cup*

/ʌ/ is a midvowel produced with a relatively relaxed tongue arched toward the middle or back of the palate. It is heard only in stressed syllables[7] either at the beginning or middle of words. The most frequent spellings are *u* as in *up, cup, but,* and *hum* and *o* as in *come, some,* and *comfort.* Less frequent spellings are *ou* as in *touch* and *double* and *oo* as in *blood.*

There is a tendency for some speakers, possibly as a result of influences emanating from the southern part of England, to substitute a vowel close to /ɑ/ in words usually pronounced with /ʌ/. This tendency appears to be especially strong for words spelled with the letter *o*. The reader may check his own practice by comparing his pronunciations of the following pairs of words:

donkey	dunk
come	cut
done	dub
some	summary
comfort	cunning

PRACTICE MATERIAL FOR /ʌ/

blood	lunge	assumption
blunder	mumble	asunder
brother	mutton	begun
bud	once	benumb
club	rubber	construct
does	sprung	discussing
double	tongue	percussion
gun	trouble	rebuff
honey	umpire	undone
love	unctuous	unsung

1. Get up, the night is done, and greet the new day's sun.

2. He grumbled and mumbled throughout the supper meal.

3. In some schools it was once a custom to identify the poor student by a dunce cap.

4. Sometimes the bee keeps on making honey because he is in a rut.

5. Numbskulls as well as witches can create double trouble by their mumbo jumbo.

6. The fight for freedom, once begun, is a fight that is never done.

---

[7] See pages 75–77 for a discussion of strong and weak forms and the unstressed "equivalent" of /ʌ/.

7. But now my task is smoothly done:
   I can fly or I can run.
          MILTON—*Comus.*

/ə/ as in *about* (first vowel) and *sofa* (second vowel)

/ə/ is a midvowel, produced with a relaxed tongue in a position slightly lower than for /ɜ/. Except as part of a diphthong, the sound /ə/ is used only in unstressed syllables as in the first syllable of the words *attend, about, alone,* and the second syllable of *sofa, soda, taken, bacon,* and *fracas.*

The vowel /ə/ though limited in use to unstressed syllables is nevertheless probably the one most frequently used in American-English speech. Two related features of American-English speech explain the high frequency of usage for the vowel /ə/. One is that most words of two or more syllables have at least one unstressed syllable. The second is that "unimportant words"—prepositions, conjunctions, etc., regardless of number of syllables—are usually spoken as if all syllables were unstressed.[8]

We may *begin* to *become* *aware* *of* how *often* /ə/ may *occur* if we read *the* pres*en*t sent*ence* *a*loud. Each of the italicized syllables may appropriately be pronounced with the vowel /ə/.

Further practice may be had by saying the following sentences aloud as if they were parts of conversations. The spellings of the words should not be permitted to exert undue influence on the pronunciations.

1. The woman was about to leave the room.
2. The paper was full of frightful items of news.
3. The older brother attended to the needs of the younger one.
4. We who are about to die, salute you.
5. It rained and rained from morning to night.

/ɚ/ as in builder, harder (General American).

/ɚ/, like /ə/, is used only in unstressed syllables. It is used in place of /ə/ by those speakers who habitually pronounce medial or final *r*'s whenever the letter occurs in the word spelling.

The vowel /ɚ/, like /ə/, is a mid-central vowel produced with a rela-

---

⁸ See page 75 for further discussion of this point.

tively lax tongue. Unlike /ə/, however, /ɚ/ is characterized by an /r/ coloring. This characteristic is produced either by raising the tip of the tongue from behind the lower gum ridge or by arching the middle part of the tongue a bit higher than for the /ə/ sound.

The reader may check his own tendencies relative to the vowels /ə/ and /ɚ/ by analyzing his pronunciations of the italicized syllables in the words tak*er*, farth*er*, wond*er*, and bitt*er*.

The difference between /ɝ/ and /ɚ/ may be brought out by attending to the vowels in the stressed and unstressed syllables in the words *murmur, murder, further* and *burnèr.*

Review Material for Central Vowels

1. Werther had a love for Charlotte
     Such as words could never utter;
   Would you know how first he met her?
     She was cutting bread and butter.

           . . .

   Charlotte, having seen his body
     Borne before her on a shutter,
   Like a well conducted person,
     Went on cutting bread and butter
                 WILLIAM M. THACKERAY—*Sorrows of Werther*

2. George M. Cohan uttered a terse complaint that we are "hurried and worried until we're buried, and there's no curtain call."

3. Hunter was perturbed about sleeping in an upper berth. He worried that if he turned or stirred an accident might occur.

4. Tom Tucker and his brother Merle sang at supper.

Questions and Exercises on the Study of Vowels

1. How do vowels differ in articulation from consonants?
2. What consonants closely resemble vowels in their manner of production?
3. Why may it be said that the consonant sounds /m/ and /n/ may well be considered nasal vowels?
4. In what way do the sounds /w/ and /j/ resemble vowels?
5. Transcribe phonetically your pronunciation of the following words: *fee, bean, people, been, pill, state, plate, hat, mat, ask, path, too, school, blood, hook, roof, broom, boat, stall, ball, hog, log, father, balm, curl, surly, above, rudder.*
6. Do any of your pronunciations vary from those of other speakers in your own social and educational class? Indicate the differences through the use of phonetic transcriptions.

7. Transcribe the italicized words of the following sentences as you would pronounce them in ordinary conversational speech.

(a) *The* race is *to the* quick.

(b) Three *and* four are the same *as* five *and* two.

(c) Is this book *for* me?

(d) *The* hour has come.

8. Transcribe each of the following according to your habitual pronunciation: *asunder, burn, curtain, furnace, further, pearl, plunder, under, upper, yearn.*

DIPHTHONGS

Diphthongs are vocalic glides which are uttered in a single breath impulse. In a strict sense, the word *diphthong,* which literally means *two sounds,* should not be used for what is actually a *continuous gliding vowel* sound. The conventional phonetic symbolization suggests that a diphthong contains two sounds. A better interpretation of the symbols would be that the first element of the diphthong represents the approximate initial sound and the second element represents the approximate final sound of the glide. For example, the diphthong /ɔɪ/ is initiated with the vowel /ɔ/. The organs of articulation are then continuously modified to produce a continuous change of sound until the diphthong is concluded with what approximates the vowel /ɪ/.

The diphthongs /aɪ/, /ɔɪ/, and /aʊ/ are phonemic. Each represents a distinctive sound unit. Each serves as a basis for enabling us to distinguish between spoken words in the same way as do vowel and consonant phonemes. Not all diphthongs, however, are phonemic. For example, though we may recognize an acoustic difference in pronunciation when *gate* is pronounced [get] or [geɪt], we would recognize the intended word with either pronunciation. Similarly, we know what day of the week is signified whether we hear *Tuesday* pronounced as [tjuzdɪ], [tɪuzdɪ], or [tuzdɪ]. The nonphonemic diphthongs include /eɪ/, /oʊ/, /ɪu/, and /ju/.

There is another group of sounds which might also be studied among the nonphonemic diphthongs. These sound combinations occur in the speech of persons who omit the medial and final /r/ in their pronunciations. This group of vowels includes: /ɪə/, /ʊə/, /ɔə/, /oə/, and /ɛə/ in words such as hear, dear; poor, sure; floor, door; horse, wore; and dare, fair. These will be briefly discussed on pages 170–174.

/aɪ/ as in *ice*

The diphthong /aɪ/ is most frequently represented orthographically by the alphabetic letters *i* at the beginning and middle of words and *y* as the final letter of words. Many persons, use the vowel /ɑ/ for the first sound of the diphthong to produce the blend /ɑɪ/. This pronunciation is frequent enough among cultured speakers to be accepted as standard.

The words *ice, ire,* and *aisle* contain the diphthong /aɪ/ in the initial sound.

In the words *mine, timely, miner,* the diphthong appears medially. In *sky, by, tie, wry* the diphthong /aɪ/ is used as the final sound.

PRACTICE MATERIAL FOR /aɪ/ OR /ɑɪ/

aisle	aspiring	aside
buy	beguiling	butterfly
diagram	declining	behind
drive	designing	byline
height	devise	despite
island	inviting	hindsight
mine	reminder	lifelike
side	requited	overripe
riot	unlikely	skyline
time	unsightly	twilight

1. Dinah made a beguiling bride as she walked down the aisle.
2. The wise use others' hindsight for their own foresight.
3. The high spires appeared to be aglow in the twilight.
4. Ina aspired to an iron clad knight.
5. We require few reminders to do things we like.
6. Simon noted that time and tide are not on the side of those who are righteous but idle.

/ɑʊ/ or /aʊ/ as in *now*

The now famous line, "How now brown cow?" contains, in each of its words, the diphthong /ɑʊ/ or /aʊ/. In this sentence, it may be noted, the diphthong is consistently represented by the letters **ow**. Another frequent spelling is **ou** as in *mouth, out, flout, bound,* and *sound.*

There is a rather strong tendency to use the vowel blend /æʊ/ rather than /ɑʊ/ or /aʊ/ in some parts of the Eastern speech areas (New York and the Middle Atlantic states) and in parts of the South. The use of /æʊ/ is usually considered substandard in the North but is generally acceptable (is less likely to attract unfavorable attention.[9]) in the south. Occasionally, the triple vowel combination /æɑʊ/ or /æaʊ/ is heard for the standard /ɑʊ/ or /aʊ/.

The combination /aʊ/ rather than /ɑʊ/ is frequently used throughout many parts of the United States. It has the prestige of usage by persons of education and culture.

PRACTICE MATERIAL FOR /ɑʊ/ OR /aʊ/

count	about	allow
doubt	announce	bow
gown	astound	brow
mouth	dismount	cow
out	impound	how
owl	profound	now
proud	rebound	plough
shout	resound	sow
south	unfounded	thou
town	ungrounded	vow

1. The threat of showers shrouded the day in gloom.
2. The horseman failed to dismount but fell to the ground.
3. However unfounded, the rumor spread throughout the town.
4. Even as thou, a cow or a sow may look profound.
5. Take counsel with yourself before deciding to mouth your thoughts aloud.
6. The scoundrel's last wish was that he might see his proud wife wearing a shroud.

/ɔɪ/ as in *soil*

The diphthong /ɔɪ/ is appropriately used in words such as *oil, toil,* and *toy.* The most frequent spelling equivalents in English are the letters *oi* at the beginning and middle of words and *oy* at the end of words.

The vowel blend /ɜɪ/ is occasionally heard substituted for /ɔɪ/ by some New York City speakers. This substitution is considered sub-standard.

---

[9] See C. K. Thomas, *ibid.,* p. 143

In the speech of some Southerners, the phonemic difference between /ɔɪ/ and /ɔ/ breaks down, the speakers using a lengthened vowel /ɔ:/ for the more generally acceptable diphthong /ɔɪ/.

The following word list and sentences are intended to provide practice material for words in which the use of the diphthong /ɔɪ/ is recommended as standard. Avoid the use of either /ɜɪ/ or of /oɪ/. The latter is a substitution occasionally heard in parts of the Middle Atlantic States.

PRACTICE MATERIAL FOR /ɔɪ/

oil	join	employ
toil	point	enjoy
soil	poison	annoy
voice	rejoice	recoil
choice	oyster	deploy
boy	coin	adroit
coy	cloy	convoy
soy	spoil	avoid

1. Memories of things once enjoyed still leave us with an aching void.
2. A slippery oyster can be enjoyed only by the well poised.
3. The oil which burns may be an ointment for the burned.
4. The cackling chicken is no longer noisy when it becomes a broiler.
5. The royal family exploited the citizens to provide themselves with the coin of the realm.
6. The spoils of battle are seldom worth the toil of battling.
7. A voice too coy may be a voice to cloy.
8. Boyd enjoyed the play at the Savoy.

/eɪ/ as in *bay*

The diphthong /eɪ/ is pronounced as the first letter of the alphabet. It may be used instead of the vowel /e/ in such words as *nail, aim, lace, fame, pray, way,* and *bewail.* It may also be heard in such words as *date, berate,* and *ache* and in the second syllable of *today.* The use of the diphthong /eɪ/ rather than the vowel /e/ depends upon speech context. The difference in pronunciation between /ə/ or /eɪ/ will not result in differences in meaning for any English word. (See page 152 for practice material.)

/oʊ/ as in *toe*

The diphthong /oʊ/ is pronounced as the alphabetic letter *o*. This diphthong, or the vowel /o/, is used in such words as *only, owner, ocean, pillow, open,* and *coal*. Whether the speaker uses the vowel /o/ or the diphthong /oʊ/ is almost entirely an automatic matter determined by the speech context. In this respect it is parallel to the use of /e/ or /eɪ/ discussed earlier. (See page 161 for practice material.)

/ɛə/ as in *their*

The diphthong /ɛə/ is used instead of the more frequently heard combination /ɛr/ by persons who omit the medial and final /r/ sound in their pronunciations. It is likely to be heard in such words as *air, fair, there,* and *scare*.

Some speakers tend to substitute the diphthong /ɛə/ for the vowel /æ/ or /a/ in such words as *last, fast, class, path,* and *bath. This substitution* is generally considered substandard.

PRACTICE MATERIAL FOR /ɛə/ or /ɛr/

air	mare	despair
bear	their	forbear
care	wear	impair
dare	affair	prepare
fair	beware	tableware
hair	compare	welfare
lair	declare	repair

1. The unwary bear was trapped in his own lair.

2. Most men forbear to express their feelings about how women care for their hair.

3. The heirloom, a fine set of silver tableware, has a rare design.

4. A bachelor, unable to bear children, may still write about their welfare.

5. The heiress seemed beautiful beyond compare.

6. Our share of night to bear,
   Our share of morning.
           EMILY DICKINSON—*First Series, Life*

/ɔə/ and /oə/

The diphthongs /ɔə/ and /oə/, are likely to be used by persons who are inclined to omit /r/ from their pronunciations except when the letter *r* is immediately followed by a vowel. These are the same speakers who use /ɛə/ rather than /ɛr/ for words such as *there* and *welfare.*

Speakers who regularly include /r/ sounds whenever they occur in the spellings of words are likely to use /ɔr/ or /or/ in the same contexts. Practice in regard to /oə/ and /ɔr/ or /oə/ and /or/ varies, though not with complete consistency, along the following lines.

The pronunciation of words such as *accord, horse, lord,* and *north* follow fairly uniform usage throughout the United States, /ɔə/ for the "r-dropping" speakers and /ɔr/ for the others.

There is greater variability between /ɔ/ and /o/ in the pronunciations of the words *board, mourning, course,* and *more.* Most Americans are likely to pronounce the words with either an /o/ or and /or/. "Native" residents of New York City are likely to use the vowel /ɔ/ for all of these words, thus making no distinctions between *horse* and *hoarse* or *for* and *four.* Except in the New York City area, most Americans are likely to use /ɔ/ for *horse* and *for,* and /o/ for *hoarse* and *four.*

The reader may check his own practice by comparing his pronunciations for the following pairs of words:

> *border* and *boarder*
> *horse* and *hoarse*
> *morning* and *mourning*
> *war* and *wore*

The following words are usually pronounced with either /ɔr/ or /ɔə/, depending upon regional tendency relative to the final /r/

cord	import	perform
course	lord	short

/ɪə/ as in *dear*

This diphthong, as noted earlier, is used by persons who omit medial and final /r/ sounds from their pronunciations of words such as *dear, fear, near, arrear, beard,* and *cheerful.* In the General American speech area, all of these words are properly and more frequently pronounced with the combination /ɪr/ rather than the diphthong /ɪə/.

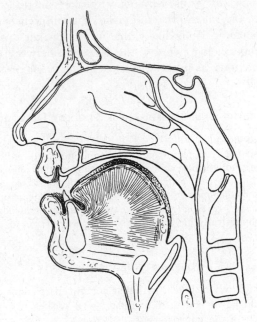

Figure 29.   Tongue position for /j/.

/ʊə/ as in *poor*

The vowel blend /ʊə/ is likely to be used in words such as *poor, cure, sure,* and *tour* by those speakers who tend to omit the /r/ except in words in which the r is followed by a vowel. Speakers who regularly pronounce the /r/ sound whenever the letter r appears in the spelling of a word are likely to use the combination /ʊr/ rather than the diphthong /ʊə/.

/ju/ as in *use*

In our study of the consonants, the sound /j/ was described as a *glide*. It should be apparent that one could easily justify listing /j/ as a vowel rather than as a consonant. In keeping with this point of view, the sound blend /ju/ may justifiably be considered a diphthong. It is pronounced as the letter *u* of the alphabet.

The combination /ju/ is heard in the words *few, feud, cube, pewter, music, use, eulogy,* and *union.* It may also be heard in *Tuesday* and *new.* Many cultured speakers, however, pronounce *Tuesday* as [**tuzdɪ**] and *new* as [**nu**].

The diphthong /ɪu/ is used by many speakers instead of /ju/ in words such as *beauty, cube, muse, fuse,* and *views.* The difference between /ɪu/ and /ju/ is not phonemic. It is likely that most speakers use both of these diphthongs without being aware of the difference between them.

In initial positions, as in the words *use, eulogy, unique,* and *union,* /ju/ is regularly used.

Questions and Exercises for Study of Diphthongs

1. Define a diphthong.
2. Distinguish between phonemic and nonphonemic diphthongs.
3. Transcribe phonetically your pronunciation of the following words: *fear, dear, pail, maze, mate, wait, pear, rarely, like, high, flow, Joe, stone, bone, rope, elope, billow, escrow, boor, gourd, Moor, soil, join, boy, Roy, more, wharves, floor, down, gown, stout, doubt, endure, skewer, fewer, news, music.*
4. Indicate phonetically any frequently heard variations in the pronunciation of these words.

Recommended Readings

The list that follows includes texts that contain discussions and practice materials that should be of help to the student who wishes to pursue further the phonetic approach to the improvement of diction.

Anderson, V. A. *Training the Speaking Voice,* 2nd ed. New York: Oxford University Press, 1961.

Brigance, W. N., and Henderson, F. *A Drill Manual for Improving Speech,* Rev. ed. New York: Lippincott, 1955.

Bronstein, A. J. *The Pronunciation of American English.* New York: Appleton-Century-Crofts, 1960.

Carrell, J., and Tiffany, W. R. *Phonetics.* New York: McGraw-Hill, 1960.

Eisenson, J. *Improvement of Voice and Diction.* New York: Macmillan, 1958.

Fairbanks, G. *Voice and Articulation Drillbook,* Rev. ed. New York: Harper and Row, 1960.

Kantner, C. E., and West, R. *Phonetics,* Rev. ed. New York: Harper and Row, 1960.

Thomas, C. K. *Handbook of Speech Improvement.* New York: Ronald, 1956.

Thomas, C. K. *An Introduction to the Phonetics of American English,* Rev. ed. New York: Ronald, 1958.

Van Riper, C., and Irwin, J. V. *Voice and Articulation.* Englewood Cliffs, N.J.: Prentice-Hall, 1958.

CHAPTER 8

SPEECH, LANGUAGE, AND MEANING

(HOW TO MEAN WHAT YOU MEAN)

> *The situations which prompt people to utter speech include every object and happening in their universe. In order to give a scientifically accurate definition of meaning for every form of language, we should have to have a scientifically accurate knowledge of everything in the speakers' world.*
>
> LEONARD BLOOMFIELD*

WHICH IS TO BE MASTER?

"When I use a word," Humpty Dumpty said in a rather scornful tone, "it means just what I choose it to mean—nothing more nor less."

"The question is," said Alice, "whether you *can* make words mean so many different things."

"The question is," said Humpty Dumpty, "which is to be master— that's all."

The conversation between Humpty Dumpty and Alice raised questions which have still not been answered. Can words be made to mean anything we want them to mean? Which is to be the master, the speaker or the words? And how does the listener know which meaning of the word is intended by the speaker?

We will be able to arrive at answers when we decide two fundamental questions: (1) What do we mean by meaning? (2) How do words get their meanings?

MEANING

In a broad sense, meaning is the way we respond to situations (things, persons, places) or ideas. Our responses vary from time to time. Strictly

---

* Leonard Bloomfield, *Language* (New York: Holt, 1933), p. 139.

speaking, we never respond the same way twice to any situation. Strictly speaking also, no situation is ever precisely the same at any two moments.

The house we live in undergoes constant change. The wood ages. New and differently colored paints are applied. The roof is patched or a new roof put on top of the old leaky one. Flowers are grown and wither and die. Time and the seasons bring changes. If we are aware of our responses to the physical features of our house, we begin to appreciate that they are subject to constant change. Notwithstanding all of these changes, however, there is a core of consistency in our responses. Our particular house is not likely to change its location to any significant degree. It is located on a given street or a road in a particular village, town, or city. We have no difficulty in recognizing it as our house despite the modifications.

When we talk about meaning, we usually have in mind the relatively constant significance that things, persons, places, or ideas have for us. The *boss*, whoever else he may be, is someone for whom we work. Our *house* is the place in which we live. The sun is a source of light and energy regardless of whether it is visible or when it rises or sets.

There is another way of considering meaning which allows for constant semantic change. We might say that meaning is the way we respond, at the moment of responding, to any situation when all its aspects are considered. The *boss* then becomes not just someone we work for, but the sum total of our responses at a given moment because of the way he behaved when we arrived ten minutes late. Our *house* may be one thing when we think of its cost and the size of the mortgage, and something else again when we think of who is living in it. Its meaning includes shoveling snow during the winter, mowing the lawn during the summer, and raking leaves in the fall. The specific meanings of our *house* are as varied and as many as the number of times we respond to it.

FACTORS WHICH DETERMINE MEANING

Most words considered alone have so many possible meanings that it becomes necessary to consider what factors determine a particular meaning. "A word is not a crystal, transparent and unchanged; it is the skin of a living thought and may vary greatly in color and content according to the circumstances and the time in which it is used."[1]

The *circumstances* and the *time* cover considerable territory. They include the external conditions at the time a word is used, the relationship of the given word to a context of words, the attitude of the speaker toward the person to whom he is speaking and/or to what he is saying. These, and

---

[1] Justice Oliver Wendell Holmes—quoted in *Yankee From Olympus* by Catherine Drinker Bowen, Boston: Little, Brown, 1944, p. 396.

at least two other factors which we shall consider, determine the meaning of a particular word.

External Conditions

Is a *fireman* a person who puts out fires or keeps them going? On a steam train a fireman keeps a fire going. In a home community a fireman is one whose job it is to help put out fires *in places where they are not wanted*. No sane fireman either starts fires everywhere or puts them out anywhere he may be. The special circumstances or external conditions help to determine the meaning of the word.

Circumstances include our expectations based upon direct or vicarious experiences with an object, a situation, or a relationship. How *fast* is *fast*? If a trip between two points is usually made in an automobile in 30 minutes, and varying traffic conditions on occasion make it possible to cover the distances in 25 in minutes, and on other occasions in 35, then is 25 fast and 40 minutes slow? A conventional automobile travels fast when it is going over 60 miles an hour, a propellor driven airplane travels fast at 200 miles per hour, and a jet-powered plane is not traveling fast unless its comparative ground-speed is at least 600 miles per hour.

Verbal Context

By this is meant the relationship of a given word to other words with which it is used.

"Are you sure you're going to marry the best man?" a radio comedian asked a bride-to-be on a quiz program.

"Yes," the bride-to-be assured him.

"That's funny," the comedian quipped. "I thought you're going to marry the groom."

Of the many possible meanings a word may have, the particular meaning usually becomes evident when the word is used in context. When context alone is not enough, the special conditions under which a word is used help to limit word meaning. There is little danger that the bride will be confused between *her* best man and *a* best man.

Some words sound alike but do not even have a common core of meaning. In context these words—*homonyms*—seldom if ever cause confusion to the literate. The number *eight* is not apt to be confused with the verb *ate*. The sentence *Two drinks may be too many drinks* contains a pair of homonyms. Verbal context helps to make their meanings clear as well as to give meaning to the sentence as a whole.

The amount of verbal context necessary to limit or clarify a meaning is highly variable. As we indicated, it is sometimes necessary to "spell out" the special conditions of a verbal formulation to bring out one meaning where several meanings are possible. For example, there are several possible meanings for the statement *John Jones watered his stock*. Some of these are brought out only if we know something about John Jones as a person. What is his vocation, avocation, and reputation for honesty? For example, if John Jones is known to be a farmer, the words *watered* and *stock* and the statement as a whole have different meanings than if John Jones is the head of a business corporation that has just issued stock for sale to the public. Still a different meaning would develop if we knew that John Jones happened to be a horticulturist who was fond of a particular *flower called stock*. If John Jones turned out to be a gentleman farmer as well as the head of a corporation, we would need to know *when* the watering took place, and to inquire about the nature of the *stock* for the statement *John Jones watered his stock* to have any particular meaning. In brief, verbal context is helpful only when it is sufficient to take care of special circumstances for limiting and defining the meanings of individual words as well as multiple word formulations. If we had a paragraph rather than a single sentence about Mr. Jones, we could keep our thoughts about him in order. For example, it should help to be informed:

John Jones, the head of the National Skyhook Corporation, was convicted of falsifying his company's assets and watering his stock. Jones was sentenced to three years on a state prison farm. Among his specific tasks was to water the stock daily and to keep the barn clean.

Attitude of the Speaker

When we know how a speaker feels about what he is saying, when we are aware of his personal attitude, we are in a better position to understand the meaning of his words. The speaker's attitude may be a momentary one or may be moderately habitual. The speaker may be irritated or annoyed at the moment he is speaking. What the speaker means by his words, at such moments, is likely to be colored by his immediate personal attitude. The "No" of an angry individual may in effect mean, "Don't ask me now."

When we know the habitual attitude, or position of a speaker on a subject or issue, we increase the likelihood that we will understand the meanings of his utterances. The words *coexistence with the communist world* have different meanings for the members of the Communist party in general than they do for members of either the Republican or Democratic parties in the United States. In the early 1960's *coexistence* seemed to express a different attitude for members of the Comunist party in good standing within the Soviet Union than they did for Communist party members in China.

We need not confine our examples of meanings as related to attitudes to citizens of nations with divergent political and social philosophies. Many American husbands insist that they have learned to compromise issues with their wives by accepting their wives interpretation of *compromise*. And some American wives insist that they have learned to *compromise* by conceding. Is the *flexible* person one who can appreciate another's point of view or is he one who lacks the courage of his convictions and bends or yields to the assertions of another who speaks with conviction, or as if he had conviction? The more we know about the speaker, his personality and his attitude, the better we are able to understand the meanings of the words he uses.

Manner of Speaking

The way in which an individual speaks his words—his manner of utterance—is intimately associated with his immediate personal attitude. Feelings are readily reflected in voice (see pages 37–38). Voice tones may belie intended meanings and reveal the speaker despite himself.

Frequently the speaker uses a vocal tone, or an inflection, or a slow rate to give special significance to a word or words. *Yes* spoken with an upward pitch glide may be a more effective way of saying "No" than the word *no* spoken with a downward pitch glide. If the sentence *Yes, I'll do it* is spoken slowly, with a slight upward pitch glide on *yes*, the speaker is probably revealing unwillingness but resignation for a task. The same words, spoken rapidly and with a downward pitch glide on *yes* and *do*, reveal willingness and determination for the task.

Manner of utterance includes more than vocal pattern. The facial expression, the gestures, the total bodily action at the time of speaking are elements which give meaning to words. These elements have been discussed in some detail in the earlier chapters (see "The Components of Speech" and "Gesture").

The Referent

Few if any words have inherent meanings. Words acquire meaning through a process of association. Through association most words come to "stand for" characteristics of the objects or actions or experiences. Still other words "stand for" relationships between actions and objects or experiences. To know the meaning of a word we must be able to determine, at any given time, what the word stands for. We must, in brief, know which association out of many possible associations the word calls forth in our minds. When we are able to do that, we have defined the *referent* of the word, and so have placed appropriate limitations on the meaning of the word.

Common Reference

Words would have little value in communication if they had meaning only for the speaker. Words are the coin of communication because they have some common meanings for many members of a group. The shared meanings are a result of common experiences which persons of a given group must necessarily have. However individual our reactions may be in regard to the weather, or our jobs, or our homes, if we live in a particular community many aspects of our reactions are approximately alike. These approximations or similarities of experience and response are the basis for the common references to words. The meanings of words listed in a dictionary represent the highest common factors of the various meanings of the words based on common experience. These may be referred to as *denotative meanings.*

APPROXIMATION OF UNDERSTANDING

We manage to get along in our social and business world through the use of words which we understand only approximately. Identity of meaning and of understanding is probably never achieved. For the ordinary purposes of living, approximations are usually adequate. Whether we would get along better with one another if a more complete understanding were possible is debatable. It may even be that we actually would love our neighbor less rather than more if we understood fully what he meant by the words he spoke.

In any event, the degree to which we understand one another's meanings is determined in part by the similarity of past experiences between the speaker and the listener. The greater the number of common experiences, the greater will be the likelihood that the speaker will respond essentially the same way to the spoken words. In brief, common meanings depend upon common responses to words and to related experiences or objects.

The blind men in the fable derived different meanings from their contacts with the elephant because at a crucial moment the blind men shared no common experiences. From the point of view of seeing persons, all the blind thought the others were wrong because no two of them were responding to the same part of the elephant, and none of them was responding to the elephant as a whole. For words to have even approximately the same meanings for two or more individuals, those individuals must be able to respond to the same situation, considered not in part but as a whole.

HOW WORDS ACQUIRE MEANINGS

Association

Words acquire meanings through a process of association. As a result of experiences, an event, an object, or a relationship becomes associated with a word. If the experience is vivid, or highly significant, or occurs frequently, a connection is made between the event, or object, or relationship and the associated word. In time the word comes to *stand for* or symbolize the associated experience.

The child learns the word *doll* after the toy object and the word are presented together often enough for the association to be formed. When the child responds to the word *doll* in much the same fashion as she (or he) responded to the object doll, the word *doll* means the object doll. So, also, the child learns other words.

As the child matures and has experiences, he continues to make associations and learn new words. Sometimes he has several different experiences associated with the same word. The child may learn that water is associated with drinking and swimming and cooking and washing. Thus he learns that a word may have more than one meaning. In time the child, as he grows up, may come to the conclusion that a word may have as many different meanings as he has ways of responding to it. He may eventually conclude that a word may have one core meaning and various shades of meaning. To the small child *mother* may mean the person who is the comforter and the feeder and the linen-changer and the lullaby singer-at-night. *Father* may mean the person who comes home in time for supper and who walks the floor with him at night and who talks roughly but usually does what mother tells him.

KINDS OF MEANING

Personal vs. Objective Meanings

If we study our responses to situations or to words, we can appreciate that some of them are highly personal and individual. We are not surprised to find that other persons do not respond as we do to the same situation. A particular tune is not just a Cole Porter melody; it is *our song* because we heard it when we began to think as *we*. But the tune, because it has a certain time and rhythm, is also a specific kind of melody. The same situation may have a *personal* or *subjective* meaning and an *impersonal* or *objective* or *informative* meaning. Words, which stand for situations, similarly may have personal meanings and objective meanings. The word *mother* has innumerable personal meanings, many of which are highly sentimental. The objective meaning of *mother* is almost rudely abrupt. *A mother is a female parent.*

Another way of arriving at the difference between a personal and objective meaning is to compare the implications of two statements that include the term *mother*. Suppose James Wilson says to his friend Tom Smith, "I think that Bob's wife is a fine mother." Such a statement might be considered a value-judgment. It is an expression of what Wilson considers to be qualities, not in any way indicated, of what constitutes *motherhood*, as well as *fine motherhood*. All we know, if we know anything at all about Wilson's statement, is that he seems to approve of Bob's wife as a mother. At a later time, Wilson may be walking down a street with his friend and meet and greet a child and a woman. As Wilson and his friend Tom Smith continue on their way, Wilson may then say, "Oh, by the way, that was young Bob Jones and his mother." In this statement mother has objective and denotative meaning. The word *mother* in this instance referred specifically to the familial relationship between two persons, without regard to any value-judgments or personal assessments about the relationship.

Meanings may be personal without necessarily being sentimental. Sydney J. Harris, whose syndicated column originates in the *Chicago Daily News*, presented several personal meanings and views to his readers in a column headed "Antics with Semantics." Included were the following:

I am nonchalant; you are devil-may-care; he is wildly irresponsible.

My remark was witty; your remark was pointed; his remark was cruel.

I am flexible; you are pliable; he is a piece of putty.

For most of us, what we call "ethics" is a sort of spiritual dress suit that we take out for formal occasions—banquets, conventions and the like—and then hang back in the closet for our workaday lives.

When a man says, "Let's look at the facts," it is reasonable to assume that he has arranged the evidence so that only those things he wants to believe are designated as "facts."

I take a sober view of affairs; you are a touch melancholy; he is depressed.

My young child is "going through a normal stage"; your child is a "bit upset"; his child is "emotionally disturbed."

Whether we are "defying the legally constituted authorities," or "striking a blow for freedom," depends wholly upon our subjective definitions—we are for "order" when it protects our self-interest, and for "liberty" when our self-interest is seriously threatened.

The people who are called "frivolous" in society are really the most serious of all; for nobody else is grimmer and more concentrated in the pursuit of amusements than "frivolous" people.

I am down-to-earth; you are somewhat pedestrian; he is utterly devoid of imagination.[2]

---

[2] Pittsburgh *Post-Gazette* (June 11, 1960).

It will be noted that despite their subjectivity, the definitions are so worded that an objective core can be recognized. Unless there is an objective core—a common ground of understanding—shared meaning is not possible.

Occasionally, a speaker or a writer may appreciate the need to define his attitude so that his position, as well as his exposition, may be understood. John Fischer, editor of *Harper's Magazine*, did this before undertaking to criticize a British writer's essay on the subject of disarmament. Wrote Fischer:

A substantial number of the British have peculiarities which handicap them in dealing with the world beyond their island. (Or so it at least seems to me, on the basis of a number of years spent living and working among them.)

First of all, they are Decent Chaps—maybe too decent. They are reasonable; they believe in fair play; they have developed compromise into an art form. For all their rudeness, they are kindly folk; when they get an opponent down, they don't kick his brains out—they help him to his feet and mutter, "Well played, old boy." They have no ideology, only their cherished instinct for Muddling Through; and if they did have, they would never dream of forcing it on other people. (Manners are something else. They simply can't understand why other peoples don't adopt British manners and customs—from tea to the committee system—since they are obviously Right.)

Second, in dealing with foreigners they are singularly lacking in imagination. Consequently they find it hard to comprehend that some nations *do not* believe in fair play and honest compromise. When confronted with an ideologue —a Nazi, a Communist, or a Mohammedan Mahdi—who is religiously dedicated to kicking *their* brains out, the British are blankly incredulous. Blessedly free of fanaticism themselves, they can hardly credit it in others. Thus, in the face of a six-year accumulation of overwhelming evidence, many intelligent Englishmen persisted until the last moment in their conviction that Hitler was really a decent chap who could be internationally housebroken by gentle handling, patient negotiation, and sweet reasonableness.[3]

Affective Connotation

Some words more than others are associated with experiences of feeling. The feelings may be pleasant or unpleasant, mild or strong. Though these words have meanings listed in the dictionary, more frequently than not the dictionary does not list among their objective meanings the responses that the words arouse in us. When we refer to people as "dogs," "buzzards," "old bats," or "squares" we express our feelings rather than our thoughts about them. Feelings of a different sort are usually expressed when we address persons as "cookie," "honeybun," "sweetness," or "little monkey." Somehow in our culture such terms are usually considered endearing.

Many words such as those listed above are especially useful when we need affective language. The variety of words that a man may use for a woman reflects his differences in feelings. It makes an affective difference

[3] "A 'Scientific Formula' for Disarmament," *Harper's,* February 1963, pp. 12–19.

whether a female person is referred to as a "woman," "young woman," "lady," "gentlewoman," "wife," "wench," or "mistress." It also makes a difference if she is referred to merely as "that female person."

Terms of respect, including *Sir, Your Honor, Your Excellency, Your Worship,* are significant for their affective implications.

Affective language makes it possible for us, in writing as well as in speaking, to reveal how we feel about what we think. The thought in the following paired sentences remains essentially the same. Our feelings about the thoughts are different:

The issue was so grave that the president was unwilling to be hurried into a decision without first weighing all the facts.

The president didn't know enough to make up his mind.

We had roast capon for dinner.

We had cooked, desexed chicken for dinner.

Her intellectual curiosity and deep sympathy naturally directed her to choose psychiatric social work as a career.

She has always been a busybody, prying into other people's affairs. No wonder she chose to become a psychiatric social worker!

Almost any word may have affective value acording to its manner of use. The sentences above illustrate the significance of word context to modify an essential idea with feeling tone. A more usual way of adding feeling to thought is through voice change. This method is considered at some length in the discussion on the components of speech (Chapter 3).

SYMBOLS, WORDS, AND LANGUAGE

Symbols

The sounds which make up our words mean nothing unless two or more human beings agree on a meaning. The agreement is usually tacit. As children we learned combinations of sounds and their associated meanings. The process is called *learning to speak.* If we wish, however, we can more actively agree that certain things will stand for other things. Two persons may formulate a code for private communications. The persons may agree between themselves that their *code symbols* will stand for whatever they choose. They may choose visible symbols such as puffs of smoke, or red lights, or white lines. They may decide that a red light means *stop* or that a double line on a highway means *do not cross.* They might just as readily have decided that a red light means *go,* and a double white line means *crossing is permitted*

Persons may agree on using symbols which require direct contact for communication. A handshake or a pat on the back, as is the case in some secret societies, may be given a specific meaning. Symbols may be of as many kinds or combinations of kinds as there are senses. Symbols may be based on smells or sights or sounds or physical feelings. Whatever the basis of the symbol system, there is seldom if ever a necessary or inherent connection between the symbol and that for which the symbol stands. The possible exceptions are the sound symbols (words) such as *buzz, hiss,* and *switch* which, when spoken, may suggest the thing for which they stand.

A *symbol* is a convenient artifice which, by tacit acceptance or active agreement, comes to stand for something. The something for which a symbol stands or which it symbolizes may be an object, a relationship, an experience, a feeling, or an attitude.

Speech Symbols

Speech symbols are audible and/or visible. They are commonly called words and gestures. *Audible symbols* are conventionalized (agreed upon) sounds produced by actions of the lips, tongue, teeth, palate, vocal muscles, and lungs. *Gestures* are conventionalized actions produced by the hands, arms and shoulders, facial muscles, and occasionally other parts of the body. Whether audible or visible, we normally produce speech symbols without the need to resort to instruments or devices outside of the human body. Instruments and devices, however, may be employed to transmit symbols (the telephone or radio) or to make them more easily discernible (the loud speaker system).

A *spoken language,* as we usually think of it, consists of a system of audible symbols. Tonal patterns, manner of articulation, and customs of sentence structure and word relationships (grammar) are involved in our concept of a spoken language. The patterns and customs differ according to the language spoken. These differences give us English and French and Chinese and all other spoken languages. A *written language* is a system of visible symbols which usually stand for spoken symbols.

Symbol Reaction

The ability to deal with symbols is a distinctive human achievement. Symbol behavior characterizes man alone. Animals as high in the scale as the chimpanzee occasionally approximate man's achievement, but the approximation is rarely close enough for the brightest chimpanzee to be able to compete successfully with a human being even of subnormal intelligence.

The distinctive difference between us and the animal in respect to symbol behavior is that we are able to reserve judgment and action. The animal is not. We are able to learn that something *may stand for* something else. We do not ordinarily confuse *stands for* with *is*. We are able to evaluate the situation which amounts to our saying to ourselves, "The symbol stands for something *only if conditions are the expected ones, only if there is nothing unusual in the present situation to call for a different reaction.*"

The workingman on a construction job may expect a whistle to blow at lunch time and at quitting time. He may, however, stop even if the whistle fails to blow. On the other hand, he may continue for a brief time *after* the blowing of the whistle if present conditions call for such behavior. The riveter with a hot rivet in his hand is not likely to drop his material merely because the whistle has blown. He is more likely either to continue putting the rivet in the metal or to place the rivet where it will be out of harm's way.

For most of us, a green light stands for "go." We do not, however, insist that a green light be present in order to make us go. Some road crossings have no lights. We "go" or "stop" according to the total situation. Occasionally, if there is urgent reason for speed, we may "go" on a red or yellow light. What we do is to evaluate the situation which involves the symbol and the usual reaction to it. If the conditions warrant it, if there is nothing unusual in the total situation, we react in the conventional or customary way. If unusual conditions prevail; if, for example, a child is crossing against a red light, or an automobile is stalled in our path, or another car is "going through" a red light, we do not feel compelled to "go" merely because we are faced with a green light.

If we were to respond to a symbol in a consistent and invariable way regardless of the set of conditions, we would then be reduced to an animal level of behavior. The symbol would then have become completely identified with the thing with which it is associated. The dog who was trained to respond to expect food at the ringing of a bell continued for a long time to salivate and show other responses to food whenever he heard the particular bell ring even though food was no longer presented to him. Another dog, having learned to recognize the sound of an opening door, would run to the door every time he was able to hear it being opened, even though he did not wish to leave the house. Such behavior reveals an inability to evaluate, to reserve judgment while conditions are being surveyed and assessed. This may be designated as signal responses.

When we respond to symbols without reservation and in an invariable manner, we are behaving below our highest level of capability. Such behavior may take place when we are tired, or emotionally disturbed, or intellectually distracted. As an occasional incident of a total pattern, nonevaluative behavior has significance according to the occasion. If, however, nonevaluative reaction characterizes the general behavior of a person, he has given up the most important feature of human behavior. He is no longer exercising the distinctively human capability to withhold or delay a response until it has been determined that conditions are appropriate for the expected response to be made. He is behaving in a low-level, *unconditional manner*.

Specific Responses

There is another important way in which our ability to deal with symbols differs from that of animals. We are able to use symbols to convey highly specific ideas and to get highly specific responses. We are able to use symbols to present shades of differences in ideas, and to respond to symbols which stand for concepts or objects nearly alike but different in some important respect. We can think and talk about water, hot water, cold water, lukewarm water, distilled water, and other kinds of water. The animal is able to make his wish for quenching his thirst known by going to his customary place for getting water and hoping that someone will observe him going there. If he is not observed, he may bark to attract attention and then repeat his action. If the dog is given water he has the choice of drinking it or rejecting it. He is not able to specify what it is about the water which dissatisfies him; nor is he able to indicate what kind of water would be more to his liking. Most human beings who have learned to speak can be more specific in revealing their likes or dislikes. We are able to ask for a drink as specialized as "a coffee soda with vanilla ice cream, whipped cream, and chocolate sprinkles."

Through our ability to deal with symbols specifically, we are able to present specific situations through words, and to get specific responses. We are able, through specific symbol use, to convey innuendoes and implications in our thinking. We are able to be either blunt or subtle, cruel or gentle, kind or unkind, according to our thoughts and feelings.

NONSYMBOLIC LANGUAGE

As human beings we are ordinarily capable of dealing with symbols in specific ways. It is, however, not always necessary or appropriate that we do so. Sometimes, and for some of us rather frequently, the situation in which the symbol is used requires that a general rather specific response be made. When acquaintances on meeting greet each other with "How are you?" a report of health status is seldom expected. The "Fine, thank you" response, even though it may be literally untrue, is nevertheless appropriate for the speech situation. This kind of word usage is not specifically symbolic. Its symbolic value is general and pertains to the situation as a whole rather than to the individual words or even to the statement per se.

Language is also used without regard to the specific symbolic value of words when we speak to express our feelings rather than our thoughts. The language of love and of hate, of tender feelings and of violent emotions, is nonspecific and nonsymbolic. If it were otherwise, persons in love would accuse one another of talking nonsense in the early stages of their romance. If words were always specifically symbolic, we would not, when angry, call one another names which are impossible of literal application.

Words, then, may be symbolic and highly specific. When there is such need, those of us who are normal are ordinarily capable of using symbols on this high intellectual level. We do not, however, always need to use words on this high intellectual level. It is frequently appropriate to use words nonspecifically and nonsymbolically. This point is considered at some length in the discussion on the functions and levels of speech (see pages 3–5).

WHICH IS TO BE MASTER?

This is an appropriate time to return to the question with which the chapter was opened. *Which is to be master*—the words or the speaker of the words? The words spoken or the person responding to the words?

Taboos

Whenever we respond to words as if they had powers and potentials other than those we give them, we are permitting the words to be our masters. To some degree, almost all speakers permit themselves to be victimized by words. There are some words which we do not speak in polite society; there are other words which we do not speak with propriety in mixed company, even though the words may be known, understood, and used by all members of the company regardless of sex. In brief, even in our highly civilized society some words are considered *taboo*. The largest number of taboo words are those referring to biological functions, sex, illness, and death.

Attributed Power

Words also become our masters when we respond to them as if they had the characteristics or powers of the things for which they stand. We react as word-victims when we avoid using words for fear that their use might somehow cause undesirable events to happen. Many small children have been hushed, scolded, or slapped for innocently asking about a sick person, "Will he die?" During any period of war or threat of war, mothers, wives, and sweethearts do not want to discuss the possibility of death or injury in combat.

Overgeneralization

In still another way we reveal that we are sometimes the victims rather than the masters of our words. In some parts of the United States a person is condemned merely because he is a Yankee. In other parts, or among certain groups, to call a person a Republican or a Democrat is to indicate his undesirability as a member of society. Among some groups of Republicans or Democrats, a person who is a liberal is, without reservation, considered undesirable. For many industrialists, a labor leader cannot possibly be considered an acceptable member of society. And many labor leaders return the compliment, or lack of compliment, to industrialists.

Southerners and Northerners; Republicans, Democrats, and Socialists; industrialists and union leaders share the fault of *overgeneralization*. When the Northerner reacts to all Southerners as he has learned, correctly or incorrectly, to react to one or more Southerners, he is overgeneralizing. When a labor leader assumes that every industrialist by virtue of his being an industrialist is necessarily opposed to the workingman, the labor leader is overgeneralizing. He is responding to the word as he did to a particular person with whom the word is associated. Unfortunately, he is also responding to the person as he responded to the word. And in each response there is considerable margin for error.

MAKING MEANINGS CLEAR

Narrowing the Approximations

The point has been emphasized that we communicate only approximate meanings. Exact communication of thought is not possible except under circumstances difficult to conceive. These circumstances would require that the speaker and listener have identical experiences in regard to the language symbols used, and identical reactions to the experiences. It is obvious that if we were reluctant to communicate except where listener and speaker showed identical experiences, there would be little or no communication. Speaking would be a lost art.

Though precise communication of meaning is not possible, moderately accurate communication is within the limits of our capabilities. The basic task is one of *narrowing* the extent *of the* approximation so that there is a reasonable chance that speaker and listener are responding to essentially the same symbol situation. This may be accomplished through at least two approaches.

Increasing Respect for Listener

The first approach calls for increasing the respect we have for our listener. If we are speakers genuinely interested in communicating ideas, we must be willing to talk in language understandable to our listeners. We must be willing to take pains to select not only words but meanings. Our words should be so presented that our meanings become apparent. That implies that when a speaker uses language he should have reason to believe that (1) the words are within the known vocabulary inventory of the listener; (2) the particular meaning of the possible meanings of the word is likely to be recognized by the listener; (3) the language context and speaking situation make it likely that the particular meaning is brought out. It makes a difference whether a statement such as "I need gas" is spoken at an automobile service station, at a dentist's office, or over the telephone to a clerk of a utility company.

All of this is another way of saying that words are symbols, and *stand for* things. If we really wish to be understood we must make our symbols stand *as near as they can* for the same things in our listener's minds as they do in our minds *at the moment of speaking*. The meanings of the word-symbols we use are not inherently in the words. They are in our minds. We must not assume that the same meaning—the same response to the symbol —will occur in the listener merely because it is present in us.

Are We Sure of What We Mean?

Unless we can, without doubt or indecision, answer "yes" to this question, we have no right to expect our listener to figure out what we mean. If we are hazy in our thinking, our approximations will be wide of the mark. If our feelings are so strong that our listeners respond to the affective tones (the manner) rather than to the words (the matter) of our speech, we will not be making our meanings clear. Our feelings will have intruded themselves in the way of our meanings.

Determining the Intention of the Speaker

Essentially, when a listener tries to determine what a speaker intends by the words he uses, he is indicating his respect for the speaker. Because words in and out of verbal context are capable of many meanings, the matter of *intention* is often crucial. Dialogues such as the following between husband and wife may suggest what may develop if either fails to recognize the intention of the other.

"Darling, mother wrote that she is coming for a visit next week. Do you mind?"

"No, not at all, why should I mind?"

"Well, if you cared for me, even if you didn't for mother, you would mind in a nice way. You might even be glad that mother is coming so I wouldn't need to worry about her."

"Oh, I didn't know you worried about your mother. Is anything wrong?"

"See, you don't even care enough for me to know when I'm worrying, about mother, or anything. No wonder you don't mind. You don't mind about mother, or what I wear, or how I feel, all you do care about is——."

Listener Attitude

Because words may have many meanings, understanding is what emerges out of a relationship between a speaker and a listener. If it is our purpose to understand what a speaker is trying to communicate by the words he uses, we must not only hear his words, but become sensitive to the intentions of the speaker. To understand a speaker, we must learn to listen to what he intends his words to mean. If our own intentions prevail, if we assume that verbal utterances necessarily mean what we would mean if the utterances were ours, understanding will suffer. If it is our sincere wish to understand the persons with whom we must talk and interact, then we must as listeners behave as generously as if we were about to be speakers. We shall have more to say on this point in our discussion of Speech and Personality.

The General Semantic Approach[4]

This approach emphasizes the use of aids and devices for narrowing the approximations to make meanings clear. The most widely used of the semantic devices is the *subscript*. The subscript is an index used to indicate that among a number or series of similar words or terms, the particular word or term is *different* in some important way or ways from the others. For example, $horse_1$ is *not* $horse_2$, is *not* $horse_3$. . . . $Industrialist_1$, is *not* $industrialist_2$, is not $industrialist_3$. . . . Union $leader_1$ is *not* union $leader_2$, is *not* union $leader_3$. . . .

A second frequently used semantic device is the *dating of terms*. In effect, dates are a special kind of index. They are used to emphasize that *meanings change with time*. We can readily understand that John $Jones^{1910}$ is *not* John $Jones^{1920}$, is *not* John $Jones^{1930}$. . . . A span of thirty years would be expected to make a difference in John Jones' appearance, physical endurance, and thinking. We should also be able to understand that United

---

[4] Semantics is a subdivision of linguistics dealing with word meanings. The *general semanticist* employs the study of symbols and meanings in an effort to improve human adjustment.

States foreign policy[1950] was *not* United States foreign policy[1960], and may *not be* United States foreign policy[1970]. . . .

A third device is the use of *modifying terms* to limit the extent of a generalized statement. Such terms would include *seems to me, I believe, I think, from my point of view, etc*. We can evaluate the effect of modifying or conditional terms by comparing the following paired statements:

John Smith is reactionary in his political thinking.

As I see it, John Smith is reactionary in his political thinking.

Living in the suburbs is dull.

I find that living in the suburbs is dull.

Moving pictures are a waste of time.

For me, moving pictures are a waste of time.

This kind of modifying terms reveals the speaker's awareness that his judgments are subjective. In effect, the speaker is saying that he has come to a personal conclusion based on his own observation and that he is speaking only for himself. Other modifying terms limit the condition or conditions according to which a statement may be valid. *Conditional terms* include *at the present time, in our country, in our culture, under existing conditions,* etc. Differences will be brought out in comparing the following:

The struggle for power between labor and capital is inevitable.

Under existing conditions, the struggle for power between labor and industry is inevitable.

Women are dependent persons.

In our culture, women frequently become dependent persons.

The use of semantic devices has serious shortcomings as well as virtues. To use them often in spoken language would result in a somewhat cumbersome phraseology. Too many modifying terms give the listener an impression that the speaker is either overcautious or insecure. It is difficult for a speaker to sound convincing if his statements are characterized by many *ifs, buts,* and *it seems to me's*. The outstanding value of the semantic devices is to create a feeling and a point of view as to the need for accuracy in language usage. This point of view is expressed by Wendell Johnson:

A considerable amount of practice in using the devices is essential—if one is to develop the "feel" for their semantic significance. Once this "feel" is acquired to a reasonably high degree, one need not use the devices outwardly or actually, except now and then when they are especially to be stressed. Otherwise, their use is a matter of mutual understanding between speaker and listener . . . , an agreement or bargain.[5]

[5] Wendell Johnson, *People in Quandaries,* New York: Harper and Row, 1946, p. 224.

Another general semantic device is the use of quotes around specific words. When a particular written word is modified by quotes, we indicate that we are using the word in a special way and an individual way, that we are aware, and are cueing our reader, of this unusual use. Unfortunately, it is difficult to hear "quotes" when one is a listener. Some speakers help the listener to overcome this difficulty by gesturing "quotes" with the index and middle fingers of the hands as a particular word is uttered. When a speaker with a general semantic orientation uses "quotes," he is trying to indicate to his listener that he is aware of his subjectivity or of the individual extended meaning he is giving to a word, and he hopes that the listener will take this into consideration as he evaluates what he hears.

PRACTICAL APPLICATIONS

At this point the reader may be posing a pertinent question. He may be asking himself and the author: "Now that I know more about the meaning of meaning, what am I supposed to do about it?" Some answers to the anticipated question were implied in the present chapter. An effort was made to establish a point of view or attitude towards speech and language which would be helpful in our thinking and in our speaking. In later chapters we will make more specific applications of our study of meaning. We will learn how to apply our information as conversationalists, public speakers, or public readers. We will see how an understanding of meaning can be of help in the preparation and delivery of spoken material. We will also see how the point of view of *proper evaluation* of language and speech situations may help us to reduce the terrifying influence of the bogey called Stage Fright.

SUMMARY

Meaning is the way we respond to situations. The meaning of a word is the way or ways we are able to respond to the word.

Words have relatively constant or core meanings and less constant subjective meanings. The meaning of a given word is determined by several factors which include:

1. The circumstances and the time the word is used.
2. The verbal context.
3. The attitude of the speaker
4. The manner in which the word is spoken

Words have little value in communication unless speaker and listener share a common reaction to them.

Identity of meaning is not possible. At best we are able to understand only approximately what we hear.

Few if any words have inherent meanings. Words acquire meanings through a process of association.

Words may be said to have personal, subjective meanings and objective meanings. Objective meanings are found in the dictionary. Personal meanings vary with the individual.

Some words are frequently associated with feelings rather than thinking. Such words may be said to have *affective connotations*.

A *symbol* is something which *stands for* something else. Human beings are intellectually superior to animals because they are usually able not to confuse *stands for* with *is*. Human beings are able to make evaluative judgments about symbol situations. Animals are not able to evaluate or reserve either judgment or action to symbol situations. In addition, human beings are able to use symbols to convey highly specific ideas and to get highly specific responses. Animals do not possess this ability. Human beings, however, do not always react or need to react to symbols on their highest level of capability.

Meanings can be made clear by narrowing the area of approximation. This aim may be accomplished by having the speaker place himself more completely at the disposal of the listener. The speaker must take the trouble to use words in such a way that (1) the words are likely to be within the vocabulary inventory of the listeners; (2) the particular meaning of the word is likely to be recognized by the listener; (3) the language context clarifies word meaning; and (4) speaker and listener respect one another's intentions.

We are not likely to make our meanings clear unless (1) we have a strong wish to do so, and (2) we are certain of what we mean when we speak.

Another way of clarifying meaning is through the approach of the general semanticist. This approach emphasizes technical devices such as *subscripts, dates, modifying terms*, and *conditional terms* and a general understanding that the speaker is saying what he has to say with "semantic modifiers" implied even when they are not specifically stated.

QUESTIONS AND EXERCISES

1. (a) What is the meaning of *meaning?* (b) What factors determine the meanings of a word? (c) Over which of the factors does a speaker have control? (d) Why is identity of meaning seldom possible?

2. (a) What is a symbol? (b) What is a symbol reaction? (c) When is language used in a nonsymbolic way?

3. How many meanings do you have for the words *case, charge, front, matter, run, shop, water?* Check your list with that of an unabridged dictionary. Bring out the various meanings of one of these words by using it in several different sentences.

4. Bring out as many meanings as you can for the word *yes* through changes in the manner of utterance.

5. What is the first reaction (meaning) you have to the words *liberal, conservative?* Check your reaction with those of five friends or acquaintances. Were the reactions consistent with their known attitudes?

6. Differentiate between the objective meaning and your personal meaning for the following words: *Chinaman, father, college, fascist, snake, lizard, statesman, winter, childhood, politician.*

7. Indicate the relationship between language and symbols. What kind of symbols do we use in spoken language?

8. Differentiate between an evaluative reaction and a signal reaction. List five words to which you are especially inclined to give signal reactions. Can you explain why?

9. Are there any words considered *taboo* in your social group? Can you account for the basis of the *taboo?*

10. What is the linguistic fault of *overgeneralization?* List five examples in which editorial writers or newspaper columnists reveal this fault.

RECOMMENDED READINGS

Chase, S. *The Tyranny of Words.* New York: Harcourt, Brace, 1938.

Eisenson, J., Auer, J. J., and Irwin, J. V. *Psychology of Communication.* New York: Appleton-Century-Crofts, 1963, Chap. 7.

Hayakawa, S. I. *Language and Thought in Action.* New York: Harcourt, Brace, 1964.

Johnson, W. *People in Quandaries.* New York: Harper and Row, 1946.

Johnson, W. *Your Most Enchanted Listener.* New York: Harper and Row, 1956.

Lee, I. J. *Language Habits in Human Affairs.* New York: Harper and Row, 1941.

Lee, I. J. *How to Talk with People.* New York: Harper and Row, 1952.

Weinberg, H. L. *Levels of Knowing and Existence.* New York: Harper and Row, 1959.

CHAPTER 9

SPEECH AND

PERSONALITY

WHAT IS PERSONALITY?

In our discussion of meanings we presented an underlying notion that meanings are the many ways persons respond to events, including verbal events. The term or verbal event *personality* is an excellent example of one with a multitude of meanings. The inquisitive student with time to investigate the meanings, the implications, of the multifaceted term personality might, time permitting, discover more than fifty definitions in the psychological literature. Investigations in the popular writings among the "How to Improve Your Personality" type of books and articles might increase the "definitions" with each writing. We shall, therefore, not undertake a survey of the literature, but instead move to our concept of *personality*

As we shall use the term *personality*, we shall emphasize two related aspects: (1) A personality is as the person behaves. (2) A personality is for the most part what the individual thinks of himself.

The behaving individual, if he is at all sensitive to his behavior, has some awareness of the effect he has on others. In some instances he may exaggerate this effect and in others underestimate it. In any event, the "feedback" influence of the individual's own behavior is an influence that determines future behavior. Personality, therefore, is a product of interacting influences, the resultant of "forces" of the individual acting upon other persons in the environment and the return influences of the environment on himself. Because the resultant is an estimate or judgment of one person, the forming and ever-modifying personality becomes and is continually becoming what the individual thinks of himself. Diagrammatically, the interacting forces may be represented thus:

[196]

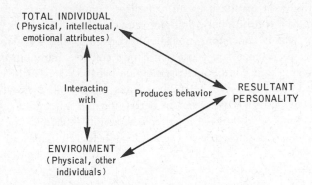

We make varying impressions and leave more or less lasting impressions upon others according to the immediate and residual effects of our behavior. Such impressions are an important product of the personalities of *the others*. An individual may be considered either aggressive or charming or inconsiderate or thoughtful by virtue of the "same" overt act. Thus, a man in a crowded bus who gets in the way of another male passenger to make it possible for a woman passenger to occupy a newly vacated seat may create several different impressions. The woman in the situation may consider the intruding man to be a gentleman because he did not take the seat for himself. The obstructed male, especially if he is not as tall or husky as our first man, may consider our "gentleman" to be an aggressive bully. Still another observer may consider him foolish for not following the—or his—principle of every man for himself. Each, according to his own light, and his own inclinations, is exercising a judgment and making his own interpretation of the observed behavior of someone else.

An individual may seem to have more than one personality according to relatively established and yet different patterns of his behavior in "typical" situations. An employee may behave as a docile Mr. Milquetoast on his job and yet be an autocratic and short-tempered Mr. Bangs in his home. An employer, by contrast, may be as harsh and indifferent as his labor-management contractual obligations permit him to be, and yet be a sensitive, considerate husband and father. These seemingly inconsistent and contrasting patterns of behavior may stem from underlying common dynamics. Some individuals must express their aggression and their hostilities somehow and somewhere. They may choose to express such feelings and attitudes according to their own judgments as to how their over-all needs are best served. So, a cold and indifferent boss may find it the better part of wisdom to be considearte husband and father in contrast to a timid employee who finds it necessary to "rule his roost."

Personality, it appears, is easier to describe than to define. It is the sum total of our reactions and interactions. It is each of us somehow identified as an *I*, acting as a resultant of an organized complexity of forces making adjustments to a continuously changing environment. Personality is neither constant nor wholly consistent, nor should constancy and consistency be the individual goal. Except for those who may confuse immobility with stability, unvarying and completely predictable behavior has little virtue. The normal adult abandons the behavior of his childhood, however successful such behavior may have been in satisfying his immediate needs. This includes the kind of talking—the speech behavior—that may be acceptable in a child but would characterize the adult as being childish and immature.

THE MAKING OF A PERSONALITY

While many factors and forces combine with temporary and maintaining influences to produce *a personality* (note the *a* to emphasize unity), there are six aspects of the question of personality we believe should be emphasized.

1. Personality is the expression of many physical, environmental, and psychological forces and influences; some are inherited and others are acquired. For example, how one is likely to look is a physical factor. How we estimate and respond to our "looks" and what appearance we present in terms of our "looks" are products of environmental and psychological factors.

2. Personality is the expression of the individual's judgments and values and the attitudes that are initially shaped and continually modified by interaction with a culture at large and a subculture, or subcultures, in particular. We are citizens of a country (culture at large) and live in a community, are members of a family, attend given schools, work at special jobs (subcultures in particular), etc., etc.

3. Personality, with its many possible meanings, nevertheless implies that there are two prevalent kinds of reactions: (a) those which determine what, at a given time and in a given situation, an individual is likely to do; and (b) those which influence the reactions or effects on others of the behaving person—the personality-in-action—with whom we happen to be concerned.

4. The developing personality anticipates certain reactions from members of his environment and modifies whatever behavior he might otherwise express in the light of these anticipations.

5. The individual's *self-concept*, the image the individual has of his own personality, is determined by his anticipation and the realization or outcome of these anticipations as he responds to the reaction he has evoked.

6. A personality is the expression of the "essence" of the individual's

relatively enduring traits organized in a relatively consistent manner so that it becomes possible to expect a line or mode of behavior from the personality in action. A *trait* may be any particular or distinguishable enduring way in which one individual differs from another.

PERSONALITY AND SPEECH: RELATED DEVELOPMENT

Personality is expressed in each act of our behavior. Beginning with the moment of birth and its accompanying cry, virtually all of our behavior is accompanied by some act of inner or overt speech. At birth, crying is purely reflexive. It is a product of physiological activity involving the muscles of the body as a whole, including those of phonation (vocalization). Cries of healthy, new-born babies sound pretty much alike. So, for a brief time at least, are their personalities, which may be characterized as indefinite or nebulous. As infants become conscious of being alive, as they become aware of physical changes and of their responses to them, as they begin to have needs, there is more vocalization. The vocalization is expressive, and the expressions of personality make their appearance. The happy baby reveals his happiness by "contented sounds." The unhappy baby keeps himself and others busy by crying; we label him a "colicky baby." If he does a fair amount of cooing but does not overlook the usefulness of vigorous crying, we may think of him as a "determined baby."

As small children learn to use words, physical activities are usually accompanied by speech; the small child behaves and talks about his behavior. He plays and talks aloud—to himself and to others. He begins to entertain ideas and to work out problems. He expresses not only his wishes and his feelings but his thinking as well. The small child reveals in his speech that he is conscious of what is going on about him. He tells us of his strivings and of his adjustments; his speech indicates that intellectually, physically, and emotionally he is functioning as an integrated entity. We become aware of the child as a personality.

The child growing up reveals his development and growth through speech. Speech development reflects intellectual, physical, and emotional "growing up"—or failure to grow up. Almost all conscious behavior is accompanied by some form of speech. Consequently, speech—words and the way they are used—begins to stand for the adult. If, through speech, a man tells us that he has not given up speaking and thinking as a child, we think of him as infantile. If a man's concepts are narrow and his abstractions inappropriate, we think of him as dull. Through the words and voice we hear, we form impressions of people we never see. The personality pictures we have of radio performers are based entirely upon their speech. If we are able to observe a man's actions, we have a more complete basis for forming a judgment of his personality. Right or wrong, we assume that the person is as he speaks.

Through speech we exercise control over our environment. The infant accomplishes control through crying. The infant has relatively few needs, so that crying is generally adequate as a method of control. Many of the infant's needs are anticipated for him, so frequently even crying is not necessary. The child has more needs than the infant, and less is done for him in anticipation of his wishes and wants. The child, therefore, must use language for a satisfying existence. The child who fails to develop adequate language must either reduce his wants or be frustrated. We know that children whose vocabularies are inadequate for their environment tend to be frustrated. They reveal frustration through crying, temper tantrums, and other nonverbal means of expression.

The maturing individual, with his complexity of wants and wishes, has an increased need to use language in order to control his environment. Through speech he satisfies some of his wants and wishes, and agrees to delay in the satisfaction of others. Through speech the maturing individual adjusts to his environment and assists the environment in adjusting to him. Maturity implies ability to make necessary adjustments. It implies knowing when to yield, when to compromise, and when to be insistent on having one's way. It implies knowing how to establish a balance between an individual's demands and the demands of his environment. The mature, well-adjusted personality does not make excessive demands on his environment. Neither does he permit the environment to make excessive demands on him.

The personality we reveal through speech is the result of a continuous process of growing. Though growth is a continuous process, it is not always a smooth and even process. Speech develops and parallels intellectual, physical, and emotional growth. When the three aspects of growth are well integrated, speech and personality are well integrated. Disturbances in growth, temporary or permanent, are reflected in the individual's speech. From time to time, minor disturbances are to be expected. They are part of the "normal personality." Perfection in speaking at all times and under all circumstances rarely, if ever, occurs. The "normal personality" does not strive to achieve perfection in speaking. Some margin for error must be allowed for speech behavior as well as for behavior in general.

THE NORMAL WELL-ADJUSTING PERSONALITY AND SPEECH BEHAVIOR

Vocabulary

In our discussion on Conversation we emphasize the need for the speaker to respect his listener if he—the speaker—is speaking to somebody with an expectation of being understood. So, a normal speaker makes an initial selection of words—says what he has to say in words the listener should be able to understand. In any speaking situation, in conversation or in public speaking, the normal speaker observes his listener for reactions, for "feedback," so that he may learn from the observed reactions whether he has been understood. If the reactions suggest a lack of understanding or of the speaker's intention, the normal speaker adjusts his words or his manner of speaking and tries again. In short, the normal speaker realizes that unless he is speaking only for or to himself, he must make verbal adjustments to his listeners. Such adjusting does not imply speaking down or using a vocabulary limited to the first thousand or two thousand words most frequently used in our language. Adjusting does imply taking the trouble, when necessary, to define unusual words or words used for a special meaning. Further, it implies the use of examples and the expansion of explanations or the rephrasing of a statement so that his message, or the point of his story, may be understood.

Voice

The voice of the speaker, the variation in its attributes—loudness, quality, pitch range, and the rate of utterance—should reveal the thinking and feeling of the speaker and be appropriate to the speaking situation. (See pages 80–82 for a review of effective voice.) The listener should not need to wonder what the speaker's vocal changes mean because the vocal changes should be consonant with the speaker's meanings. It should sound emphatic when the speaker wishes to be emphatic, without suggesting aggression or hostility. The speaker's voice should be able to invite attention to an idea or a shade of meaning or a state of feeling, and yet not be obvious or infantile. The speaker's voice should be easy to listen to and readily heard and yet not be overloud. Control of the attributes of voice requires inner control and a constant response to the listeners' reactions. Ordinarily, the speaker's wish to accomplish these objectives is sufficient to insure the accomplishment.

Gestures

The speaker who is well adjusted has probably incorporated gestures as part of his expressive verbal behavior. Gestures are used to reenforce his meanings and to communicate his feelings. In any speaking situation, the well-adjusting speaker uses gestures as he does his words, with an attitude of respect for his listeners. If the gestures get in the way of his ideas, if the response to them is negative or inappropriate, the use of gestures must be modified. Occasionally, speakers reveal anxiety or discomfort through the repeated use of a movement or an action that is ticlike and distracting. If this is the case, the gesture should be controlled. For the most part, however, gestures tend to be produced "naturally" and accompany the speaker's verbal behavior without need for conscious concern.

NORMAL SPEAKER-LISTENER RELATIONSHIPS

A normal relationship between speaker and listener necessarily implies a wish for mutual understanding. Underlying this wish, or attitude, as we have emphasized elsewhere, is an obligation to appreciate the intention of what is uttered. This means that the speaker must have insight into his own intentions. He must know not only what he is saying, what he wishes his listeners to understand, but also what he really intends by his utterances. The listener, for his part, must not ignore intention if, for some reason, the utterance—the words used—seems not to be consonant with the intentions. Words have many meanings, and words in sentences may have special meanings. The well-adjusting speaker should be able to project himself into the role of the listener and to be objective about whether what he is saying and the manner of his speaking are likely to communicate his thoughts, his feelings, and his intentions. The listener, in turn, should be fair minded. Such state of mind becomes possible if the listener does a bit of projecting on his own and assumes that what he may have to say when he becomes a speaker may also be understood or misunderstood, according to the listener-to-be's ability to appreciate intention as well as literal meanings.

A well-adjusting person is aware that some words and some ways of saying some words are likely to produce negative emotional reactions. The well-adjusting speaker avoids these words, or at least the "loaded" way of using some words.

We shall try to highlight some of the difficulties we have with our verbal behavior in the discussion of personality maladjustments and speech. We hope that from this approach the reader will gain insights as to what might be avoided if he wishes to be considered a well-adjusting person.

PERSONALITY MALADJUSTMENT AND SPEECH

Speech of the Moderately Maladjusted

How, through speech, do we recognize the not-so-well-adjusted individual? We learn much from the voice we hear. There is the voice that whines when there is no occasion for whining. There is the voice that apologizes for being heard when the speaker has a right to be heard. There is the voice that "shouts down" even in the face of no opposition. There is the voice of the irritable and the voice of the plaintive. There is the voice of the person who for too long has enjoyed ill health and only regretfully admits being well. All these, and others, are the voices of not-so-well-adjusted personalities.

The not-so-well-adjusted tell us much about themselves in the words they speak and in their responses to the words they hear. Language content may be narrow and limited. The not-so-well-adjusted individual may specialize in a single subject which is laboriously presented in pseudoconversation without regard to time, place, or number of previous repetitions. Listeners may have to hear, for the nth time, about the oh-so-big-fish that got away, or about numerous allergies, or about a precocious grandchild, nephew, or niece. What the speaker has to say may be interesting or even fascinating—but only the first or second time at an appropriate place.

The one-topic specialist frequently makes a poor listener. He speaks his piece but reveals no willingness to listen. Over the telephone he has his say and then, perhaps even rudely, cuts the conversation short. The listener is left with a mouthful of unspoken words and an elevated blood pressure. If we interpret the behavior of the one-topic specialist as mere rudeness, we may be wrong. Probably a more nearly correct interpretation is that this kind of speaker feels that he cannot make adequate responses on another person's level of thinking. Narrowness of language content is probably a reflection of a speaker's limited ability in a world of words other than his own.

Not all the not-so-well-adjusted are one-topic specialists. Some avoid words on any topic. Their part of a conversation consists of a begrudgingly emitted "uh-uh," or an occasional "umm." Still others are experts on almost any topic. You start it and they take it over. They listen just long enough to take off with a "now, let me tell you about my experience." From that time on the conversation becomes a monologue. Some of it may be entertaining or even funny, but essentially it is a pseudoconversation with a giving or at least a production of words, but without a willingness to be receptive, to listen to the words of another.

These speakers reveal considerable difficulty in getting along in a world of words, at least when the words are not, for the most part, their own. The nonverbal grunter is probably insecure about what his verbal responses should be. He avoids saying the wrong thing by saying next to nothing. He reveals, however, that he is aware of social proprieties by punctuating what he hears with his occasional grunts. The expert-on-any-topic speaker does not take a chance on misunderstanding what someone else may have to say to him. By taking over, he makes his further understanding of speech unnecessary. What he fails to understand is the give-and-take nature of conversation; what he succeeds in making his listeners understand is that, as a speech personality, he is inadequate.

Somewhat related to the nonverbal grunter is the speaker whose conversational responses consist of a few set but not always pat phrases. Instead of an "uh-uh," we might get a "how nice," or "lovely" or "you don't say" to what we do say. A response from a limited inventory of responses is made to a speech situation without regard to the nature or intent of the situation. Occasionally, the set phrase may have a grandiose ring to it and include a "Why, that's just devastating," or "isn't it simply divine!" Profanity and slang are other resources of the speakers of set phrases. This kind of limited language usage, if it is characteristic of the speech responses of an individual, may indicate rigidity of personality. It may also indicate the individual's inability or unwillingness to attend to speech closely enough to make appropriate rather than set or stereotyped responses.

The Literal Speaker

Of another kind is the speaker who insists that the words you speak and he presumably is trying to understand must mean what he means when he uses the words. He will take a word out of context and argue with you about its meaning. Frequently he forgets that the context includes the manner of speaking, the nature of the speech situation, and the sequence of events that led up to the use of the word. For this occasionally verbose but almost always rigid personality, words may mean only what he or the dictionary permits them to mean. This speaker may know many words, but he does not know the ways of words. He may even pursue the study of words as some persons pursue the accumulation of money. A large vocabulary, a memory for literal definitions of words, an exactness and precision of speech, round out the picture. Unfortunately, formalized rigidity of thinking and of language usage are the products of the study. Conversations with such a person are not easy. One must be on guard not to use a word in any but the conventionally accepted sense. A conversation becomes a verbal inspection. Each meaning must be in its expected place, or else. . . .

The Non-Communicative Speaker

For those of us who are at least moderately well adjusted, or adjusting, and who use speech for social contact and communion, it may come as a surprise that some less well-adjusted persons speak only to communicate. Because of this limitation, these persons seem noncommunicative. In effect, they are, because speaking for them is generally a one-way affair. A message is spoken, information is verbalized, or a directive given. Unfortunately, because there is no personal contact, the speaker does not find out whether he has been understood. Often the "message" is presented without adequate preparation or opportunity for the listener to become ready for what he is to receive. There are no social amenities. There is no verbal equivalent of the Navy's "Now hear this, now hear this." The noncommunicative speaker goes directly to his task; he speaks his piece and thinks that he is through.

If the listener indicates that he has not understood this speaker, perhaps only because the listener was not quite ready for the message, the speaker may repeat verbatim what he said the first time. The utterances are likely to be logical, precisely articulated, with each word meaning what the dictionary denotes it to mean. Because some listeners may be somewhat less logical and more adjustable, they may not be able to appreciate the appropriateness of this speaker's remarks. All too often the remarks of those who speak presumably only to communicate fail to show an awareness of the situation—the time, the place, and the background and interests of the listener or listeners.

It is quite likely that the noncommunicative speaker is not aware of his own intentions in speaking. He speaks to empty his mind, to get rid of thoughts and words rather than to share them with others. Perhaps he may feel that his job, if not his duty, is done. He seems to speak to say what he must, rather than to establish contact and so become more truly involved in a communicative situation.

Misevaluations

The not-so-well-adjusted individual is what he is in part because of the way he evaluates what he hears. His evaluations are self-centered. Too often this person fails to determine the intentions of the speaker to whom he is presumably listening because his own intentions get in the way. In contrast, the well-adjusted personality evaluates what he hears in terms of the particular speaker and the background and occasion of the speech. He does not confuse words with the host of meanings which words may have. The well-adjusted personality recognizes that few if any words have inherent meanings, that his use of a word may differ in significance from another person's use of the "same" word. The well-adjusted personality would not feel slighted or insulted because a neighbor's child called him a "silly-willy." First, he would consider that a child is using the phrase. Then he might conjecture that, for this particular child involved, "silly-willy" may be a term of endearment. Finally, he might ask himself what "silly-willy" meant to him. If after pondering the question, he could come to no conclusion, he would decide that this question was one not really worthy of an answer, and so why bother about it after all!

The special aptitude most of us have for misevaluating the words of others is dramatically presented by Dorothy Parker in her story *"Here We Are."* The scene is a compartment on a train. The characters are two newly-weds. One of the predicaments they talked themselves into follows:

"I guess I will take this darned old hat off," she said.
"It kind of presses. Just put it up on the rack, will you, dear? Do you like it, sweetheart?"
"Looks good on you," he said.

"No, but I mean," she said, "do you really like it?"

"Well, I'll tell you," he said. "I know this is the new style and everything like that, and it's probably great. I don't know anything about things like that. Only I like the kind of a hat like that blue hat you had. Gee, I liked that hat."

"Oh, really?" she said. "Well, that's nice. That's lovely. The first thing you say to me, as soon as you get me off on a train away from my family and everything, is that you don't like my hat. The first thing you say to your wife is you think she has terrible taste in hats. That's nice, isn't it?"

"Now, honey," he said, "I never said anything like that. I only said——"

"What you don't seem to realize," she said, "is this hat cost twenty-two dollars. Twenty-two dollars. And that old horrible blue thing you think you're so crazy about, that cost three ninety-five."

"I don't give a darn what they cost," he said. "I only said—I said I liked that blue hat. I don't know anything about hats. I'll be crazy about this one as soon as I get used to it. Only it's kind of not like your other hats. I don't know about the new styles. What do I know about women's hats?"

"It's too bad," she said, "you didn't marry somebody that would get the kind of hats you'd like. Hats that cost three ninety-five. Why didn't you marry Louise? You always think she looks so beautiful. You'd love her taste in hats. Why didn't you marry her?"

"Ah, now, honey," he said. "For heaven's sakes!"

"Why didn't you marry her?" she said. "All you've done, ever since we got on this train, is talk about her. Here I've sat and sat, and just listened to you saying how wonderful Louise is. I suppose that's nice, getting me all off here along with you, and then raving about Louise right in front of my face. Why didn't you ask her to marry you? I'm sure she would have jumped at the chance. There aren't so many people asking her to marry them. It's too bad you didn't marry her. I'm sure you'd have been much happier."[1]

Levels of Significance

The newlyweds in Dorothy Parker's story involved themselves in difficulty because of the failure to appreciate that speech has varying levels of significance. Their states of mind and feeling brought about a verbal entrapment from which neither could escape without the help of the other. Their special situation could and should excuse their dilemma, their temporary, we hope, inability to distinguish between speech as an emotional expression and speech to convey and interchange thought. Faced with the overwhelming situation of the first hours of their marriage, they forgot the importance of the trivial. But many not so newlywed husbands and wives continue to make comparable errors and verbal misevaluations. For some, there is no such occasion as a casual conversation. "How are you?" spoken as a social gesture evokes a detailed account of their medical ailments, past and present. A parting, "So long, hope to see you soon" is likely to result in an actual visit the next day. Feelings may be hurt if the unwitting extender of the invitation did not seem to expect or be prepared for

---

[1] From "Here We Are" in *The Portable Dorothy Parker*. Copyright 1943 by Dorothy Parker. Used by permission of The Viking Press, Inc., New York.

the visitor. All too often, words spoken in jest are remembered and taken literally and seriously. Weeks after a conversation, the not-so-well-adjusted individual recalls the precise words he has heard and confronts and confounds others with them.

PERSONALITY ADJUSTMENT THROUGH SPEECH

A well-adjusted personality responds to language as part of a total situation in which the language is used. The not-so-well-adjusted individual, and especially the neurotic personality, overlooks one or more significant parts of the situation, and responds inappropriately. Faced with a problem, the neurotic does not have a thorough enough talk with himself. Evidence of research workers reveals that neurotics actually resist a complete verbalization of their problems. The neurotic fails to recall important elements in the situation which created the problem. This memory failure limits the amount of information he must have to arrive at a proper solution. It reduces the likelihood of arriving at a normal, discriminative response.

Insight and Speech

Both well-adjusted and poorly adjusted persons talk to themselves. The important difference is that the well-adjusted persons know when and how to do the talking. It is only through talking things over with oneself that insight is attained Insight is nothing more than a verbalization of a person's problems so that he appreciates how he should relate to them. If the not-so-well-adjusted personality seeks better adjustment, he must learn how to talk to himself. Well-adjusted persons control their behavior through the use of language. Some of the language is subvocal and some is gesture. Adequate adjustment can take place when the individual learns how to speak to himself and for himself in ways appropriate to the situation. Fortunately, man can do more with language than talk himself into quandaries and dilemmas. Through speech he can solve his problems and make adjustments to the world in which he lives. In essence, therapy for self-adjustment is a learning process. The learning is achieved when the person knows how and when to speak to himself in appropriate ways to control his own conduct.

Objective Listening to One's Self

It is important for us not only to be well adjusted, but also to sound and act the part. Though we do not yet have the gift "to see ourselves as others see us" we can hear ourselves as others hear us. A variety of recording and playback devices make hearing ourselves possible. The most desirable setup for hearing ourselves as others hear us is to be recorded "candidly." But even an intended recording may have great therapeutic values. One adolescent boy with a "cracked, falsetto, soprano voice" cringed when he heard his voice played back for him. He pleaded for the help he resisted before he had the opportunity to hear himself. By hearing ourselves we may be able to learn why our listeners do not interpret us as we would like. We may begin to appreciate why the thin voice with the oversupply of rising inflections is not a persuasive voice; or why our listeners took in deadly earnest something we intended in fun. In short, if we are not satisfied with the personality picture others seem to have of us, hearing ourselves as others hear us may provide a basis for making changes.

Reflected Behavior

In one sense, we are able to see ourselves as others see us. We tend unconsciously to imitate the physical behavior of those we observe. Looking at a tense individual makes us feel tense and may make us feel uncomfortable. If we regularly become uncomfortable in the presence of another person, we may avoid the person who is the cause of the discomfort. Further, we may conclude that the individual who is the cause has an unpleasant personality. We may come to the same conclusion in regard to persons who are overrelaxed and "sag." Such persons make us feel tired. It is well to remember that we do unto others as they do unto us. If others fidget in our presence, it may be because we make them fidget. If they become tense, it may very well be that they have "caught" the tensions from us. If our listeners slump when we talk to them, they may merely be reflecting our own appearance.

Our gestures as well as our voice and words reveal our personalities. Gestures, as part of the total act of speech, influence communication and help to determine the response we get in speaking. Our actions may contradict our words. A facial grimace or a smile may reveal our attitude more truly than the words we use. The relaxed appearance, the tense look, the tired or bored look, all reveal attitudes which are parts of personality. Through our actions, whether or not accompanied by words, others make assumptions about us and adapt to us. Unfortunately, we cannot study our own actions as well as we can our voices and our words. We can, however, study our responses to the actions of others, and then apply some of the conclusions to ourselves.

SUMMARY

Personality is the impressions we make on others and ourselves as a result of our behavior. Personality is most readily expressed in our speech.

Through speech we not only express our personalities, but also make adjustments and modifications of behavior which reflect growth and change. Our use of language, voice, and gesture reveals our abilities to get along in our environment. Through speech we can talk ourselves into maladjustment. Fortunately, speech is also the means of modification for correcting maladjustment. A proper evaluation of speech, from the point of view of the speaker as well as the listener, will prevent maladjustment. Sensitivity to the effects of our speech behavior on others should help us to modify undesirable personality aspects.

QUESTIONS AND EXERCISES

1. What is your concept of personality? Explain how it is possible for one individual to have more than one personality. How do you form your judgments of the personalities of persons you meet for the first time?

2. Tune in to a television "soap opera." As soon as you hear each performer speak, form an immediate estimate of his personality. Is your estimate that which the script writer would want you to have?

3. Explain how disturbances of speech and personality are related.

4. Read one or more speeches of three of the following persons: (a) Abraham Lincoln, (b) Harry S Truman, (c) Franklin D. Roosevelt, (d) Dwight D. Eisenhower, (e) Richard Nixon, (f) John F. Kennedy, (g) Winston Churchill.

Indicate how the men reveal their personalities through their words. For those you have seen on television, or in person, describe characteristic gestures and how they are manifestations of the speaker's personality.

5. Are there any radio speakers who irritate you? Why?

6. Are there any newspaper columnists to whom you object because of the way they write? Indicate, by specific quotations, what you find objectionable.

7. Describe briefly the personalities of people you know who fall under the following headings:

    (a) The infantile individual,

    (b) The person with a minute speaking vocabulary,

    (c) The grunter,

    (d) The whiner,

    (e) The expert-on-any-topic speaker,

    (f) The single-topic speaker,

    (g) The noncommunicative speaker,

    (h) The "Caspar Milquetoast" type,

    (i) The speaker who insists that words be used only as defined by the dictionary,

    (j) The person who regularly overlooks the intentions of another speaker.

8. What speech activities would you recommend for each of the above as aids in the improvement of personality?

9. *A characteristic of the neurotic personality is his inability to state clearly the problem or problems which trouble him.* Cite instances in support of this statement. What speech or language exercises would you recommend to overcome this aspect of neurotic behavior?

10. Contrast the essential difference in verbal behavior between a well-adjusted and a somewhat maladjusted person you know.

Recommended Readings

Eisenson, J., Irwin, J. V., and A'uer, J. J. *The Psychology of Communication.* New York: Appleton-Century-Crofts, 1963, Chap. 19.

Guilford, J. P. *Personality.* New York: McGraw-Hill, 1959.

Hayakawa, S. E. *The Fully Adjusted Personality,* in S. I. Hayakawa (ed.), *Our Language and Our World.* New York: Harper and Row, 1959.

Johnson, W. *Your Most Enchanted Listener.* New York: Harper and Row, 1956.

Merloo, J. A. M. *Conversation and Communication.* New York: International Universities Press, 1952.

Oliver, R. T., and Cortright, R. L. *Effective Speech,* 4th ed. New York: Holt, Rinehart and Winston, 1961, Chap. 3.

CHAPTER 10

CONVERSATION

*Conversation is an exchange of thought that
leaves all parties to it a grain the wiser.*
DR. A. WHITNEY GRISWOLD*

If we interpret Dr. Griswold's statement literally, we might well begin with a feeling of awe or apprehension that perhaps we are not always capable of generating wisdom in our conversations. Dr. Griswold did not intend the participants in a discourse to do so with a grim determination to act and sound profound, to chart a course with a fixed objective, and to avoid any incidental port of pleasure that may be derived from engaging in talk. Quite the contrary. Conversation may well begin in the realm of trivia, and possibly conclude on a note of trivia, or, if the participants are fortunate, on a note of levity. Somehow, however, those of us who still believe in talking to one another may manage to touch or be touched by wisdom. It is important that when this contact is made, the participants have no fear of exploration, that all participants be carried along without fear of getting somewhere.

More than 2,000 years ago Socrates established the basic principle of conversation. He did so by example and by precept. The principle was that conversation should take place among friends, with shared interests in a congenial atmosphere. The best conversations, according to Socrates, are ones in which the friends share wisdom as a common interest. Wisdom we shall characterize as the product that evolves when men with ideas and ideals are willing and able to share their innermost thoughts and are capable of translating their thoughts and feelings into language as plain as that habitually used by Lincoln.

When our civilization was young and still without books, it was conversation that brought out its essence and conversation that maintained and transmitted the essence for generations until written recordings could be made. When, finally, books were available, their contents required conversa-

---

* Dr. A. Whitney Griswold in his Convocation at Brown University's 191st academic year.

tion to bring forth their meanings. This, we hope, continues to be the purpose of those relatively formalized and structured conversations known as classroom recitations. Conversation, then, is the first, the oldest, and still the most prevalent form of instruction. This is how we learned to talk as children, and how we learned what talking is about as we matured.

SOCIAL CONVERSATION

Early in this text we indicated that one of the purposes of speech is the enjoyment of utterance. We converse because most of us find it more enjoyable to talk to somebody than to talk to ourselves. In order to talk to somebody we need to talk about something of interest, or having the potential of being of interest for all the participants. The immediate purpose of most social conversations is shared pleasure of talking—and of listening.

Social conversation, at least at its outset, is not intended to provide an opportunity for expounding a point of view, or to solve the problems of the day. If the opportunity does come, it should not be shunned, but neither should the conversation be abruptly ended because no obvious profound note is sounded. Good men, and even wise ones, have the right to indulge themselves by sharing their light thoughts and their light moments, to have a good time together. When we participate in conversation, we may incidentally learn or share something of more lasting significance—we may arrive at wisdom—but our primary purpose is the sheer enjoyment of the occasion.

Whatever else a social conversation might be, the participants must avoid making it either an occasion for holding forth at length or a sharp debate. This observation does not imply that differences of opinion should not be aired, or that one participant in discourse should not try to persuade others about his point of view or even try to get the others to accept or initiate a particular line of action. Nor does it mean that a speaker's erudition is to be concealed when he has an urge to reveal and to share. The, observation does mean that when a point of view is expressed, however persuasively, or a bit of learning revealed, it should be done amiably rather than aggressively. A participant in a social conversation should never be made to feel ignorant because he is sharing knowledge or insights. Neither should he ever feel that he is being made to yield to another's viewpoint despite inclinations to the contrary. Persuasion should be practiced as a gentle art when it takes place in conversation. If persuasion ceases to be gentle, then it is out of place in conversation.

SUBJECT MATTER OF SOCIAL CONVERSATION

Except as limited by good taste, there are no limits to the subject matter of social conversation. The subject that is of greatest interest to people is "people." And the people most conversationalists are interested in talking about are themselves. This, in an important sense, is as it should be if knowledge of subject is a criterion for its selection. Often, indeed, the speaker with knowledge as well as insight about himself has a fascinating topic for conversation, providing he is not fascinated too long at a time, and is capable of appreciating that other speakers may entertain a comparable fascination. Next to themselves, most persons are also likely to be interested in talking about their friends. In a sense, this topic is a projection of the one of primary interest—still themselves.

How much we are interested in ourselves and in our friends can be estimated from the results of an analysis of conversations overheard in England two days after Hitler marched into Austria. Hitler's army entered Austria on Saturday, March 13, 1938. On the following Monday, of 310 recorded conversations, almost three times the number of persons in the survey talked about friends than did those who talked about politics and current events. And the weather as a subject of conversation was almost twice as frequent as was politics and the vital news![1]

Are Americans different from the English with respect to favorite topics of conversation? Americans may be a bit more politically minded. On the whole, however, the American's favorite topics are the highly personal ones of his family, his home, and his health, followed by politics and matters of national and international interest. The major emphasis continues to be on the important pronoun *his*. There seems little question that topics which touch upon personal interests and are related to the things for which we strive are those which are most frequently discussed.

People are of interest to the butcher, the baker, the candlestickmaker— and the college student of either sex. The psychologists Landis and Burtt[2] found that female college students conversed about persons 37 per cent of the time compared with 16 per cent of the time for men.

In a conversation of any length, more than one topic is likely to be touched upon. In women's conversation, persons, clothes, and social affairs tend to become intermingled. Among men, research findings indicate that money and business affairs tend to be chiefly discussed. The weather and sex, for all our inability to do anything but accept them, are leading topics of conversation among men and women through middle age. Beyond

---

[1] T. H. Pear, *The Psychology of Conversation,* London: Nelson and Sons, 1939, p. 120.
[2] Cited in Pear, *op. cit.,* p. 114.

middle age, the weather tends to be more frequently discussed than sex, though sex, in the matters of babies and scandal, is by no means completely neglected.

OCCASIONS FOR SOCIAL CONVERSATION

Social conversation takes place whenever persons meet, by accident or by design, and feel the need to say something. The occasions may range from the chance meeting of acquaintances on the street or in any public place, when all that is interchanged is a nod, a smile, a hand gesture, or the single word "Hello," to the anticipated and prearranged gathering at the home of a friend or a meeting hall.

Social conversations vary in their degree of informality. Probably the most informal, in terms of possible place, dress, subject, behavior, and language used, takes place between members of a family. On the relatively formal side are the conversations which occur among relative strangers who arrive ahead of time to a specified meeting place for a particular purpose.

Conventions in Conversation

The behavior of the speakers, their choice of topics, their manner of speaking, the words used, and the clothes worn should all be dictated by the conversational situation. Sport clothes and slang may be appropriate at a big league baseball game, but both would be definitely out of place at a formal banquet for the dean of a college. A topic suitable at a gathering of men may not be suitable if a woman is present. Similarly, the talk about clothes, which features the conversation of many women, may lose its appropriateness if men are present. It may be of interest to note that in mixed groups American women tend to adapt their conversations to the interests of men more than American men do for women.

Pear, in discussing the difference in manner of social speaking, observes:

To an English ear—here I tread warily—American speakers, even professional lecturers, seem to attribute little importance to the way things are said. Some Australians and New Zealanders assure me that, in their country, to speak in a way obviously different from the average would be considered undemocratic, so if one's hearer's are not fussy, why bother?[3]

Professor Pear continues his observations by asking,

---

[3] T. H. Pear, *Personality, Appearance and Speech,* London: Allen and Unwin, 1957, p. 38.

Am I right then, in assuming that in this respect people in the younger English-speaking countries are relatively insensitive to speech nuances?

We do not consider Pear's observations to be correct, even if we could accept his lumping, or should we say grouping, of millions of persons throughout the world as belonging to the "people in the younger English-speaking countries." Nuances in speech, as in dress and in manners in general, vary as cultures vary. American "nunances," the words spoken and the way they are spoken, differ as they also do among other English speaking peoples. They differ individually according to the personalities of the individual speaker and the sensitivities of the speaker to the conversational situation. There is no lack of nuances in the conversations of people who speak English in the many ways English is spoken. They are not, of course, the nuances of London and Manchester or of Oxford and Cambridge. To be sure, video and wireless in England and television and radio in the United States have served as levelers of diction and perhaps have given us stereotypes, if not prototypes worthy of emulation, of what and how conversational speech should sound.

NATURE OF GOOD SOCIAL CONVERSATION

Social conversation is unplanned discourse. It is a speech excursion in an uncharted sea of thoughts-about-to-be expressed. Good social conversation is a cooperative enterprise among speakers who are eager to communicate and willing, if not actually eager, to listen. Any reluctance a speaker has to listen must be balanced by a realization that unless he is willing to hear others he has no right to expect to be heard. Cooperative communication entails a willingness to put aside what we may want to say in order to follow through what somebody else is saying. Responses should reveal understanding and appreciation of what is being said. Social conversation fails if it becomes a series of synchronized and barely related monologues, with each speaker waiting for an opportunity to say his piece and then consider his job done.

CHARACTERISTICS OF A GOOD CONVERSATIONALIST

Social conversation can be no better than its participants. It can, however, be much worse. We can engage in good social conversation only if we are talking with persons who are sensitive to feelings other than their own and who are as reluctant to give hurt to others as they are to be hurt by others. Wit and the apt rejoinder have their place in social conversation only if they are as enjoyable to the listeners as to the speaker. Oscar Wilde and James Whistler may have been brilliant speakers but they were poor conversationalists. Their remarks, scintillating but caustic, were more pleasurable to overhear than to hear. Their "retorts perfect" were stoppers to conversation. As such they were out of place in genial society. What, then, are the characteristics of good conversationalists?

Adequacy as a Human Being

To begin with, a good conversationalist must be an adequate human being. In addition to other things, he must be aware of his own strivings and appreciate that others, too, have strivings. Above all, the good conversationalist is one who realizes that normal human beings want to enjoy living, and he must be willing to do his part to make living enjoyable. The egocentric, self-absorbed person may succeed in being an effective public speaker, but he is not likely to become a good conversationalist.

Tolerance

A good conversationalist must be tolerant. He must appreciate that we all have weaknesses and shortcomings. He must not assume that a person who disagrees with him is necessarily wrong. Neither will he feel compelled to "show up" another person even if he knows that the other speaker is mistaken. High on the list of insufferable individuals and inadequate personalities is the one who is always right, who makes undeniable assertions, and who, moreover, has the facts to prove it. The good conversationalist is aware that there may be a wrong time for being right, and does not confuse being right with being righteous.

Experience and Knowledge

We must not overlook the need to have something to say which is worth saying as a requisite for a good conversationalist. It is obvious that the broader the person's experiences, the greater his background becomes for conversation. The person who knows well his own job and who knows moderately well the jobs that are related to his, the person with curiosity as to the significance and interrelationships between his job and others, has indirectly prepared himself for the art of the conversationalist. But knowing one's job is not enough. The more one knows about life and people, the better acquainted one is with literature, art, music, history, and all that makes up human knowledge, the better prepared one is for conversation. It becomes clear, then, that there is no prescribed preparation or training for becoming a good conversationalist. The substance of conversation is human experience, direct and vicarious. The ability to verbalize experience and the desire to share with others go a long way towards the making of a conversationalist.

Ability as a Listener

The good conversationalist is a good listener. Listening is an active process. Effective listening requires that we let our speaker know that we are responding to him. Our posture, our facial expressions, our nods of assent or approval, are elements in good listening. The listener is not necessarily a silent person. Listening permits comments, but the comments should be brief and of a nature which encourages rather than interrupts the speaker. Questions which draw out the speaker, and which reveal a genuine interest in what is being said, are always in order. They are included in active listening.

What are some characteristics of the good listener? We will briefly state what we consider the most important traits.

1. From what we have already said, it should become clear that a good listener accepts the *spirit* of *mutuality*. As such he appreciates that communication, if it is to be realized in conversation, is a two-way avenue.

2. A good listener truly wishes to understand what he hears. His ears are receptive, willing, and free. He will, for example, not attempt to refute a position unless he can restate, to the satisfaction of the first speaker, the · position he is about to refute.

3. A good listener, as we have stated elsewhere at greater length (see page 205), tries to appreciate the intent as well as the literal meanings of the speaker. He is attuned to ideas, to nuances, to mood, and to feelings. His responses are to the over-all content of the situation rather than to a selected part of the content which may be in keeping with his own more limited needs.

Listenability

All of us are aware that it is easier for us to listen in some situations than in others. On some occasions the difference is in the speech. On other occasions the difference is in the time, or the place and the physical environment. Occasionally, however, the difference may be in ourselves. Nichols[4] did considerable research on factors that were conducive to listening comprehension in public speaking situations. Many of the factors apply to conversation. We shall list those we consider especially relevant as they pertain to the listener, with our own brief comments.

---

[4] Ralph G. Nichols, "Factors in Listening Comprehension," *Speech Monographs,* **XV,** 2 (1948), 161–62.

1. Intelligence. Here, probably, no comment is needed.

2. Size of vocabulary. We assume that the number of meanings and the ability to discern the correct meaning of the speaker's words, as well as the total number of words, are implied.

3. Ability to make inference. Here, we assume, is included the willingness to make the correct (from the speaker's viewpoint) inference.

4. Listening for main ideas, not merely for specific facts. Words, statements of "facts" are conveyors and supporters of ideas. These are what the speaker wants us, to listen for and to understand.

5. Real interest in the subject discussed. Do not prejudge a subject. It may turn out to be as interesting as the one to which you wish to change when your turn arrives.

6. Emotional adjustment to the speaker's thesis. The speaker has a right to his point of view. Try to be objective about the speaker's subjectivity, as you hope he will, in turn, be about yours.

7. Ability to see significance in the subject discussed. The "truth" may often be revealed in seeming trivia, in light treatment of a subject, in the choice of an anecdote. Assume that virtually nothing is really said by chance, and much will become significant. Don't, however, take the attitude of an analyst who becomes constantly concerned with "What did he really mean by that remark?" Be patient, and you may find out.

8. Physical fatigue of the listener. If you are tired, try not to accuse the speaker of being tiresome. Assume an attitude of attention, look at the speaker and some of your own fatigue may pass away.

Nichols also found that males, on the average, are better listeners than females. We shall refrain from any comment on this finding.

Irving Lee, in his excellent little book *How to Talk With People,* sums up and defines the listener's role in a conversation.

> The listener has a job to do, too. He must make the effort to come to terms with the speaker to keep from assuming that he inevitably knows what the speaker has in mind. At the very least he must temper his arrogance with a question now and then just to make sure.[5]

The listener about to be a speaker as well as the speaker who must be prepared to be a listener must both bear in mind that conversation, in common with all communicative efforts, requires at least two persons engaged in interacting roles. Whether the conversation has as its purpose the clarification of an issue to arrive at "the truth of the moment" or the enjoyment of an anecdote, at least two persons are needed. At any given time only one can be a speaker and the other must be a listener.

---

[5] Irving Lee, *How to Talk With People,* New York: Harper & Row, 1952, p. 20.

Avoidance of Boredom

A final requisite of a good conversationalist is that he must, above all else, avoid boring people. A bore has been defined as a person who talks about himself when you wish to talk about yourself. Few, if any persons, have ever been accused of being boring by encouraging others to talk about themselves while they listened attentively and with evident interest.

Another attribute of the bore is his inability to know when to stop talking or how far to pursue a topic. If what a speaker has to say is sufficiently interesting to warrant his prolonged talking, his listeners will insist that he resume after he stops. It is safe to assume that if the listeners are satisfied that they have heard enough from an individual speaker, he has said at least enough. Any further speech would be at the risk of becoming a bore. As long ago as the early seventeenth century, Francis Bacon recognized that ". . . it is a dull thing to tire, and, as we say now, to jade, any thing too far."

In summary, a good conversationalist is an adequate human being. He is sensitive to the feelings of others, has genuine interests outside of himself and appreciates that others may disagree with him without being wrong. The good conversationalist recognizes that human behavior is characterized by strivings which include the wish for pleasurable living. He does whatever he can to make living pleasurable. In brief, a good conversationalist is a good human being who knows how to talk, when not to talk, and how to listen so that the pleasure of talking may be shared and further conversation may be created.

CHARACTERISTICS OF A GOOD CONVERSATION

Given two or more well-adjusted persons who are willing to share the pleasure of talking, *and of listening,* good conversation should easily be achieved. The chances for success are enhanced if one of the participants is willing, as the occasion may demand, to assume the responsibility for guiding the talk and for helping all participants to observe the "rules" of conversation. Some of these rules may be stated as follows:

1. Choose an initial subject that should give no offense to any normal participant. The subject should, of course, be one of potential interest to the participants and one about which they are informed.

2. Encourage participation from all present—including drawing out the shy and discouraging the overenthusiastic talker from indulging in too many or too lengthy speeches.

3. Avoid prolonged periods of silence, but do not become anxious because of moments of quiet. This attitude involves knowing how to ask a

pertinent question and knowing when and how to change from one subject to another.

4. Do not drag out a topic so that discourse becomes either boring or strained.

5. Each participant must make an effort, and a point, of relating and addressing himself to all members of the conversational group. Each must avoid the occasional temptation, by words, tone, or gesture, of speaking to selected members as if they were special initiates of a subgroup. Each must avoid an air that he is "tipping his verbal load" and letting the words fall where they may. At all times the prevailing attitude and spirit must be one of talking with and not of talking at others.

6. Underlying all "rules" or "principles" is that a conversation, to be "good," must start on a good-natured tone and that the tone must remain good natured.

Some of the characteristics of a good conversation are exemplified in the excerpts from the story "Summer Is Another Country" by Christine Weston. In these excerpts we are able to note the changing of topic, the essential good nature of the speakers, and the underlying pleasant mood. Despite the apparent inconsequential nature of what seems to be said and thought at any moment, deep insights are revealed and perhaps the objectives of Socrates, the sharing of wisdom in a congenial atmosphere, are reached.

Early this morning Danny Tracy came to mow the hay in my field. As he turned off the town road into mine, I felt rather than heard the ponderous tread of his horse's great fringed feet on the ground, and the delicate creak and jingle of the mowing machine, for Danny is the only man in our neighborhood who still uses a horse and old-fashioned rig for his heavy work.

When Danny reached the steps where I stood, he paused to say hello and I saw the tobacco juice trickling down his face, which, at seventy-six, had taken on the color and texture of old, weevil-ridden wood.

"Nice day," he said. "Wind in the nor'west, looks like we're in for a stretch of fine weather."

Country people deal in the obvious as they deal in small coin. It is often all they possess.

"You're late this year, Danny," I said. "I was beginning to wonder whether you would ever get around to taking the hay."

He laid the reins on the horse's back and looked at me.

"Been awful busy this fall. Hattie, she suddenly got one of her spells of wanting something new, and nothing would do but what we got to put in a *bathroom.*" He brought it out with intense deliberation, as though speaking of childbirth or a serious operation. "A bathroom, mind you. After fifty years of doing without one, she's suddenly got to have a bathroom for no better reason but that Nita Merrit just got one."

I asked Danny whom he had employed to install the new bathroom, and before answering he sent a jet of tobacco juice over the off-wheel, then: "Hollis Merrit from Machias. Best there is, and I figured we going to sink all that money in a drain, might as well do it right."

Hero changed feet and flipped his long blond tail and Danny went on: "One reason I been so long getting around to your field, I been helping Hollis with the ditching for the bathroom drain. Takes two men and it ain't rightly Hollis's job nohow. Wasn't he's cousin to Hattie, he never would lay a hand to a shovel, what with his education and all."

"But what about you, Danny!" I exclaimed. "Should you be doing such hard work?" He looked as if he might crack in two like an old dried-out plank. I went on: "Can't you get one of the younger men around to lend a hand?"

"Lend a hand digging a drain?" His laugh was toothless and interior. "You ever tried to get one of them young ones to do chores around here for you? No. sir. They got other ideas, and I can't say that I blame them. Driving trucks or working at a filling station is more to their taste, and that's like it ought to be."

I started to disagree, but he continued as if he hadn't heard:

"Take my own two boys. Junior's with that bus outfit as a driver and pulling down a good salary, and Paul's working in a coffin factory over to Boston, Mass. Why should they be wanting to hang around home, breaking their backs shoveling manure or working off their taxes fixing the state highways like I have to?"

He picked up the reins and looked at me with tiny bright blue eyes. "You given any thought to what you're going to do about having the hay cut after I'm gone?"

"Gone?" I echoed, uncomprehending. Where in the world are you planning to go, Danny?"

He laughed and slapped the reins on Hero's broad back.

"Well, we all got a choice between one of two places, ain't we? Guess I've lived a good clean life, so I ain't worrying too much."[6]

QUESTIONS AND EXERCISES

1. What is the relationship between the most usual purpose of social conversation and the functions of seech? Which speech functions does social converstation serve?

2. Cite five kinds of social conversation which vary in degree of formality. Choose an appropriate starting topic for each conversational type.

3. What qualities characterize the behavior and the speech of the person with whom you would most prefer to engage in conversation? What are the characteristics of the person you prefer to avoid?

4. Recall a recent conversation you enjoyed. What made it enjoyable for you?

5. Recall a recent conversation you found trying. What made it so?

6. List five topics of conversation which would be suitable for mixed groups of educated men and women, five which would be more suitable for men than for women, and five which would be especially suitable for women. Justify your selections.

7. Anticipate your role as a host in a conversational situation. How would you start a conversation going on each of the following general subjects: (a) the season's most popular play; (b) modern music; (c) men as cooks; (d) women in politics; (e) modes of traveling; (f) What is college for?

8. Write three questions a host might be prepared to ask on each of these topics in order to keep the conversation going.

9. Samuel Johnson, the English literary figure, was recognized as a great conversationalist. He has been described as a person ". . . of large heart and

[6] From Christine Weston, "Summer Is Another Country," *Harpers*, (July 1961), pp. 27–30. Reprinted by permission of the author.

frame, proud and humble, tender and just, hungry for all that is human, radiating wisdom which was fresh from life." Do you know any person who might be similarly described? Describe a conversation held with him (or her).

10. Write out one or more interesting items of information which you might be able to incorporate into conversations on the following general topics:

    (a) Advances in medicine,
    (b) The place of athletics in college,
    (c) Changes in political parties,
    (d) Educational television,
    (e) Making television worthwhile,
    (f) How to get along with parents.

11. Reread the example of conversation in the closing pages of the chapter. Find three places where the conversation might have taken a turn to cause the feelings of a participant to be hurt. How was offense avoided?

12. Recall a conversation in which you were involved or that you overheard in which something did go wrong. Why? How could it have been avoided?

13. Francis Bacon in his essay *Of Discourse* wrote: "And generally, men ought to know the difference between saltiness and bitterness. Certainly, he that hath a satirical vein, as he maketh others afraid of his wit, so he had need be afraid of others' memory."

    (a) What did Bacon mean?
    (b) What is the proper place of wit in conversation?

14. Do you agree with the point of view that "knowledge is the death of talk"? Comment on your reaction.

15. What is your favorite radio or television program that employs conversation as a medium for instruction or entertainment? Are any other purposes served by the program? What are the "tasks" of the recognized "leader" in this program?

16. How does the moderator of your favorite conversation-discussion program help the participants to observe the practices or rules that govern conversation-discussion? How does the leader make certain that all who are present participate?

17. What are the chief differences and objectives between relatively unstructured "open-end" conversation programs on radio or television and those which use conversation as a format but are structured or controlled?

18. How do you and your friends manage a long-winded talker in a bull-session?

RECOMMENDED READINGS

Biancolli, L. (ed.). *The Book of Great Conversations.* New York: Simon and Schuster, 1948.

Eisenson, J., Irwin, J. V., and Auer, J. J. *The Psychology of Communication.* New York: Appleton-Century-Crofts, 1963, Chaps. 15, 19, 20.

Johnson, W. *Your Most Enchanted Listener.* New York: Harper and Row, 1956.

Lee, Irving J. *How to Talk with People.* New York: Harper and Row, 1952.

Oliver, Robert T. *Conversation: The Developmenet and Expression of Personality.* New York: Thomas, 1961.

Pear, T. H. *The Psychology of Conversation.* London: Nelson, 1939.

Priestley, J. B. *Talking.* New York: Harper, 1937.

Taft, H. W. *An Essay on Conversation.* New York: Macmillan, 1927.

Wright, Milton. *The Art of Conversation.* New York: McGraw-Hill, 1937.

CHAPTER 11

DISCUSSION

Men are never so likely to settle a question rightly as when they discuss it freely.

LORD MACAULAY

Frequently during a social conversation, we mention items on which, as individuals, we might like to linger. We may desire more information, or our awareness of a problem may demand analysis and, perhaps, appropriate cooperative action. Usually, the course of social conversation changes too rapidly to permit a full exchange of information or more than a cursory examination of possible solutions. More often, too few members of the social group have adequate knowledge of a subject or a recognized leader capable and willing to coordinate the discussion. Often the mood and the time or the place are not right for pursuing a topic in depth. But when several participants feel the need to pursue a topic, to search out the facts, to explore possible courses of action, the conversation becomes directly and specifically purposeful. We have then left social conversation and are ready to engage in discussion.

Discussion that emerges from social conversation is unanticipated and unplanned. The dangers of a superficial analysis based on insufficient information thus leading to false solutions is an ever-present hazard. Despite its impromptu character, several features of formalized, planned discussion are likely to appear. To begin with, the participants feel the need for answers impossible to obtain through social conversation. Second, they wish to share their information, to seek additional evidence, to interchange opinions and perhaps, to discover methods of resolving their common problems. Third, one of the participants of the original conversation group usually assumes temporary leadership, guiding the more formal behavior of the conversationalists turned discussants.

Most formalized discussions—and those with which we shall be concerned in this chapter—are planned and anticipated. The participants know

[223]

they have come together for purposeful talking, for pooling knowledge and for sharing experiences relative to a problem of common concern. These formal discussions and debates operate at all levels of government, business, and society. Indeed, free discussion and debate constitute a way of life in the democratic world. Admittedly, the process is imperfect, due in large measure to the inadequacies of the participants. Before discussing this process and methods for its improvement, we need to state the basic premises underlying our philosophy of discussion and debate in a free society.

We believe that:

1. Discussion and debate furnishes the best method of objective inquiry into questions of policy or value.

2. Men reach the most satisfactory solutions to problems when issues are resolved through unlimited discussion and debate.

3. In times of crisis and emergency discussion may prove impractical; nevertheless, when solutions are achieved democratically, they are inherently superior to authoritarian and autocratic decisions.

4. Discussion and debate functions most satisfactorily when employed by mature, educated, responsible participants.

5. The techniques of discussion and debate must be learned and developed through training and practice.

6. No one type of discussion or debate is inherently superior to any other. The determing factors are the problem, the audience situation (if any), the knowledge of the participants, the time limits, and the degree of necessity for an immediate decision.

Objective Inquiry

Discussion at its best becomes a project in group thinking. If it is to be of value to the participants, the discussion process must be motivated by an orderly, systematic, objective approach. Most authorities recommend some form of reflective thinking patterned after John Dewey's familiar five steps. Ewbank and Auer hold that "the adaptation of the scientific method has been made by formalizing the techniques of discussion and debate along a continuum of inquiry and judgment. . . ."[1] Essentially *one process,* then, discussion and debate follows the five logical steps of reflective thinking embracing the essentials of the scientific method.

These steps are:

1. locating and defining the problem
2. exploring the problem

---

[1] H. L. Ewbank and J. J. Auer, *Discussion and Debate,* New York: Appleton-Century-Crofts, 1951, p. 33.

3. examining suggested solutions
4. choosing the best solution
5. securing the acceptance of the best solution.

Decision-Making

Clearly, few discussions accomplish all five steps at a single session. Some may conceivably begin with step three. Few discussions plod slavishly through all five steps. Informal debate may occur at almost any stage of the process, but usually assumes a more formal character at about step four or five. On a particular problem, it may take months or years to achieve the acceptance of a workable solution. It occasionally becomes necessary for discussants to realize that some problems have no apparent solutions. To insist on finding a solution to every problem may result only in finding a poor one. The best solution is sometimes no solution.

The decision to reach no decision is more likely to result from informal discussion arising out of social conversation than it is from planned discussion. When people get together for the purpose of finding a remedy for a problem, one or more of the participants is likely to have a workable solution in mind. But even in planned discussion, all proposed plans are often weak in one or more important respects. One community found its present water works defective and inadequate. After a long series of discussions and investigations, at least four methods were offered as solutions to the problem:

1. Patch up and expand the present plant.
2. Purchase water from an adjoining community.
3. Run pipe to a nearby Great Lake.
4. Build a completely new reservoir, using an adjacent river as the water source.

No one scheme satisfied all the citizens or the town council who finally selected plan four as less than perfect but probably the best possible solution.

Open-Mindedness

Persons intent upon inquiry have points of view of their own, but should try to maintain the attitude of an earnest seeker intent on giving fair attention to every idea presented. Open-minded without being empty-minded, discussants may hold strong contentions and opinions but intently avoid a contentious or opinionated attitude. They cheerfully agree to disagree without becoming disagreeable.

CHARACTERISTICS OF EFFECTIVE DISCUSSION

Preparation and Participation

In discussion, where from three to twenty persons share the responsibility for talking, the temptation is strong to be incompletely prepared, comfortable in the thought that "George" will carry on somehow. Few other attitudes are so well designed to sabotage a discussion session. While not necessarily preparing in the same way, the discussant must equal the public speaker in the thoroughness of his preparation. No discussion will ever achieve merit until each participant prepares fully for his task.

Communication

To promote a relaxed atmosphere conducive to effective communication, the chairman and the participants should give careful attention to the physical environment. For guided conversation, the seats should be arranged for easy exchange; for the panel or symposium, the tables, chairs, and speaker's stand must occupy positions conducive to optimum viewing and subsequent audience participation.

During the discussion the participants should strive to employ all the techniques of effective communication. They share equally the responsibility of transmitting ideas clearly and vigorously to members of their group and to any audience that may be present. When the situation permits, the speaking manner should resemble excellent social conversation. If possible the discussants for a public program should meet in advance and employ every opportunity to converse about the problem under consideration. Even where the discussion opens with formal speeches, the chairman should introduce the program in a manner designed to promote informality and to encourage audience participation. The speeches themselves, in the best tradition of public address, should follow the conversational mode of delivery.

Many of the personality conflicts during discussion sessions stem from our failures to communicate or to employ the language of conciliation. "Every thinking person knows that . . ." we say as we brand by implication as stupid or unthinking all who disagree with us. Or we ask, "Do you have any other suggestions to offer?" implying by our inflectional patterns and facial expression that we hope not, if they are as absurd as the previous ones.

Successful communication likewise implies satisfactory interpersonal relationships. Discussion brings to the table persons possessing a wide assortment of personalities, age groups, social, racial, and religious backgrounds. The search for truth is intermixed with status seeking, ego fulfillment, concealed loyalties, and conflicting interests. As we glance around the table, we are apt to see the expert in one-up-man-ship across from the timid soul, the supreme optimist next to the prophet of gloom, the axe-grinder along side the conciliator, and the reflective thinker near the conclusion-jumper. While it is comforting to think of ourselves as one of the few "normal" persons at the table, we may also recognize most of these character types present in ourselves. The effective discussant makes every effort to keep the discussion idea-centered, to suppress the tendency to consider criticism of his ideas as personal attacks, and to avoid attacking individuals whose ideas are distasteful. Successful discussion does not necessarily require a sterile atmosphere free from the germs of dissention, where only sweetness and light prevail, but it does thrive best in an environment of mutual respect.

Effective Leadership

If the discussion session accomplishes its purposes, careful planning and participation in cooperation with a trained leader is vital. The leader must understand the various types of discussion, master the techniques of each, and possess a keen appreciation of the philosophy of discussion. While it is not necessary to select an expert on the subject under consideration, it is important to find a liberally educated person, skilled in communication and possessing a sympathetic understanding of human relationships. Sometimes an expert on the topic makes a poor discussion leader because of his impatience with less well-informed participants and possibly his resulting desire to dominate the discussion.

Obviously, the leader needs to possess as many of the so-called desirable personality traits as possible. Tact, poise, confidence, a sense of humor and the ability to make quick decisions are among the important characteristics. He must possess the talent for guiding the discussion courteously and fairly, drawing facts and inferences from the group, thus insuring a final product that reflects group thinking at its best. In one study,[2] Wischmeier found that discussions under the guidance of a group-centered leader produced a greater degree of cooperation and more substantive contributions than those employing a leader-centered moderator. Some contrasting characteristics of each type of leadership are noted in the parallel columns:

	Group-Centered		*Leader-Centered*
1.	Leader clarifies and reflects member ideas without attempting to influence.	1.	Leader interprets, rephrases, and modifies a member's contributions to conform with what he considers most important.

---

[2] Richard R. Wischmeier, "Group-Centered and Leader-Centered Leadership: An Experimental Study," *Speech Monographs,* **XXII** (March 1955), 43–48.

Group-Centered	*Leader-Centered*
2. Leader makes few evaluative statements.	2. Leader freely evaluates the statements of the members and expresses approval or disapproval.
3. Leader is concerned with utilizing all of the human resources of the group and thus encourages all members to participate.	3. Leader makes little apparent effort to bring all members into the discussion so long as he feels that the group is progressing satisfactorily.

Paradoxically, a majority of the discussants in Wischmeier's study felt that the more autocratic leader did the better job, perhaps suggesting that a leader must risk his own reputation as a so-called "dynamic" personality in the interests of group accomplishments. Inevitably some situations arise which seem to demand leadership bordering on the autocratic, but we can be sure when this happens that democratic decision-making has suffered some degree of setback. In general, the more nearly free and democratic the process becomes, the more successfully the discussion progresses. Moreover, discussion on this level requires greater self-discipline, clearer thinking, and more individual effort than is required under more autocratic control.

TYPES OF DISCUSSION

If we consider all modifications of the discussion format, a nearly unlimited variety exists. They range all the way from the informality of the guided conversation to the formality of traditional debate. The audience in some instances consists merely of the discussant, while in other types, spectators may witness and ultimately join in the discussion. Those carried on without a witnessing audience include: *guided conversation, the study group, classroom discussion,* and *the conference.*

The Guided Conversation

Often referred to as *informal discussion,* the guided conversation sometimes emerges from a social situation. During a social gathering a group discovers a problem of mutual concern and resolves to investigate, study, and discuss it together under the direction of a leader. Occasionally, they invite experts or resource persons with special information on the topic to join the group. This does not absolve group members from study and preparation. Moreover, inviting experts may actually turn the meeting into a lecture-forum, thus radically changing the discussion method.

Groups intent on guided conversation may also find it helpful to meet for an organizational session, elect a leader, and subdivide the topic. All members should read and study the subject broadly, but each also should assume individual responsibility for seeking factual information and opinion in special areas. The so-called *study group* and *classroom discussion* often follow the format of the guided conversation. When special experts are added, the discussion is usually referred to as a *colloquium*. Further suggestions for organizing and participating in the *informal discussion* are:

1. a small group numbering twenty or less
2. an informal atmosphere, marked by good fellowship and punctuated with good humor
3. short, spontaneous remarks, preferably a minute or less
4. a leader who keeps the discussion moving by stimulating the shy and reticent while patiently and tactfully discouraging the overtalkative
5. frequent summaries and assessments by the leader or other members to help insure a unified, coordinated discussion
6. avoidance of the temptation to tarry over interesting nonessentials to the exclusion of prosaic essentials.

The Conference

Although the term *conference* is used in various ways, often to describe a convention or the organizational form for ecclesiastical bodies, we are limiting our use of the term to small private discussion groups intent on finding a solution to a common problem. The conferees may seek answers to personal problems or they may attempt to find solutions to problems affecting widely divergent groups. During labor-management disputes the conferees often represent the union, the industry, the government, and the public. Occasionally, conferees with no personal interest in a controversy are selected to insure objectivity. Such is the case when an impartial board of arbiters seeks to settle disputes or make adjustments affecting the welfare of others. Often a major obstacle is the selection of persons satisfactory to all parties in the controversy.

Determinants of a Successful Conference

The successful conference operates in the best tradition of the *round-table discussion*. All members are relatively equal, insuring a balanced group in terms of the potential importance of each participant. If any member sits at the table merely for the sake of form and his point of view is dismissed by common, tacit agreement of opposing members, the conference is unbalanced. If, for example, in a faculty-student conference on campus social problems, the faculty representatives are willing to listen to student suggestions, but have made up their minds in advance to accept no changes, only the superficial appearance of a conference exists. A conference is successful only when all members listen with flexible as well as polite minds. This same "balance of power" must prevail in larger conferences where all legitimate, though divergent points of view, require fair representation.

A successful conference tolerates no inactive members. Each conferee is selected with the expectation that he will contribute substantially to the

Figure 30. The group appears to possess many of the essential characteristics of participants in an effective conference. Concentration, interest, sincerity and a willingness to share ideas are essential to a productive round table discussion.

solution of the problem. Thus, whenever possible the number of participants is kept as small as is consistent with a fair representation of factions and opinions. A group larger than fifteen may lose the air of informality necessary for the easy give-and-take of opinion.

The chairman of the conference must be a respected person, capable of dealing impartially and tactfully with persons holding divergent views. Of great strategic importance is the chairman's timing ability. He must know how to avoid wasting time, and yet not appear to hurry any of the participants into reaching decisions which they may not be ready, either intellectually or emotionally, to make or to accept.

PUBLIC DISCUSSION

The discussions we have considered so far may be thought of as *private* since the participants themselves comprise the audience. Another form with roots deep in American culture is the public discussion held and conducted by one group of participants for the benefit of another group. The listener may be actually present and constitute an audience before whom the speakers carry on their discussion, or he may be at home listening and watching while the discussants appear before a microphone or a television camera. In either case we have *public* rather than *private* discussion.

In most public discussions the participants wish to stir up questions and comments from the audience. Every communicative situation demands a two-way exchange, but in public discussion, the dialogue is usually more audibly vocal than in public speaking. Indeed, the number and the quality of the questions and comments from the audience may well serve as indicators of the success or failure of the discussion. Even in radio and television programs, conducted without a studio audience, the listeners or viewers are often encouraged to phone in their questions. And all of us have caught ourselves during a radio or television program inserting our own comments or continuing the discussion in the family circle.

QUESTIONS FOR DISCUSSION

Current events, social and personal problems, economic crises, and religious, educational, and political events furnish the milieu from which discussion questions develop. Like the topics for a public speech, discussion questions follow the needs and interests of the participants. The audience, if any, should influence the precise selection. The questions themselves are usually classified as *fact, value,* or *policy;* all are possible types for private or public discussion.

1. Questions of Fact.   We sometimes consider questions of fact as poor topics, since in many instances we can consult a source such as the *World Almanac* or an authoritative encyclopedia for the answer. "Has the United States put more Sputniks in orbit than the Soviet Union?" as a discussion topic will probably lead nowhere. On the other hand, a consideration of the question "Are we losing the race for outer space?" calls for a wide assortment of fact and opinion, coupled with a careful analysis and an interpretation of all the available evidence.

2. Questions of Value.   When we discuss questions such as "Is the trimester preferable to the quarter system?" or "Should teenagers go steady?" or "Is desegregation of public housing desirable?" we are dealing with questions of value. We are seeking answers to educational philosophy, standards of personal conduct, moral issues, and the rightness or wrongness of certain practices.

3. Questions of Policy.   Questions of policy usually offer the best avenues for discussion, including in their structure a consideration of subsidiary topics of value and fact. For example, the question "What should be the United States policy in outer space?" will include a consideration of such questions as "Of what scientific value are manned moon flights?" "Can scientific instruments answer all our questions about outer space?" and "Are manned flights employed principally for their circus value?" Before action is taken on any question of policy all the available facts, alternative proposals and possible solutions must be examined and evaluated.

Question Form

It may be noted that all the above subjects were cast as questions rather than as declarative sentences or mere topics. This is important and consistent with the point of view that *inquiry* is a fundamental objective. While a profitable discussion might ensue from such topics as "Progressive Education," "Outer Space," and "The Common Market," the question form helps delineate, prescribes the limits, and points toward a specific area of investigation. The declarative sentence or proposition "the Free Nations should form an economic community" implies debate or advocacy rather than inquiry.

Timely or Timeless Questions

Questions concerning outer space and manned flights to the moon are comparatively recent topics but will probably remain timely for years. The timeless questions are in a somewhat different class, for example, "How can we best avoid economic depression?" and "What is the best education for good citizenship?" In picking the timeless question, the group must make sure that the relevance of the subject is as apparent to the audience as it is to the discussants. The study group may thrill to new revelations about the philosophy of Spinoza, but the topic would offer special problems in timeliness for a public discussion. Problems demanding immediate answers—for example, "which of the candidates shall this city select for the town council?"—will usually promote a lively, stimulating session.

Provocative Questions with Widespread Popular Appeal

Questions for discussion should be controversial, thought-provoking and of genuine interest to the audience as well as to the speakers. Sometimes questions are of concern to selected audiences with specialized interests. "How can the curriculum of X College be vitalized?" is probably of greater concern to the students, teachers and administrators of that institution than to the general public. The skill and insight of the program planners into the concerns and needs of the group will determine the success or failure of the discussion.

Clear, Precise, Fair Phraseology

Lengthy, double-barrelled, involved questions lead to confusion rather than to understanding and thought. "How can the government promote the development of communication satellites and should they ultimately be turned over to private enterprise?" is a two-pronged question and is better stated as two separate questions for purposes of discussion. "Should we adopt a radical program of socialized medicine?" not only begs the question with two loaded adjectives, "radical" and "socialized," but also implies a yes or no response, usually leading to debate rather than to inquiry. If stated, "How can we best meet the health needs of our citizens?" the door opens to a fair discussion of voluntary and compulsory health insurance and their various modifications.

SETTING THE STAGE

The *procedures* and the precise *form* of public discussion are determined by the purpose of the meeting and the size and nature of the audience. The following techniques, as a means of stimulating, coordinating, and promoting group action, often prove helpful.

Physical Arrangements. Beyond hiring the hall and publicizing the meeting, someone must take the responsibility for arranging the tables and chairs to provide maximum audience viewing and participation. The "theatrical" elements in public discussion make it imperative that the planners and participants recognize and utilize the dramatic possibilities in each type of discussion.

Warm-up Sessions and Advanced Planning. Although participants in public discussion are selected because of their special knowledge in a particular field, prior planning is necessary to coordinate and insure a meaningful and organized presentation. In the panel discussion and symposium, participants should meet in advance to set up an outline and clarify the divisions of the question.

Balanced Participation. Lodges, church groups, industrial organizations, and various closed groups sometimes employ discussion to indoctrinate the membership. We would warn that discussion under any circumstances may prove a poor propaganda tool, since heretical doctrines may inevitably intrude. We consider indoctrination as the basic purpose of public discussion to be an inappropriate if not unethical practice. Those in charge of a discussion have an obligation to make certain that all points of view are fairly represented.

Promotional Devices. An imaginative planning board or chairman can devise various means to promote a lively discussion and stimulate audience interest and participation. Film strips, movies, case studies, role-playing, or recordings coordinated skillfully with the chairman's opening remarks often help to dramatize the problem and stimulate the discussion.

FORMS OF DISCUSSION

Although the varieties of form in public discussion are unlimited, most follow one of four basic patterns that we shall consider. These are the *panel,* the *symposium,* the *lecture-forum,* and the *buzz session.* In a public-speaking exercise, you may already have participated in a lecture-forum if a question period followed one of your speeches.

The Panel

The panel is a guided conversation held in the presence of an audience. The speakers, usually two to six in number, are highly interested persons possessing special information on some phase of the problem. Seated on a platform in full and easy view of the audience, the panelists, under the direction of the chairman, engage in conversation among themselves, but expressly for the benefit of the audience. Indeed, during most panel discussions the audience is ultimately invited to ask questions or to make comments. In a brief introductory talk the chairman outlines the procedures and introduces the topic and panelists to the audience. Since each panel member usually develops a special aspect or point of view relative to the topic, he may outline this theme in a short opening statement. The dangers of this procedure sometimes offset the advantages by turning the panel into a symposium and thereby destroying the spontaneity and conversational informality of the discussion.

The *objectives of the panel* are to give the audience a better understanding of the problem under discussion and in some cases to encourage

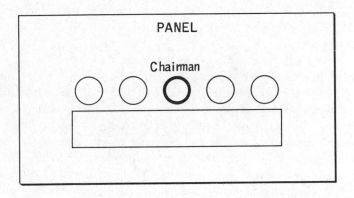

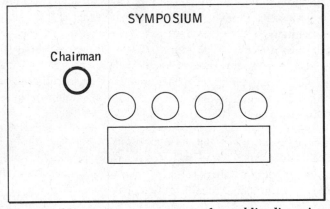

Figure 31. Possible seating arrangements for public discussions employing the panel or the symposium. A lectern is often preferable to the table in the symposium.

them to consider possible courses of action relative to the problem. The panelists may feel the need to fight their way through to some definite conclusions. More often, however, they are content with the creation of audience concern and the clarification of preliminary information about the problem. An incidental but still exceedingly important contribution of a panel is to help persons realize that well-informed speakers may entertain different points of view and maintain respect for one another despite their differences.

The *chairman* bears a major responsibility for the success of the panel. His duties include:

1. Creating a friendly, informal atmosphere conducive to a lively, good-natured discussion.
2. Clarifying procedures for the panelists and the audience.
3. Guiding tactfully the discussion toward previously established goals.
4. Phrasing questions designed to probe and draw out discussion on unexamined areas.
5. Keeping panelists aware of the audience.
6. Sensing the opportune time to open the discussion to the audience. (Spaced suggestions, implying later audience participation often help. "In a few moments a member of our audience may want to comment or question us about the statistics we've just presented." No sharp break in the discussion need occur at the point of audience participation.)
7. Recognizing himself as the prober, organizer, mediator—not as the chief contributor, authority, or source of all wisdom. (The discussion should move easily and freely among panelists with no necessity for formal recognition of each speaker. If the chairman enters the conversation after each contribution, the discussion session may be considered a failure.)
8. Alleviating hostilities if they arise through tact and possibly through self-directed humor.
9. Sustaining a clear, purposeful discussion by encouraging speakers to summarize the outstanding points as they develop. (The chairman may summarize or encourage other panel members to assume some of this responsibility. He should not, however, call on any member to summarize without a forewarning.)

The *panelists* share the major responsibility for the substance of the discussion. The chairman's burden is considerably lightened if the speakers assist him in carrying out their roles.

The duties of the panel members include:

1. Preparation and research no less thorough than is required of the public speaker. (In some respects, the panelist, if he performs well, faces a more demanding task than the public speaker; for he is required to shift, adapt, and integrate his ideas with those of four or five other persons.)
2. An understanding of the dramatic elements in the panel discussion. (Too many panels become oppressively dull because members seem unaware of the audience and of the necessity to "appear" interested, alive, and alert. The danger of underplaying is far greater than any tendency to "ham it up.")

3. Recognition of the need for vocal projection and more precise diction.

4. Skill in speaking fluently and translating technical concepts into readily understandable words.

5. Tact, a sense of humor, and a willingness to engage in a controversial discussion without losing his good nature.

Audience Participation: The Forum.   Ultimately during the panel discussion the audience is invited to participate. They may direct questions to the speakers or submit their comments. No formal break need occur between the so-called panelists' portion of the program and the wider discussion including the audience. Indeed, the moment for audience participation will be determined by the interest of the audience and the awareness of the chairman to audience desires and his sense of timing. The chairman continues to direct and coordinate the discussion and recognizes the speakers from the audience. He may have to rule tactfully on the relevance of questions, reword if necessary, and sometimes direct them to specific panel members. At the conclusion of the forum the chairman should make a final statement, informally and briefly summarizing the areas covered.

The Symposium

The major distinguishing feature of the symposium is its reliance on set speeches, carefully prepared in advance. Usually, three or four experts prepare five-to-ten-minute speeches on a specific phase of a general topic. Following the presentation of the prepared speeches, the speakers may enter into informal discussion, questioning and cross-questioning each other. Eventually, the audience is invited to participate in a forum, in which questions are directed to individual speakers.

The questions asked by audience members usually fall into one of three categories:

1. those calling for more detailed explanation or further information from a speaker

2. those intended to give a speaker who is in essential agreement with the questioner an opportunity to expand or support an argument already stated

3. those intended to reveal weaknesses in the arguments of a speaker with whom the questioner is in disagreement.

The *objectives* of the symposium are similar to those of the panel. In general, the purpose is either to provide the audience with information or to give the listeners an opportunity to consider and compare the merits of two or more solutions to a problem. The symposium is better adapted to larger audiences and is conducive to a more orderly, formal presentation than is the panel.

The *success* of the symposium, like that of the panel, is determined largely by what has taken place during the preparatory stages. Usually, a number of interested persons engage in the preliminary planning. Items they should consider include:

1. The choice and wording of a topic most likely to arouse audience interest. Questions often need to receive headline treatment. Instead of the prosaic "How can we best meet the medical needs of all our citizens?" a more lively and provocative title might read "Is your health the nation's business?"

2. Deciding on the basis of audience knowledge whether the objective should be to provide information or to consider the relative merits of solutions to a controversial issue.

3. The selection of speakers who can best contribute to the achievement of the objectives of the symposium. Care should be exercised to insure adequate, fair, and balanced representation to all points of view.

4. The selection of a chairman acceptable to all factions and completely familiar with the discussion method and the precise techniques of the symposium.

5. Giving the chairman and the speakers an opportunity to become acquainted with one another as well as with the nature, objectives, and plan of the meeting.

The *duties of the chairman of a symposium* resemble in some respects those of the panel chairman. They include:

1. Presiding at the meeting. [This responsibility involves (a) a short, provocative introduction of the general topic; (b) an explanation of the ground rules, governing time limits and audience participation; (c) introducing each speaker; (d) making certain the rules and time limits are observed; and (e) recognizing members of the audience.]

2. Unifying the discussion by pointing up relationships between the speeches.

3. Eliciting questions and statements during the forum which will direct attention to different aspects of the problem.

4. Restating inaudible audience questions and rewording them when the meaning is obscure.

5. Concluding the meeting according to the prearranged schedule with a summary that ties together the main ideas in the discussion.

Lecture-Forum

The lecture-forum is perhaps the most widely used type of public discussion, probably because it requires less preplanning by fewer individuals than any other type. It is also the least likely to generate a profitable discussion. It consists of a prepared lecture by a specialist, followed by audience questions. A chairman usually presides over the meeting, introducing the speaker and conducting the forum period.

If it were possible for people with formed opinions to be completely objective, the lecture-forum might be an excellent way of presenting points of view as well as information on a controversial problem. Because objectivity is difficult if not virtually impossible to achieve once a speaker has formed an opinion, the listeners will likely hear a talk weighted or slanted toward the speaker's private opinion. Some discussion clubs remedy this problem by securing a series of speakers for successive meetings, each representing a different point of view on the same subject.

Some of the following suggestions will help to stimulate a profitable discussion during the forum period.

1. The sponsoring organization should select a chairman who is alert to the dangers and possibilities inherent in the lecture-forum.

2. In his introduction of the speaker, the chairman should create an atmosphere conducive to discussion by alerting the audience to the forum period and inviting them to formulate their questions during the lecture period. Cards distributed in advance to the listener-participants may help them remember to write out their questions.

3. The chairman should design his own questions to point up areas of controversy.

4. In advance of the meeting the chairman might encourage various members to come prepared to ask questions. Once the ice is broken, audience questions usually flow freely.

5. The chairman should formulate a plan for the forum period designed to promote discussion of the significant points and prevent aimless wandering.

The advantage of the lecture-forum is the ease of arrangement. The disadvantages are its lack of objectivity and the dangers inherent in loose structuring. These include the possibilities of no questions, poor questions, and "sounding off" speeches rather than questions. The result may be a dull, random discussion period involving no real group thinking. A good speaker may occasionally "save the day" by saying, "If I were a member of the audience, I would ask this question. . . ."

Buzz Sessions

Often called "Phillips 66 buzz session" and named for its originator J. D. Phillips, this specialized technique is often employed with large groups as a method of stimulating the widest possible participation.[3] Although

<hr>

[3] See J. D. Phillips, "Report on Discussion 66," *Adult Educational Journal,* **VII** (October 1948), 181–182.

numerous variations in method are possible, buzz sessions usually follow this pattern.

1. During the introduction the chairman explains the discussion procedure and outlines the problem. His remarks may be followed with a panel, a symposium, or one or two experts who supply background information. From this discussion a single, specifically stated question such as "What is the most important contribution of X organization to our community?" is placed before the whole assembly.

2. The audience is divided into clusters of six persons who merely shift their chairs closer together and then take six minutes to find as many answers as possible. Speed is of utmost importance, so groups quickly select the chairman and secretary and proceed immediately to formulate their answers.

3. After six minutes the general chairman calls for order and asks each group spokesman (secretary or chairman) to submit a one-minute report of its answers. These are usually synthesized and recorded on a blackboard. Discussion then may continue, involving a selected panel or the whole audience. The leader continues to direct and integrate the discussion.

Obviously, the buzz session demands a leader who has planned the whole program with meticulous care—a person with contagious enthusiasm and one possessing a thorough familiarity with the entire discussion process. It likewise demands a high degree of homogeneity in the participating group. A primary virtue of the buzz session is the stimulus it offers toward 100 per cent participation in a large group. Further, the atmosphere of informality tends to carry over to the larger group, thus setting the stage for a lively discussion. Its drawbacks include the time-consuming process of explaining and setting up the mechanics of the program and the dangers of superficial answers based on less than adequate information.

LIMITATIONS OF DISCUSSION

Discussion is a mode of speaking—and thinking and living—possible only in a democracy. Its characteristics, basic philosophy, and limitations are also those of a democracy. Discussion is often slow and time-consuming. It does not always enable people to arrive at decisions or to formulate a course of action. It gives persons with limited knowledge a chance to talk. (Fortunately, it also gives them a chance to learn.) Discussions and the behavior of people taking part in them are unpredictable and sometimes unpleasant. What happens cannot always be anticipated. Most of these criticisms are probably valid. But they are criticisms of the characteristics inherent in a democratic society.

Even the most enthusiastic advocate of discussion would hesitate to recommend the full discussion process from investigation to consensus as the best method for emergency action. Times of crisis may demand quick action under the direction of a person recognized as superior in a given situation. But even during the Cuban crisis in the Fall of 1962, President Kennedy and his advisors engaged in lengthy discussion before making the decision to set up the blockade. We can conclude that some emergency situations cannot wait for complete or even partial consensus. Often the leader must take action (or no action) opposing at times the best judgment of some members.

Discussion, because of its relative informality, often makes sustained and logical presentation of argument difficult. Listeners wishing to hear a concise and orderly presentation of argument either in favor of or in opposition to a proposition are not likely to get it in discussion. Neither are they likely to be presented with clear-cut alternatives to a recommended course of action. When action is necessary and the group has failed during the discussion to reach a general agreement and they wish to hear or engage in argument pro-and-con on a specific possible course, the time for preliminary discussion has ended and we are ready for debate.

SUMMARY

As contrasted with social conversation, discussion demands careful planning, skilled leadership, and intensive preparation by the participants. The purpose of discussion may be to impart information to an audience or to seek solutions to problems in any area vital to the participants and to any observers present.

Ideally, the process of decision-making through discussion closely approximates the scientific method, including *location, definition,* and *exploration* of the problem, coupled with the *examination* and *selection* of the best solution.

Discussion may occur on a private level in *guided conversation, study groups, classroom* discussion, and the *conference.* Many forms and variations appear in public discussion, the most common being the *panel, symposium, lecture-forum,* and *buzz session.* The nature of the proposition under consideration and the size and circumstances of the meeting will help determine the most appropriate type of discussion form.

QUESTIONS AND EXERCISES

1. If you were going to set up a discussion program for an audience of 700 persons, which type of format (i.e., panel, symposium, lecture-forum, buzz

session) would you employ? Be prepared to defend your choice. What special circumstances would influence your selection?

2. Divide the class into groups of four to six and let each group pick a topic suitable for a panel discussion. The instructor or the group may wish to designate one person in each group to serve as the leader. If possible, record the panel discussion and then ask each participant to criticize the discussion according to the following factors:

    (a) Was the chairman successful in keeping the discussion organized?

    (b) Which member or members of the group offered the best contributions?

    (c) If you were to use this same topic again for a panel discussion, what changes would you make in your preparation and participation?

3. After your experience in the panel discussion, what qualities do you consider most necessary for the leader?

4. Listen to a radio or television discussion program. Can you classify it according to any of the types mentioned in this chapter? Would another format have accomplished the purpose more satisfactorily? Were the major points of view adequately represented?

5. Select the campus issue you consider most timely and most desperately in need of a satisfactory solution. If you were to organize a public discussion on this question, what kind of discussion form would you employ? Who would you select as the leader? Participants? Be prepared to defend your selections.

6. Take the five steps in the process of reflective thinking and break each one into three subheadings. For example, under the second step, "Exploring the problem," you might include: (a) the causes of this problem, (b) the economic factors, and (c) the political nature of the situation.

7. Select a general topic for discussion. Phrase the topic into a discussion question for a symposium. In a one-minute speech explain and defend your phraseology.

8. Attend a lecture-forum and then write a short paper in which you discuss and evaluate the following:

    (a) The moderator's introduction of the topic and the speaker.

    (b) The question and answer period. Did the moderator use any devices to encourage questions? Was the speaker clear in formulating his answers? To what extent, if any, did the moderator participate?

    (c) Summaries. Did the speaker or moderator summarize at any point? Was the summary helpful?

9. Select a topic of current public interest or campus concern and assume that you will serve as the chairman of a panel preparing to discuss this question. In outline form set up the specific subtopics and the order you would attempt to follow during the discussion. In a short speech be prepared to defend your selection of the subtopics and the order.

RECOMMENDED READINGS

Bryant, Donald C., and Wallace, Karl R. *Fundamentals of Public Speaking*. New York: Appleton-Century-Crofts, 1960, Chaps. 25 and 26.

Cartwright, Dorwin and Zander, Alvin (eds.). *Group Dynamics: Research and Theory*. New York: Harper and Row, 1960.

Cortright, Rupert, and Hinds, George L. *Creative Discussion*. New York: Macmillan, 1959.

Ewbank, Henry L., and Auer, J. Jeffery. *Discussion and Debate*. New York: Appleton-Century-Crofts, 1951, Chaps. 15, 16, 17, 18, 19, 20, 21 and 22.

Howell, William S., and Smith, Donald K. *Discussion*. New York: Macmillan, 1956.

Keltner, John W. *Group Discussion Processes*. New York: Longmans, Green, 1957.

Utterback, William E. *Group Thinking and Conference Leadership*. New York: Holt, Rinehart and Winston, 1950.

Walter, Otis M., and Scott, Robert L. *Thinking and Speaking: A Guide to Intelligent Oral Communication*. New York: Macmillan, 1962, Chap. 13.

White, Eugene E. *Practical Speech Fundamentals*. New York: Macmillan, 1960, Chaps. 18 and 19.

CHAPTER 12

DEBATE

*It's better to debate a question without settling
it than to settle a question without debating it.*
JOSEPH JOUBERT

On September 26, 1960, for the first time in history, the two leading
candidates for the office of President of the United States met in face to
face debate. An estimated audience of seventy million watched and listened
as Senator John F. Kennedy and Vice-President Richard M. Nixon outlined the issues, submitted to cross-examination, and engaged in refutation
and rebuttal. They were unconcerned with the preliminary stages of discussion, namely, the investigation of all possible solutions. Each man thought
or at least behaved (spoke) as if he thought that his party had discovered
the right answer, and each was feverishly attempting to persuade the American electorate to accept his party's choice as the commander-in-chief for the
next four years.[1]

When the citizens of the nation approach a moment of decision, either
on a national (with international implications) or on a local level (striving
to solve a water supply problem or determining methods of raising funds),
the citizens may engage in a long series of discussions, perhaps calling in
experts to define as well as help to solve their problems. The community
may examine a wide variety of solutions. But eventually the citizens directly,
or their representatives must exercise their choice and make some decision.
In one community a discussion of the city's financial plight reached the
referendum stage and the voters ultimately decided the fate of the proposition: "Resolved, That a 1 per cent gross income tax be levied on all residents." Citizens' committees for and against soon sprang up and the
articulate argued the question informally at homes, at places of business, and

---

[1] See *The Great Debates,* Sidney Kraus (ed.), Bloomington: Indiana University
Press, 1962, for a thorough analysis. The Gallup Poll estimated eighty-five million heard
at least one of the debates (*idem,* p. 148.)

at service clubs. A few days before the election two representatives for each side clashed in public debate, attempting to persuade the electorate to cast their ballots for or against the new tax.

During any discussion a considerable amount of the talk approximates debate. Even in the panel or conference the discussants may proceed through the process of reflective thinking, engage in an informal debate, and ultimately select one solution to the problem. We need to recognize that no sharp dividing line separates discussion from debate. These are not two distinctively and diametrically opposed concepts, but essentially an intermixture of two complementary elements of one process—democratic decision making.

NATURE OF DEBATING

When persons seeking a solution to a problem have reached a point in their consideration where they are prepared to hear arguments *for* and *against* a specific proposal, they are ready for debate. We may define formal debate then as a clean-cut, pro-and-con argument between two persons or sides who are advocating a specific proposal for the solution of a problem. One side—the affirmative—supports or argues for (affirms) the proposition. The other side—the negative—argues against (denies) the proposition.

If we analyze the thinking process taking place *before* a group is ready for action, four fundamental characteristics of discussion and debate become apparent:

1. In discussion we usually begin with a problem and, through group thinking, strive toward a solution. When the group fails to reach a general agreement or a consensus during their discussion and the membership is clearly divided in its acceptance of a solution, the moment for debate has arrived.

2. Formal debate may then be the final step in the process of reflective thinking.

3. Debate begins with a proposed solution; a discussion member turns debater after he has selected a solution and is prepared to support it with evidence and argument.

4. We usually phrase the solution as a resolution, a proposition, or a motion. In formal debate a proposition is always explicitly stated.

THE PROPOSITION

In discussion we are usually concerned with a general question, for example, "What kind of sewage disposal system is best for our town?" The topic implies general dissatisfaction with present arrangements. After a thorough investigation, including, perhaps, expert analysis, several solutions may claim our attention. Additional discussion may produce a specific point of view, stated in declarative form and constituting the proposition "Resolved, That a chemical disposal plant be constructed for the purpose of sewage disposal." At this point speakers line up their evidence and arguments for and against a definitely stated point of view. Like discussion questions, debate propositions may concern *fact, value,* or *policy.* "Joe Smith murdered his wife" (fact). "Free enterprise is preferable to socialism" (value). "The United States should extend diplomatic recognition to the communist government of China" (policy).

Effective debating requires a good proposition, recognized by the following qualities:

1. *Debatable.* A proposition is debatable when it has two clear-cut sides. Unless sufficient evidence and argument permit individuals of intelligence and integrity to take opposing sides, the proposition is undebatable.

2. *Complete assertion.* A good proposition demands a complete assertion. A phrase or term such as "Compulsory Health Insurance" is incomplete and not debatable. The statement "Resolved, That the United States should adopt a program of compulsory health insurance for all citizens" is complete and debatable.

3. *Brevity.* A good proposition is stated in as brief a form as possible without sacrificing clarity. The following is an overworded proposition: "Resolved, That subsidies on agricultural products of American farmers be continued for the welfare of the United States as a whole and for the economic betterment of the farmers." The same proposition is more briefly and effectively worded: "Resolved, That subsidies on American farm products be continued."

4. *Single.* Avoid multipropositional statements. A good proposition necessarily centers about a single problem. We should not, for example, attempt to include a nuclear test ban, peaceful uses of atomic energy, and general disarmament in one question. Although these problems are closely related, only one should appear in the phrasing of a proposition.

5. *Affirmative.* A good proposition is stated *declaratively* and asserts the position of the affirmative. The affirmative argues for a change in the existing state of affairs. It recommends the establishment or the abolition of a situation depending upon existing conditions. For example, students at a college with intercollegiate football might debate the question "Resolved, That intercollegiate football be dropped at X College." At another school without intercollegiate football, the proposition would be stated: "Resolved, That intercollegiate football be established at Y College."

6. *Impartial.* Keep the proposition free from emotional, question-

begging terms which give special advantage to either side. We should avoid, for example, a wordy one such as "Resolved, That the United States should stop poisoning the atmosphere and condemning unborn generations to untold misery by unilaterally stopping all further testing of nuclear weapons." So stated, the proposition argues the case for the affirmative. A fairer statement might be "Resolved, That the United States should unilaterally stop all further testing of nuclear weapons."

ARGUING THE PROPOSITION

Before the debaters appear in public, they face the intensive demands of analyzing the question and finding the evidence with which to build the strongest possible cases. The initial preparation requires both sides to perform the following tasks:

1. *Definition of all terms.* Even if the proposition is clearly stated and free from technical jargon, we can save needless talk in discussion and debate by defining our terms. Unless all words and phrases appearing in the debate are clear and mutually acceptable to both sides, it is impossible to grapple with the major issues themselves.

2. *Determining the specific issues.* Issues are like swinging doors, opening the way to both the affirmative and negative cases. Correctly phrased they pose questions to which the affirmative always answers yes and the negative usually answers no. In propositions of policy, the affirmative must establish the validity of all the so-called *stock issues:*

(a) Is there a need to change our present policy? Is the body politic sick?

(b) Will the change recommended by the affirmative remedy the condition? Will this remedy effect a cure?

(c) Is the proposed change practicable and workable? Is this "wonder drug" free from harmful side effects?

(d) Is the proposed change the best available solution? Is this cure better than any other possible remedy?

(e) Will additional benefits result from the adoption of the affirmative proposal? Will this remedy also serve as a tonic?

The stock issues are valuable to both the affirmative and negative mainly in the early stages of analysis. During the debate itself, the skillful debater avoids talking about the "need" and "our plan," phrasing each issue according to the specific proposition he is debating. On the question "Resolved, That Congress should be given the power to reverse decisions of the Supreme Court," the first stock issue (NEED) might include: "Has a small group of nonelected men usurped legislative functions, thereby thwarting the will of the people?" Since the proposition in this instance does not spell out the means of congressional reversal, the affirmative must also present a specific plan. They might advocate the overriding of Court decisions by a two-thirds vote of the Congress. If the question were on the abolition of capital punishment, the affirmative plan is included in the statement itself. The affirmative must establish (prove) the validity of all the issues. The negative may deny (rebut) all the issues or it may admit some and refute others.

Burden of Proof and Burden of Rebuttal

Since the affirmative is the complaining party, it must accept the burden of proving its indictment of the *status quo* (present situation). It must also demonstrate that its proposal will satisfactorily remedy the ailment. Logically, unless a protesting voice is raised, the audience is obliged to accept the affirmative proposal. The negative, then, must assume the burden of rebuttal. In meeting this responsibility, it enjoys a wider range of choices than the affirmative, who must keep its complete fortress intact during the entire debate. The negative on the other hand, may concentrate its fire on the weakest bulwark (issue), and if that issue fails, the affirmative loses the debate.

Possible Negative Stands

The negative may reject the entire affirmative case, denying the existence of a problem and perhaps even maintaining that were one to exist, the affirmative program still would not work. Or the negative may recognize some weaknesses in the present structure, but insist that a few minor changes will remedy the problem. Using a different tack, the negative may admit the evils in the present system, but insist that the affirmative measure will not correct the ills. Further, the negative may brand the affirmative cure as worse than the illness. While the negative speakers are under no obligation to present a remedy, even when they share the affirmative's distaste for the present system, they may find it advantageous to offer a *counterproposal*. The negative then assumes the burden of proof and must demonstrate that the counterplan not only is superior to the affirmative remedy but also cannot under the statement of the proposition be adopted by the affirmative. On the Supreme Court question, for example, a negative proposal to permit three-fourths instead of two-thirds of the Congress to override the Court is not a counterplan. The affirmative would simply agree with the negative and win the debate under the statement of the proposition. On the other hand, President Franklin D. Roosevelt's proposal to increase the membership of the Supreme Court as a way of insuring his legislative program would constitute a counterplan, albeit, as Roosevelt discovered, not a popular one.

TYPES OF DEBATE

Formal Debate

In traditional, formal debate, an equal number of speakers, usually two, support each side. The speaking order and time limits usually follow this pattern.

Constructive Speeches

First affirmative	10 minutes
First negative	10 minutes
Second affirmative	10 minutes
Second negative	10 minutes

Rebuttal Speeches

First negative	5 minutes
First affirmative	5 minutes
Second negative	5 minutes
Second affirmative	5 minutes

To meet various audience situations, it is possible to employ a multitude of forms, including problem-solving debate, heckling debate, debate-forums, two-man debate, documentary debate, and courtroom debate.[2] The most commonly used variations are the following:

Cross-Examination Debate

Sometimes called the Oregon Plan because of its development at the University of Oregon,[3] it gives each speaker an opportunity to cross-examine the opposition and in turn to submit to cross-examination. Except for the first affirmative, the speakers step from cross-examination to the

---

[2] Most standard texts in argumentation and debate include complete explanations of each type. See H. L. Ewbank and J. J. Auer, *Discussion and Debate,* New York: Appleton-Century-Crofts, 1951, pp. 394–404; and Austin J. Freeley, *Argumentation and Debate,* San Francisco: Wadsworth, 1961, pp. 305–324.

[3] J. S. Gray, "The Oregon Plan of Debating," *Quarterly Journal of Speech Education,* **XII** (April 1926), 175–180.

speaker's stand for their constructive speeches. A typical debate appears as follows:

Speeches	Minutes
1. First affirmative speech	8
2. First negative cross-examines first affirmative	4
3. First negative speech	8
4. Second affirmative cross-examines first negative	4
5. Second affirmative speech	8
6. Second negative cross-examines second affirmative	4
7. Second negative speech	8
8. First affirmative cross-examines second negative	4
9. Negative summary (either speaker)	4
10. Affirmative summary (either speaker)	4
Total time	58

Aptly designed for audience situations, the cross-examination debate insures close attention through the rapid give and take and the opportunity for direct clashes of the participants. Indeed, the debaters need to recognize and may exploit all the legitimate dramatic elements inherent in this type of speaking. But a word of caution is in order too! They must guard against the emotionally histrionic exhibition that plumbs the depths of *argumentum ad hominem* and descends to mere bickering and browbeating. Below are some suggestions for the cross-examination debater:

1. Intensive preparation and practice to insure clear, relevant, well-phrased questions.

2. Questions concentrated on one issue rather than scattered over the whole case.

3. Questions phrased to elicit short responses, preferably yes or no.

4. Questions designed to expose feeble evidence or specious reasoning.

5. A realization that the cross-examiner must know the answers to all his questions. He is not seeking information, but attempting to establish or weaken a contention.

6. Little or no editorial comment from the cross-examiner.

7. A close integration of the answers revealed during cross-examination with the development of the constructive speeches. (Too often the cross-

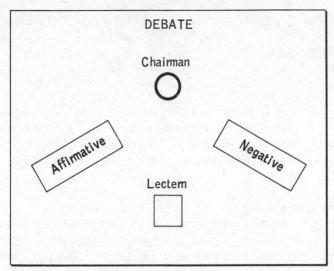

Figure 32. A typical platform arrangement for the cross-examination or the formal debate.

examination and the constructive argument bear little relationship to each other.)

Direct Clash Debate

This modification encourages a careful analysis of the specific issues and promotes a direct pro-and-con consideration of one issue at a time. Using a traditional debate question and two to five persons on a side, the procedure is as follows:

1. *The analysis period.* With the affirmative opening the debate, each side takes six minutes to clarify its stand on *definitions, major issues, plans,* and *counterplans.* The purpose of the initial speeches is to clarify the issues and determine those on which both teams agree to clash. If necessary both sides may have an additional three-minute speech to support its analysis. Neither team needs to use all of its time, and the only evidence introduced is to establish the validity of definitions or the importance of the issues. It helps at this stage to place all the issues on the blackboard.

2. *The judge's evaluation.* The judge then comments on the issues, definitions, and plan, suggesting any necessary clarifications. He may select the issues for the clashes or permit teams to choose their own from the accepted list.

3. *The clashes.* The affirmative initiates the first clash with a four-minute speech designed to establish an issue. A negative speaker follows with a two-minute answer. Alternating two-minute clashes continue until

each side has spoken an agreed number of times or until the judge declares one side the victor. In the second clash, the negative initiates the issue with a four-minute speech and concludes the clash with the final two-minute speech. The affirmative opens and closes the last clash and the team winning two out of three wins the debate.

Clearly, this style of debate places a premium on issue analysis, direct adaptation, incisive, extempore speaking, and immediate refutation. Indeed, when a team fails to answer directly or adequately the judge is asked to stop a clash and award the decision to the other side.[4]

Parliamentary Debate

This modification of traditional British debating provides a stimulating type for classes, literary societies, and forensic organizations. The Oberlin College Forensic Union regularly uses this form to introduce the membership to a new topic and to give all members maximum opportunity to speak briefly to the proposition. Presumably, all participants have studied the question in advance. The procedure is as follows:

1. As members enter the room, those favoring the motion sit to the chairman's right and those opposing to his left. The chairman calls for order, announces the motion, e.g., "This House Would Rather Be Red Than Dead," and introduces the first speaker who has seven minutes in which to support the motion.

2. The chairman presents a speaker for the opposition who likewise has seven minutes. He is followed by pro-and-con seconding speeches of three minutes each.

3. The chairman then recognizes speakers from the floor, alternately for and against the motion, who may speak for not more than three minutes.

4. Any speaker except the first may be interrupted "on a point of information." The speaker may refuse to answer or even give a member the chance to ask his questions.

5. Only the following points of order are permitted: objections to irrelevant remarks; objections to unsuitable language; objections to behavior of a member.

6. At the end of a specified time, eighty or ninety minutes, the chairman recognizes speakers for the final summaries, first against and then for the motion. Each side has two minutes.

7. The chairman calls for a division of the house (vote) announces the winner and adjourns the meeting.

---

[4] J. Garber Drushal, "Direct Clash Debate as a Teaching Procedure," *The Gavel*, **41** (November 1958), 5–6, 14, 16.

Obviously, this style of debating requires a chairman with a heavy gavel and a complete knowledge of parliamentary procedure. It helps speakers develop a facile, extemporaneous style. There is a danger, however, that it may also encourage the speakers to count on and to develop verbal facility rather than to concentrate on the essentials of research and an analysis of the issues.

PREPARATION FOR DEBATE

Everything we have said up to this point should help you prepare for a specific debate. Presumably, before taking sides, you engage in serious inquiry, examining the problem and the various solutions. After the selection of a proposition, you then face the task of developing a unified case and a speech that is coordinated with the constructive argument of your partner. These additional suggestions should prove helpful.

Investigate Both Sides

No debater is completely prepared to defend his own position until he thoroughly understands the arguments of the opposition. He must, therefore, find all the evidence (facts, opinion, motivations) supporting every possible contention on both sides of the question. Finally, he must concentrate on discovering all the available proof for his own contentions. Unhappily, too many debaters place their faith in unsupported assertion, developing arguments and drawing conclusions based on inadequate or faulty evidence. While the affirmative must prove its indictment of the status quo, *every debater, affirmative and negative, must assume the burden of proof for all of his assertions.* To assert with vigor or vehemence is not enough.

Record the Evidence

The old-fashioned picture of debate teams lugging huge stacks of books to the tables prior to the debate, while quaintly romantic, probably served no useful purpose. A better method is to devise a uniform system of note-taking, following a prearranged format satisfactorily to both debaters. Then as the debate progresses, each can exchange readily understandable items of evidence. Each debater should develop a consistent system of note-taking, perhaps like those shown in Figure 33, which can also serve as a useful research tool for any type of public speaking. The first item is an example of *evidence of opinion* and the second, *evidence of fact*.

Subject: Impact of the Common Market, E.E.C. on U.S. economy	Author: Louis Cassels	Title: Management skill will determine our future	Source: Nation's Business, 50 (May 1962), pp. 34–5.

H. Ladd Plumley, President of State Mutual Life Assurance Company and President of the U.S. Chamber of Commerce, is quoted as saying: "Tariff adjustments . . . are necessary . . . if the United States is to become a trading partner rather than an outmatched competitor of the powerful new Common Market which has emerged in Western Europe."

Subject: Hospital cost per patient day	Author:	Title: Source Book of Health Insurance Data, 1959	Source: Health Insurance Institute, New York, N.Y., p. 52

According to the American Hospital Association the cost per patient day in nonfederal, short-term general and special hospitals was:

Year	Average cost per patient day
1946	$ 9.39
1952	18.35
1958	28.17

These figures exclude psychiatric and tuberculosis hospitals.

Figure 33. A typical system of note-taking.

During your research keep the following rules in mind:

1. The above form represents only one of many ways to record evidence of fact and opinion. It is important, however, for teams to select a precise form and adhere strictly to it. *Be consistent in your note taking.*

2. Select a uniform sized card (4×6 or 6×8). A 3×5 card is usually too small.

3. Place *one item* only on each card.

4. Use your own words whenever possible. Save direct quotation for

authorities whose opinions carry real weight and whose words and phrases are in themselves impellingly persuasive.

5. Be sure to set off direct quotations with the appropriate marks. For your own words within a quotation, use brackets.

6. Identify the author and source. For many audiences, one name and source is just like another. Simply because a writer made a statement and had it published does not give it the weight of actual authority. Establish the basis for the authoritativeness of your source.

Formulate a Complete Brief

The name *brief* seems to be a contradiction in terms since it is far from short or lacking in length. It is the debater's complete logical outline of all the contentions on one side of the question. It likewise includes all the evidence of fact and opinion, placed in proper logical relationship to each premise or contention. It is not intended as the speaker's outline for his debate speech. If the speakers followed the complete brief for their presentations, their speeches would be stiff and colorless. We shall cover the "debate speech" in the following section of the chapter. Additional helps on outlining the actual speech are in the chapter on Synthesis and Organization (see pages 329–336).

The following briefs were developed for a new variation in forensic competition, designated by its originator, J. Garber Drushal of the College of Wooster, as *Appellate Debate*. Students from Wooster and Oberlin Colleges introduced this new type of debating at the Symposium of the North east Ohio Debate Conference held at Oberlin on October 10, 1959.

Prior to the debate each team submitted its four-page brief to the opposing team and to a panel of three judges. The format, patterned after legal debate as used in the appellate courts, was organized as follows:

First affirmative	15 minutes
First negative	15 minutes
Second affirmative	12 minutes
Second negative	12 minutes
Negative rebuttal	5 minutes
Affirmative rebuttal	5 minutes

The judges cross-examined the speakers during their constructive speeches, but were asked not to interrupt during the first and last two minutes. Following the debate the chief judge anounced the decision and gave his reasons. The other judges were also asked to present a short opinion of concurrence or dissent.[5]

---

[5] See Austin J. Freeley, *Argumentation and Debate*, San Francisco: Wadsworth, 1961, pp. 314–15 for a more complete discussion of Appellate Debate.

SAMPLE BRIEF

PROPOSITION: Resolved, That Congress should be given the power to reverse decisions of the Supreme Court.

AFFIRMATIVE
by
Betty Boyd and Roger Johnson, Oberlin College

Introduction

I. Immediate cause for discussion:

    A. Controversial decisions rendered by the Supreme Court over a long period of our history make it necessary to define more clearly the Court's power.

    B. Many state justices have advocated a reduction of the Supreme Court's power. "What 36 State Chief Justices Said About the Supreme Court," in *U.S. News and World Report,* October 3, 1958, pp. 92–102.

    C. Continued growth of judicial power, coupled with the extension of executive power, suggests a reappraisal of legislative responsibility.

II. Origin and history of the question:

    A. The framers of the Constitution failed to confer the power of judicial review on the Supreme Court, a power the court itself assumed. Carr, Robert K., *Democracy and the Supreme Court* (1936), p. 15.

    B. The growth of the Supreme Court's powers is most noticeably expressed in the *Marbury* v. *Madison* case, the *Dred Scott* case of 1857, the interpretation of the "due process of law" clauses in the 1880's, and the 1918 *Hammer* v. *Dagenhart* decision. *Ibid.,* pp. 16–18.

    C. In the 1930's, following the nullification of much New Deal legislation, an effort was made to limit the Court's power.

    D. Recent Court decisions have limited Congressional power to deal with subversives and have reversed historic Court positions on separate but equal facilities in public schools.

III. Definition of terms:

    A. "Congress" refers to the two federal legislative houses.

    B. "Should" means ought to, and not necessarily will.

    C. "Power" means the granting of legal sanction.

    D. "To reverse" means to annul, to set aside, or to vacate.

    E. "Decisions" refers to rulings on constitutionality in cases tried.

    F. "Supreme Court" refers to the highest judicial body in the government.

IV. Admitted matter:

    A. Since Congress already has the right and power to reverse decisions of the Supreme Court in cases concerning statutory construction, this proposal would concern only those cases dealing with the constitutionality of state and federal laws.

    B. The purpose of this debate is to discuss the broad implications of the Supreme Court's role in our democratic government.

V. The main issues evolve from the following questions:

    A. Have the Court's decisions throughout history revealed startling inconsistencies?

B. Is the Court, in reality, a political body, exercising legislative power as well as judicial authority?

C. Should the Court's power be limited to promote more democratic ideals of government?

D. Can this need best be met by making Congress the final authority as to the interpretation of the Constitution?

VI. Points in partition:

A. The Supreme Court's exercise of the final judicial veto over legislation is not justified, is undesirable, and calls for a change.

B. Giving Congress the right by a ⅔ majority to reverse decisions of the Supreme Court will meet these problems.

C. The adoption of the affirmative proposal is not disadvantageous to the operation of our government.

Discussion

I. The Supreme Court's exercise of the final judicial veto over legislation is not justified, is undesirable, and calls for a change, because:

A. The Court, itself, is vague on fundamental decisions which it hands down, for:

1. Unanimous decisions are rare and multiple opinions common. *U.S. News and World Report,* October 3, 1958, p. 102.

2. The Court hands down many 5–4 decisions. *Ibid.*

3. Frequently a majority of the Court cannot be mustered on one viewpoint and a compromise must be made to render a decision. *Ibid.*

4. The Court has frequently overturned its own decisions. *Ibid.; Adkins* v. *Children's Hospital,* 261 U.S. 525 (1923); *West Coast Hotel Co.* v. *Parrish,* 300 U.S. 379 (1937).

B. A small group of nonelected men has usurped legislative functions, thereby thwarting the will of the people, for:

1. The Court overturned progressive legislation at the turn of the century and in the 1930's. Corwin, Edward S., *Court Over Constitution* (1938), p. 87; Carr, *op. cit.,* p. 140.

2. They now espouse a clearly liberal legislative viewpoint. *U.S. News and World Report,* July 18, 1958, pp. 81–82; Speech to Senate on July 10, 1958 by James O. Eastland.

3. We cannot tell what their legislative position may be in another decade.

II. Giving Congress the right by a ⅔ majority to reverse decisions of the Supreme Court will meet these problems, because:

A. The affirmative plan, while not changing the make-up or selection of the Court, will put reins on the Court's power and will more nearly represent the will of the people, for:

1. It will allow the people, through the voice of ⅔ of their Congressmen, to reverse Court decisions.

2. It will review the power of the Court to legislate.

3. It will stop this march of "judicial supremacy" that has evolved from almost nothing. Carr, *op. cit.,* pp. 15–18.

B. The affirmative plan will allow the Court to be more closely connected with the philosophy of the times in which it exists, for:

1. The judges, now complacent in their life terms, will become more

aware of the opinions of the people in the democratic electorate. *U.S. News and World Report,* October 3, 1958, p. 102.
2. The Court will not have the opportunity to impede progress and will be more adapted to meet the changing times ahead. Carr, *op. cit.,* 125.
C. The affirmative plan will allow a larger representation and a more democratic segment of the population to speak on those questions that have shown themselves hardest to be decided, for:
1. It will be those close 5—4 and, possibly, 6—3 decisions that will be most vulnerable to reversal by Congress.
2. The records which show the number of reversals of Supreme Court decisions clearly indicate that the basis for deciding in the first place was not clear-cut. *U.S. News and World Report,* October 3, 1958, p. 102.

III. The adoption of the affirmative proposal is not disadvantageous to the operation of our government, because:
A. Our proposal does not do away with judicial review, for:
1. The Supreme Court will still have the power to declare laws unconstitutional.
2. Since a ⅔ vote in both houses of Congress will be required to reverse a decision of the Supreme Court, this will be a very difficult power to abuse.
3. Our proposal is not really as drastic as some make it out to be, since Congress can already reverse decisions of the Supreme Court except in those cases dealing with the constitutionality of laws.
4. Our plan will inhibit irresponsible attacks on the Supreme Court, and on the process of judicial review, by members of Congress.
B. Our proposal does not harm the system of checks and balances, but in fact enhances it for a new check has been added.

Conclusion

Therefore, since:
I. The Supreme Court's exercise of the final judicial veto over legislation is not justified, is undesirable, and calls for a change, and
II. Giving Congress the right by a ⅔ majority to reverse decisions of the Supreme Court will meet these problems, and
III. The adoption of the affirmative proposal is not disadvantageous to the operation of our government.

It is to be concluded that the Congress should be given the power to reverse decisions of the Supreme Court.

NEGATIVE
by
Carol Stine and Larry Caldwell, College of Wooster

Introduction

I. One of the outstanding features of the development of a free and efficient political state has been the right, even duty, of the public to discuss and evaluate governmental institutions and practices.

II. Thus, the Supreme Court has often been the subject of discussion.

III. The definitions of the terms of the proposition are:

A. "Congress": Senate and House of Representatives, (U.S. Constitution, Art. X.)

B. "Should be given": Ought to but not necessarily will be vested with. (*Competitive Debate,* Musgrave, p. 11, Rule 2d.)

C. "Power": Necessary authority.

D. "To reverse": "To overthrow, vacate, set aside, make void, annul, repeal, or revoke, as to reverse a judgment, a sentence or decree, or to change to the contrary or to a former condition." Black's *Law Dictionary,* 4th ed., p. 1482.

E. "Decisions": "Determination of a legal controversy or issue upon the laws and facts involved by a judicial or similar tribunal." A. J. Zurcher in *A Dictionary of American Politics,* Smith and Zurcher (1944), p. 92.

F. "Supreme Court": Highest Court in the American federal system and the only one provided for directly in the constitution.

IV. Position of the negative in this debate:

A. In this healthy situation of a debate concerning the Supreme Court and its role, the negative contends that the *status quo* as it has evolved meets the needs of the present complex democratic society.

B. Following procedures supported by the negative, decisions of the Supreme Court have been and may now be affected by:

1. Constitutional amendments. See *Chisholm* v. *Georgia,* 2 Dall. 419 (1793) and the eleventh amendment; *Pollock* v. *Farmers' Loan and Trust Company,* 158 U.S. 601 (1895) and the sixteenth amendment.

2. Congressional revision of statute to meet judicial requirements. Note Guffy Coal Act ruled unconstitutional in *Carter* v. *Carter Coal Co.,* 298 U.S. 238 (1936), reenacted in 1937, and upheld in *Sunshine Anthracite Coal Co.* v. *Adkins,* 310 U.S. 381 (1940).

3. The Court's own later decisions. Compare *Hammer* v. *Dagenhart,* 247 U.S. 251 (1918) and *U.S.* v. *Darby,* 312 U.S. 100 (1941).

Discussion

I. There is no need for a change, because:

A. Procedurely, over the years the presently operative federal judicial system has provided the most effective expression of due process of law. ". . . Someone must interpret the Constitution and declare its meaning. No one is better suited to the task than the Supreme Court, and no process is better adapted than the judicial process to the function of determining constitutional meaning and effective constitutional limits and guarantees." John R. Dethmers, C. J. Sp. Ct. of Michigan, in "What a State Chief Justice Says about the Supreme Court," *U.S. News and World Report,* December 12, 1958, p. 91.

B. Substantively, the system of laws developed by the government of the United States has provided an effective and satisfactory level of justice. "The Supreme Court is the embodiment of judicial power and under its evolving interpolation of the great constitutional clauses—commerce among the states, due process of law and equal protection of the laws, to name examples—we have achieved national unity, a nationwide market

for goods, and government under the guarantees of the Bill of Rights."
"Statement by 100 Leading Lawyers," in *The New York Times,* October
28, 1956. Quoted in *Liberty and Justice,* Smith and Murphy, Knopf, 1958,
p. 564.

II. The affirmative proposal is not practical, because:

   A. Judicial decisions cannot be expeditiously achieved through the legislative
process, for:

      1. Such decisions would be subject to delay and neglect through charac-
teristic Congressional procedures. "Fuss over the Filibuster—What
It's All About," in *U.S. News and World Report,* January 9, 1959,
p. 49.

      2. The fate of such decisions would depend too much upon the committee
assignment. F. A. Ogg and P. O. Ray, *Introduction to American
Government,* 1951, pp. 319 ff.

      3. Congress lacks familiarity with the intricacies of case law. Learned
Hand, *Bill of Rights,* Harvard Univ. Press, 1958, p. 12. Federalist,
No. 81. ed. by Max Beloff, Blackwell, Oxford, 1948, p. 413.

   B. Many decisions of the Supreme Court are not amenable to reversal, for:

      1. Some decisions are orders for retrial. On May 21, 1955, the Supreme
Court remanded the segregation cases to courts of first instance.

      2. Various cases brought to the Supreme Court are disposed of on the
bases of jurisdiction. See concurring opinion in *Ashwander* v. *T.V.A.,*
297 U.S. 288 (1936) and *Colegrove* v. *Green,* 328 U.S. 549 (1946).

III. Affirmative Proposal is undesirable, because:

   A. The balance of power, eliminated or drastically curtailed under the
proposal, is essential to the American form of government, for:

      1. Checks and balances have been the keystone of the system. *American
Democracy in Theory and Practice,* Carr, Berstein, Morrison, Snyder,
McLean, Rinehart, 1955, pp. 280–82. Tresolini, *American Constitu-
tional Law,* Macmillan, 1959, p. 82.

      2. Though the influence of each of the three branches of government is
qualified, the effective cooperation depends upon each having strength.
See *Ex Parte Grossman,* 267 U.S. 87 (1925).

   B. By placing the ultimate decision with the legislature, the affirmative
proposal destroys belief in the finality of law, for:

      1. The prestige of the decision, which is an important basis of acceptance,
is seriously reduced. Louis Lusky, 52 *Yale Law Journal* (1942), pp.
18–21. Robert H. Jackson, "The Supreme Court in the American
System of Government," in McKay, *An American Constitutional Law
Reader,* Oceana Publications, 1958, p. 43.

      2. It seriously lengthens the process.

      3. It makes virtually impossible the rendering of decisions that have suf-
ficient finality.

   C. It destroys the insulation of some branch of the government from hasty
political pressures, for:

      1. The Supreme Court occupies a unique position of isolation from
momentary whim on the part of the public. Woodrow Wilson, *Constitutional Government in the U.S.,* 1908, p. 165.

      2. The Supreme Court is designed to represent the will of the people,
not at any given time, but in the long view. Felix Frankfurter, in

dissenting opinion in *W. Va. State Bd. of Ed.* v. *Barnette* 319 U.S. 624 (1943).

Conclusion

I. The nation has progressed under the present system which has provided procedural and substantive benefits.

II. The negative urges that the proposition not be adopted.

THE DEBATE SPEECH

In traditional debate with two-man teams, each speaker shares the responsibility of developing a part of the complete case. Combined with his colleague's speech, it constitutes the constructive argument on one side of the question. The general approach for typical debate speeches will appear somewhat as follows:

First Affirmative Constructive Speech

I. Introduction
   A. Focus attention on the topic, demonstrating its timeliness and importance; if possible select evidence or develop an illustration designed to encourage a sympathetic audience response to the affirmative position.
   B. State the proposition for debate.
   C. Define only the ambiguous terms or those which may lead to misunderstanding or controversy.
   D. Outline the entire affirmative case, indicating the major contentions each affirmative speaker will establish.
   E. Restate your major contentions.

II. Body
   A. State the first contention (a part of the need issue).
      1. Establish through reasoned argument based on examples, analogy, statistics, and authority.

To develop the complete need issue, the first speaker may offer two or three but never more than five contentions. After he establishes these contentions (need issue) he should probably outline the specific nature of the plan, if such is necessary. It is unfair to the negative and to the audience to withhold the affirmative plan until the second affirmative speech. Furthermore, the second affirmative needs most of his speech to demonstrate how the plan will remedy the inadequacies in the present system.

III. Summary

Every speaker in the debate should save sufficient time to restate succinctly the team case and his own contentions. It is likewise helpful to insert summaries, during the body of the speech, briefly restating each contention following the proof. Skillfully executed, the internal summary also helps to build the transition to the next contention. For example, "Thus, we can see that many states lack adequate resources to support public education. This brings us to our second contention that the lack of funds produce substandard schools."

First Negative Speech

1. Introduction
   A. Adaptation to the case of the affirmative. Acceptance, rejection or reinterpretation of the affirmative definitions. If the speaker challenges the definitions, he must prove that the negative's interpretation is valid.
   B. Presentation of the entire negative case. This will depend on the negative approach (see Possible Negative Stands, pages 248–249). The remainder of the introduction, body, and conclusion will follow the same general plan as the first affirmative's speech.

Second Affirmative Speech

The second affirmative speech depends largely on the negative stand. Still the speaker must complete the affirmative case by proving that the affirmative plan is the best possible remedy for the weaknesses of the existing structure. If the negative admits the need issue and presents a counterplan, the major focus of the second affirmative will consist of an attack on the negative plan, coupled with a defense of the affirmative proposal.

Second Negative Speech

This speaker completes the negative contentions through direct adaptation to the affirmative case. With absolute fairness and accuracy, he indicates which negative arguments the affirmative has failed to recognize or answer adequately. By this point in the debate, the issues should be sharply drawn and the area of conflict narrowed.

Rebuttal Speeches

With the exception of the first affirmative, all speakers should use a part of their constructive time for direct refutation of the opposition's contentions and arguments. A team that reserves all of its refutation for the rebuttal period, will find itself hopelessly behind. During the rebuttal neither team may add major contentions to its case. For example, the affirmative can not present its plan at this point, nor can the negative raise a new objection to the affirmative case. But new evidence, continuing adaptation, and fresh reasoning are necessary for an effective rebuttal. A major breakdown occurs when teams exhaust their ammunition during the constructive argument and are reduced to parroting "what my colleague just said." They need an abundance of "stopper" evidence.

A common error in rebuttal is a speaker's futile attempt to answer every piece of evidence and every shred of argument thrown against his case. He produces at best a shot-gun, scattered defense or an attack that scarcely damages the opposition. The skillful debater sifts the mountains of evidence to discover the major objections or issues, rarely more than two or three, and meets these squarely with his strongest evidence and reasoning. The following outline will prove helpful, if the debater realizes that he must adapt it to the particular circumstances of each debate.

I. Introduction
   A. Refute one of the issues covered by the previous speaker.
   B. Indicate which issues still remain in contention.

II. Body
   A. Take each issue singly and state clearly.
   B. Indicate how the opposition attempted to establish it.
   C. Present your counter evidence and indicate the flaws in your opponent's reasoning.
   D. Summarize and show how this issue now affects both cases.
   E. Treat the remaining issues similarly or indicate that your colleague will deal with them.

III. Conclusion
   A. Summarize the entire debate.
   B. Contrast the advantages of your position with that of your opposition, appealing at the same time for the adoption or rejection of the proposition.

COMMON ERRORS IN DEBATE

Attempting to Convince the Opposition. This is a waste of time and yet debaters frequently deliver most of their speeches to the other team. An occasional remark directed to the opposition for its dramatic effect may be in order, but the primary target for your persuasion is the audience. Each team needs to show what acceptance or rejection of this proposition will mean to each member of the audience.

Use of Technical Debate Jargon. Debate is essentially persuasive speaking designed to win the approval of the average person. It is not an esoteric exercise for the select few. As a debater you should understand what is meant by *burden of proof, status quo,* and *post hoc ergo propter hoc,* but you will be wise to avoid using any of these terms in the actual debate.[6] The same applies to the technical terms of a particular question. If you have to employ any of these terms, you must make sure that your audience understands the meaning. We often forget how long we studied to acquire an understanding of a technical term and erroneously expect our audience to grasp the concept immediately.

Use of Memorized Speeches. The so-called "canned" speech rarely succeeds in debate. After the first affirmative speech, all others must constantly shift and adapt their remarks to preceeding speakers. All debate speeches are most effectively delivered extemporaneously, that is, thoroughly prepared, outlined, and rehearsed in advance, but neither memorized nor read from manuscript. In addition to the difficulties of adaptation, a memorized speech usually lacks the directness and spontaneity necessary for effective delivery. To anticipate arguments and devise rebuttal cards in advance are wise measures as long as the debater recognizes the necessity of adapting every argument to the precise case of the opposition.

A Sarcastic, Contentious Attitude. Sarcasm in any speech is a highly explosive substance, prone to injure both the giver and the receiver. A debater can be vigorous and enthusiastic without exhibiting bad manners. Moreover, a team that can maintain its poise, emotional equilibrium, and kindly sense of humor during the heat of argument adds immeasurably to its own persuasive appeal. An overemotional, sarcastic attack often incites audience sympathy for the victim and contempt for the promoter.

Fabrication of Evidence. Debaters are sometimes accused of employing dishonest methods in their unholy desire to win an immediate verdict. A few may have succumbed to such temptation. To their dismay the audience or their opponents usually discover the deceit. Debate and discussion, as we have indicated earlier, are not the favored tools of the dema-

---

[6] See p. 248 for the definition of Burden of Proof. *Status quo* means literally "the state existing." It is thus ridiculous for debaters to say as they often do "The *Status quo* can remedy the existing condition." *Post hoc ergo propter hoc* means "after this therefore because of this." The rooster who thought his crowing caused the sun to rise committed this fallacy.

gogue. He and the charlatan flourish best in an atmosphere where they are free from exposure.

Unwillingness to Concede an Issue or Argument. "He must be a great debater," runs the familiar axiom, "because he contradicts everyone on everything." Nothing could be further from the truth. The skillful debater knows how much of his opponent's argument to accept without losing the debate. He is then in a stronger position to push his attack or strengthen his defense at the strategic points.

Reliance on Limited Types of Evidence. A common error is to place too much reliance on one type of evidence. Debate speeches sometimes appear as a mere recital of opinion. The wise debater looks for as wide a variety of evidence as possible, employing facts, witnesses, instances, statistics from which to draw his inferences. He searches for analogies, comparisons, and illustrations with which to make his arguments vivid.

Failure to Identify Authority. When available, fact is always superior to expert opinion. But on questions of probability we are sometimes forced to rely on opinion. Simply to attach a name to an opinion, however, lends no special significance to the opinion. The audience needs to know *who* the authority is and *why* his opinion makes a difference.

Failure to Evaluate and Verify the Evidence. In our cliche-ridden world we often speak of the "simple fact of the matter." We would caution any speaker that even a so-called "well-known fact" may finally prove to be pure fiction. Often a declarative statement which sounds like a fact is instead merely an inference. *Fact*: We observe a man stagger. *Inferences*: That man is drunk? Crippled? Sick? None of these inferences may constitute a fact. He may, in fact, be "putting on an act." Thus, debaters need to generate a deep-seated suspicion of all sources and witnesses, rigorously testing them to determine their accuracy and reliability. Finally, we can safely draw one conclusion—facts are rarely "simple" and almost never "well known."

SUMMARY

Although debate often begins where discussion ends, it is frequently difficult, if not impossible, to draw a sharp dividing line. These two democratic techniques constitute cooperative, continuous forces in decision-making. But when we reach that stage of deliberation that requires action or no action and the participants need to hear clean-cut, pro-and-con arguments, they are probably ready for debate.

Like discussion, debate demands a fairly stated proposition of *fact, value,* or *policy.* Most often, debate concerns policy decisions and requires a formal question that is: (1) debatable, (2) complete, (3) brief, (4) single, (5) affirmative, and (6) impartial.

Debaters on both sides of the question share the responsibility of *defining the terms, determining the issues,* and *assuming the burden of proof* or *rebuttal.*

Many different forms of debate are possible, the most commonly used being: *formal debate, cross-examination, direct clash,* and *parliamentary.*

Preparation for debate involves the construction of a *case,* thoroughly supported with evidence of fact and opinion. The *brief* helps the debaters draw logical inferences and serves as a reservoir of evidence for each contention. The debate speeches usually include the *constructive argument* and the *rebuttal.* While carefully prepared and rehearsed, the speeches are always distinguished by careful adaptation to the arguments of the opposition and directed to the interests and concerns of the judges (audience).

Questions and Exercises

1. Explain what is meant by the statement, "Debate begins when discussion ends." Can you find exceptions to this general principle?

2. Distinguish between propositions of *fact, value,* and *policy.* Write an example of each.

3. Formulate debate propositions of policy on the following problems:

    (a) State control of medicine,
    (b) Federal aid for education,
    (c) Labor legislation,
    (d) United Nations police force,
    (e) Control of nuclear weapons,
    (f) Reduction of minimum age for voting,
    (g) Disarmament,
    (h) Free trade.

4. Find a newspaper editorial with which you disagree. Develop a four-minute rebuttal speech. You will find it helpful to review the material on pages 262–263 dealing with rebuttal.

5. The modifications of traditional debate procedure covered in the preceding chapter are only a few of many in existence. Work out a "new" plan of debate and be prepared to defend your "modification" in a short speech to the class.

6. Select a proposition suitable for debate and indicate specifically (avoid stock issue phraseology) the issues. Take one issue and develop an affirmative or negative brief of that issue.

7. Using the same proposition define the terms. Do you believe that the affirmative and negative might disagree on the definitions of any terms?

8. Bring to class three examples of *evidence of fact; evidence of opinion.* In a three-minute speech indicate how you verified the facts and how expert or authoritative you consider the items of opinion.

9. Set up a series of classroom debates on vital topics of public or campus concern. The teams may consist of one or two persons and the time allotments for individual speeches may vary, but each side should receive equal time.

10. Select three of the propositions you formulated for question three. Assume that you are a negative debater and work out legitimate *substitute plans* for each. Be prepared to defend your plans as bona fide alternate proposals.

RECOMMENDED READINGS

Baird, A. Craig, and Knower, Franklin H., *General Speech: An Introduction.* New York: McGraw-Hill, 1963, Chaps. 17 and 19.

Ehninger, Douglas, and Brockriede, Wayne. *Decision by Debate.* New York: Dodd, Mead, 1963.

Ewbank, Henry L., and Auer, J. Jeffery. *Discussion and Debate.* New York: Appleton-Century-Crofts, 1951, Chaps. 23, 24, 25, 26, 27, and 28.

Huber, Robert B. *Influencing Through Argument.* New York: McKay, 1963.

Kruger, Arthur N. *Modern Debate: Its Logic and Strategy.* New York: McGraw-Hill, 1960.

Mudd, Charles S., and Sillars, Malcolm O. *Speech: Content and Communication.* San Francisco: Chandler, 1962, Chaps. IV and X.

Thompson, Wayne N., and Fessenden, Seth A. *Basic Experiences in Speech.* Englewood Cliffs, N. J.: Prentice-Hall, 1958, Chaps. 10, 13, and 14.

CHAPTER 13

STAGE FRIGHT

THE NATURE OF STAGE FRIGHT

Stage fright is a much-used term for a comparatively rare phenomenon. Few of us are really frightened by an audience. If we were, the inevitable would more frequently take place. Flight would follow fright, and we would run away. Most of us, rather than being frightened, are more truly stimulated by an audience and the thought of having to face one. We may be excited and nervous, and somewhat concerned about our performance. But these elements do not of themselves constitute fear. To be sure, what happens to us physically and mentally when we are stimulated by an audience includes changes which we also experience when afraid. A *fearlike* element is undoubtedly present. But the same element is present when we are experiencing pleasurable excitement and when we anticipate good things. We are not afraid when we watch a well-played baseball game, and we are not afraid while waiting for the seconds to tick away before the time for our big date. We are intensely stimulated and we are excited. This is normal. Why, then, the confusion with fear or fright?

Physical Symptoms

We confuse intense stimulation with fear because parts of the picture are the same. The physical symptoms of fear may include rapid pulse, strong heart beat (palpitation), excessive perspiration, dryness of the mouth, trembling of the limbs (hands and legs), and disturbances of secretion and excretion. All of these physical symptoms need not be present to cause the reaction known as fear, but usually two or more are present. In stage fright the overt manifestations may include trembling of the arms and legs,

[268]

quavering of the voice, random movements, and a general lack of controlled and poised appearance. In general, the performer feels unstable; occasionally he looks unstable.

Intellectual Changes

In addition to the physical symptoms, fear includes an outstanding mental change. A person afraid is suffering from *intellectual disorganization*. A person afraid is one whose thinking has gone astray. Not knowing how to think, he does not know *what to do*. A person who is experiencing true fear either does nothing, or behaves in ways which are inappropriate. Fear may cause a child to run into the path of an on coming automobile. A well-organized adult, observing the behavior of the child, may experience an intense, fearlike feeling. This feeling will not, however, prevent him from snatching the child out of the path of danger. In fact, the physical changes he experiences enable him to act more vigorously and quickly in the accomplishment of his task. In stage fright, the performer may be blocked in his thinking and so find himself unable to go on with what he had planned to say or do. His internal behavior may be basic to the overt expressions of his inability to mobilize and integrate his inner forces. In extreme stage fright, as in an extreme state of emotion such as fear, the individual is suffering temporarily from the dynamics of disintegration.

Heightened Feeling

The difference between the behavior of the child and the behavior of the well-organized adult is the difference between fear and heightened feeling. The child suffered from fear because he did not know what to do. The adult experienced heightened (fearlike) feeling because *he did know what to do*. Heightened feeling prepares the body for vigorous emergency activity. The feeling results mostly from an increase in the amount of adrenalin supplied to the blood stream. The athlete preparing for a contest has such a feeling. So do we as speakers when we anticipate appearing before an audience. It is not only good but necessary for us to have some feeling about facing an audience. It makes us more alert and alive. We sound and act interested in our job of speaking.

Perhaps we can approach the matter of stage fright as one of *degree* rather than of kind. We may then accept the term *stage fright* to mean any notable degree of psychological and physiological arousal experienced by a performer before an audience. Mild arousal may be stimulating and helpful. A severe amount of arousal may be disrupting and disorganizing and impair rather than improve a performance.

RESEARCH FINDING OF STAGE FRIGHT

In the growing literature on stage fright[1] the following generalized findings seem to be warranted:

1. All speakers, regardless of length and amount of experience, undergo some degree of psychological and physiological arousal before or during their speaking efforts.

2. Observers (listeners) are often less aware of disruption than the speaker anticipates or believes is taking place.

3. There is no significant relationship between stage fright, reasoning ability, and level of intelligence.

4. There is no significant relationship between personality traits, or aspects of personality, at least as these components are measured or are measurable by standard personality inventories.

5. Stage fright is no sparer of sex. Both men and women experience stage fright, but men are more likely to show overt and obvious manifestations of this state of feeling or emotion than are women.

6. A reduction in stage fright, at least as far as its disruptive influences are concerned, is associated with improved speaking ability, increased experience in speaking, and with age. These factors may, of course, be interrelated.

CAUSES OF STAGE FRIGHT

Faulty Evaluation

True fear of an audience may develop out of heightened feeling if the speaker fails to evaluate the physical changes occurring within him for what they are worth. A speaker may suddenly become aware of a palpitating heart or a dry mouth. He may also, consciously or unconsciously, recall that these symptoms were also present when he was frightened. If he fails to recognize that the cause of his old fright is nonexistent in his present situation, he may give way to fear. In effect, such a speaker is responding to two elements —palpitating heart and dry mouth—as he originally did to a total but different situation which happened to include these two elements. The other fear symptoms such as trembling and excessive perspiration may make their appearance. If the speaker then becomes overwhelmed with the physical changes taking place within him, he may forget what he has to say. Random

---

[1] See J. Eisenson, J. J. Auer, and J. V. Irwin, *The Psychology of Communication*, New York: Appleton-Century-Crofts, 1963, Chap. 18, for a review of the literature on the subject of stage fright.

talking and random, disorganized movement may take the place of organized thoughts and gestures. True fear—stage fright in a real sense—has set in.

Inadequate Preparation

Besides faulty evaluation, there is one other basic cause for stage fright. The cause is insufficient preparation. The speaker has reason—good reason —to be afraid. Not having organized his thoughts in advance, the speaker, especially the inexperienced speaker, becomes suddenly aware of his inadequacies. Fear arises when we feel ourselves inadequate to meet a situation. Stage fright is fear in a situation involving a speaker and an audience.

Intensification of Feelings

Though extreme stage fright is a comparatively infrequent phenomenon, the intensification of feeling and a state of "arousal" in anticipation of an audience, or while facing an audience, is a common experience. Most professional performers on stage, radio, television, or public platforms admit to such feelings. We can go back to Cicero and find that even he admitted to turning pale at the outset of a speech. Among our contemporaries, Winston Churchill admits to an occasional discomfort he described as a feeling of "a nine-inch square block of ice in the pit of his stomach." Fortunately, in most instances, the ice melts away as the performance is pursued, and often exhilaration replaces the initial state of discomfort.

Although professional performers use the term *stage fright* for their intensified feelings, they are not frightened by either the term or the feelings. In fact, many performers contend that unless they feel somewhat tense, aroused, or "pepped up," their performances may fall flat. We may quite properly conclude that the internal changes, as well as some of the external ones, that result from the increased flow of adrenalin serve a useful purpose in supplying extra energy and muscle tones necessary for an effective performance.

STAGE FRIGHT EXPLAINED AS
AN APPROACH-AVOIDANCE CONFLICT

It is common for many of us to ask commitments for future responsibilities and then do whatever we can to avoid the deed and the day of reckoning. There are many situations that have both desirable and undesirable features. We may enjoy being at the beach but dislike the arduous trip to the beach. Attending an athletic event may be highly enjoyable, but not the necessary travel to and from the stadium. If an event is far enough away, our wishes to participate may dominate our behavior, and so we may make a positive commitment regarding the event. As the time for the event approaches, so do our counterinclinations relative to it. Then avoidance behavior is increased, and we may look for ways out.

We believe that there is a tenable anology between approach-avoidance behavior in general and reactions to public speaking situations in particular. Many persons who have a choice about accepting or refusing public speaking engagements are likely to accept them if the time is not too near. The wish to speak—to perform and to impress—dominates the drives and determines the immediate behavior—acceptance of an engagement. As the time for speaking draws closer, then avoidance drives may set in. Unfortunately, such drives may result in a failure to prepare for the speaking situation, and this may strengthen the avoidance drive. Theoretically, if a speaker arrives at the time for the execution of his responsibilities with approach and avoidance equal in strength, he is in a state of impasse. If circumstances, or his conscience or his sense of responsibility, result in strengthening the approach, he may meet his commitment but possibly without adequate preparation and with shaky confidence in the performance to come. The result may be more avoidance on the next occasion and possibly more conflict, and with this state an increased likelihood for a severe case of stage fright.

HOW TO PREVENT STAGE FRIGHT

Evaluation of Situation

The first suggestion for overcoming the effects of stage fright is to evaluate what we are experiencing. In all probability, it is heightened feeling and not fear. The physical changes in heightened feeling, though they resemble the change in fear or fright, are, as we have indicated, useful to us. Moreover, they are common and shared by public performers of all degrees of ability and practice.

We should go beyond recognizing the changes when they ocur. We should anticipate their occurrence so that the element of surprise is not present. To be able to say, "Oh, yes, that's what I expected would happen" is much less disconcerting than to ask, "What's happenig to me?" when the knees shake and the hands begin to quiver. An athlete expects his heart to beat fast while engaged in a contest. He does not get caught by surprise at changes he anticipates! The public speaker, similarly fortified by expectation, would not mistake feeling for fear. Fear is a response to the unknown. The familiar for which we can prepare should command respect rather than fear. "Nervousness" may be induced, but nervousness is not fear.

Preparation

Preparation, in all respects and with thoroughness, is probably the best direct equipment against stage fright. Preparation includes dress, audience analysis, and familiarity with speech material, including the sound of the words, the turn of the phrase, and the meaning of every utterance. If the need is felt for written notes, these should be prepared and available.

Notes should be written so that they can be easily read. They should be phrased so that they readily recall ideas to mind. The question of how much written help is necessary must be answered by each speaker for himself. Usually, as the speaker gains experience and confidence, he is able to get along with fewer notes and more reliance on memory. Many speakers gain confidence in the knowledge that notes are available if they should be needed.

Notes are best written on small filing cards which can be handled inconspicuously. The cards should be numbered according to the order of the speech material. Inexperienced speakers will probably find it helpful to have card #1 contain the complete opening sentence. The last card should have the tentative closing sentence. Intermediate cards should contain key ideas and transition sentences. Statistics should always be available in written form.

Confidence in Subject Matter

We must have confidence in our facts as well as in our notes. As speakers, we should be free of worrying about the validity of our statements. If we entertain doubt or feel insecure about assertions we are about to make, we should avoid making them. To lack confidence is to court fear. If facts are in proper order, they are deserving of confidence.

As speakers, we should avoid speaking on a topic which calls for greater qualifications than we possess. That does not mean that we should be an authority before we entertain an opinion. It does mean that we should not *pose as an authority* when merely presenting an opinion. If we are not qualified to speak, we should avoid appearing in public to display our lack of qualifications.

Interest in Subject

As speakers, we should feel an urge to speak on the topic we select. The urge need be no greater than that of wishing to share a humorous anecdote or the experiences of a trip, but some *wish to communicate* must be present for the communication to be effective. The speaker who has an urge to share an idea and who has confidence in his idea will have little reason to have fear of fear. On the other hand, the speaker who lacks interest in what he is saying is probably correct in assuming that his audience will lack interest in listening to him.

Movement

The muscular tensions which accompany heightened feeling, if not released, may immobilize a speaker. A rigid, unmoving speaker is likely to produce tensions in his audience. The effect is disturbing to both speaker and listener. Fortunately, the muscular tensions can be put to use. Tension may be drained off through movement. As speakers, it is our task to engage in movements which have meaning and which reinforce rather than interfere with our task of communicating ideas. Adjusting clothing, twisting a handkerchief, shuffling notes, playing with a watch, rocking on the toes, walking for the sake of walking, are movements which have significance *not* related to the purpose of the speech. Controlled gestures, walking toward or away from a speaker's stand according to the import of the spoken material, movements which serve as punctuation and as emphasis are recommended. This, however, should be remembered: almost any movement is better than no movement. If a speaker feels tense and not intellectually equal to the task of using a meaningful gesure, he ought then to move for the sake of movement. With the draining off of tension and the regaining of intellectual composure, the speaker will find himself able to use appropriate action to enhance communication.

Shifting Focus of Attention

In our discussion of the role of the speaker as a listener, we emphasized the need for the speaker to be aware of the reactions of the persons to whom he is talking. The public speaker does not ordinarily anticipate an immediate verbal response to his remarks. He should, nevertheless, be more concerned with what he has to say to his listeners, and with their possible reactions, than he is with his own feelings. The speaker who assumes a mental attitude and set of talking to and with his listeners, who is actively engaged in communicating, will find less time and opportunity for excessive introspection and reaction to his own internal reactions. Such a speaker will gain confidence from the realization that his listeners are indeed listening and responding to his ideas. With such confidence, intensification of feeling will serve to stimulate the speaker rather than to produce disintegration and true stage fright.

Practice

Heightened tension to a degree which becomes disturbing tends to disappear with repeated performances. For almost every public performer—

actor, teacher, or public speaker—a first performance is likely to be something of an ordeal. Repeated performances reduce the severity of the ordeal. In time, little more than mild excitement may be felt. The public speaker who has really experienced stage fright should follow the practice of the aviator who has crashed his plane. The aviator who wants to continue flying goes up again just as soon as he can. The public speaker who wants to continue speaking should find another occasion to perform just as soon as he can. Obviously, there is much less real danger in repeated performance for the public speaker than there is for the aviator.

SUMMARY

True stage fright—fear in a speech situation—is a rare phenomenon. Heightened feeling, which shares physical symptoms in common with fear, is what most speakers experience while facing an audience. Fear is disruptive; heightened feeling is useful in speaking.

The speaker can avoid having heightened feeling become fear by following several suggestions. These include: (1) evaluating the speaking situation; (2) anticipating the physical changes which accompany heightened feeling; (3) preparing thoroughly; (4) using notes; (5) speaking only on subjects on which he is qualified to speak; (6) being interested in his topic; (7) using action to drain off tension; and (8) shifting focus of attention from himself to his listeners.

QUESTIONS AND EXERCISES

1. What is stage fright? How is it related to other emotional states? How does so-called stage fright resemble and how does it differ from an actual state of fear?

2. What are the most frequent causes of stage fright? How can you prevent intensified feeling from developing into stage fright?

3. What is the value of knowing the nature of the physical and mental changes in the prevention of stage fright?

4. How can you overcome the effect of stage fright?

5. Prepare a two-minute talk on the relationship of muscle tensions to stage fright. In your talk, prepare to use *movement* to demonstrate its usefulness in "draining off tension."

6. Prepare a two minute talk on one of the following topics or on a topic of your own choosing. Outline your talk. Commit the opening and closing sentence to memory.

  (a) Why be educated?
  (b) Fear—and its usefulness.
  (c) One of life's anxious moments.
  (d) A television personality I can do without.
  (e) A relative I would like to disown.

RECOMMENDED READINGS

Eisenson, J., Auer, J. J., and Irwin, J. V. *The Psychology of Communication.* New York: Appleton-Century-Crofts, 1963, Chap. 18.

Oliver, R. T., and Cortright, R. L. *Effective Speech,* 4th ed. New York: Holt, Rinehart and Winston, 1961, pp. 65–71.

Robinson, E. R., "What Can The Speech Teacher Do About Students' Stage Fright?" *The Speech Teacher,* **8,** (1959) 8–14.

Watkins, D. E., and Harrison, M. K. *Stage Fright and What To Do About It.* Boston: Expression Co., 1940.

CHAPTER 14

SPEAKING IN PUBLIC

The dumbness in the eyes of animals is more touching than the speech of men; but the dumbness in the speech of men is more agonizing than the dumbness in the eyes of animals.

HINDU PROVERB

Why speak in public? Quite frankly, a large percentage of those persons occupying the public platform should talk to themselves or to their forgiving friends who in some instances have developed a tolerance for poor public speaking. As one cynic expressed it: "If you never go to hear a speech you'll miss a lot of poor ones." Yet, most ineffective speakers are capable of developing satisfactory speech habits. A person with normal intelligence, an idea worth communicating, and a knowledge of the basic principles of public speaking can become an effective speaker if he is willing to prepare and practice. While some of us enjoy greater intelligence, a wider background of experience, a more flexible, sensitive speech mechanism, and a commanding physique, anyone, through study and training, should be able to share an idea with a group of listeners. The need is not for more public speaking, but for improved public speaking. The only substitute for poor speaking is better speaking.

Effective, responsible public speaking is difficult but challenging. Unlike the popular magazine advertisement, we cannot promise immediate success through any "magical formula" which will "make people listen the moment you start to talk" and continue their listening for a significant time thereafter. We know of no way to succeed "without really trying" in business or public speaking. Excellent public address demands time, thought, effort, and sensitivity. Harry Emerson Fosdick, long-time pastor of Riverside Church in New York City, made it a rule of thumb to spend one hour in the study for every minute in the pulpit, and Mark Twain ob-

[277]

served slyly that it usually took him three weeks to prepare a good impromptu speech.[1]

Ideally, the world of listeners and speakers would be spared much mutual suffering if everyone held his tongue until inspired by noble thoughts. Such a perfect state is clearly unattainable. The listener, however, should enjoy certain inalienable rights. Among these are: speakers of character, opportunities to hear worthwhile messages, and speakers capable of sustaining audience attention. The candidate unwilling to submit to a regimen of concentrated study, planning, and practice should avoid inflicting his speeches on audiences that may be too polite to accord him the reception he deserves.

Yet, the citizen of a democracy must not shirk the responsibility of developing completely his full potential as a public speaker. Free government depends on free speech and if this form of self-rule is to survive, we must learn to speak and to listen. The same is true for science, business, and industry. White-collar workers spend seven out of every ten minutes of the average day attempting to communicate through speaking, writing, or reading. Conservative estimates indicate that more than 75 per cent of our communication experiences occur on the oral level—in speaking or listening.[2] In a world, still bent on settling issues by force rather than forensics, where failures to communicate exact a frightful toll in science, business, society, industry, and government, an alert citizenry must learn to speak and listen effectively, intelligently, and responsibly.

The Greeks in the fifth century B.C., the first to enjoy the fruits of democracy, understood the indispensable tie—the linking of effective public address with free self-government. As in our world today, theirs was also divided between Western democracy and Eastern autocracy. Yet, in the midst of a life and death struggle and with the enemy advancing to the gates of Athens, free speech remained unrestricted and final authority rested on the Assembly where every Athenian citizen enjoyed the privilege of free speech. It is hardly surprising then that we look to the Greeks for our first systematic treatment of the art of public address. Indeed, the principles of public speaking formulated by Corax, Isocrates, Plato, and Aristotle, later restated and amplified for the Roman World by Cicero, Quintilian, and St. Augustine, form the basic foundation for modern speech theory.

---

[1] Winston Churchill, acknowledged as a master of the apparently informal and non-oratorical style of public speaking, is nevertheless painstaking in his preparation. He has admitted that his effects of informality are produced by careful rehearsing and dependencies upon notes while pretending with more or less success to be making it up as he goes along. (From Samuel T. Williams, "Speeches and Speakers," *New York Times Magazine,* October 3, 1948, p. 30.)

[2] Ralph G. Nichols, "Do We Know How to Listen? Practical Helps in a Modern Age," *The Speech Teacher,* **X** (March 1961), 118.

Greek and Roman rhetoricians established five canons of rhetoric, essential skills every public speaker must master:

1. *Inventio* (the discovery of logical, emotional, and ethical proofs).
2. *Dispositio* (analysis, synthesis, organization, and outlining the proofs).
3. *Elocutio* (words, phrases, language—clothing the proofs with an appropriate style).
4. *Memoria* (the treasure-house of ideas).
5. *Pronuntiatio* (delivery—proper management of the voice and body).

The classical canons furnish the substance for seven fundamental questions every speaker faces. The completeness and accuracy of his answers will determine the quality of the delivered speech.

1. What *responses* do I want from the audience?
2. What *proposition* will best express these responses?
3. How will this particular *audience* on this specific *occasion* affect my choice and treatment of the proposition?
4. What *supporting materials* (logical and psychological, ethical and emotional proofs) will motivate the desired responses?
5. What plan of *organization* will promote the desired responses?
6. What *style* (words, phrases, figurative language) will stimulate the audience to make the appropriate responses?
7. What mode of *delivery* (extempore, manuscript, memorized) will most effectively produce the selected response?

GENERAL AND SPECIFIC PURPOSES

Every successful speech takes accurate aim at securing an appropriate audience response precisely attuned to the speaker's *general* and *specific* *purposes*. Frequently, the principal cause for ineffective public address is our failure to determine or to analyze accurately our own motivations for speaking. Too many speakers suffer the same affliction as the artist in *Don Quixote*. When asked what exactly he was painting, he declared, "That is as it may turn out." If the listeners ever wonder where the speaker is heading, the chances are he and they are on their way to nowhere. As Billy Sunday once observed, "To shoot without taking aim is a waste of powder." The speaker who would increase our knowledge, add to our enjoyment, rekindle our faith, strengthen our courage, or change our beliefs must possess a complete comprehension of his precise purpose for speaking.

Usually, the general and even the specific purpose lies in part beyond the speaker's control. His selection is dictated by the times, his position, and the particular audience he is addressing. The same limiting conditions also prevail in the so-called practice or classroom situation. In many cases your instructor will determine the *general purpose,* leaving you free to select your own *specific purpose.* During the course you may be asked to speak to a number of general and specific purposes, just as the lawyer, teacher, or businessman faces a similar task in his appearances before the same audience. Even for the individual who speaks only occasionally, the conditions of the invitation often force him to limit his direction toward one goal—one *general purpose.* Within the framework of external or self-imposed limits the speaker is then free to exercise his talents as a creative artist, moulding and shaping his specific message.

INTERMIXTURE OF GENERAL PURPOSES

The *general purposes* for the speech are not rigid or mutually exclusive. While every speech contains *one* general purpose, it may also contain subsidiary aims as long as they tend to support and promote the one goal. The speaker who favors the adoption of a city income tax has as his general purpose *to convince.* His *specific purpose* is to win votes for the new tax measure, and his proposition, thesis, or purpose sentence may be stated: "All citizens should support the income tax to provide improved police and fire protection, better streets, and needed recreational facilities." To accomplish his *general purpose, to convince,* he must likewise sustain audience attention, perhaps through his ability *to entertain.* With most audiences he must also deliver a speech *to inform,* supplying his listeners with the facts, rationalizations, and inferences necessary to promote their acceptance of an additional tax burden. Finally, he must arouse popular enthusiasm and enlist the support of those who agree with his proposal through a speech *to stimulate.*

Clearly, whether our tax proponent fuses all these *purposes* into one speech or concentrates on one purpose, his general aim is *persuasion.* He hopes his listeners will accept and understand his ideas, perhaps enjoy his wit, renew their faith in the cause, and respond favorably to his appeals. For convenience and greater clarity, however, it is helpful to subdivide the speech purposes,[3] which in turn furnish convenient names for the possible types of speeches. Authorities use a large variety of names to designate the possible general purposes, including speeches to interest, entertain, inform, inquire, persuade, convince, actuate, stimulate, impress, arouse, instruct, explore, and even, confuse.

---

[3] Cicero's threefold aim for every speech, namely, *docere, delectare, movere* (instruct, win, move) received a new interpretation through the centuries, particularly by George Campbell who considered the *ends* in terms of the *audience response,* thereby paving the way for modern classifications.

With the exception of the speech to confuse, an element that a speaker may accidentally or deliberately inject into any address, we would consider all of the other types as legitimate. We are not here concerned with the speaker who intentionally and demagogically muddies the stream in an effort to befuddle his audience into making illogical decisions based on lies, a studied distortion of the evidence, and appeals to hatred and bigotry. While we consider this attempt to pervert public address highly unethical, we also share Aristotle's belief in the inherent superiority of truth. When error prevails, the blame rests mainly on the unpersuasive speaking of the advocates of truth. We likewise share Quintilian's faith in the good judgment of the jury and in its ability to detect a charlatan. We also recognize that all truth is rarely found on one side of a question. Both the advocates and the opponents of a proposal for a city income tax may have a legitimate cause and case. The audience must base its decision on the action it deems as *probably* the best in the light of immediate or ultimate interests.

Although the speaker may select any of a dozen general ends for his address, we feel that for greatest clarity four *general purposes* are sufficient. Those four purposes, in turn, supply convenient names for the types of speeches, namely, *to entertain, to inform, to stimulate,* and *to convince.* Beyond emphasizing the flexibility of speech purposes, we would stress the audience role in determining the actual objective of the speech. Even in the same audience, an address designed *to stimulate* one listener may constitute a speech *to convince* for another. The after-dinner speaker whose primary aim is *to entertain* may also *stimulate* his audience to increased devotion to home, church, or state.

THE SPEECH TO ENTERTAIN

Some authorities consider the speech to entertain the least difficult to prepare and rank the speech purposes in order of increasing difficulty from entertainment through conviction. Such an analysis may be misleading. It is also probably erroneous to consider humor as an indispensable and necessary component of a speech to entertain. The listener may hold his sides or smile faintly or not at all. Speeches to entertain are often quite properly soberly serious.

The entertaining speech is sometimes less complex in structure than the speech to convince, but it is not necessarily easier to prepare or deliver. Indeed, if the speaker decides to employ humor, he will wisely heed the advice of many professional comedians who will usually testify to the effect that "being a funny man is no laughing matter."

Speakers who find it relatively easy to develop the speech to inform or convince often succeed merely in impaling themselves on their own wit when they attempt to entertain. A mayor of Chicago once introduced Chauncy Depew, perhaps more famous for his after-dinner speaking than his political addresses, as an automatic machine. "You put in a dinner and up comes a speech." In his response, Depew noted the difference between his after-dinner speaking and the mayor's. "He puts in a speech and up comes your dinner."

It is likewise misleading to equate the speech to entertain with the holding of audience interest or attention. Every successful speech sustains audience attention. The superior speech to entertain holds attention through those subtle, elusive substances of wit, repartee, and all the histrionic elements that have held men spellbound in the theater and music hall. The excellent entertaining speaker becomes one with the master story-teller. While he may not increase the world's storehouse of knowledge or move men to momentous decisons, he helps reduce tensions, offers keen insights into human and national problems, often unmasks pompous sophistry, and certainly adds immensely to the sheer enjoyment of living. While individual television performers supply a large percentage of the speeches to entertain, this general purpose forms the staple diet for many social and service organizations. Entertainment may actually constitute the aim of the speaker offering his listeners an account of his travels to a foreign country or even explaining a new process developed by his company. It is apparent that the nature of the audience and the occasion as well as the speaker's intent determines the actual speech purpose.

THE SPEECH TO INFORM

Much of our speaking in public hall and school, in business office and factory, in church and home requires the precise, accurate transmission of information. Costly, tragic breakdowns in government, industry, and society result from our continual failures to exchange information understandably. The speech to inform is often more complex than the speech to entertain; it is almost always more precise in its aim to impart useful information. While a speech on the habits of the headhunters in South America might contain novel, interesting information, this speech for most mixed audiences serves largely as entertainment. If on the other hand the listeners are planning a scientific expedition to the Ecuadorean Amazon where survival depends on an accurate knowledge of the headhunter's tactics, the speaker's purpose transcends mere entertainment to the imparting of vital information. What may be entertainment for one listener is lifesaving instruction for another. The truly informative speech answers the *who*, *what*, *why*, *when*, *where*, and *how* questions vital to the listener's needs in any area.

Speeches to entertain and inform deal mainly with expository materials. An unbiased radio or television newscaster informs us through his factual account of the day's occurrences. Information ends with the speaker's interpretation of the material or his forecast of the probable consequences of the events, e.g., the implication (prediction) of President Kennedy's quarantine of Cuba. The "commercial" following the news sounds factually instructive and strives hard to entertain, but its real objective is to increase sales by creating favorable attitudes toward one product and sometimes hostile reactions toward all rivals. The last two general purposes concern the speech whose central intent is persuasive rather than expository, whose purpose is to change the attitudes, beliefs, and behavior of the listener.

THE SPEECH TO STIMULATE

The distinctively persuasive speech usually falls into one of two classes. It is either directed toward those actively opposed to a proposition or to those who through apathy or human frailty respond at best with something less than genuine enthusiasm. In the speech to stimulate, the speaker is not attempting to change beliefs or attitudes, but tries instead to promote increased exertion for a cause. He seeks to win from those who are already convinced a devotion that goes beyond mere lip service. For many the spirit is willing but the flesh is weak. Some walk the high road and a few the low, while most are content to remain on the misty flats where action is indefinitely deferred. All too frequently the "convinced" behave in the manner of the congressman who assured an inquiring reporter for a college newspaper: "Yes, I often change my mind as a result of debate on the floor of the house. But as for my vote, son, almost never."

The so-called *speech to impress*[4] is a type of speech to stimulate which lifts up the accomplishments of a hero or the significance of an event or concept in a way designed to inspire the listener to an appreciation of his heritage. The implications of such a speech are obvious. Often the speaker in the speech to stimulate appeals directly for increased devotion to the church, the party, or the fraternity.

Most individuals accept certain ethical principles, believe that honesty is the best policy, the life they save may be their own, that a stitch in time saves nine. Most persons also require periodic reminders and stimulation through speech, drama, religion, and various art forms to help them raise their everyday performance to more acceptable levels. The ministers in almost all faiths seek to strengthen beliefs rather than to convert their listeners. The vast majority are already convinced, believing, and acting

[4] See W. E. Gilman, Bower Aly, and Hollis White, *The Fundamentals of Speaking*, 2nd ed., New York: Macmillan, 1964, Chap. 10.

with various degrees of enthusiasm. Even sermons whose primary purpose seems doctrinal, expository, or devotional usually carry overtones, implications, or direct appeals for greater personal dedication and more active stewardship. The preacher often furnishes the rational foundation for emotionally held personal convictions. In times of crisis and national emergency leaders frequently rise to articulate a message the ordinary man feels but cannot express. When Churchill growled out his matchless prose to a frightened, isolated, beleaguered Britain, the most timid soul on the island took heart, determined to join his comrades in their finest hour.

Political conventions, often boring or amusing to the independent and aggravating to the opposition, seem to thrill and inspire the party faithful. With the innovation of nationwide television coverage, political parties might profit from a more carefully planned convention, one designed to convince as well as to stimulate. But the type of convention designed to win converts to the party might also strike the party worker as a drab and colorless affair. Much of the hoopala, the planned "spontaneous" demonstrations, the emotionally charged oratory, constitute attempts to stimulate the faithful but weary party patron to redouble his efforts in behalf of the party.

The never-ending task of inspiring audiences to increase their devotion to worthwhile causes presents the speaker with unusually difficult problems. The already committed listener is sometimes ashamed of his less than satisfactory achievement. Yet, the speech to stimulate may impress him as the "same old stuff," a dull recital of cliches and pious pronouncements. Perhaps more dangerous, the speaker in his effort to inspire may provoke an argument, thus driving the already convinced into the position of defending an opposing position. How often in our penchant to serve as "devil's advocate" do we end up embracing the evil we previously had deplored. The so-called nagging wife rarely needs to convince her erring spouse that his performance is unsatisfactory, that he ought to clean up the yard, take a more active interest in the PTA, or spend more time with the children. Her task, never an easy one, is to stimulate him toward activities he is already admittedly convinced he should undertake.

THE SPEECH TO CONVINCE

The most complex, though not necessarily the most difficult, speech attempts to change attitudes, shift opinion, or promote overt behavioral changes in the listeners. It requires a delicate intermixture of all four general purposes. Obviously, the speaker must sustain attention throughout. Indeed, early schools of psychology considered attention a causative persuasive element and William James' famous dictum, "What holds attention determines action,"[5] inspired James Winans to shape his philosophy of persuasion around the concept of attention. "Persuasion," wrote Winans "is the process of inducing others to give fair, favorable, or undivided attention to propositions."[6] While a necessary first step and the common denominator in all speeches, attention in itself is not the motivating element in persuasion. Conviction demands the precise application of logical, emotional, and ethical proofs to the listener.

Increasingly, listeners demand evidence (the speech to inform) before they will accept the speaker's proposition. The advertisers' use of nasographs. sandpaper beards, chalk dust germs, and animated drawings of our insides, often an insult to our intelligence, is nevertheless a way of satisfying the popular demand for "proof." For college assemblies a speaker's most effective emotional weapon is often his expressed intention of employing logical proofs for an audience which makes or believes it makes its decisions on the basis of facts and evidence. Even the hardest-headed logician, rarely behaves logically in all situations. Most of us are like the dowager in the cartoon who in the midst of an argument with her spouse shouted across the room, "It's going to take more than facts to convince me!"

The speaker who would convince must begin by appealing to attitudes the audience possesses at the outset. He stimulates previously accepted responses and may wait until late in his speech to move into areas of disagreement. As much as possible he attempts to associate the acceptance of his proposition with the fulfillment of previously held attitudes and beliefs. Thus, the speech to convince becomes a delicate blending of speeches to entertain, to inform, and to stimulate.

Again, we must emphasize the role of the audience in determining the speaker's purpose and precise subject treatment. For example, a speech urging support of or resistance to the Supreme Court's decision on school integration will differ markedly in purpose if delivered to a YMCA college audience in Ohio, the White Citizen's Council in Mississippi, or the Chamber of Commerce in Nashville, Tennessee. Indeed, it may be virtually impossible for the speaker to receive a fair hearing before any of these audiences if the group realizes the speaker's position in advance.

The table on page 286 illustrates the possible blending of speech purposes which might occur in speeches delivered before the particular audiences listed. The relative weights given to entertainment, information, stimulation, or conviction, would, of course, vary with individual speakers and the specific purposes they selected.

In nearly every listening situation involving a controversial topic are some individuals who already accept the speaker's proposition. For them the speech is one to stimulate. For the unenlightened the speech may be

---

[5] William James, *Psychology—Briefer Course,* New York: Holt, 1892, p. 449.
[6] James A. Winans, *Public Speaking,* New York: The Century Co., 1917, p. 194.

THE BLENDING OF SPEECH PURPOSES

Audience	Topic or speaker	Entertain	Inform	Stimulate	Convince
PTA	New methods of teaching reading	+++	+++++		
Teachers' convention	The best method of teaching reading	+	++	++	+++
Rotary Club	Travel talk on Africa	+++++	+++		
College YMCA	Join Peace Corps	+	+++	+++	+
College YMCA	World religions	++	++++++		
Kiwanis Club	Highlights of Kiwanis International	+++	+++	++	
White Citizen's Council	Pro-Integration	+	+++	+	+++
NAACP	Pro-Integration	+	+	++++++	
Am. Medical Association	New treatment for diabetes	+	+++++	+	+
Am. Medical Association	Pro-Socialized Medicine	+	+	+	+++++
Lions Club	New treatment for diabetes	+++	+++++		
TV andience TV audience	Bob Hope Jack Benny	+++++++			

one to inform. For those on the fence and for the actively opposed the speaker seeks to convince. He may want the audience to accept his point of view or he may seek more overt changes of behavior—a contribution, a favorable vote, or another vocal supporter. A change of mind is as much an action as a change of vote. The particular audience and occasion will determine in large measure the type of response the speaker may legitimately seek. His courage and skill will determine the degree of audience response. To measure the success or failure of a speech we must consider the obstacles encountered as well as the resultant shift in attitudes or behavior. A speech to convince may succeed even if it merely promotes the listener to say, "I'm still opposed, but now I can see the other point of view." The response does not necessarily measure the excellence of a speech.

We must further recognize that circumstances, seemingly beyond the speaker's control, may render a technically superior speech powerless.

It may fail to achieve its intended goal because of insuperable obstacles, while a less ambitious effort may win over meager opposition.

Contemporary judgment of excellence in speech-making is tenuous at best. In situations where one speaker has failed, another facing the same obstacles, may succeed through a more skillful approach to his subject and his listeners. Moreover, we can never assume that audience behavior immediately following a speech is in fact a direct product of that speech.

In determining the degrees of success or failure, we must like-wise consider the long-range as well as the immediate effects of the speech. Probably no speaker ever aimed his rhetorical shafts solely toward future generations. Those who fail on the contemporary scene sometimes attempt to console themselves with the thought that future generations will somehow appreciate them. Who would not say for example, that Woodrow Wilson's heart-breaking attempt to win United States support for his League of Nations, even though it failed, did not pave the way a quarter of a century later for a more mature and chastened public to embrace the United Nations?

Every speaker also faces the question: "Shall I fix my goal at an easy, attainable level or set my speech purpose on a higher plane, thereby risking possible failure?" We offer no easy answer. Every speaker must make his own choice. This decision, however, will reflect in large measure his traits of character and that elusive, but highly persuasive quality the Greeks called *ethos*—that proof which springs directly from the speaker.[7] Certainly, after setting his goal, no speaker ever dares succumb to the easy temptation of blaming his rhetorical failures on the stupidity of the crowd. Even Wilson, grand though his rhetoric was, might have won more "willful men" to walk the pathway toward world order if he had been as astute a student of persuasion as he was of style.

DELIVERY (BODILY ACTION)

As we indicated earlier in this chapter, the fifth canon of rhetoric concerned the actual presentation of the speech. Yet this skill which the Greeks seemed to place at the end of the preparation process is of immediate concern to the beginning speaker. The learning process forces him to step before an audience well before he has had an opportunity to study or master the others skills (invention, organization, or style). Thus, it seems appropriate at this point to include a discussion of delivery, answering in particular some of the questions concerning the use of gesture. The student may also wish to review Chapter 4 on gesture (see pages 47–55)

---

[7] See the next chapter, pages 306-307, for a discussion of *ethos*, ethical proof.

and may perhaps want to look ahead to Chapter 15 for a discussion of the vocal and physical forms of support (see pages 311–312).

Gestures In Public Speaking

Although gestures are an integral part of all our speech behavior, we generally are more aware of gestures when engaged in public speaking or in listening to a public speaker. We begin to become aware that some speakers look timid or afraid and tell us so before even making a sound; others appear defiant or aggressive; some look relaxed and friendly. There are speakers who distract us through the use of meaningless movements. We may begin to feel more concerned about whether a speaker's buttons will stand the strain of his frequent handling, or about what he may pull out of his pockets, than we do about what the speaker is trying to tell us through his words.

The gestures of the public speaker are not so highly conventionalized as the articulated movements of organized gesture language. For the most part, the speaker's gestures reveal attitudes, consciously or unconsciously entertained, and belong to the expressive aspect of speech. For example, an attitude of friendliness is expressed when a public speaker steps toward his audience; one of abhorrence (usually for the idea being presented) when the speaker steps back or away from his audience.

Hand gestures are generally more conventionalized than gestures involving the body as a whole. Examples of these include an open-hand, *palm-up* gesture to signify *agreement* or acceptance of an idea. It may also mean friendship or willingness to join in a friendly relationship. A *palm-down* gesture, on the other hand, signifies *negation*. More emphatic negation than the palm down is the *thumb-down* hand movement. The pointed-index finger is used to help point out an object or to single out an idea. *Strong feeling* and unity of purpose are revealed through the *clenched fist*.

Two gestures of the head are highly conventionalized. A nod of the head means approval; a lateral shake of the head means disapproval.

Facial expressions, that is facial gestures, can be used with great effectiveness to reveal degrees of feeling. The speaker may smile with pleasant approval, or sneer in scornful or contemptuous rejection; his eyes may open wide in surprise or wonder, or half close in anger or hate; he may knit his brows to show concern or concentration, or smooth his brows to reveal relaxation.

Empathic Responses

At this point we might pause to consider a basic principle of expressive behavior which will help us to appreciate why action is so important in public speaking. Any performer who can succeed in having an observer do and feel in a manner in accord with his purposes increases the likelihood that he will succeed in his objective. If the doing and feeling can take place on an unconscious basis, the speaker further increases the chance of success. If we identify with athletes we are observing in competition, we tend, as far as we are physically able, to imitate the behavior of those being observed. So, we may tense our muscles and "jump and roll over" while watching a high jumper; we buck the line with our favorite ball carrier at a football game; sometimes we actually kick the person in the stand immediately below us while watching a kick-off or field goal attempt. The underlying principle of this projective behavior is *empathy*. In essence, empathy is sympathetic, kinetic response. The speaker who succeeds in evoking empathic responses from his listeners almost literally has his listeners acting with him. To the degree that the actions are expressive of states of feeling, listeners feel as the speaker feels and, we hope, as he wishes them to feel according to the intentions of his speech.

The importance for the speaker to control his movements so that he may direct the empathic responses of his observers should be apparent. If the speaker is himself poorly controlled, if his actions are directed to no purpose but a manifestation of his own state of discomfort, his observers, while they continue to observe, will feel uncomfortable. Members of an audience may cease to look as well as to listen to avoid this state. Once a negative reaction is evoked, the speaker may lose his audience and from that point on speak to no purpose. Fortunately, most members of an audience are sympathetic as well as empathic, and so may make allowance for initial fidgetiness or random movement. But a speaker should not count on sympathy to be indefinitely maintained. Listeners in a public speaking situation should not be taxed beyond easy endurance. If a speaker is deserving of an audience, the members of an audience are deserving of a controlled speaker who can quickly get on with his job of doing and saying what the occasion requires.

Extent of Action

The term *extent* shall be used in two ways: (1) to indicate how much action is appropriate in a public speaking situation, and (2) how broad, how much sweep, should any action be. Hamlet's advice to the players may well serve as a guide for the public speaker. He may recall that Hamlet advised a group of actors to be sure to "suit the action to the word, the word to the action," with this special observance, "that you o'erstep not the modesty of nature." How much action is appropriate depends, of course, on the time, the place, the occasion, and the performer.

The amount of action, how much obvious gesture is employed, is

A   B

Figure 34.   The impassioned arm-swinging of Lady Nancy Astor and the fist-pounding of Senator William Proxmire contrasts sharply with the more restrained actions of the other two speakers. Of even greater importance is the appropriateness of the gesture to the idea and emotion being expressed.

C   D

determined by the nature of the occasion and the specific nature of the speech. A member of Congress, when called upon to give a commencement address at a college or university, should endeavor to sound more like a statesman than a politician. As a statesman, he would be more restrained though not inhibited in his use of gestures than he would at a political rally. We would hope, also, that his choice of topic would be one that would not be impaired by a modest use of gestures devoid of podium-pounding and pointing to give significance to platitudes. The member of Congress speaking at a political rally may let himself go. The audience members expect action and will be disappointed if it is not produced and evoked. By and large, older persons expect more restraint in the use of gestures than do younger persons. Should the older persons attend a ceremony where relative abandon rather than control is the mode, as they might at a college reunion, then gestures might be used more freely.

The size of the room, as well as the size of the audience, should determine the sweep of the gestures, as well as the amount of gesture used. A small group in a small room calls for speaking in a conversational mode, and so for gestures that are essentially those used in conversational situations. A larger audience, a scattered audience in a large room, or an audience at a distance from the speaker in a moderately large room would dictate the use of gestures with a broader sweep than those in conversation. In general, we may follow the principle that gestures should be readily visible to the members of an audience at the greatest physical distance from the speaker. If the gesture cannot be discerned, it may serve as an expressive movement for the speaker, but it will not help materially in communicating the speech content to the listener-observers.

Suitability

We have already anticipated one aspect of suitability in our discussion of the speech occasion. The other aspect of suitability to be considered is directly related to the specific speech content—the suiting of the action to the word. Gestures, we have indicated, are used to convey meaning. As such they either reinforce oral words or are substitutes for words when they are insufficient to communicate the speaker's thoughts or feelings. If gestures are not used for either of these purposes, they must at least serve to release speaker and audience tension. This objective is sometimes necessary when either speaker or listeners have become tense and need release from tension to avoid physical discomfort.

Gestures used to convey meanings are usually used to emphasize a point. The point should be worthy of emphasis. If this is not the case, then the speaker is in effect misleading his listeners and so getting in the way of his own communicative effort. Too much emphasis may easily become equivalent to no emphasis. Random movements suggest random thinking. Controlled movement, in general, and controlled gestures, in particular, suggest selection. Such movements constitute a speaker's nonoral way of highlighting the thoughts he wishes most to be remembered.

Timing

The timing of gestures, as we have indicated, should be related to the over-all content of the speech and "distributed" so that main thoughts are reinforced. There is another aspect or principle of timing that we shall consider briefly. A specific gesture should be timed to *precede the words* to be reinforced. In a sense, a speaker's gesture serves to "point" to the idea about to be presented in words. Beyond this, of course, the gestures give emphasis to the words. When a speaker moves or leans toward the audience, it should be to bring the listeners closer to the thought to come because it is a particularly important thought. If a speaker wishes to indicate a transition in thought or a major division of his speech, he may accomplish this by a vocal pause and by moving during the pause from one part of the platform to another. If this is not possible because the speaker is "mike bound" or "podium bound," this purpose may be served by a shift in position. Movement of this sort is the approximate equivalent of the use of punctuation and division of a page into paragraphs and sections in written communication.

Emphatic gestures should also precede the words to be highlighted. Thus, the movement of an arm, the use of a pointed finger on an extended arm, the closed hand gesture, should precede the words worthy of such emphatic behavior.

An exception to the general principle that the gesture precedes the words is the one used to replace words. The gesture then should terminate the thought and be followed by a pause so that there is no confusion that action did not suit the word. Thus, if a speaker wishes to act out rather than say "oh well, what can one do" by shrugging his shoulders, a pause should follow the gesture before oral speech is resumed.

Practices in the Use of Gesture

We shall conclude our consideration of the language of action for the public speaker by suggesting some guides for the execution of movements and gestures with maximum effectiveness.

1. *Gestures begin with every movement that brings the speaker to the platform, as well as with movements while he is on the platform.* This includes the way the speaker sits while waiting to be introduced, the way he walks to the part of the platform where he will "take his stand" for his

engagement, and whatever he does beyond that point. So, don't slouch while sitting and waiting or while standing or moving. Sit easily but upright and walk with ease and alertness to your first position. If you slouch it should be to suggest a slouchy idea to your listeners. If you become hypertense, it should also be to suggest a feeling or meaning that calls for hypertension.

2. *Permit your movements to be natural and free of inhibitions.* If the gestures you employ are an extension of those you would be inclined, unconsciously, to use in conversation, they are likely to be both natural and appropriate. Once a gesture is initiated, do not inhibit it. Inhibition will produce jerky movements and will evoke feelings of discomfort in the observers. Few beginning speakers are likely to "o'erstep the modesty of nature," so let yourself go.

3. *When you execute a gesture, as you "let yourself go" be sure that all of you is involved and coordinated in the going.* A gesture of the hand should involve the whole arm, and the arm in turn be part of the movement of the body as a whole. If your gesture is one of offering something to your audience with outstretched hands, the offering should involve the entire body. If it does, it will be a free and generous giving and likely to be well received. Every gesture should be, or at least suggest, a complete movement unless there is an intention to suggest inhibition or incompletion.

4. *Use variety in gestures as you use in words.* An effective speaker who wishes to maintain attention avoids the use of repeated phrases or of sentences all cast in the same pattern. Do not use the same gesture in such close sequence that the listener-viewers obtain the impression that your "vocabulary of gestures" is limited and inadequate for the ideas you are trying to communicate.

5. *Avoid self-conscious movements and random behavior.* Do not "play" with any object unless you are using it for illustrative purposes. If you are not certain about your hands, just let them hang by the arms at your side. They will then be readily available for use when a hand-arm gesture is needed. By all means keep your hands out of your pockets unless you are really trying to extract something to show to your audience. Avoid any repetitive or ticlike action such as scratching part of your face or arranging and rearranging part of your attire. Come dressed for the occasion and assume that you will continue to be so dressed throughout your performance.

6. *Establish contact with the members of your audience by looking directly at them.* If your audience is large and the members spread out, shift

your glance from time to time so that none will feel ignored. Do not, however, shift with rhythmic regularity. This is not an effective or appropriate way to sway your listeners.

7. Bear in mind that every movement has a meaning and make certain that it is the meaning you wish to convey.

SUMMARY

A democratic society demands an alert citizenry, skilled in the techniques of public address. Essential to effective public speaking is a mastery of the classical elements in speech preparation, namely (1) *invention,* (2) *organization,* (3) *style,* (4) *memory,* and (5) *delivery.*

The speaker's specialized treatment of these five essential skills will depend in large measure on his selection of the *general* and *specific purposes* of the speech. The purpose itself is directly correlated with the type of response or responses the speaker seeks from his audience. The objective of all effective public speaking is an appropriate response, either physical (vote or contribution) or mental (change of attitude or belief). The responses in turn furnish us with convenient names for the different kinds of speeches, usually classified under four headings:

Speech to Inform	⎫
Speech to Entertain	⎬ Expository
Speech to Stimulate	⎫
Speech to Convince	⎬ Persuasive

The visible elements of delivery, particularly the speaker's ability to employ gestures meaningfully, will determine in part the audience response.

QUESTIONS AND EXERCISES

1. Following the plan of the table on page 286 showing the blending of speech purposes, set up a similar chart for the topics listed below. Select a potential audience for each topic.
    (a) Pro-legalized gambling,
    (b) Anti-low-cost governmental housing,
    (c) Soil Conservation,
    (d) Juvenile Delinquency,
    (e) Common Market,
    (f) Anti-foreign aid,
    (g) Campus social regulations,
    (h) The English educational system,
    (i) Anti-intercollegiate Athletics.
2. Attend a public lecture and analyze the speech for the following:

(a) The speaker's *general purpose*. How much blending of general purposes occurred?

(b) The speaker's *specific purpose*. State this purpose in one sentence. If you find it impossible to state the specific purpose, can you decide why?

(c) Did the speaker accomplish his specific purpose? Why? Why not?

3. Prepare a two-to-three-minute speech *to entertain* using an autobiographical approach.

4. What factors determine the success or failure of a public speech? Construct a four-minute manuscript speech to defend your point of view.

5. Choose a subject and then phrase four *purpose sentences* or *propositions*, one for each of the four general purposes—i.e., entertain, inform, stimulate, and convince.

6. Distinguish between the speech to inform and the speech to convince. Prepare a three-minute talk explaining the differences. Use at least three possible speech topics or subjects as illustrative supporting material for your talk.

7. Prepare a two-or-three-minute speech to inform on a topic of your own choice to be delivered to your class. Using the same topic, construct and deliver a speech to convince.

8. In a three-minute speech to inform, explain the essential differences in the potential general purpose and response in social conversation as contrasted and compared with public speaking.

9. Study an address from *Vital Speeches* and after you have determined the speaker's purpose, rewrite the introduction, keeping the same topic but radically changing the general purpose.

RECOMMENDED READINGS

Arnold, Carroll C., Ehninger, Douglas, and Gerber, J. C. *The Speaker's Resource Book,* Chicago: Scott, Foresman, 1961, Part I.

Brigance, William N. *Speech: Its Techniques and Disciplines in a Free Society.* New York: Appleton-Century-Crofts, 1961, Chap. 9.

Bryant, Donald C., and Wallace, Karl R. *Fundamentals of Public Speaking.* New York: Appleton-Century-Crofts, 1960, Part I.

Gray, Giles Wilkeson, and Braden, Waldo W. *Public Speaking: Principles and Practice.* New York: Harper and Row, 1963, Parts I and V.

Hildebrandt, Herbert. *Issues of Our Time,* New York: Macmillan, 1963.

McBurney, James H., and Wrage, Ernest J. *The Art of Good Speech.* New York: Prentice-Hall, 1953, Chap. VI.

Monroe, A. H. *Principles and Types of Speech,* 5th ed. Chicago: Scott, Foresman, 1962, Chap. 3.

Oliver, R. T., and Cortright, R. L. *Effective Speech,* 4th ed. New York: Holt, Rinehart and Winston, 1961, Chap. 13.

Parrish, Wayland Maxfield, and Hochmuth, Marie. *American Speeches.* New York: Longmans, Green, 1954, Chaps. 1 and 2, "The Study of Speeches" and "Lincoln's First Inaugural."

Pei, Mario. *The Story of Languages.* New York: Lippincott, 1949.

Reid, Loren. *First Principles of Public Speaking.* Columbia, Mo.: Artcraft Press, 1962, Chaps. 1, 4, and 6.

CHAPTER 15

FINDING AND FORTIFYING

THE PROPOSITION

Few more perplexing problems ever face us as prospective speakers than the one of finding the "right" subject. We may derive some comfort from the knowledge that this condition is nearly universal, even among those who prepare frequent, even weekly public addresses. While the more experienced speakers may possess a deeper reservoir of knowledge, a wider background of experience, less fear of the platform, and greater verbal facility, all speakers—the novice and the seasoned alike—must follow the same general processes of selection and preparation.

Good speech topics rarely flash into the speaker's mind spontaneously or easily. They come only after conscientious prompting and as a result of systematic techniques. Happily, as we develop correct research practices, we often discover more topics than we can find audiences. And just as the beginner may find it difficult to "keep talking" for two minutes during his first speech, so he may later find it painful to stop at the end of ten or more minutes.

ANALYZING THE AUDIENCE AND OCCASION

Our first step in finding a topic is to determine the kind of response we can legitimately seek from a particular audience at the precise moment we speak to them. In the previous chapter we discussed the *general* and *specific purposes,* and our task now is to determine the suitability of the purposes for potential audiences. A primary cause of failure in public speaking, perhaps the major cause, is the speaker's inaccurate appraisal of the tenor and temper of his audience and the occasion. His speech, we say, would have succeeded if he had only addressed the National Association of Manufacturers instead of the CIO-AFL.

The members of the same audience, if it were possible to duplicate an audience, might behave and react in one way during a message on Sunday morning and in a quite different manner at a Wednesday noon luncheon. The subject matter of a speech should reveal awareness of the time, place, prospective listeners, as well as contents *per se*. Thus, a talk on a subject such as "The European Economic Community" should vary widely in style, organization, and delivery, depending on whether we are addressing a high-school audience, the farm bureau, a college seminar in economics, or a particular Chamber of Commerce. Additional elements influencing our topic selection and its treatment will stem from the limitations imposed by the time of day and the events (other speakers, business meetings, songs, and ritual) immediately preceding or following our remarks. The formality or informality of the occasion, the physical conditions of the room and the time allotted to our speech are all items to consider. After an appraisal we may even decide that some topic other than the Common Market would fit one of these audiences more satisfactorily. But, if our invitation specifically requested the Common Market, then we are under an obligation to make this complex topic clear, provocative, and relevant to that group. Clearly, the same speech will seldom be equally appropriate for the farm bureau, a high-school assembly, and a college seminar.

Our analytic exercise is further complicated by the heterogeneous complexity of most audiences. They often include smatterings of widely divergent social, economic, and political groups, diverse elements making it virtually impossible to satisfy every person. In one address Adlai Stevenson, with his characteristic flair for self-directed humor, pictured the familiar dilemma always plaguing the commencement speaker. Like other June orators, Stevenson confessed, he could never decide whether to direct his remarks to the graduates or to their parents and teachers. The accepted formula of aiming somewhere in between would, he feared, only assure him a perfect miss.[1]

While recognizing the impossibility of achieving perfect audience adaptation, the wise speaker will nevertheless strive to discover the probable answers to these questions:

1. What is the educational, social, and cultural background of the audience?
2. Is this a predominately professional, social, or religious group?
3. What professional and occupational groups are represented?
4. What is the general economic level of the audience?
5. What age group, if any, predominates?

---

[1] Commencement Address at Oberlin College, June 15, 1955.

6. Is the audience composed of men, women, or both?
7. What is the general political orientation of its members?
8. Is race or creed a significant factor?

After the speaker has selected his specific proposition, he must investi-gate the potential attitude of his audience toward his subject. Will they be likely to have an apathetic, friendly, open-minded, or hostile attitude toward his proposition? In the *speech to inform* we must give particular attention to the background knowledge of our potential audience. We dare not bore them with the "same old stuff." Neither can we risk confusing them with technical material beyond their comprehension. In the *speech to convince* we must base our arguments on premises they are willing to accept and draw our inferences from evidence they can understand. No matter how important, vital, or interesting we may consider the topic, it must, first and foremost, contain materials within the comprehension and the frame of reference of the particular audience we are addressing. Specifically we must ask ourselves:

1. What kinds of background information does the audience possess which is directly and indirectly related to the proposition?
2. What basic attitudes does this audience hold toward the subject under consideration?

SELF-ANALYSIS

Finally, the selection, as well as the treatment of the topic, will depend to some degree on the audience's attitude toward the speaker. This is closely related to that form of support known as *ethical proof* which we shall discuss more fully in this chapter. Here it is sufficient to ask ourselves:

1. Because of my background, training, or experience do the listeners anticipate a particular kind of speech? You may in some instances wish to deliver a radically different kind of speech from the one they expect. But you should project and be aware of their potential reactions.
2. Will the audience accept me as an authority in this area? A negative answer will not necessarily rule out a topic, but you may be forced to use more documentation or employ special forms of proof.

FINDING THE SPECIFIC TOPIC

Subjects often spring directly from self-analysis or from the audience and the occasion. The groups and the situations themselves create the stimuli and provide the atmosphere, but the speaker must still find the precise topic and phrase the specific proposition. This is the problem every student speaker faces after his instructor has assigned a speech to inform. The student has a better than average opportunity to analyze his audience and appraise the occasion. Yet, in complete desperation he often says to his instructor or his roommate, "I can't find a topic; I have nothing worth saying." At that moment he is completely honest, if inaccurate. Usually a cursory investigation of three or four areas turns up more likely topics than he can immediately use.

1. Look to Yourself. At first glance it would seem that there is no other place to begin. Unfortunately, we are so close to our own experiences that they often strike us as too commonplace. Subjects from far-away lands and highly technical topics for which we have little background often hold a fatal attraction. No one should be discouraged from doing research on esoteric topics, but the student must recognize that unless he has some initial background knowledge, he will probably succeed in merely confusing himself and his audience. The beginning speaker will do well to look to his own *interests, hobbies, past experiences, travels,* and *work experiences* for speeches to inform. A subject on which you have some basic knowledge, either through first-hand experience or through course work makes the best starting point. From there you move into research, increasing and enriching your original fund of knowledge.

2. Look Around. When one student turned in a fairly good outline for a speech on the slums of New York City, her instructor asked if she had ever examined the housing conditions in their own small middle-western town. Her natural response was, "What is there to investigate?" Yet within easy walking distance of her dormitory there were slumlike conditions (unknown to the average student) nearly paralleling on a smaller scale the worst of New York or Chicago. After a visit to this area that student prepared a pertinent, dynamic speech, far more vital to her audience than any she might have developed on the housing conditions in New York City. Unfortunately, only a handful of college students heard her speech. The more influential speakers in the community who had larger audiences remained silent on the subject of slums until a tragic fire swept a bedroom hovel, too small for even one child, and snuffed out the lives of seven of the nine children sleeping there. After the tragedy, everyone, on and off campus, had a speech ready to deliver at the mushrooming public indignation meetings. Every campus and community are filled with available subjects. But we need the insight and imagination to spot them.

3. Look to Courses. Students are constantly engaged in research, but they are not always sensitive to the potential speech topics lurking within an economics, history, foreign language, or zoology assignment. From a psychology course one student developed an interest in cybernetics, pursued the topic with additional research and ultimately developed an excellent speech on the implications of cybernetics to modern psychology. Another student discovered a topic in geology, and gave his speech on "Our Water Supply in the Future." In history and government classes we are exposed to a multitude of problems bearing directly on all our lives. The alert student continually jots down topics and tentative outlines, which through further research and study, might become vibrant, meaningful speeches. A word of caution is also in order. Often student speakers attempt to cover all of Economics 101 in an eight-minute speech, resulting in a discussion so thin it fails to say anything new or else one so entangled in economic theory that it only confuses the listeners.

TESTING THE TOPIC

From the moment a speaker begins his search for a topic and begins his investigation, he ought consistently to test his subject. Some of the inquiry will apply to all topics; other parts will bear directly on the particular speech under consideration. During his preparation for any speech he will want to ask himself the following questions:

1. *Is the topic one in which I am vitally interested?* While the *sine qua non* of an excellent choice is always the speaker's enthusiasm, many potentially good subjects are cast aside before the speaker has realistically examined them. Seemingly drab topics, upon careful investigation, take on genuine luster. On the other hand, many subjects lose some of their initial glamor after close examination. Thus, we often need to refreshen and revitalize our enthusiasm. Above all, it is essential to maintain the feeling that our topic is important and necessary for the audience.

2. *Is the topic timely or timeless?* Other factors being equal the timely topic is preferable to one that is "timeless." As long as man puts other men to death, the subject of capital punishment will remain as a timeless topic. On the eve of an execution involving a nationally or internationally publicized criminal, for example, Adolf Eichmann, an age-old topic takes on new and immediate significance.

3. *Is my topic relevant for my audience?* If the listeners ask themselves during the speaker's remarks just why they are receiving a talk on this particular topic, the chances are the speaker has overestimated its relevance. A denunciation of fraternities on a campus where they are already forbidden and where no sentiment prevails for their establishment will probably strike a student audience as totally irrelevant. The speaker is in effect attacking a "straw man" and developing his speech around an artificial issue.

4. *Is the topic suitable for oral discourse?* A skillful speaker can adapt most subjects to the platform. Complications often arise, however, when we attempt to treat a highly technical topic. Some subjects require several thousand words to be understood when written for a reader. Such topics, even if they can be presented for listeners, are likely to require longer rather than shorter treatment than they would for readers. The speaker who undertakes to present a complex topic in too few words and with an insufficient number of concrete illustrations is inviting inevitable failure. He likewise risks disaster, if he assumes a background of information his audience does not possess. Even an audience with some college background in mathematics would probably find itself at sea during a discussion of "Geometrical Algebra."

A few topics, depending on audience make-up, may fall into the classification of taboo subjects. The list has shrunk markedly over the years and subjects once discussed in "closed" sessions are now freely discussed in mixed groups. However, if the speaker is merely hoping to shock his listeners or striving to prove that he is free from puritan shackles, he is likely to fail even in this objective. Before venturing into these areas, the beginning speaker needs to analyze his audience and his own capabilities.

POSSIBLE TOPICS

While the topics below are listed under two general headings, *Expository* and *Persuasive,* they can serve almost any speech purpose, depending on the specialized treatment given to them. Each speaker must *narrow* and phrase his own *specific proposition.*

EXPOSITORY

(Entertain and Inform)

1. My trip to (England, Africa, India, etc.)
2. Indian Customs
3. History of (baseball, the UN, a town, cause, etc.)
4. Personal History
5. Space Explorations
6. Physical Fitness Program
7. Music Lessons
8. College Social Rules
9. Mock Conventions
10. Procrastination
11. The Weather and I
12. Camping

PERSUASIVE

(Stimulate and Convince)

1. Support the Red Cross
2. Federal Aid to Education
3. Highway Safety
4. Public Health Programs
5. Censorship
6. Pornography
7. Common Market
8. College Athletics
9. Legal Reforms
10. Red China (UN Membership?)
11. Slum Clearance
12. Civil Rights
13. Foreign Aid
14. Peace Corps

EXPOSITORY (*Entertain and Inform*)	PERSUASIVE (*Stimulate and Convince*)
13. Poetry or "How much verse can it be?"	15. Juvenile Delinquency
14. Quacks	16. Church-State Relationships
15. A Ring on the Hand	17. Free Enterprise
16. Blunders	18. Liberty—Justice
17. Existentialism	19. Tariffs
18. Extrasensory Perception	20. Medical Care
19. Japanese Haiku Poetry	21. Water Pollution
20. NATO	22. Federal Housing
21. Bird Navigation	23. Collective Bargaining
	24. Disarmament

FORTIFYING THE PROPOSITION

Whether the speech is designed to inform, entertain, stimulate, or convince, the speaker's major obligation is to secure sufficient supporting evidence to promote the desired inferences and responses from the audience. His general techniques of research differ little from those of the debater or the discussant.[2] To establish his proposition and win the desired audience response, he is wise to employ as wide a variety of supporting forms and materials as possible. Moreover, the steps in finding supporting materials closely approximate the steps used in finding a suitable topic. The best starting place is the speaker's own fund of knowledge. Even after he has apparently drained his own resources, he often finds to his surprise, if he starts early with his preparation, that he will continue to receive a flow of seemingly new ideas. Even during the actual presentation, the precise illustration he needs may suddenly occur to him. While no one should rely on last minute inspirations, they occur most frequently and successfully to speakers who are thoroughly prepared.

After the speaker has forumlated a tentative outline based on his own background resources, he then moves beyond the narrow border of his own experience. The excellent speaker never neglects neither does he depend solely on his personal storehouse of information, but looks to the well-known indices to periodical literature for articles, to the reference books for factual support, and to the varied sources catalogued in the library card file. If individuals near at hand possess special knowledge on his subject, he searches them out for interviews. To the traditional forms of support —*logical, emotional*, and *ethical*—he seeks *expository* and *stylistic* methods of rendering the final product clear and vivid as well as persuasive. As

---

[2] See Chapters 11 and 12, pages 223–267.

we shall presently observe, no dividing line separates the various forms of support; they overlap at many points, and ultimately the speaker blends them into a unified speech which, if artistically designed, moves toward the establishment of the proposition. Finally, he places his evidence before the audience in a form best suited to his listeners and the specific occasion.

Logical Forms

Basically, the speaker employs two logical patterns to support his propositions—the *inductive* and the *deductive*. Although we sometimes consider these two as separate approaches, they are in reality inextricably interwoven and wholly dependent on each other. The scientific method proceeds inductively, moving from specific items of evidence toward a general truth. The police inspector follows the inductive process when he finds a cigarette that bears lipstick traces, a mink stole, and a lady's perfumed handkerchief in the same room with a murdered man. From these specific clues he may conclude, rightly or wrongly, that some female was mixed up with the homicide. Another inspector may attack the case deductively. When he receives the call at headquarters that a man has been murdered, he may remark, "No doubt a woman in the case. There always is!" He begins with the general premise that all murder cases include a woman. In deductive reasoning, then, we move from the general to the particular. From the general premise "Back of every successful man there stands a woman," we might conclude, rightly or wrongly, that the successful Mr. Smythe must have received his inspiration from his wife, mother, or another woman. But this particular Smythe may have been a woman-hater.

Clearly the most precarious, least reliable form of logical proof is probably the deductive. Since it begins with the generalization or a so-called "universal truth," the speaker must be sure he has established the validity of his premise. Books on public speaking and debate often spend much time examining the structure of deductive logic, i.e., the syllogism and enthymeme.[3] It is probably important to understand the various tests for the syllogism, cause and effect relationships, and the analogy. It is even more important to make sure the premises (generalizations) are substantiated by the facts. If all syllogisms were as infallible as the logicians' favorite concerning the mortal nature of man in general and of Socrates in particular, we would experience little difficulty.[4] But our major premises are

---

[3] The enthymeme is often called the rhetorical syllogism. Aristotle explained that since audiences were too impatient to follow the complete syllogism, the orator shortened and omitted certain steps. The enthymeme might best be explained as a maxim, a general truth the audience will accept as valid.

[4] All men are mortal. (*Major premise*)
Socrates is a man. (*Minor premise*)
Therefore, Socrates is mortal. (*Conclusion*)

seldom based on so universal a truth. At best we can usually establish only a probability of truth for our premises and thus for our conclusions. "All apples contain seeds," we say basing our generalization on rather widespread inductive evidence. The trouble is that it is not universally true. Seedless apples as well as grapes, grapefruit, oranges, and even watermelon do exist. At one time, no doubt, a generally accepted universal truth was: "All grapes contain seeds."

H. L. Mencken branded this kind of deductive logic, "sillygisms" listing some of the following among his favorites:

That Anglo-Saxons are a superior race.

That Americans are God's chosen people with a divine mission in the world.

That progress must be always upward and onward.

That obedience to constituted authority is the prime requisite of good citizenship.[5]

We do not mean to imply that the speaker should avoid premises and inferences. He must use this form of support; he has no other choice. Indeed, his proposition is the fundamental deductive premise in the speech. It is the primary assertion or generalization he attempts to establish through specific facts, instances, and testimony. From these facts (induction), he draws further generalizations, points to causes and effects, constructs analogies, and hopes through this mixture of specific instances (induction) and general conclusions (deduction) to establish the validity of his major proposition. But the excellent speaker tests every fact and every tentative generalization, recognizing his assertions and inferences (even his so-called facts) for what they are, namely, possible truths.

Every four years with the arrival of a new student generation some magazine writer attempts to classify the present college crop. In one quadrennium they are "Beat" and in the next "Lost," and most recently they are "Concerned."[6] To test the validity of these premises (inferences) "College students are 'beat' 'lost' 'concerned' " we need to ask some questions:

1. Are the alleged facts gleaned through testimony, statistics, and examples sufficiently abundant (how many colleges, students) to warrant a probable inference, generalization, premise, or contention?

2. Are the instances representative? (Ivy League, state schools, denominational schools?)

3. Does a direct relationship exist between the facts and the conclu-

---

[5] C. Merton Babcock, "H. L. Mencken: Of Horse-Laughs and Syllogisms," *ETC: A Review of General Semantics,* **XIX** (February 1963), 430–431.

[6] See Harold Taylor, "Portrait of a New Generation," *Saturday Review* (December 8, 1962), pp. 10–12.

sions? In cause and effect relationships is the cause sufficient to produce the effect? (Progressive education, life adjustment courses may have produced a generation of mental midgets.)

4. Are our facts substantiated by a wide variety of sources? Do the witnesses (books, magazines, TV and radio reports, personal interviews, personal experience) tend to agree on the facts?

5. Were the facts (statistics, instances, examples) gathered by a responsible agency and can they be verified and supported by other sources?

Emotional Forms

No clear-cut line separates logical from emotional proof. Just as inductive and deductive logic support each other, so the emotional strands of an argument interlace the logical, thus making it difficult, if not impossible, for even the trained rhetorical critic to identify and isolate the elements. The amount of emotion in any logical appeal depends on the treatment (word choice, phrasing, delivery) the speaker gives his facts and illustrations. The coldest statistic on a ticker tape may inspire some to wild, emotional responses and others to suicidal depression. George Whitefield's vocal control was such that he could supposedly bring tears to the eyes of his listeners with the mere repetition of the word "Mesopotamia."

When the chairman of the Federal Communications Commission, Newton Minow, delivered his famous TV "Wasteland" speech, he stirred up one kind of emotional response in his immediate audience, the National Association of Broadcasters. He appealed to another kind of motive and received a radically different reaction from the television viewers who read his remarks. Many in his immediate audience took offense and were deeply hurt and resentful, while 98 per cent of the reading public enthusiastically supported him. Certainly in the following passage from Minow's speech, we have trouble separating the logical and the emotional appeals. "When television is good, nothing . . . is better. But when television is bad, nothing is worse." We could state these generalizations syllogistically. They constitute some of the premises, maxims, and enthymemes fundamental to Minow's speech. To establish the validity of his assertion that TV was bad, indeed a "vast wasteland," he pictured a typical TV day, citing the following emotionally loaded specific instances (induction). "You will see a procession of game shows, violence, audience participation shows, formula comedies about totally unbelievable families, blood and thunder, mayhem, violence, sadism, murder, western badmen, western good men, private eyes, gangsters, more violence, and cartoons. And, endlessly, commercials —many screaming, cajoling, and offending. And most of all, boredom."

Usually when people complain about an emotional address, they really mean that the speaker's appeals (premises) failed to coincide with their particular wants or drives. We need to recognize that emotional appeals are as logical or illogical, as sound or as specious as the entire argument. Moreover, it is wholly inaccurate to consider emotion as synonymous with fallacious argument. Man is an emotional as well as a reasoning being. These two elements are not mutually exclusive, but complementary features of his total character. And he who would persuade through language must make his appeal through logic and emotion. Indeed, any appeal to reason which runs counter to emotionally held attitudes will rarely if ever succeed.

But let us make one idea clear. We do not believe that every emotional appeal is legitimate and ethical or that we should condone the demagogue and the huckster when he appeals to every primitive trick to promote irrational decisions. Appeals to class hatred, the big lie, the half truth, noisy repetition, name calling, and the suppression of evidence lie outside the realm of ethical persuasion. The end, however noble, never justifies the use of these means. On the other hand, we do not consider all appeals based on emotion as unethical. Man's wants and drives range from his narrowest selfish concern to his noblest aspiration for the liberation of all peoples. Keeping in mind our earlier contention that it is virtually impossible to separate logical appeals from emotional appeals, we would still caution the speaker to ask himself one fundamental, soul-searching question: "Should my audience accept this proposition solely on the basis of the best logical proof available?" If the answer is affirmative, the speaker may then seek the *ethical motivation* that will promote audience acceptance of the proposition. In the next chapter we shall examine in greater detail the potential appeals.

Ethical Proof

This form of proof Aristotle considered as "almost" the most "potent of all the means to persuasion." It contains an illusive mixture, many so subtle that they defy analysis. This proof which comes from the speaker includes more than "goodness" and "sincerity." Many honest, upright men have failed utterly to develop ethical proof. It seems to include personality, appearance, reputation, character, nuances of delivery, word choice, vocal quality, and a host of intangibles. "Image" is perhaps the popular term for ethical proof, particularly when used with a favorable connotation.

Every speaker hopes his ethical appeal is high and usually strives consciously or subconsciously to increase his stature. A student speaker often wonders what he, a relative unknown, can do in the classroom situation to develop this illusive quality, one that is seemingly reserved for persons with wider experience. While the development of this quality is frequently the task of a lifetime, most observers recognize the presence of varying degrees of ethical proof in student speakers. We can isolate some of the reasons:

1. By demonstrating a complete command of the subject each time he appears before the class.

2. A thoroughly prepared speech, including a mastery of ideas, organization, style, and delivery.

3. Absolute fairness in treating the evidence and in drawing his inferences.

4. The use of recognized authority to support matters of opinion.

5. A manner free on one hand from negative suggestion and unnecessary apology and on the other from a "know it all" attitude.

6. A friendly, relaxed poised presentation.

7. Dress and bearing suitable to the subject, audience, and occasion.

8. A strong sense of communication with the audience and a willingness to respond to cues he receives from the audience.

9. In summary, the speaker strives to develop those qualities which prompted Quintilian to describe the perfect orator as a "good man skilled in speaking."

Expository and Stylistic Forms

A common lament of the speaker to his listener who misunderstands or fails to grasp an idea is the oft-repeated excuse, "But I said it." And equally distressing to both the speaker and the listener is the recorded proof. The speaker did say "It." In hurt tones the speaker then complains, "People just don't listen." And again he is right. Most people listen with only half an ear and with an efficiency rating of 50 per cent or less.[7] And unless they hear essentially the same message at least three times the percentage may drop even lower. In the area of organization they often need an initial summary, an expanded discussion, and a final summary.[8]

The supporting material throughout the speech also needs *amplification* through restatement, explanation, concreteness, figurative imagery, and all the stylistic devices which add vividness to our speaking and ease to our understanding. If necessary, a reader may reread a passage. An idea stated once may suffice for him. The listener, on the other hand, may need to hear the same message repeated—the more complex the material, the greater the need for amplification and restatement.

Restatement. Repetition is probably our most important single device for reinforcing an impression. For many, Madison Avenue learned this lesson too well, but irritating though the noisy, repetitious radio and television commercial may be, it attracts our attention, making it difficult to

---

[7] Ralph Nichols, "Do We Know How to Listen? Practical Helps in a Modern Age," *The Speech Teacher,* **X** (March 1961), 118.

[8] See Chapter 16 for a discussion of organization.

forget the name of a particular product when we stop by the corner drug store.

We hope that speakers will avoid a commercial-like repetition, but we likewise emphasize the necessity for generous amplification through re-statement—not through mere repetition. The idea is subtly restated in fresh phraseology, insulting neither the most sophisticated listener nor losing the ear of the least perceptive. Notice how Adlai Stevenson, for example, ampli-fies the concept of democracy through apt restatement.

And I suppose that most of us, if we were asked to name the most profound issues at stake in the world today, would say the issues of freedom and de-mocracy. We would say that the Western World, for all its errors and short-comings, has for centuries tried to evolve a society in which the individual has enough legal, social, and political elbow room to be not the puppet of the community, but his own autonomous self.[9]

Explanation.   Another form of amplification is explanation. Clearly most speeches contain a generous intermixture of repetition, restatement, and explanation. In the same speech quoted above, Stevenson explains what he means by the assertion: "There is precious little dignity or equality in our natural state."

Most human beings have to spend their lives in utter vulnerability. All are murderable and torturable, and survive only through the restraint shown by more powerful neighbors. All are born unequal, in terms of capacity or strength. All are born to the inherent fraility of the human condition, naked and helpless, vulnerable all through life to the will of others, limited by ignorance, limited by physical weakness, limited by fear, limited by the phobias that fear engenders.[10]

Concreteness.   Only a small fraction of the population can think in abstractions. No one can speak clearly to another in abstract terms. And when two or more do talk with each other in the abstract, neither can ever be sure that he understands precisely what the other is talking about. If they speak of "truth" and "justice," these concepts evoke widely different sensory images in each person. When Disraeli said in a speech, "Justice is truth in action," he made them somewhat more concrete. When John Galsworthy compared justice to "a machine that when some one has once given it the starting push, rolls on of itself," we see more clearly. Then if we can wrap these abstractions in human personalities and specific illustra-tions, they take on a vivid accurateness.

Statistics.   The best as well as the poorest parts of a speech are often those fortified with statistics. Capable of lending concrete liveliness, they can also assume the deadly and confusing inhuman visage of the most

---

[9] *Vital Speeches* (March 1, 1963), p. 306.
[10] *Ibid.,* p. 307.

foreboding mathematical equation. Yet the dullest figures, when classified, compared, and integrated with the proposition, can take on real color. Bob Hope demonstrated how specific data given the human touch can be highly entertaining:

Today my heart beat 103,389 times, my blood traveled 168,000,000 miles, I breathed 23,040 times, I inhaled 438 cubic feet of air, I spoke 4,800 words, moved 750 major muscles, and I exercised 7,000,000 brain cells. I'm tired.[11]

By using the exact figures (inaccurate though they were) Hope managed to heighten the humor. The speaker is often puzzled over the question of whether to use the complete statistic or round off the figures. In the serious speech, absolute accuracy is necessary and yet the complete statistic may only confuse. For situations where exactness is important, the speaker must avoid overwhelming his listeners. He can sometimes accomplish this by using the round number in association with the exact numbers. An additional restatement in *percentages* may further amplify his point.

In all instances the raw figures must be put in terms the audience can comprehend. When a speaker announces with vigor the astronomical figures in the national debt, most listeners, whose checkbooks rarely carry a balance beyond three figures, have no frame of reference in which to place these billions. The naive listener may be impressed, but the serious student will resent the confusion resulting from the speaker's failure to interpret his statistics. On the other hand, a commonly used device of putting the debt on a "per person" basis increases the understanding of all listeners.

If a speaker points out that the total cost for public education in elementary and secondary schools for the year 1962–63 cost United States taxpayers 19.5 billion dollars, an all time high, the audience might conclude we were spending a tremendous sum. Putting this sum in perspective through comparison may change our attitude. The National Educational Association translated the figure to show that we were actually paying 45 cents an hour for each enrolled pupil or about 10 per cent less than the going rate for teenaged baby sitters.[12]

In presenting figures and statistical data it is essential that they be authoritative and that the listener be so impressed. He will not get such an impression if statistical data are introduced with a vague and evasive statement such as, "Records show that . . ." or "Statistics prove that. . . ." Instead, the precise source of the data should be presented in such a way that any listener may check their authenticity should he so desire.

Figurative Imagery. "Man is a creature who lives not upon bread alone," wrote Robert Louis Stevenson, "but principally by catchwords."

---

[11] From "Quotable Quotes," *Reader's Digest* (January 1949), p. 131.
[12] *NEA Reporter* (Washington, D.C.: February 22, 1963), p. 3.

We would add to this—figurative phraseology. President Kennedy packed his Inaugural Address with vivid imagery, as a writer in *The New Yorker* pointed out.

The oration is so rich in figures of speech—the many metaphors include a torch, a beachhead, jungles, a trumpet, a tiger—that we can imagine students of the future studying it for examples of antithesis ("If a free society cannot help the many who are poor, it cannot save the few who are rich"), personification (". . . the hand of mankind's final war"), and anaphora ("Not as a call to bear arms, though arms we need; not as a call to battle, though embattled we are . . ."). "Battle" and "embattled"—an excellent example of paronomasia.[13]

A word of caution may be necessary in the use of stylistic devices. Excellent oral style should be *clear, appropriate,* and *vivid.* We must also recognize that style appropriate for the Kennedy Inauguration would be out of keeping in an after-dinner address or a lecture on the federal budget. Moreover, style that calls attention to itself usually needs reworking. Adjectives and adverbs, metaphors and similes, through overuse, turn into cliches. As G. L. Mehta, Indian Ambassador to the United States, in an editorial entitled "Spare That Adjective" points out: "Times are always 'critical,' sessions of conferences 'momentous,' and tests 'acid' . . . policies have to be 'firm' and 'enduring' but statesmanship (of opponents) is usually 'bankrupt.' "[14] All of us too easily adopt the once vivid figures of the past, turning them into the cliches of the present. For example, *"Each* and *every one* of us is *wiser but sadder* as we *point with pride* to the *perilous* waters through which our *grand old ship of state* has sailed." We need further to watch lest we mix our figures as did one unidentified sacred orator who compared the church to a ship and then asked, "Why does our ship sail on so grandly? Because it is grounded on a rock!"

AUDIOVISUAL SUPPORT

Certain types of speeches, particularly those designed to inform, are often improved by the skillful use of audiovisual aids—by charts, graphs, pictures, enlarged models, film strips, movies, tape recordings, and records. Modern projectors now permit the use of audiovisual presentations, once possible only in a small room with a blackboard. Overhead viewers can enlarge the speaker's pictures, charts, graphs, and writing and place them within easy viewing for an almost unlimited audience. The speaker does not break contact by turning his side or back to the audience as required by use of the blackboard or easel. The energy invested in preparing slides and securing the projector and screen frequently pays rich dividends in

---

[13] Reprinted by permission; © 1961 The New Yorker Magazine, Inc.
[14] *Saturday Review* (August 10, 1957), p. 18.

audience interest and comprehension. But whether using conventional means or electronic assistance, the speaker needs to consider these suggestions:

1. If you decide to use an audio or visual aid, it is important to plan its use carefully. A visual aid can easily degenerate into a frustrating block. Few practices are more annoying than to bring an aid too small to be seen in row one or to wave a chart or picture in front of the audience so rapidly that none can see it.

2. Keep the aids clear and simple. They need not to be artistic unless you are demonstrating your own or another's pencil sketching or oil.

3. Omit all unnecessary detail and complicated sets of figures. Round off statistics and where possible use percentages.

4. Remove the aid when you have finished using it; otherwise the listener may continue studying it rather than listening to you. This situation may also prevail if you pass a visual aid around the audience.

5. Make sure that your aid will actually promote the purpose of your speech.

Vocal and Physical Forms. The answer to the oft-asked question, "Shall I use gestures?"[15] is that you cannot avoid using them. No action (if that is possible for a speaker) constitutes a vivid, meaningful gesture. It is probably incongruous if not ludicrous, contradicting rather than reinforcing the speaker's message. But just as you cannot deliver a speech without voice (we would direct your attention to the first part of the text again for assistance in pronunciation, articulation, and vocal control), so the public speech is incomplete until the speaker achieves the proper management of his body.

The appropriateness and effectiveness of a speaker's physical presentation is determined by the *empathic reactions* it touches off in the audience. We may define *empathy* as our muscular, emotional and mental reactions to the audible and visible stimuli we receive from a speaker. For example, while listening to a person with a husky voice, our own throats tend to become scratchy. The fidgety speaker, all "tied up in knots," makes his audience nervous and ill at ease. On the other hand the man who is relaxed and in command of himself places his audience at ease and in a receptive state to respond to his appeals. The question is, "How does the speaker achieve a satisfactory empathic relationship with his listeners?"

We do not propose to enter the age-old controversy between the natural and artificial schools over the best methods of improving the physical aspects of delivery. The so-called artificial school lays heavy emphasis on the study and practice of gesture. The other school places less emphasis on the actual gesture, maintaining that if the speaker understands his ideas and truly

[15] See pages 288–294 for a discussion of gestures in public speaking.

feels the emotion at the moment of speaking, he will naturally employ the "right" action. Both groups devoutly hope to produce an artist with no trace of artifice in the final production.

Taking a position somewhere between these two extremes, we would suggest the following premises:

1. The *idea, organization,* and *style* must form the basic structure for any study of delivery. No amount of training in gesture will ever enable

Figure 35.   The speaker is demonstrating the effective use of one kind of visual aid. The chart is simple, easy to read and should serve to reinforce and clarify the speaker's words. Unlike many persons who employ charts, he understands the importance of maintaining eye contact with the audience.

a speaker to present empty thoughts effectively. An empty bag will not stand upright; it also needs more than hot air. *We can never divorce the teaching of speech delivery from speech content.*

2. All bodily action, facial expression, and movement must start from within, receiving their motivations from the speaker's thought and feeling.

3. Speech preparation is an active, vigorous process, never an enterprize carried on exclusively in the seclusion of the closet. While the speaker may need moments of quiet meditation and research, the final stages call for

vigorous vocalizations. He even prepares much of the speech on his feet, pacing the floor, employing uninhibited gesture. As he reheases his speech orally, before facing his audience, his gestures will become less random and self-directed; ideally they should always reinforce and clarify the idea.

4. Public speaking calls for a total reaction of the entire body toward the reinforcement of the thought and feeling of the speaker.

5. During the actual speaking experience, the *idea* and the *desire* to communicate with the audience takes precedence over any subsidiary thoughts about gesture or action. A basic rule is to avoid "holding back." If the rehearsal and preparation has been thorough, many of the gestures will come forth quite naturally. And as the speaker becomes more accustomed to using gestures, they will come more spontaneously.

6. Every speaker needs criticism from the audience. If he is sensitive, he will receive unmistakable feedback. But, unhappily, the gods denied us the power to see ourselves as others see us—even when we look in a mirror. Thus, your instructor and classmates will serve as corrective influences, pointing out the virtues and shortcomings in your ideas, their organization, the language you employed, and the vocal and physical presentation.

SUMMARY

Appropriate topics for speeches usually spring directly from the speaker's personal experiences and vital interests. They also arise from the specific occasion and are in all instances governed by the audience and the setting for the speech. In testing a potential topic the speaker must always make his evaluation according to the *timeliness,* the *relevance* for a specific audience and occasion, and the *suitability* for oral presentation.

After the speaker has selected his topic and phrased his proposition, he calls first of all on his own storehouse of knowledge. Continuing his research, he consults expert authority through the interview and library sources. Throughout this preparatory stage he seeks the *logical, emotional,* and *ethical* forms of proof to strengthen the proposition. He further fortifies his topic with *expository* and *stylistic* materials, thereby adding color and vividness to the subject. Additional forms of support available include: *restatement, explanation, concreteness, statistics, figurative imagery,* and *audiovisual aids.* We shall consider the speaker's special problems in organization in the next chapter. Finally, to bring his proposition to the listener, the speaker must select and practice an appropriate and effective mode of delivery.

Questions and Exercises

1. Rewrite the description of a typical day on television (read Newton Minow's indictment once more on page 305) as one of the television executives might have written it. Indicate the kind of audience he might be addressing.

2. Prepare and present extemporaneously a two-to-three-minute speech to clarify the abstract. Your instructor will assign an abstract term (truth, freedom, beauty, democracy, love, etc.) as the general topic. Your job is to limit and illuminate the subject, avoiding cliches and empty generalities. Use at least three different forms of support.

3. Attend a public lecture and analyze the speaker for evidence of *ethical proof*. After listening to the speaker, write a two-minute talk to be read to the class on the elements that added or detracted from the speaker's *ethos*. You may want to discuss some of the following:

   (a) The effect of his appearance, dress and general bearing,
   (b) His voice,
   (c) His pronunciation,
   (d) Direct or indirect references to his background, experience, or qualifications,
   (e) The use of supporting materials.

4. Bring to class five propositions which might serve as the major premise in a syllogism, e.g., "All men are prone to make mistakes." Try to find premises you believe are "Universal Truths." Be prepared to defend your selections in class.

5. Distinguish between restatement and repetition. Select a simple proposition and "restate" the idea in at least three ways without employing "repetition."

6. Listen for examples of mixed imagery in ordinary conversation or look for some in literature. Even Shakespeare was guilty when he had Hamlet "take arms against a sea of troubles." Bring five examples to class.

7. Make a list of ten common cliches. How can you express the same concept just as clearly and vividly with fresh phraseology?

8. Prepare and present to the class a four-minute speech to inform, using visual aids. Make sure the aids are merely supplemental help and that the speech does not turn out to be merely a visual aid.

9. At the next athletic contest you attend, analyze the empathic responses of the audience to the game. Describe in a two-minute speech to the class the physical responses of the spectators to the tense game-situations.

10. Give a two-minute speech in which you employ statistics. With each statistical support you use, restate the statistics by means of a comparison. For example, Albert J. Nevins said in one speech: "If our military budget for a single year was spread back over this same period, we would have spent more than $40 a minute since the birth of Christ. We no longer measure bombs in pounds as we did in World War II, nor even in tons. Today we speak in megatons. One megaton equals 166,000 block busters of World War II. It would take 20,000 box cars to carry enough TNT to make a single megaton bomb." (*Vital Speeches,* December 1, 1962, p. 117.)

11. Take an editorial on a current issue and analyze it for the *proposition* and the *supporting* material. State the writer's proposition in one sentence and classify the supporting evidence.

RECOMMENDED READINGS

Brigance, W. N. *Speech Composition*. New York: Appleton-Century-Crofts, 1953, Chaps. II and VI.

Monroe, Alan H. *Principles and Types of Speech*. Chicago: Scott, Foresman, 1962, Chaps. 3, 9, 11, and 12.

Sarett, Lew, Foster, W. T., and Sarett, Alma Johnson. *Basic Principles of Speech*. Boston: Houghton Mifflin, 1958, Chaps. 12, 13, and 14.

Walter, Otis M., and Scott, Robert L. *Thinking and Speaking: A Guide to Intelligent Oral Communication*. New York: Macmillan, 1962, Chaps. 2, 3, 6, 10, and 11.

White, Eugene E. *Practical Speech Fundamentals*. New York: Macmillan, 1960, Chaps. 5, 10, and 11.

CHAPTER 16

SYNTHESIS AND
ORGANIZATION

*But to avoid all display of art in itself
requires consummate art.*

QUINTILIAN

Even after considering our startlingly new discoveries, the writer of
Ecclesiastes was nearly accurate in his cynical observation that "there is
nothing new under the sun." Most speech topics are old. A few members
of the audience will recognize even the most obscure supporting material.
But the speaker's *organization* and *style,* if his speech is to succeed, must
impress the audience as fresh and new, a creation distinctively his own.
Above all, it is the speaker's treatment of organization and style that distinguishes the scholar from the plagiarist.

First, the speaker selects his topic (proposition or purpose) and then
collects the supporting materials (facts, illustrations, testimony). Next, he
faces the highly personal task of synthesizing, discarding, limiting, subdividing, and finally ordering the usable evidence in a way designed to promote the desired audience responses. If he depends on one source for his
facts, his organization, and even his style, he not only plagiarizes but usually
bores his listeners with an ill-digested, oversimplified analysis. Even if he
acknowledges his reliance on one source and thereby avoids the stigma of
plagiarism, his speech is likely to degenerate into "vanity" and a "striving
after wind." The audience may be and often is familiar with that one source.
From the speaker they deserve a study in depth and breadth, a mature analysis including the speaker's own individualistic interpretation, phrasing,
and organizational pattern.

SPEECH ORGANIZATION

Ancient and modern writers agree on the necessity for larger divisions in the speech, but differ markedly on the number. Aristotle, perhaps in revolt against excessive subdivisions, stripped speech organization of all but its two essential parts: (1) the *proposition* and (2) the *proof*. Yet, he also recognized the practical necessity of additional parts, audiences being "what they are."[1] Thus, he recommends four parts: *Proem* (introduction), *Statement* (proposition), *Argument* (body), and *Epilogue* (conclusion). The Roman rhetoricians Cicero and Quintilian recommended five to seven divisions depending on the type of speech (forensic, deliberative, or ceremonial) and the circumstances under consideration.[2]

Modern authorities tend to favor Plato's three-divisional plan which he described in his matchless analogy in the *Phaedrus:* "Every speech ought to be put together like a living creature with a body of its own, so as to be neither without head, nor without feet, but to have both a middle and extremities, described proportionately to each other and to the whole."[3] We recommend then that for greater clarity and convenience the speaker use three major divisions: *Introduction, Body,* and *Conclusion.* More important are the elements in each division and the various methods of developing each major part.

THE INTRODUCTION

Most speeches contain a rather clearly defined introduction. One possible exception is the humorous speech to entertain in which the speaker weaves together a series of loosely connected illustrations. A special type of introduction often accompanies the speech to convince in which the speaker examines all the available solutions for a problem, finally rejecting all except

---

[1] Lane Cooper, *The Rhetoric of Aristotle.* New York: Appleton-Century-Crofts, 1960, p. 224.

[2] The seven-fold classical Roman divisions included: (1) exordium (introduction), (2) narration, (3) proposition, (4) partition (listing main points), (5) proof, (6) refutation, (7) peoration (conclusion). The ancients were particularly sensitive to the need for audience adaptation in the organization of the speech. Writing on the major divisions of the speech, Quintilian declared, "Let no one however demand from me a rigid code of rules," citing "the all-important gift for an orator . . . a wise adaptability since he is called upon to meet the most varied emergencies." Nevertheless, Quintilian proceeded to establish many rules. We would emphasize, however, that the student must understand the rules *before* he knows how to deviate from them. (*The Institutio Oratoria*, trans. by H. E. Butler, Bk. II, Chap. XIII.)

[3] *Plato . . .* , Lane Cooper (trans.), New York: Oxford University Press, 1948, p. 51.

one. The plan here is sometimes called "this or nothing," or the method of "residues,"[4] and will be discussed later in this chapter.

Irrespective of the speaker's general and specific purpose, his opening statements or introduction must accomplish the first three and usually all four of the following objectives:

1. Secure the *immediate attention* of the audience.
2. Promote *long-range, continuous* attention.
3. Establish a *favorable rapport* between the speaker and the audience.
4. Provide the audience with a *forecast* of the specific purpose and the general direction of the speech.

The speaker must, of course, sustain the first three objectives throughout the speech. In the opening minutes they are crucial. Nearly all members of the audience are willing to attend during the first sentence or two; a few will hang on doggedly to the end, hoping even if in vain, for some new thought or inspiration. Most will decide during the introduction whether to listen or to amuse themselves with more pleasant pastimes. During the introduction, the speaker must earn his right to be heard. We do not imply that audiences bear no responsibility. Ideally, both the listener and the speaker should contribute a 100 per cent effort to maintain the dialogue essential to communication, regardless of the virtues or vices of the other party. But the speaker, through his special position on the platform, bears the major responsibility and possesses the potential to analyze his listeners and apply the appropriate measures to hold their attention.

The wise speaker avoids certain fatal temptations when developing his introduction. We have all heard persons handicap themselves during the opening moments by assuming the role of an *apologist,* the *humorless humorist,* an *abstract philosopher,* or the *cliché artist.*

The Apologist. While most listeners dislike the egotistical speaker and consider modesty a virtue, overt attempts to demonstrate a humble mien are often mere expressions of self-love. The subtle qualities of modesty are usually reserved for the truly great. A respected scholar, after a lifetime of research, may suggest to his audience that he possesses only a fraction of the available knowledge in his field. The average speaker who advertises his inadequate knowledge, incomplete state of preparation, lack of platform skill, or diseased larynx probably has no right to waste the listener's time. But even the best prepared speaker sometimes entertains a doubt about his adequacy on certain occasions. He is usually wise to keep these self-doubts to himself. By apologizing he administers what may turn out to be a fatal

---

[4] See W. N. Brigance, *Speech Composition,* New York: Appleton-Century-Crofts, 1953, pp. 102–109; also W. E. Gillman, Bower Aly, and Hollis White, *The Fundamentals of Speaking,* 2nd ed., New York: Macmillan, 1964, p. 98.

dose of negative suggestion. He may succeed only in planting attitudes and concepts in the conscious or subconscious thinking of the audience that he least wants them to accept. While negative suggestion is best avoided at all times, it is particularly detrimental during the introduction. The wise speaker prepares as thoroughly as possible and then presents his speech confidently, without excuses or apology.

The Humorless Humorist. Happily the erroneous assumption that a speaker should begin with a humorous story is no longer widely held. Indeed, any humor which does not contribute to one of the four previously mentioned objectives for the introduction or does not relate to the topic or the occasion has no legitimate place in any part of the speech. Humor is a powerful attention catcher and used wisely can win the respect and attention of the audience. Ineptly employed, it can seriously damage the effect of the speech.

Self-directed humor in the introduction, while dangerously negative, is often effective in dispelling hostility toward a speaker whose reputation with a particular audience is less than attractive. When the chairman of the Federal Communications Commission, Newton Minow, addressed the National Association of Broadcasters for the first time, some members of his audience were suspicious of him and fearful of what he might say. As it turned out, their fears were not groundless. But before Minow branded television "a vast wasteland," he employed humor rather effectively to win the good will of his audience. In words adapted to the radio or TV industry, he said, "I seem to have detected a certain nervous apprehension about what I might say or do when I emerged from that locked office for this, my maiden station break." (laughter) He followed this with two more instances of self-directed humor first by denying the rumor that he regarded himself "as the fastest draw on the New Frontier" and second by suggesting that the FCC assume a name similar to a current TV crime serial: "I may even suggest that we change the name of the FCC to the Seven Untouchables!" (applause and laughter).[5]

The Abstract Philosopher. One listener remarked on leaving an auditorium that he "understood every word of the speaker and not a single sentence." Circumlocution is sometimes further complicated with abstract, technical jargon understandable only to the initiated. Such phraseology is rarely acceptable to a general audience. Notice for example, the following abstract passage:

Therefore even if consciousnesses are only pure conceptual connections of phenomena, even if the rule of their existence is the *percipere* and the *percipi*,

---

[5] A complete text of Minow's address is in *ETC: A Review of General Semantics*, Vol. XVIII, (July 1961), 134–147. It also appears in the *Congressional Record*, 87th Congress, 1st session, and in *Vital Speeches* (June 15, 1961), pp. 533–537.

the fact still remains that the *multiplicity* of these relational systems is a multiplicity in-itself and that it immediately transforms them each into a system in-itself.[6]

It may be that the author can express this thought in no other words. We find it difficult to judge, since we are not sure what the author is trying to say. But if this is the only way to express this idea, the speaker might as well save his words.

The Cliché Artist.   Special occasions demand particular types of introduction. Every speaker faces the problem of expressing his appreciation for the opportunity to speak and often labors under the illusion that he must pay his audience some kind of compliment. If he can accomplish the feat easily and naturally, he probably has achieved a degree of rapport with his audience. Too often, in the style of Senator Snort of cartoon fame, speakers thoughtlessly, though not so obviously declaim: "I said it before and I'll say it again . . . this is the most intelligent audience I've spoken to on my campaign tour. . . ." "It gives me great pleasure. . . . I am delighted with this great opportunity." Even a casual glance at *Vital Speeches* reveals speakers who overwork these tired phrases and who should know better. If a compliment or a reference to the occasion is necessary, it is best kept brief and correlated, if possible, to the theme and purpose of the speech. Clichés, while impossible to avoid entirely, are best used sparingly and whenever possible given a special face-lifting operation.

Securing Attention

While one of the main purposes of the introduction is the focusing of attention on the topic and the successful crossing of the interest barrier, a word of caution is necessary. The overly dramatic, bizarre opening, even though electrifying an audience, may defeat the speaker's long-range purpose. Every attention-catching effort must bear a direct relationship to the speaker's topic. The speaker who stepped to the platform, smashed a phonograph record and then exclaimed, "Our company has been breaking production records for years," strained the pun and misunderstood the purpose of the attention-getting device. If the speaker opens sensationally, he should be prepared to sustain an unusually high degree of vividness throughout. This is not an excuse for the many prosaically dull introductions, but following a foretaste of the exciting, the audience often demands as its price of attention nothing less than the extravagant.

The supporting materials used in the introduction to secure immediate and long-range attention are not markedly different from those employed

---

[6] Sartre, Jean-Paul, *Being and Nothingness,* Hazel E. Barnes (trans.), New York: Philosophical Library, 1956, pp. 229–230.

throughout the speech. Some of the more effective methods of developing the introduction include the use of *illustrations,* the *vital,* an *apt quotation,* and the *novel.* Every speaker should recognize the necessity for a generous intermixture of these components.

The Illustration or Narrative. Everyone loves a good story. It is the basic ingredient of the speech to entertain. It is the seasoning element in every speech. Well constructed, it contains the basic attention-catching elements—conflict, specific detail, and the unusual. It often dramatizes our vital concerns, and if the illustration is a personal one, the speaker and audience immediately identify with each other. Charles Grandison Finney, one of the truly great evangelists of his day, ridiculed preachers who thought illustrations destroyed their ministerial dignity. Said Finney in defending the sermon illustration, "You have Jesus Christ and common sense on your side!"

The Vital. Every introduction, if it is to hold the audience and inspire continuous attention, must contain some references vital to the listeners' wants and desires. It may not always be wise or even possible to place an audience in a position of impending disaster or bliss. But the speaker with the imagination to develop an introduction touching the listeners' highest or lowest concerns will best hold interest. Prior to our entry into World War II, Robert Hutchins employed the vital effectively in a nationwide radio address.

I speak tonight because I believe that the American people are about to commit suicide. We are not planning to. We have no plan. We are drifting into suicide. Deafened by martial music, fine language, and large appropriations, we are drifting into war.[7]

Apt Quotation. Even brilliant phrase-makers often find that someone else has expressed a key idea better than they. The pithy epigram, the provocative question, the line of poetry often serve to heighten the effect of the introduction. President M. Norvel Young of Pepperdine College in a speech on federal aid to education combined a biblical paraphrase and question in his opening remarks to a group of teachers: "What will education be profited if it gains billions of dollars in Federal aid and loses its own freedom? What should a teacher or a school give in exchange for its freedom?"[8]

The question, direct or rhetorical, is always provocative and usually serves as an effective attention-catcher. It can also provide the transitional

---

[7] *American Issues.* Vol. One: *The Social Record,* Willard Thorp, Merle Curti, and Carlos Baker (eds.), Chicago: Lippincott, 1944, p. 1031.

[8] *Vital Speeches* (June 1, 1961), p. 492.

sentence, bridging the gap between ideas. Even so, every speaker needs to recognize the danger of destroying his effectiveness through the overuse or misuse of the question. Opening a speech with an "Are you aware" question relating to a condition or an event on the level of Columbus' discovery will usually prompt an inaudible but sarcastic audience response.

The Unusual. The novel possesses limited attention value. Indeed we are incapable of attending to the absolutely new for more than a short period of time. On the other hand, the old soon bores us. But a judicious mixture of the familiar and the unusual with a twist of paradox can produce a lively provocative introduction. Richard J. Babcock, the president of the *Farm Journal,* in the introduction of his speech at Kansas City, Missouri, effectively intermixed the unusual with a paradoxical twist.

When a Connecticut Yankee comes to Missouri to speak on the subject of agriculture, surely one must wonder if this isn't carrying coals to Newcastle. Perhaps not necessarily so. Way back in 1877 when a forward thinking man by the name of Wilmer Atkinson began to publish a little farm paper called the *Farm Journal* it was dedicated, as he said, "to serving the interests of farm families within a day's ride of Philadelphia."
Farm Journal is still published for farm families who live within a day's ride of Philadelphia. Thanks to the jets, that day's ride now includes the 900-odd farm families who read *Farm Journal* in each of our two newest states, Alaska and Hawaii, as well as the 3,000,000 subscribing families who live in the 48 contiguous states.[9]

Favorable Rapport

In his first State of the Union message, President Kennedy recognized the necessity of developing a working relationship with the Congress. Calling on his past experience in both Houses, he extended a genuine compliment to members of both parties.

Mr. Vice-President, members of the Congress, it is a pleasure to return from whence I came. You are among my oldest friends in Washington and this House is my oldest home.
It was here, more than fourteen years ago, that I first took the oath of Federal office. It was here, for fourteen years, that I gained both knowledge and inspiration from members of both parties in both houses—from your wise and generous leaders—and from the pronouncements which I can vividly recall, sitting where you now sit—including the programs of two great Presidents, the undimmed eloquence of Churchill, the soaring idealism of Nehru, the steadfast words of General de Gaulle. To speak from this same historic rostrum is a sobering experience. To be back among so many friends is a happy one.[10]

A year later, facing an even more hostile audience in the Sixty-sixth Congress of American Industry, President Kennedy attempted through self-

---

[9] *Vital Speeches* (February 15, 1961), p. 269.
[10] *Vital Speeches* (February 15, 1961), p. 258.

directed humor and a gentle jibe at his listeners to reach common ground. His frank recognition of audience hostility and his direct appeal for co-operation between business and government "to advance the common interest" was an attempt to secure a fair hearing.

Mr. President and gentlemen. I understand that President McKinley and I are the only two Presidents of the United States to ever address such an occasion. I suppose that President McKinley and I are the only two that are regarded as fiscally sound enough to be qualified for admission to this organization. . . .

I have not always considered the membership of the N.A.M. as among my strongest supporters. I'm not sure you have all approached the New Frontier with the greatest possible enthusiasm and I was, therefore, somewhat nervous about accepting this invitation until I did some history—studying of history of this organization.

I learned that this organization had once denounced—on one occasion, our "swollen bureaucracy" as among the triumphs of Karl Marx, and decried on another occasion new governmental "paternalism and socialism."

I was comforted when reading this very familiar language to note that I was in very good company. For the first attack I quoted was on Calvin Coolidge and the second on Herbert Hoover.

I remind you of this only to indicate the happy failure of many of our most pessimistic predictions—and that is true of all of us.[11]

The Forecast

Some speeches leave the listeners with that lost feeling of having just completed a harried expedition through an uncharted Sahara. They realized simply that they were adrift on a sea of sand, totally devoid of directional markers. The speaker who is careful to state his proposition clearly and who subdivides his topic with an *initial summary* in the introduction takes an effective step in avoiding this "uncharted desert" effect. Moreover, if he employs some stylistic subtlety in his forecast, he can even heighten the enthusiasm of the audience, creating genuine anticipation for the rest of the speech. Any time the speaker omits a statement of his purpose and a forecast of his major divisions, he should make sure that he has a legitimate reason.

If the speaker faces a sharply hostile audience, one he is sure would reject his proposition at the outset, he may state the proposition in question form or even omit it completely. The speech to inform and to stimulate nearly always demands an initial summary and a direct statement of the proposition. The same is true of the speech to entertain, although the speaker enjoys a much wider latitude in this type of speech. Naturally, the development in the body of the speech must conform to the forecast. Few errors in organization are more confusing than to set up one order in the introduction and another in the body.

---

[11] *Vital Speeches* (January 1, 1962), p. 162.

THE CONCLUSION

Getting off the platform gracefully constitutes a serious problem if the speaker fails to prepare adequately in advance. The feeble, negative, apologetic "thank you" gives the audience a less than satisfactory impression. If the speaker has completed his task successfully the audience should thank him with their applause.

The conclusion ought to include one or more of the following:

1. A short but complete summary. This is essential in the speech to inform, if the speaker entertains a serious hope that the audience will carry away the factual material.

2. An appeal for increased devotion to an ideal or an institution. The speech to stimulate usually concludes on such a note.

3. An appeal for a change of attitude, perhaps for a specific course of action. In the speech to convince, the speaker hopes to produce a change of belief. If he can also ask for overt physical action (vote, write, protest, support), the decision is likely to be more lasting.

The specific types of supporting material for the conclusion do not differ in kind from those used in the introduction. An appeal at this point is usually a more emotional part of the speech, and many speakers rely rather heavily on the epigramatic quotation, a verse, line of poetry, or a directly phrased question. Occasionally, a speaker will conclude with an extended illustration whose implications the listener cannot ignore. Above all, the speaker must keep the conclusion as brief as possible. Nothing so exasperates an audience as the speaker who missed a good place to stop. Otherwise excellent speeches are sometimes marred with the anticlimactic "just one more thing," "finally," "and so in conclusion."

THE DISCUSSION OR BODY

The second major division, the discussion or body, contains the full development of the speaker's proposition. In this section he expands, illustrates, amplifies, and establishes the validity of his proposition in the persuasive speech or clarifies it in the expository speech. The process involves selecting and synthesizing the evidence and dividing and subdividing the supporting materials. Finally, he must determine the proper order for the main heads, arranging each part to lend proper balance to the whole speech.

Every good speech is essentially a *one-point speech*. The one point, as we have previously emphasized, is the proposition, thesis, purpose, aim, end, or objective. Occasionally, a speaker states his proposition and completes his speech with an extended illustration. Or he may employ the more indirect approach and by implication open with the illustration and conclude with the proposition. Many speeches to stimulate follow this formula. The popular safety slogan, "The Life You Save May Be Your Own" readily lends itself to a one-point development through a single illustration or a series of them.

Main Heads and Subheads

Most speech propositions, including the one on safety, lend themselves to a major subdivision or two. If your proposition appears to contain more than two to four main heads, you should reexamine your proposition to determine the scope of your speech. Either the topic is too broad or a number of subheadings have erroneously assumed the stature of a main head.

The average listener is able to retain about three or four of the ideas he hears in a speech. We hope he will remember the main ideas. If the major supporting heads for the proposition are phrased clearly and impellingly, he should remember these and may even recall some of the subpoints and illustrative materials. We can be sure that with any complex or simple subject where the divisions and transitions are obscure and where the relationships of idea to idea are cloudy, the listener will succeed in carrying home only confusion. The length of the speech in no way determines the number of major divisions. Longer speeches simply contain additional supporting illustrations and facts.

Kinds of Arrangement

Probably no two speakers, even when facing the same audience and using the same topic, will employ precisely the same plan. Yet, the speaker's purpose, his specific topic, and the response he seeks from his audience must influence and dictate the general over-all organization. Moreover, he may employ several types of organization in the same speech. But, if his speech does seem to call for more than one type of organization, he should reexamine his topic to determine whether he is actually speaking to two propositions rather than to one. Although some intermixing may occur, one of the following methods usually predominates:

Topical
A. Chronological
B. Spatial
C. Logical
   1. Problem-solution

2. Cause and effect relationships
3. This or nothing

Topical.   Broadly considered, every speech is organized topically. The *main heads,* whether expressing time sequence or spatial, logical, or psychological relationships, are stated as topics. The organizational pattern, frequently described as *topical,* will be discussed with the logical forms of arrangement.

Chronological.   The time-order or time-sequence is easily adapted to the historical subject or to any part of the speech calling for the developmental history of a product, an idea, or a movement. A speech on the customs of the Hopi Indians entitled "The Journey from Birth to Death" covered topically the practices and rites of the tribe and followed an over-all chronological pattern : birth, childhood, adulthood, and death.

Spatial.   As with the chronological method, the spatial is perhaps best suited to the expository (informative) type of speech. A talk on television might employ the time-order plan. A somewhat similar talk might be set up spatially as follows :

I. Commercial television
II. Educational television
III. Pay television

We may also decide, after surveying commercial, educational, and pay television, that our original plan is too broad and decide to concentrate on one of the areas. Clearly, any of the three lends itself to chronological development. The spatial order best fits geographical topics and subjects calling for a division of a large area into more comprehensible parts. It is the (1) first floor, (2) second floor, (3) third floor type of speech. Sometimes it is called the *simple list,* which may be misleading to those who fail to recognize that a meaningful spatial, chronological, or logical relationship must exist between the listed topics.

Logical.   Speakers often employ the chronological or spatial plans in developing the speech to stimulate or convince. Indeed, Franklin D. Roosevelt's message to Congress following the Japanese attack on Pearl Harbor and President Kennedy's demand for an arms' quarantine of Cuba[12] used chronological order with devastatingly persuasive force. In attempting to

---

[12] *Vital Speeches* (November 15, 1962), pp. 66–68. (For the complete text of Roosevelt's Pearl Harbor address see the section on Bringing Print to Life, pages 359–360.)

demonstrate the seriousness of the farm problem and the plight of the farmer, one speaker organized his speech spatially around three heads:

I. The commercial farmer
II. The subsistence farmer
III. The migrant farmer

In most instances, however, the speaker will use the *logical* or *psychological* development for the speech to convince. Indeed, he may use both forms in the same speech. They are not distinctively different from each other or mutually exclusive. Logical and psychological more accurately describe the phrasing, the use of motive appeals, and the substantive matter contained in the topical heads.

When the speaker attempts to demonstrate the "Why's" of a course of action or attempts to discover the "causes" or the "effects," he looks for supporting *main heads* or *topical statements*. The main heads sometime follow a logical pattern and at other times a psychological one with appeals related directly to our wants and desires. Most speeches to convince and stimulate contain an intermixture of logical and psychological headings.

Problem-Solution. The logical organization often follows a pattern similar to those we outlined in the chapter on debate.[13] The speaker outlines the *problem* (need for a change) and then presents his *remedy*. Usually both the problem step and the solution are developed topically. For example, we face the problem of finding the kind of educational system that will best enable each child to achieve to the full extent of his capabilities. We may set up the problem as follows:

I. Unusual children both bright and dull, face problems the conventional school cannot meet.
   A. Bright children do not work up to capacity.
      1. They soon get bored and lose interest.
      2. They may develop intellectual sluggishness.
   B. Dull Children are forced to work beyond their capacity.
      1. They become frustrated and insecure.
      2. They cease to try for fear of failure.

Cause and Effect Relationships. Cause and effect relationships also furnish the speaker with his main topical heads for the persuasive speech. Again, we would warn of the dangers involved in the use of cause to effect and effect to cause reasoning, urging the speaker to examine carefully the alleged relationships he attempts to establish. It is easy to draw unwarranted inferences from the facts and to conclude hastily that because two events

---

[13] See pages 247–249 for a review of the material as related to debate techniques.

occurred simultaneously or in close sequence that they are joined causally.[14]

When the stock market declined sharply in 1962, laymen and experts alike searched for the probable causes. Since the "crash" came close on the heels of President Kennedy's stinging rebuke of the steel companies' announced price increase, some immediately placed the blame directly and solely on the President's shoulders. Rarely is any occurrence, particularly one as complex as a decline in the economy, the result of a single act. Most economists could point to a number of probable causes other than the action of the executive branch.

Unhappily, political parties seem to thrive on the oversimplified causal relationship. Following "Cleveland's Panic," for example, the Democrats were labeled as the party that "causes" depressions until 1929 when the Republicans assumed that unenviable role. Even though three major wars in the Twentieth Century occurred during Democratic administrations, it is hardly logical, as is often done in the heat of a political campaign, to blame the wars on the Democrats. Nor were the Democrats fair in their post-1929 oratory in linking the Republicans causally to depressions.

If we understand the limitations and hazards of causal reasoning, we can employ three types in setting up the organization in expository and persuasive speeches: *effect to cause, cause to effect,* and *effect to effect.*

The speaker who attempts to analyze the stock market crash phrases his topical headings according to an *effect to cause* relationship. The *effect* (economic decline) is known and he seeks the possible or probable *causes.* In the second type the *cause* is known or contemplated and the speaker predicts the probable consequences (*effect*) of such action. In his second State of the Union message in 1963, President Kennedy employed this kind of *cause to effect* reasoning when he proposed a tax cut. Such a measure, he maintained, would stimulate business and the economy sufficiently to compensate eventually for the initial loss of revenue. Others questioned the probable effect predicted by the administration, insisting that unless another cause were coupled with the tax cut—namely, a cut in governmental spending—the entire economic structure of the government would suffer. Some observers doubted that the tax cut would improve the economy sufficiently to bring in the promised new revenue.

The third approach, known as *effect to effect,* is a combination of the first two. The rat has cancer (effect) caused by the application of nicotine tars. Reasoning from this situation, we conclude that nicotine tars will cause cancer in human beings. The *effect to effect* relationship then appears as follows: rat cancer (effect) to nicotine tar (cause) leads us to the assumption that nicotine tar (cause) will lead to human cancer (effect).

---

[14] Check again the pertinent materials in the section on Debate, pages 264–265, and the section on Finding and Fortifying the Proposition, pages 303–305.

By setting up a series of cause and effect relationships we can construct a chain of circumstances seemingly triggered by a single cause. The familiar nursery rhyme that joins causally the lost kingdom with the need for a horseshoe nail employs this kind of relationship.[15] But we need to remember that such reasoning is no stronger than its weakest causal link. The argument falls if a cause is insufficient to produce the desired or alleged effect.

This or Nothing. The speaker employing this method examines in an expository manner all the possible solutions for a problem. If the listeners accept the speaker's analysis, they are finally left with no alternative other than to accept "This" (remedy) or "Nothing" (the impossible or inadequate solutions). During his campaign for governor of Indiana, Clifford Townsend used this method successfully with college audiences in defending a recently enacted gross income tax law, branded by its opponents as a "gross injustice." Using the manner of an economics professor, Townsend gave every impression of delivering a speech to inform, talking about the general state tax structure and the various methods of increasing state revenues. He examined each potential and actual tax, and by the time he reached the conclusion his listeners suddenly realized they had been placed in a position where they were virtually compelled to accept the tax, despite their opinion that it was grossly unjust.

The primary advantage of this plan is that it provokes no argument but stays on common ground with the audience throughout. The disadvantage includes the danger of missing a possible solution. The audience may also stubbornly reject "this" as worse than "nothing." "Convinced against their will, they hold the same opinion still."

OUTLINING THE SPEECH

The outline is the speaker's blueprint. No end in itself, its principal purpose is to assist the speaker in constructing an orderly address. Without it, the speech is likely to degenerate into a hodgepodge of unrelated, disjointed ideas. With it, the speaker can determine in advance whether his platform effort will meet the essential rhetorical tests of unity, coherence, and emphasis, and whether he has structured his proposition logically and psychologically for the maximum persuasive effect.

------

[15] For want of a nail, the shoe was lost,
For want of a shoe, the horse was lost,
For want of a horse, the rider was lost,
For want of a rider, the battle was lost,
For want of a battle, the kingdom was lost,
And all for the want of a horseshoe nail.

Most experienced speakers find it desirable to write out their outlines in rather complete form, making it easier to examine and alter their plans as the situation demands. Through practice and experience, every speaker, develops those habits of preparation which work best for him. No one, however, should deceive himself with the thought that if he is "full of his subject" little outlining in preparation for the speech is necessary. Indeed, the more information the speaker possesses, the greater the necessity for careful outlining, to insure the transmission of the maximum quantity of information during the allotted time. No matter how astute an authority the speaker is, he faces the exacting task of ordering his thoughts on paper in outline form. A few rare geniuses may construct and carry outlines in their heads. More often we witness the depressing spectacle of the famous authority, apparently unwilling to take time from his research to organize his storehouse of information. He usually succeeds only in boring and confusing his listeners.

Novice and experienced speakers alike usually find it helpful to incorporate most of the following features in their outlines. Your instructor will probably indicate his preference for the inclusion of specific elements. We do not insist on one type of outline as the only correct form. But we would caution that deviation from the following format should occur only after mature consideration.

Begin with the Title.   Although the completed outline and the speech itself begin with the title, the speaker may actually discover the "right" phrasing for the title at any point in his preparation. During the research period, it is wise to jot down appropriate wording that will set forth the topic *briefly, relevantly,* and in a way designed to excite the *expectations* of the listeners. Too often the selection of a title is a last-minute affair, resulting in a mere cliché—"The Challenge of Our Age" or "The Hope of the Future." Best titles usually strike a happy medium somewhere between the flamboyantly novel and the prosaically dull.

State the Purpose.   The necessity of stating in one clear declarative sentence the purpose of the speech may prevent the selection of a subject too broad for adequate treatment. If the purpose is to stimulate or convince, the speaker should phrase his purpose in terms of the specific audience responses he seeks. For example,

Speech to Stimulate: "Buy more Christmas seals to help care for the chronically ill and stamp out the White Plague."

Speech to Convince: "To save your money and your lungs stop smoking now."

In the speech to inform and entertain, the audience response is no less important, but the purpose is often expressed as follows:

Speech to Inform: "To explain the origin, the aims, and the future outlook for UNESCO."

Speech to Entertain: "To amuse the audience with some ways of fooling the faculty and passing any course without cracking the text."

Use Indentation and Uniform Symbols.   Be consistent throughout. This will help you maintain the logical and normal sequence and will serve as a check on the logical relationships between your main heads and the evidence and reasoning you have used as supporting material. A generally acceptable plan is as follows:

I. Main Head
    A. First supporting division of the main head
        1. Logical subdivision under (A)
        2. Second subdivision of (A)
            (a) First supporting division under (2)
            (b) Second supporting division of (2)
    B. Second supporting division of the main head
        1. Supporting evidence for (B)
            (a) First supporting item under (1)
            (b) Second supporting point under (1)
        2. Second supporting division under (B)

II. Second Main Head

The major divisions of the speech—that is, *introduction, body,* and *conclusion*—should follow this general plan, each beginning with Roman numeral I. The actual number of main heads and supporting subpoints will vary from speech to speech, depending on the nature of the subject. It is often wise to include *transitional sentences* between major divisions.

Use Complete Sentences.   Words and phrases as supporting subpoints are often vague. A full-content outline will enable your instructor to criticize your style and transitional phrasing as well as your over-all plan of organization. Experienced speakers may later depend on less than the full-content outline. Many continue to find the discipline of the complete outline a rewarding experience.

Employ Direct Phrasing.   The outline should contain an oral sentence structure similar to the actual language of the speech. Instead of "Explain Joe's situation at the plant," support for the main head should appear as follows:

I. Many employees at the Reed Company have fared well.

    A. Let's look, for example, at the case of Joe Moore.

        1. He has worked for the company for fifty years.

           (a) For the first three years he worked as a stock boy in the lowest paid job in the corporation.

           (b) He was then promoted to the machine shop.

           (c) Three years later he was made foreman over ten men.

           (d) For the past twenty years he has served as the plant superintendent.

        2. Joe now looks forward to the "Golden Years."

           (a) He owns his home.

           (b) The company will grant him an ample pension when he retires.

           (c) In addition he and his wife will receive social security payments from the government.

    B.   (The second supporting subpoint under I.)

One Item per Symbol. Include only one item in each main head or supporting subpoint. Notice the problem in the following student outline:

I. Television offers wide opportunities in the future.

    A. It enables Presidents to meet the public in a more personal way than in the radio speech; it has given the nation a better means of securing information; and it has been used as a tremendous aid to teaching.

Obviously, subpoint A needs to be broken down into three parts. And probably for an effective speech, each of the "opportunities" needs additional support.

Support Each Heading Adequately. One of the virtues of the outline is that it enables the speaker to see clearly how much supporting material he has included under each heading. If we are dividing a main head, it is obvious that the minimum number of subpoints is two. Even if we are simply supporting with evidence or an illustration, one supporting instance is rarely sufficient. Additional testimony, facts, and illustrations are nearly always necessary to give strength and substance to the speech.

Full-Content Outline

If the speaker has followed the previously stated instructions he will have developed a full-content outline. He will have included all of the major and supporting divisions, his evidence and illustrations. A word of caution, however, about the uses of the full content outline may be necessary.

1. The full-content outline is *not a manuscript* of your complete speech broken down by symbols and indentation.

2. It should contain the main heads and supporting evidence, but is *not a verbatim report.* Without additional amplification and restatement your speech will sound stiff and will lack life and vigor.

3. Under *no* circumstances should the full-content outline serve as your "speaker's notes."

4. If you need notes, construct a *key word outline,* based on the complete form. Place long quotations and statistics, too complex for memorization, on research cards.[16] This advice on the use of notes, when your instructor permits them, is particularly pertinent for the beginning speaker who should develop an *extempore mode of delivery,* i.e., a thoroughly prepared and practiced speech, delivered with the aid of a few notes, perhaps, but *not memorized.*

The following student outline illustrates many of the foregoing principles. This outline was designed for a five-to-six-minute speech given with the help of visual aid drawings of the phonetic symbols. The speech contains three main heads: (1) Shaw's dream of a new alphabet, (2) a description of the Shaw-Read alphabet and (3) an evaluation of the new system.

THE ABC's OF SHAW-READ[17]

General Purpose: To inform.
Specific Purpose: To describe and evaluate the new Shaw-Read phonetic alphabet.

Introduction

I. These written symbols [visual aid] you've seen popping up in coded messages on campus this week are not the work of some misguided Greek or Hebrew student.
   A. They stand for the famous George Bernard Shaw quotation—"The more you study, the less you know. Why study?" written in the new Shaw-Read phonetic alphabet.
   B. A study of the essential features of this new alphabet may prove valuable.
      1. We will constantly encounter, as in the past, various proposals for simplified spelling.
         (a) Benjamin Franklin tried to reform our spelling.
         (b) Teddy Roosevelt attempted to force a new spelling system for governmental publications, including Presidential messages.
         (c) *The Chicago Tribune* attempted to promote a more simplified spelling of some words like "thru" and "nite."
      2. As students of speech we are concerned with new methods of improving pronunciation and spelling.
      3. If you take phonetics next year, you can get the jump on the class.

---

[16] See pages 253–254 for a sample research card and suggestions for recording evidence.

[17] Outline prepared by Jayne Ann Richards for Speech 1 at Oberlin College, January 29, 1963.

4. As finals draw to a close you can join your friends in this pleasant form of artistic procrastination.

Transition: What then are the ABC's of the Shaw-Read phonetic alphabet?

Discussion

I. The new alphabet is the realization of a Shavian dream.
   A. In his play, *Pygmalion* and its familiar musical counterpart, *My Fair Lady*, the action centers around a dialectician who could record in his own phonetic system any vowel or consonant sound.
   B. With the trust fund Shaw set up in his will, he provided the finances for the establishment of a new phonetic alphabet.
   C. In his plan for the new alphabet, Shaw characteristically suggested that we scrap our present system and begin from scratch.
      1. The new alphabet was to have 48 symbols, including 24 separate vowel sounds.
      2. Each symbol was to represent a separate sound, pronounced the same way no matter where it appeared in a word.
      3. Shaw asked that the new alphabet be easy to write.
   D. English phonetist Kingsley Read set out to devise the new alphabet.
      1. Read based his work on the Shavian stipulations, corresponding with Shaw before his death concerning the proposed alphabet.
      2. After 15 years, he produced the first sample last November in the form of a transliteration of Shaw's "Androcles and the Lion" with the famous play written in "Old" English on one side of the page and the Shaw-Read version on the other.

Transition: Now, that we've seen Shaw's dream, the plan and the originator, let's take a closer look at the actual changes and the structure of the new alphabet.

II. The Shaw-Read alphabet, following Shaw's stipulations, does start afresh with new symbols and the required 48 characters.
   A. Its "letters"—the most common English sounds—come in several matching-size categories [visual aid].
      1. For example, the voiced consonants—such as "b," "d," "g," "v," and "z"—are known as "deeps."
      2. Their voiceless counterparts are called "talls," or "deeps" turned upside down.
   B. The most commonly used words in English, "the," "of," "and," and "to" are represented economically by one-symbol forms.
   C. It is now theoretically possible to write every word in English just as it is pronounced.
      1. Now, as Shaw hoped, the phonetic vagaries of our language can be eliminated.
      2. It is also possible to do away with Shaw's own favorite example of the phonetic madness of our language.
         (a) He pointed out that "ghoti" spells "fish," pronouncing the "gh" as in "cough" the "o" as in "women," and the "ti" as in "nation."
         (b) Thanks to the new Shaw-Read, "fish" is clearly "fish" and "ghoti" is written "g-hoti."

Transition: Although it appears to be a step in the right direction phonetically, we might look at some of the shortcomings.

III. The Shaw-Read phonetic system seems to have at least four drawbacks.
   A. It is virtually impossible to duplicate every sound variation as Shaw recognized when he stated in his will: "I desire my Trustee to bear in mind that the Proposed British Alphabet does not pretend to be exhaustive as it contains only [24] vowels, whereas by infinitesimal movements of the tongue countless different vowels can be produced, all of them in use among speakers of English who utter the same vowels no oftener than they make the same fingerprints."
   B. This statement by implication indicates another pronounced difficulty— (pardon the pun) the fact that it is a British phonetic alphabet.
      1. There are obvious differences between British and American pronunciations.
      2. The dialects in our own country pose a barrier.
         (a) A Southerner writing about the "floors" in a house might confuse a Northerner who thought the word being used was "flaws."
         (b) A native of New Jersey might be hard to understand in another part of the country since he might write the name of his state phonetically as "Noo Joisey."
      3. The "old" English alphabet presents words in forms familiar to everyone in spite of local accent.
   C. Our friend from New Jersey or "Joisey" would also have trouble transcribing the new alphabet.
      1. As indicated earlier, Shaw wanted to make the system easy to write.
      2. With the Shaw-Read system, however, the writer must lift his pencil after each character of a word, rather than writing them in a flowing script.
   D. Several phonetic alphabets already exist, making Shaw-Read just one more system.

Transition: To all the criticisms Shaw would undoubtedly have answered: This standardized alphabet would eventually standardize spelling and pronunciation faster than our present system.

Conclusion

I. Be all this as it may, the Shaw-Read alphabet with its advantages and its shortcomings is a noteworthy addition to our language.
   A. Time alone will measure its value.
   B. And, anyway, *Androcles and the Lion* makes interesting reading, whether written phonetically or in the "old-fashioned" English.

Sources

Fuller, J. G. "Trade Winds," *Saturday Review* (October 13, 1962), p. 14.

Knowles, Melita. "New Alphabet Makes Debut," *The Christian Science Monitor* (September 23, 1962), p. 1.

Read, Kingsley, and Shaw, George Bernard. *Androcles and the Lion*. London: Penguin Books, 1962.

"Oh Pshaw!" *Time* (December 7, 1962), p. 96.

SUMMARY

After the speaker has selected his general and specific purposes and has found most of the supporting material (illustrations, facts, testimony) to amplify and illuminate his proposition, he must then synthesize and organize his materials. Usually, he finds it helpful to consider the organization of his speech around the three major divisions or parts: *introduction, body, conclusion.*

The speaker may further divide his proposition into from two to four main headings. These topical heads and their subheadings usually lend themselves to one or a combination of the following arrangements: *chronological, spatial, logical* (problem-solution, cause and effect, this or nothing) and *psychological.*

The construction of the outline is an important preparation step. The precise type will depend primarily on the experience of the speaker and the purpose for which the outline is designed. The *full-content outline,* including the use of complete sentences, direct phrasing, appropriate, and consistent symbols and indentation serves as the best form for preparation. If the speaker plans to use notes, the *key-word* outline is most satisfactory for the extemporaneous mode of delivery.

Questions and Exercises

1. How does the quotation by Quintilian at the head of this chapter apply to the study of speech organization?

2. Write out and come to class prepared to read a one-minute introduction to a speech. Be sure the introduction contains:
   (a) An attention catcher.
   (b) Direct adaptation to the audience—the answer to the question, "Why bring us this subject?"
   (c) A forecast of the general or specific direction of the speech.
   (d) The proposition or purpose sentence. This may appear at a point in the introduction you deem most appropriate. Be prepared to defend your introduction.

3. Select three introductions from speeches in current issues of *Vital Speeches* and after considering the specific purpose, the audience, and the occasion, determine the answers to the following questions:
   (a) Did the speaker cross the cliché barrier? Indicate which phrases were in need of reworking.
   (b) Did the speaker omit any of the four elements listed under question 2 above? Was he justified in this omission?
   (c) What changes would you have made in the introduction if you had been in the speaker's shoes?

4. Examine the conclusions to the three speeches you previously studied for the structure of the introduction. What type of conclusions did the speakers

employ? Summary, appeal, overt action? What changes would you have made in the conclusions?

5. Write three different conclusions to the speech for which you constructed the introduction in exercise 2.

(a) Make the first conclusion largely a summary.

(b) Include in the second an appeal for direct action.

(c) In the third, employ one of the following forms of support, *illustration, rhetorical question, quotation, line of poetry.*

6. Prepare a two-minute, *one-point* speech, using *one* extended illustration as supporting evidence.

7. Work out three possible *titles* for speeches on the following topics. In each case indicate what the *specific purpose, audience,* and *occasion* for the speech is:

(a) The Separation of Church and State,

(b) Fraternities on the College Campus,

(c) The United Nations,

(d) Federal Health Insurance,

(e) Procrastination.

8. Select two speeches from *Vital Speeches* or from a collection of speeches, e.g., Ernest J. Wrage, and Barnet Baskerville, *Contemporary Forum: American Speeches on Twentieth-Century Issues,* New York: Harper, 1962. Outline the main speech structure and answer the following questions:

(a) Is the speech organized chronologically, spatially, logically or psychologically? Is there an intermixture of types?

(b) How would you have changed the order if you had delivered this speech?

9. Attend a public lecture and make as detailed a key-word outline as possible during the address. At your room make a more complete outline, including a critical evaluation of the speaker's organization:

(a) Did the speech have clearly stated *main topical headings?*

(b) Were the *transitional sentences* adequate to bridge the gaps between the main heads?

(c) Was the *supporting material* for the main heads arranged in an orderly way?

(d) If you found it difficult or impossible to outline the speech, how might the speaker have arranged his materials for greater clarity?

10. Select a general topic and then formulate five propositions or purpose sentences which call for at least three different kinds of organizational patterns. Write a paragraph in defense of the plan you selected in each case.

11. Bring to class two examples of *cause to effect, effect to cause,* and *effect to effect* reasoning. Be prepared to defend or question the validity of the causal relationships in each case.

12. In the outline in the text of the "ABC's of Shaw-Read" (pages 333–335), what changes or additions would you make in the introduction and conclusion? Why? For which of the *general speech purposes* is the conclusion best suited? Why?

RECOMMENDED READINGS

Brown, Charles T. *Introduction to Speech.* Boston: Houghton Mifflin, 1955, Chap. 8.

Buehler, E. C., and Linkugel, Wilmer A. *Speech: A First Course*. New York: Harper and Row, 1962, Chaps. 8 and 9.

Gilman, Wilbur E., Aly, Bower, and White, Hollis. *The Fundamentals of Speaking,* 2nd ed., New York: Macmillan, 1964, Chaps. 2, 4, and 5.

Lomas, Charles W., and Richardson, Ralph. *Speech: Idea and Delivery*. Boston: Houghton Mifflin, 1956, Chap. 5.

Thompson, Wayne N., and Fessenden, Seth A. *Basic Experiences in Speech*. Englewood Cliffs, N.J.: Prentice-Hall, 1958, Chaps. 1, 2, and 6.

Smith, Raymond G. *Principles of Public Speaking*. New York: Ronald, 1958, Chap. 6.

CHAPTER 17

SECURING THE
APPROPRIATE RESPONSE

*To study persuasion intensively is to
study human nature minutely.*
CHARLES H. WOOLBERT

Persuasion is the central objective and the ultimate aim of all public speaking. It constitutes, in essence, the essential reason for nearly all spoken discourse, even when the purpose appears uncertain and the techniques of the persuader scattered and ineffective. Thus, nearly everything we have written up to this point applies directly or indirectly to the securing of an appropriate response from the listener.

As persuaders and as the objects of persuasion, we inhabit a wide variety of different worlds—personal, social, religious, economic, national, and international. In each one, regardless of whether we relish, despise, or master the process, we find ourselves under the dominion of an inexorable law which says, in effect, "persuade or perish." The voices and appeals are often blatant and crude on the one hand and subtle and sophisticated on the other. At one moment they speak to our noblest stirrings and highest aspirations and in the next may plumb the depths of greed and malice. A demagogic madman, preaching a doctrine of racial and religious hatred, inspired a nation to enslave its neighbors. At the same moment two world statesmen drew up the Atlantic Charter, boldly proclaiming "that all the men in all the lands may live out their lives in freedom from fear and want."

In nearly all of our worlds we witness this curious paradox of persuasive perversity and contrasting utility. Our democratic government, dependent for its very existence on persuasive speech, seems to rely on elections, won or lost with half-truths, catchwords, and slogans. Yet through the centuries man has also developed a higher concept of persuasion in the courts where all men are considered equal and where a man is presumed innocent until he is proved guilty. And while men under the guise of religious persuasion have sometimes put other men to the rack, they have also developed a tradition based on brotherhood, a reverence for human life, and a profound respect for the human personality.

Fortunately, the weapons of international persuasion are now too explosive, forcing nations to rely on subtler methods of force and to verbal rather than violent persuasion. Slowly and painfully, the world is grasping (often under duress) the truth that at last it must talk out rather than shoot out its differences. Were the United Nations only a debating society, as some erroneously imply, the concept of a world parliament of men ruled by verbal persuasion would in itself justify the UN's existence.

Still the techniques and motives, the appeals and devices both brutal and sublime sometimes become so intermixed and confused that men almost despair of the persuader and the process. Such dismay is neither modern nor the product of this century. Through the ages men have echoed a Platonic lament, condemning the persuader and the teachers of persuasion as diabolical prophets who make the true appear false and the false seem true. As we have indicated earlier we do not consider every technique and device of persuasion legitimate or ethical (see pages 306–307). At the same time the difficulty of formulating valid generalizations in the realm of ethical persuasion continues to plague the best minds. Most of the persuasive techniques and devices are amoral, unfeeling, subject to the whim of the persuader. The axe can build or destroy the dwelling. Further complicating the process is the utter impossibility of determining absolute "truth." Perhaps the best safeguard against the unscrupulous demagogue remains the open and free discussion of all issues. While some explosive situations may demand the silencing of a rabble-rouser, we can, in general, say that "error" may take the stand as long as "truth" is granted equal time. This condition of "free speech" should furnish additional stimulation for those who feel they possess some degree of truth, to arm themselves with skills that transcend mere "righteous indignation."

In previous chapters, we discussed the role of the scientific method and logical proof in decision-making and persuasion. We reiterate our faith in reason. We also indicated the virtual impossibility of separating logical from emotional proof (see pages 305–306). In this chapter, however, we propose to consider those aspects of proof, sometimes considered nonlogical or pathetic, the wants and desires, the motivations which profoundly influence our decisions. When the emotional is blended with the logical, the speaker develops his strongest appeal, emotion serving as the catalytic agent, energizing and stimulating man *to want* to make the decision that logically he ought to make. We will consider then the motivating forces and their relationship to attention and suggestion.

NATURE OF ATTENTION

In a previous chapter, we indicated that attention once occupied a central position in the study of persuasion (see pages 284–285) and was considered by earlier authorities as the actual instrument of persuasion. All will agree that persuasion is impossible without attention, but it is no longer considered the motivating agency. More accurately, attention furnishes the atmosphere, the climate, the environment in which persuasion may occur. The securing of attention does, however, constitute the necessary first step in the process. The speaker who would gain acceptance for his ideas must first capture and then sustain the attention of his audience.

Unless we have established unfortunate reputations for dullness we may assume at the outset a maximum of listener attention. Some will pay initial attention out of sheer curiosity. All listeners need special treatment if the speaker expects to hold their attention throughout his speech. Thus, an examination of the nature of attention is the first step toward securing the appropriate response.

Increased Awareness. An object, a figure, a sound, or a movement catches our attention when it stands out in contrast with all background stimuli. Attention in this situation serves functionally to make clear— to make one idea or group of ideas stand out vividly at the expense of all competing ideas.

A Special Bodily Set. The runner waiting for the shot of the starter's gun illustrates both the bodily set and the purpose of this physical state during periods of attention. The stance enables the runner to respond as quickly as possible. While he is waiting for the shot, his responses to surrounding situations are considerably reduced. He becomes only dimly aware of other sounds or actions and is only marginally aware of persons near-by who may be talking or moving about. But he is keenly aware of the starter whose every sound and gesture becomes clear and significant.

Because it is important to the runner to attend, he pays strict attention to the starter. The greater his desire to win, the more closely he is likely to attend. We are not, as public speakers, concerned with winning a race. We are concerned, however, with winning a clear right-of-way to the minds of our listeners. In a sense, the speaker is to the audience what the starter is to the runner. He must somehow make his listeners want to attend because it is to their best interests to attend. To do this, he must overcome the effects of all competing elements in the surroundings and become, himself, the main source of stimulation. How can this be done? A review of highlights in studies of the psychology of attention will give us part of the answer.

PSYCHOLOGY OF ATTENTION

Attention Span

How long can we pay continuous and unwavering attention to a situation? Experimental evidence indicates that the duration of a single act of attention varies in length from as little as three to as long as twenty-four seconds. Most of us attend continuously to a situation for from five to eight seconds. We pay attention in spurts. Between spurts we experience both physical and intellectual lapses. We may blink our eyes and shift position, but are still probably able to get some meaning out of the material under discussion. During the lapses we are also more susceptible to competing stimuli, either external or self-generated. We may suddenly remember the examination we are taking next hour or decide to start making plans for the next weekend. Moreover, experimental studies indicate that we are capable of absorbing material when delivered to us two or three times faster than any person is capable of speaking. Thus, during every minute of a speech, we enjoy several hundred extra words of thinking time.[1]

The trouble is that members of an audience all too rarely use these "spare" moments for constructive listening. Instead, they pick a gap as a moment to pursue some subject other than the speaker's, and if their own thoughts prove interesting, they may never return to the speaker. The audience is always paying attention to something. We hope that at the conclusion of each ten-second interval the listeners will return to us rather than succumb to more attractive stimuli. We must also remember that the "length" of an expressed thought is still circumscribed by the short attention span of a few seconds. This is true in spite of our rapid potential listening speed. As speakers, we need, therefore, to keep our spoken thought units short, breaking up longer units through appropriate phrasing.

What is ordinarily thought of as continuous attention is in reality the cumulative effect of brief and successive periods of attending. Since attention is not steady but comes in spurts, the speaker must consider the best means of sustaining or renewing the listener's attention. A knowledge of the *factors of attention* should help.

---

[1] Ralph G. Nichols, "Do We Know How To Listen? Practical Helps in a Modern Age," *The Speech Teacher*, **X** (March 1961), 123.

Change or Variety

Probably the best method of securing and sustaining attention is through the use of ever-changing stimuli. This change includes variety in *idea, language, voice,* and *action.* Sameness of idea or phrasing, a monotone or static delivery will eventually destroy even the most eager listener's will to attend. The ideas of the speaker, especially the ones he restates for emphasis, should usually contain variety in wording and phraseology.

Vocal Variety. Fortunately, the speaker can employ changes in pitch, quality, and loudness to sustain attention as well as to clarify meanings and promote emotional responses. He can always attract attention, with a marked or sudden change in voice. But he may also defeat his purpose of sustaining long-range attention unless the vocal variety coincides with the emotional and intellectual significance of what he is saying.

Animation

Each change of bodily position and each gesture serves as an attention-catcher. Our primary concern is that they not only promote attention, but also reinforce and amplify the idea and feeling we are attempting to project. Change, not necessarily the movement itself, is the actual attention-catcher. The extremely active speaker, for example, may secure attention by suddenly stopping all action—just as the teacher often catches attention by a lengthened pause in speech.

Repetition

It is difficult to ignore a situation if it is repeated several times at unpredictable intervals. A word or phrase spoken once may not attract attention. The same word or phrase repeated is difficult to ignore. Too frequent repetition, however, may result in irritation, and unless the speaker wishes to irritate his listeners with a particular thought, he should employ repetition in moderation. The reiteration of a word or phrase, accompanied by a change in vocal pattern and reinforced with bodily action, serves both to hold attention and add emphasis.

The speaker then who would gain and hold attention must offer his listener constantly changing stimuli—visual and auditory cues—of differing intensity, animation, and quality. A word of caution, however, may be necessary. Any device used deliberately to secure attention must conform with the customs of the groups and the circumstances of the occasion. Above all, it must tend to promote the general and specific purposes of the speech. The whistle, while appropriate to the basketball court, is probably out of place in the banquet hall.

INTEREST

The factors just considered are largely methods of delivery we use to attract and to maintain attention. Equally important is the public speaker's treatment of the content and his employment of supporting materials (see pages 307–310) that will make his listeners *want* to pay continuous attention. All of the previously mentioned factors of attention will remain impotent and short-lived if the content fails to attract and interest.

While content that holds one person may bore another, certain *natural values,* despite individual differences, will tend to stimulate attention in most listeners. We refer to the *factors of interest,* including *vitalness, suspense, conflict, familiarity, novelty, concreteness,* and *humor.* We have already discussed most of these elements in preceding chapters (see pages 320–322) but would emphasize again that unless the speaker can sustain attention both through delivery and content treatment, nothing else really matters. If the speaker can accomplish this feat, he may then link his proposition to the motivating forces inherent to his theme and present in his audience. Indeed, as we turn to a discussion of motivation, we shall observe how closely it and attention are related.

THE NATURE OF MOTIVATION

Most human action is based on desire. Much of our so-called reasoning is merely self-justification (rationalization), the finding of good reasons (not necessarily the real reasons) for believing or acting in a particular way. When our thinking and our actions enjoy social approval, are sanctioned by authorities we respect, and are phrased as convenient slogans or in stereotyped words and phrases, we find it easier to justify a course of action or a belief. On the other hand, we find it difficult to carry out an action that lacks social approval. Persons with strong consciences and keen social awareness may abandon contemplated actions when they fail to secure appropriate social or group approval. Housewives, the advertisers discovered, sometimes hesitate to purchase kitchen labor-saving devices and cooking short-cuts because they feel guilty in their neglect of their culinary responsibilities. By showing the lady of the house how the new method would enable her to spend more time with her family (a legitimate desire) the advertisers managed to soothe the feminine conscience and to win wider acceptance for the product.

We would not want to give the impression that people are motivated solely by desire or that desire establishes credibility regardless of how incredible the situation may be. As Minnick[2] has shown, desire influences belief and action most strikingly when the means for establishing proof are unsure, vague, and uncertain. Where little or no empirical evidence exists, we tend to follow our desires. But even where the situation is uncertain, desire may exert little influence in rendering extreme statements believable. If a particular belief is highly important to a person, he tends to look for facts to confirm or deny his position. The degree to which wants and desires influence belief will, quite naturally, vary from person to person. We do not deny the strength of belief, but we would caution the persuader that he cannot expect his statements to receive acceptance simply because they are associated with the wants and beliefs of his audience. He must seek as wide a variety of methods and forms of proof as possible to establish the validity of his proposition.

Even so, one task of the public speaker, if he is to persuade, is to align the mode of action or the pattern of behavior he seeks to promote in his listeners with the motivating forces that will meet with approval. The approval must come from his listeners and from those persons with whom his listeners will have contact. To accomplish this he must first understand the nature of the fundamental drives that motivate and help to determine human conduct.

FUNDAMENTAL DRIVES

As normal persons, we share many wants, interests, and attitudes. We may or may not recognize their presence or their potency, but nevertheless strive continually for their fulfillment. Some of the basic drives, necessary to our biological existence, include the desire for self-preservation, the relief of hunger, thirst, and fatigue, the need for sexual expression, and the elimination of wastes. We eat and fight illness to keep alive and to perpetuate life. In some instances our strivings are immediate and impelling, at other times they are ultimate and long range. For example, we save money to buy food, to educate our children, to secure insurance for the accident we hope won't occur, or to devise a scheme for our early retirement with a comfortable income. Of course, our present and future objectives often conflict, and then we face the alternative choices of an early marriage or a career, an immediate position or graduate school.

From the biological drives, we could probably glean a nearly endless list of our specific physiological, psychological, and sociological wants. Vance Packard in *The Hidden Persuaders*[3] indicated that the motivation

---

[2] See Wayne C. Minnick, *The Art of Persuasion,* Boston: Houghton Mifflin, 1957, pp. 198–202.

[3] Vance Packard, *The Hidden Persuaders,* New York: McKay, 1957.

research practitioners attempt to discover all the unconscious cravings and hidden desires that prompt us to smoke, buy big cars, and patronize the supermarket. We doubt that the speaker need pursue the subject quite as intensively as the depth psychologists who decided that air conditioning satisfied our unconscious desire to return to the controlled climate of the womb. We even suspect that our purchase of a unit might be the obvious desire to keep cool during hot weather. Still the speaker needs to study his proposition and its relationship to such widely divergent needs as ego satisfaction, health concerns, reputation, esthetic enjoyment, power, security, ownership, freedom from restraint, and any of a multitude of other wants and value patterns present in his listeners. Most of these fall under one of several categories we shall briefly discuss.

1. Physical Well-Being.   The long lines of persons waiting to drink an ounce of fluid from a paper cup on Sabin Oral Sunday and the nearly universal concern over the health hazards of nuclear explosions testifies to the potency of this want. At fifteen-minute intervals, day and night, radio or television commercials seem endlessly to proclaim the efficacy of some product designed to save our teeth, aid our digestion, or soothe our aching heads and muscles. We must, of course, secure food, shelter, and rest and, if possible, avoid situations endangering our health or producing pain, hunger, or physical deprivation. Closely tied to our desire for physical well-being is our need for economic security and our ability to earn a livelihood.

2. Altruism.   One of our strongest drives is to serve others. It has sometimes been called "enlightened selfishness," because we actually derive more real pleasure from helping others than we receive from the purely selfish desire to "get" for ourselves. The biblical injunctions "He that loses his life [in service to others] shall save it" and "It is more blessed to give than to receive" are still true. The response to CARE, the program of "adoption" of a war orphan, the United Appeal, the response to President Kennedy's Peace Corps are all evidence of this strong motivation to serve others.

3. Mental Well-Being.   We do not live on bread alone. Included among the satisfactions we seek are those giving us mental well-being. We strive to attain social security, peace of mind, freedom from worry, and freedom from fear.

4. Belonging.   We are by nature "joiners," striving to belong and to be wanted. If possible, we also seek the respect and admiration of our associates. Usually, this includes identification with a group enjoying "status" in the community. The businessman *belongs* if he is accepted by respectable business organizations. So we have local, state, and national chambers of commerce, medical associations, scientific societies, and service clubs such as Kiwanis, Rotary, Elks, and Lions.

On some college campuses, for a student to belong he or she must receive an invitation to join a fraternity or sorority. On other campuses, it may be the drama club, debating society, or student government which are the marks of status. Children constantly form clubs. If not accepted, they may join gangs. The need to join, *to belong*, is exceedingly important and as a motivating drive can scarcely be overemphasized.

5. Love.[4]   Closely allied to our need to belong is our desire to be loved by someone we love. In a sense, being loved fulfills our desire to belong. It is a need fulfilled in an intimate, personal way. To be scorned by those we love, to feel not wanted, constitutes a cruel punishment. Psychiatrists tell us that the child who feels unwanted, who is not loved becomes a problem child and a difficult adult.

6. Zestful Living.   Most of us strive not only to live in peace and security, to be well physically and mentally, but also to live zestfully. An almost perennial campaign slogan, as old as John Adams and as new as the latest keynote address is "Peace and Prosperity." We want not only a chicken in every pot, but also two cars in every garage. We want not only clothes, but the latest styles as well. We want shelter, but also want to travel and leave our shelter, even on a go-now, pay-later basis—as long as the payments are easy and we can always return home. In short, we strive for a life which has sufficient novelty to be interesting, which combines safety and security with occasional new experiences.

MOTIVATION IN PUBLIC SPEAKING

Persuasion may occur on an individual or group level, and while there may be no such thing as a "group mind," individuals do behave differently when they are in groups. We need to consider some of the characteristics of the audience, and the way individuals behave when members of an audience.

Conformity of Behavior

As we assume a position as the member of an audience, our behavior and our thinking tend to take on the coloring of the group. When we are

---

[4] Love of country—patriotism—as a motivating power may in part be explained as a combination of *love* and *wishing* to *belong*.

aware that others are observing our behavior, we are inclined to conform to the standards we think are expected of us. We become less individualistic and more conforming in our thinking and acting. To a speaker's humorous remark we are likely to laugh only as heartily as our neighbors. On the occasions when we miss the speaker's point, we will still laugh a little if everyone around us in laughing. Indeed, in the midst of our laughter, we often turn to our neighbor and ask him to repeat the speaker's humorous quip.

Several psychological studies indicate that we are more inclined to accept the opinion of the majority or the group in preference to the opinion of an expert. Marple found that students on the high-school and college levels as well as adults were more strongly influenced by group opinion than by expert opinion.[5] Unfortunately one expert in the "right" does not seem to constitute a majority for the group. We should bear in mind, however, that the older adults in Marple's study were less influenced by the group. Other studies found some evidence to support the stronger prestige of the expert,[6] and while we can draw general conclusions about the nature of the group, we never dare lose sight of the deviants. A recent volume in *The Psychology of Communication* concludes "that group opinion is probably strongest in influencing individual attitudes and beliefs, but that the subject under discussion and the prestige of a particular expert may make for exceptions."[7]

Psychology of Group Behavior

In terms of the psychology of group behavior, we can understand this usual tendency of individuals to conform to the "mode of behavior" of the audience. Students of public speaking, discussion, and social psychology continue to study the behavior of people in groups and some of their conclusions are especially relevant to persuasion.[8]

1. *People in groups think less logically than individuals alone.* We rationalize, tend to allow desire to predominate, respond more readily to

[5] Clare H. Marple, "The Comparative Susceptibility of Three Age Levels to the Suggestion of Group *vs.* Expert Opinion," *Journal of Social Psychology,* 4 (May 1933), 176–186.

[6] See D. H. Kulp, "Prestige, as Measured by Single-Experience Changes and Their Permanency," *Journal of Educational Research,* 27 (1934), 663–672; also I. Lorge, "Prestige, Suggestion, and Attitudes," *Journal of Social Psychology,* 7 (1936), 386–402.

[7] Jon Eisenson, J. Jeffery Auer, and John V. Irwin, *The Psychology of Communication,* New York: Appleton-Century-Crofts, 1963, p. 234.

[8] See David Krech, Richard S. Crutchfield, and Egerton L. Ballachey, *Individual in Society: A Textbook of Social Psychology,* New York: McGraw-Hill, 1962, pp. 215–273, 383–530, for an excellent discussion of groups and individual behavior in group situations.

personal appeals, and generally accept specious argument even more easily than we do as individuals.

2. *Persons in groups avoid extremes in judgment.*   Unconsciously, we tend to moderate our judgments to conform to group standards. At the same time, an individual member of an uncontrolled mob may commit extreme acts under the influence and sanction of the crowd that he would not consider as an individual.

3. *The conformity of persons increases with group homogeneity.*   The more nearly persons are alike in occupation, earning power, and social, political, and religious beliefs, the more readily they will conform as members of the group.

There are, of course, exceptions to these generalizations. Persons disinclined to conform on any grounds would probably continue as nonconformists when in a group. Highly intelligent and well-educated persons are less likely to conform, in part, perhaps, because they are constantly urged to "think for themselves." Persons inclined to be negativistic might very well maintain and exercise their negativism even when in a group.

One of the tasks of the persuader then is to select the motivating drives that are especially applicable to the constituents of a given audience. The previous discussion on analyzing the audience (pages 296–298) should prove useful in directing the speaker in his selection of motive appeals. In his analysis of audiences in general the speaker will also discover that the individual in a group is usually more susceptible to the use of suggestion.

SUGGESTION

For the public speaker, suggestion consists in evoking thoughts in the listener through a process of association. We may define suggestion as the uncritical acceptance of an opinion as the basis for belief or action. Basically, much advertising is pure, direct suggestion; most is largely suggestion intermixed with a dash of pseudologic to "prove" the value of a product in satisfying some need. Following a supposedly scientific demonstration, the announcer declares, "This proves that ozone pills will relieve your hay fever twice as fast as any other remedy." The slogans that usually follow or are sometimes the sole advertisement are direct suggestion: "There's a Ford in your future." "When better cars are made Buick will make them." "Good to the last drop." In the commercial world the huckster's "purpose," as *Time* expressed it, "is to condition customers —recalling Pavlov's dogs which salivated at the sound of the dinner bell— so that they will drool at the sight or sound of a selling gimmick with the symbolism that appeals to the unconscious. M[otivation] R[esearch] practitioners are convinced that most shoppers buy irrationally to satisfy unconscious cravings."[9]

Two features of suggestion are revealed in this quotation. As far as the listener is concerned, suggestion is an unwitting process of arriving at a conclusion, the conclusion being one the speaker had in mind. The second is the close relationship of motivations, inner drives, latent attitudes, and beliefs. For suggestion to operate successfully, the idea, belief, hidden craving must be present. Suggestion has little or no effect in *changing* beliefs or attitudes. It merely uses already existing motives to promote the course of action the speaker desires. He can employ suggestion more successfully by using the following guides:

1. Spontaneity. Suggestion gains strength if it appears to originate spontaneously with the listener. "Those are my sentiments, exactly!" spoken by a listener probably means the speaker has applied suggestion successfully. The so-called "hidden" persuasion, popularized by Vance Packard, reveals Madison Avenue's effort to discover the motivational drives mentioned earlier and to associate a product with this drive through subtle suggestion. For example, the screen pictures a rugged, virile mountain climber, a deep sea diver, or racing driver pursuing his dangerous, exciting hobby and then lighting up his favorite cigarette—or better still is surrounded by a bevy of lovely ladies, one of whom gives him a light. In some of the more blatant advertisements, the announcer says, "The girls will all pursue you," but in the subtler approach, the announcer never says, "You too can be a big he-man, popular and successful if you use our brand." Instead, the idea is wholly implied that we too would share something with the great athlete or movie star if we also smoked his cigarette. If the listener, particularly the sophisticated member of the audience, recognizes that he is being offered a straight forward suggestion, its motivational force is considerably decreased.

2. Prestige of Source. The potency of a suggestion is directly related to the *prestige* of the source. It pleases most of us to know that a prominent industrialist, politician, athlete, or actor holds the same point of view as we do. Moreover, we tend to accept suggestions more readily from persons we admire and respect. We would hope that students of persuasion, at least, would demand that the prominent person be recognized as an authority in the field of thinking which encompasses his testimony. A famous scientist may possess no more than a layman's knowledge in theology, and what a movie star says about the alleged health value of a cigarette is probably

---

[9] *Time* (May 13, 1957), p. 51.

less important than the testimony of a physician. The opinions of a noted physicist such as Edward Teller on the implications of nuclear energy and fall-out shelters should hold greater significance than those of the manager of a major league baseball team. We often have difficulty, however, when the opinions of the natural or physical scientist come into conflict with the political scientist on such matters as nuclear testing, and fall-out hazards. As listeners we need to review the tests for authority. And as persuaders, we can still recognize and employ the prestige of authority without committing the obvious practices of the hucksters. Certainly, we must understand and appreciate that better educated audiences are less likely to confuse popularity with authority.

3. Positive Approach. In our discussion of the introduction to the speech (see pages 317–323) we warned about the dangers of negative suggestion. While it may be impossible, as this sentence and the previous one demonstrate, to keep all suggestions positive, persuasion operates most effectively in a positive atmosphere. As much as possible we need to keep the desired course of action uppermost rather than the undesired, lest our listeners perversely decide to taste the forbidden fruit. The parent who warns junior not to put beans up his nose is probably asking for trouble, and the student who says to the Dean of Women, "Of course, you wouldn't be in favor of liberalizing the social rules on campus," is not necessarily right, but to her sorrow may get the answer she demanded. "I didn't do very well on this one," the student says as he hands his blue book to the teacher, thereby implanting a negative suggestion, the one idea he least wants his teacher to accept. The advertiser who declares his product "less fattening" or "less irritating" is in a positively negative fashion suggesting that his product will indeed increase your weight and does contain an irritant.

Habits and Attitudes

In using suggestion we should avoid violating the lifelong habits or fixed moral feelings of our listeners. Indeed, a suggestion running counter to the listener's deep-seated prejudices or values will have little desired effect. Religious toleration, for example, was brought about in the United States, not by suggesting the "legitimacy" of all religious persuasions or the "shortcomings" of any particular sect, but by convincing each group that a part of his true religion included the concept of tolerance for others. When the notion of tolerance is reinforced with the more selfish wish to preserve one's own right to worship, vote, or speak without undue restriction, the likelihood of establishing tolerance is increased. We need a realistic view, however, and an understanding that the changing of long-standing attitudes or ways of behaving, however socially desirable, is seldom a single-speech accomplishment. We can cite numerous studies to show that attitudes can be modified by a single speech, but more often the way is long and the process slow.

The Language of Suggestion

What is the most effective way to phrase a suggestion? The difference between the right word and any word, as Mark Twain observed, is the difference between lightning and the lightning bug. The more vividly the suggestion is offered, the more powerful the suggestion. But we need also to consider another fact which on the surface may seem to contradict this idea. In general, a wording the listeners will not interpret as a command will be more effective than a direct wording. Direct commands are likely to meet with opposition. An indirect wording usually includes the speaker as well as the listeners in the recommended action. The speaker who says, "I urge you to join me in signing this petition . . ." will create less resistance and is likely to obtain more signatures than one who informs his audience that "petitions are available—sign them."

Occasionally, a directly worded suggestion may be effective. If the speaker is a person who commands great respect and is accepted as a leader by his audience, if the listeners have assembled to hear directions and to follow them, then directly worded suggestions are likely to be effective. In such circumstances the tactful "Let us . . . " approach may be changed to the "Here is what we ought to do" order. A speaker may then conclude his address with a directly worded statement along the lines of "Sign the petition before you leave the hall," or "Do not leave this hall without signing the petition."

Whether the suggested action is directly or indirectly stated, the actual wording should be as specific as possible. If a letter is to be written to a Congressman, the name and address of the Congressman should be given. If the audience is one not given to the writing of letters, a sample letter may be read or actually given to the listeners. In short, the suggestion should be one readily understood and easily executed.

MOTIVATION AND SUGGESTION

We have considered attention, motivation, and suggestion as three essential and interrelated components for the initiation and direction of the activities of the listener. When, as speakers, we succeed in holding the attention of the listeners and motivating them to act on our suggestions, we have succeeded in persuasion. We may define persuasion then as a process of initiating certain action patterns in our listeners and of blocking off others which might interfere with our securing the appropriate audience response.

Previously we have discussed the factor of *ethical proof* (see pages 306–307), and we need at this point to emphasize once again the potent force in persuasion that is found in the personality of the speaker. When we can, through voice, language, and behavior, succeed in making our listeners comfortable, we have taken the first step toward securing acceptance for the proposition. Attitudes of enthusiasm, combined with sincerity and confidence, if devoid of any trace of cockiness, communicate themselves to listeners. If we can add to these the speaker's reputation for wisdom and truthfulness, listeners will be predisposed to agreement.

Listeners are not usually conscious of their impressions of the speaker's personality. Neither are they generally aware of a predisposition to the acceptance of a point of view because it is associated with a speaker. If nothing is done to disturb this favorable listener state of mind, the speaker will have made effective, even if unwitting, use of his personality as a factor in persuasion.

DEVELOPING THE PERSUASIVE SPEECH

As we have indicated earlier, the speech to convince or persuade may be organized topically according to a logical (problem-solution or cause and effect) plan. The speech may also follow a psychological pattern, using a "this or nothing" approach or a greater reliance on blending the emotional with the logical when setting up the main topical heads. In this chapter we have concerned ourselves primarily with the psychological approach and the discovery of the motivational appeals. We would emphasize again the inevitable intermixture of the logical and the emotional and of the necessity and importance of a strong logical foundation for the speech.

By way of review, we would remind the speaker intent on persuasion to keep the following steps uppermost in the planning and developing of his proposition.

1. Secure immediate and sustain long-range attention.

2. Establish audience rapport, seeking a common ground of understanding.

3. Find those main supporting heads that will in themselves promote the desired response. Support your arguments with evidence, established fact, and authoritative opinion.

4. Make sure the foundation of the speech is logically sound.

5. Seek the motivations (wants and desires) present in the audience that will promote the desired response.

6. Use as wide a variety of appeals (logical, emotional, and ethical) as are appropriate for the subject, audience, and occasion.

7. Use the language of persuasion.

8. Reinforce ideas with appropriate delivery (language, voice, bodily action).

SUMMARY

Our most frequent purpose in public speaking is to effect a change of action or thought in our listeners. While this change appears to be the result of many forces—logical, emotional, and ethical—it is perhaps best accomplished through an appeal to the listener in terms of fundamental human drives. These drives are directed toward the satisfaction of our biological, psychological, and sociological needs and wants. They include (1) physical well-being, (2) altruism, (3) mental well-being, (4) belonging, (5) love, and (6) zestful living.

Persuasion operates in an atmosphere where the listener's attention is focused on the speaker's proposition. Since attention is of short duration, it must be constantly renewed by using the natural *factors of attention*: (1) change or variety, (2) animation, (3) repetition, and through the *factors of interest*: (1) vitalness, (2) suspense, (3) conflict, (4) familiarity, (5) novelty, (6) concreteness, (7) humor.

Intermixed with attention and motivation is the third factor in the persuasion process—*suggestion*. We may define suggestion as the uncritical acceptance of an opinion as the basis for belief or action. A suggestion gains strength when (1) it appears to be of spontaneous origin with the listener, (2) it is associated with a person of prestige, (3) it is presented positively, (4) it does not violate the listener's lifelong habits or fixed moral feelings.

Persuasion is a process, operating through attention, of initiating certain action patterns in our listeners and blocking off others which might interfere with our objectives. Motivating techniques and suggestion, fortified by the speaker's personality, are primary forces in the securing of an appropriate response from the listener.

QUESTIONS AND EXERCISES

1. Prepare a two-to-three-minute speech announcing a forthcoming event on campus. Include several of the *factors of interest* and *attention* discussed in the chapter.

2. Select an advertisement from one of the "slick" magazines such as *Fortune* or *Harper's* and from a "pulp" magazine. Compare the two for the following:

    (a) Basic motivating appeals,
    (b) Appropriateness of the advertisements for the probable reading audience,
    (c) Methods each used to catch attention.

3. Select a speech topic, e.g., Federal Aid to Education, Disarmament, United Nations, or Legalized Gambling. Phrase a proposition designed to establish a point of view. In a three-minute speech give the names of three persons you might employ as authorities to back your point of view. Evaluate your three authorities, indicating why their opinions would be persuasive. With what kind of audiences would each witness carry the *greatest* impact? The *least*?

4. During the next round of speeches in class construct a list of the annoying mannerisms that distracted your attention from the speakers. Make another list of techniques or devices, either in content or delivery, that recaptured your attention.

5. Select a speech designed to change the listener's attitudes that appears in a current issue of *Vital Speeches* and analyze for
   (a) the speaker's use of negative suggestion,
   (b) the speaker's use of positive suggestion,
   (c) instances of direct suggestion.

6. What kind of advertising appeals are most likely to influence you to buy a product? Why? What appeals do you generally object to? Why?

7. Bring to class two advertisements, one illustrating predominately non-logical, emotional appeals and the other mainly logical forms of support.

8. Look through a recent issue of *Vital Speeches* for a speech with which you are in complete disagreement. After reading the speech were you more strongly opposed? Less strongly opposed? About the same? Can you account for any shift in your attitude? Did you consider the speaker's general approach to be ethical?

9. Develop a five-minute talk in which you indicate the three main reasons why you decided to go on to college. Analyze each reason for logic and emotion.

10. During the past year you have probably changed your attitude toward different subjects. Think of an instance when a speaker helped to promote this change. How much influence did the speaker's personality play in bringing about this change? In what other ways do you account for your shift of opinion?

11. Analyze five radio or television "commercials" which annoy you. Indicate specifically why. Reword the commercials so that they become more acceptable to you.

RECOMMENDED READINGS

Brembeck, Winston L., and Howell, William S. *Persuasion: A Means of Social Control.* Englewood Cliffs, N. J.: Prentice-Hall, 1952.

Brigance, William N. *Speech Composition.* New York: Appleton-Century-Crofts, 1953, Chap. V.

Eisenson, Jon, Auer, J. Jeffery, and Irwin, John V. *The Psychology of Communication.* New York: Appleton-Century-Crofts, 1963.

Ewbank, H. L., and Auer, J. Jeffery. *Discussion and Debate.* New York: Appleton-Century-Crofts, 1951, Chap. 14.

Hovland, Carl I., Janis, Irving L. and Kelley, Harold H. *Communication and Persuasion.* New Haven: Yale University Press, 1953.

Minnick Wayne C., *The Art of Persuasion,* Boston: Houghton Mifflin, 1957.

Oliver, Robert T. *Psychology of Persuasive Speech.* New York: McKay, 1957.

Reid, Loren. *First Principles of Public Speaking.* Columbia: Artcraft Press, 1962, Chaps. 17 and 18.

CHAPTER 18

READING ALOUD

(BRINGING PRINT TO LIFE)

All poetry, and all good prose, invite me to utterance.
I hope I do not sit muttering in public places; but if I
cannot give voice, my ear harkens to unheard melodies.
ROBERT WILLIAM CHAPMAN

Black marks on white paper represent one kind of communication. Giving sound to these symbols alters radically the nature of that message. The oral reader may utter his own words or he may attempt to translate into sound someone else's thoughts and emotions. Regardless of who placed the symbols on paper, reading to others is a highly complex process involving a delicate blending of thought, feeling, and technique. It is never primarily an action of lungs, larynx, and articulators.

To convert the printed word into a meaningful, interesting and perhaps an esthetic experience is the fascinating and practical art nearly everyone at some time attempts in a multitude of ways and in widely different places.

For ministers, teachers, lawyers, actors, radio and television personalities reading aloud is an almost daily part of their professions. Nearly as often, persons in the home—the parents who read stories to their children—are certainly trying to bring print to life. For many, formal training in silent and oral reading ended abruptly in grammar school and perhaps this is one reason Johnny can't read—to *himself* or to *others*.

WHEN AND WHY WE READ ALOUD?

We read aloud whenever we say (try to recall audibly) the precise words once written by anyone—the speaker himself or someone else. But why should we read aloud? What circumstances and occasions make reading preferable to impromptu or extemporaneous speaking?

Special Thoughts and Precise Words

We often read because another person has written a better story or poem than we. Rather than recall or recite, we read it, because the exact words carry the essence better than the approximate words. By memorizing the precise phraseology, some persons are even better equipped to tell the story or interpret the poem. But they are still reading. They are reading from memory—words other than their own. Under these circumstances a speaker sometimes becomes an actor or impersonator.

We also read because we want to convey the *precise words* and so the thoughts of the writer. We read a newspaper or magazine article because we are impressed with the nicety of the thought or because we want to make clear our agreement with or our opposition to the writer's opinion. We may embrace his idea or take strong exception to his point of view and then go on to explain, in our own words, why we agree or disagree.

Unusual Circumstances

Special situations sometimes demand the manuscript speech. Most radio and television talks are read directly from a script or a teleprompter. Rigid time limits and the necessity for some degree of "content control" prompt most stations to demand a script. No one should deceive himself, however, with the notion that script reading is easier than extemporaneous speaking. If the reader must also compose his scripts he may experience double trouble. Few talks are more deadly than the obviously "read" message with its stilted phraseology and unnatural inflections. Moreover, in radio, television, and even on stage, where reading from the script or from the memory is the approved procedure, the superior speaker is able to think on his feet and *ad lib* in crisis situations. On some occasions speakers are justified in using a manuscript. As a general rule we would consider the extemporaneous mode preferable, but in times of national emergency or when exactness of language is essential, the speaker may insure accuracy through the use of a carefully prepared manuscript. Presidential addresses in times of national crises call for precise, careful phraseology. President Kennedy's nationwide television address on October 22, 1962 in the face of Russian-based missiles in Cuba was a moment when the wrong word or an ill-turned phrase could have ushered in a nuclear holocaust. Reading to a tense world, the President concluded with these words:

Seventh, and finally, I call upon Chairman Khrushchev to halt and eliminate this clandestine, reckless and provocative threat to world peace and to stable relations between our two nations.

I call upon him further to abandon this course of world domination and to join in an historic effort to end the perilous arms race and to transform the history of man.

He has an opportunity now to move the world back from the abyss of destruction by returning to his Government's own words that it had no need to station missiles outside its own territory, and withdrawing these weapons from Cuba, by refraining from any action which will widen or deepen the present crisis, and then by participating in a search for peaceful and permanent solutions.

This nation is prepared to present its case against the Soviet threat to peace and our own proposals for a peaceful world at any time and in any forum—in the O.A.S., in the United Nations, or in any other meeting that could be useful without limiting our freedom of action.

We have, in the past, made strenuous efforts to limit the spread of nuclear weapons. We have proposed the elimination of all arms, and military bases in a fair and effective disarmament treaty. We are prepared to discuss new proposals for the removal of tensions on both sides including the possibilities of a genuinely independent Cuba free to determine its own destiny.

We have no wish to war with the Soviet Union for we are a peaceful people who desire to live in peace with all other peoples.

But it is difficult to settle or even discuss these problems in an atmosphere of intimidation.

That is why this latest Soviet threat or any other threat which is made either independently or in response to our actions this week must and will be met with determination.

Any hostile move anywhere in the world against the safety and freedom of peoples to whom we are committed including in particular the brave people of West Berlin will be met by whatever action is needed.

Finally, I want to say a few words to the captive people of Cuba to whom this speech is being directly carried by special radio facilities.

I speak to you as a friend, as one who knows of your deep attachment to your fatherland, as one who shares your aspirations for liberty and justice for all.

And I have watched and the American people have watched with deep sorrow how your nationalist revolution was betrayed and how your fatherland fell under foreign domination.

Now your leaders are no longer Cuban leaders inspired by Cuban ideals. They are puppets and agents of an international conspiracy which has turned Cuba against your friends and neighbors in the Americas and turned it into the first Latin-American country to become a target for nuclear war, the first Latin-American country to have these weapons on its soil.

These new weapons are not in your interests. They contribute nothing to your peace and well being; they can only undermine it.

But this country has no wish to cause you to suffer or to impose any system upon you. We know that your lives and land are being used as pawns by those who deny your freedom. Many times in the past the Cuban people have risen to throw out tyrants who destroyed their liberty.

And I have no doubt that most Cubans today look forward to the time when they will be truly free, free from foreign domination, free to choose their own leaders, free to select their own system, free to own their own land, free to speak and write and worship without fear or degradation.

And then shall Cuba be welcomed back to the society of free nations and to the associations of this hemisphere.

My fellow citizens, let no one doubt that this is a difficult and dangerous effort on which we have set out. No one can foresee precisely what course it will take, or what course or casualties will be incurred.

Many months of sacrifice and self-discipline lie ahead, months in which both our patience and our will will be tested. Months in which many threats and enunciations will keep us aware of our dangers. But the greatest danger of all would be to do nothing.

The path we have chosen for the present is full of hazards, as all paths are. But it is the one most consistent with our character and courage as a nation and our commitments around the world.

The cost of freedom is always high, but Americans have always paid it. And one path we shall never choose, and that is the path of surrender, or submission.

Our goal is not the victory of might, but the vindication of right; not peace at the expense of freedom, but both peace and freedom here in this hemisphere, and, we hope around the world.

God willing, that goal will be achieved.[1]

President Roosevelt's war message to Congress on December 8, 1941 is also illustrative of a speech delivered at a time when democratic civilization faced its severest test:

Yesterday, December 7, 1941—a date which will live in infamy—the United States of America was suddenly and deliberately attacked by naval and air forces of the Empire of Japan.

The United States was at peace with that nation and, at the solicitation of Japan, was still in conversation with its Government and its Emperor looking toward the maintenance of peace in the Pacific.

Indeed, one hour after Japanese air squadrons had commenced bombing Oahu, the Japanese Ambassador to the United States and his colleagues delivered to the Secretary of State a formal reply to a recent American message. While this reply stated that it seemed useless to continue the existing diplomatic negotiations, it contained no threat or hint of war or armed attack.

It will be recorded that the distance of Hawaii from Japan makes it obvious that the attack was deliberately planned many days or even weeks ago. During the intervening time, the Japanese Government had deliberately sought to deceive the United States Government by false statements and expressions of hope for continued peace.

The attack yesterday on the Hawaiian Islands has caused severe damage to American naval and military forces. Very many American lives have been lost. In addition, American ships have been reported torpedoed on the high seas between San Francisco and Honolulu.

Yesterday the Japanese Government also launched an attack against Malaya.

Last night Japanese forces attacked Hongkong.

Last night Japanese forces attacked Guam.

Last night Japanese forces attacked the Philippine Islands.

Last night the Japanese attacked Wake Island.

This morning the Japanese attacked Midway Island.

---

[1] The conclusion to President Kennedy's speech and other long excerpts in this chapter are included with the thought that in addition to their illustrative value, they may also be used as practice reading material. Some of the selections in the chapter on Improving Your Voice may be used for the same purpose. The complete text of President Kennedy's address is in *Vital Speeches* (November 15, 1962), pp. 66–68.

Japan has, therefore, undertaken a surprise offensive extending throughout the Pacific area. The facts of yesterday speak for themselves. The people of the United States have already formed their opinions and well understand the implications to the very life and safety of our nation.

As Commander-in-Chief of the Army and Navy I have directed that all measures be taken for our defense.

Always will we remember the character of the onslaught against us.

No matter how long it may take us to overcome this premeditated invasion, the American people in their righteous might will win through to absolute victory.

I believe I interpret the will of the Congress and of the people when I assert that we will not only defend ourselves to the uttermost but will make very certain that this form of treachery shall never endanger us again.

Hostilities exist. There is no blinking at the fact that our people, our territory and our interests are in grave danger.

With confidence in our armed forces—with the unbounding determination of our people—we will gain the inevitable triumph—so help us God.

I ask that the Congress declare that since the unprovoked and dastardly attack by Japan on Sunday, December 7, a state of war has existed between the United States and the Japanese Empire.

ADVANTAGES OF READING

Accuracy

Reading aloud has certain advantages over speaking without benefit of manuscript. The reader need not worry about word choice, forgetting, the unintended remark, or a misplaced emphasis on a trivial matter. He is usually saved from grammatical errors and the hazards of the *faux pas* or the "slip of the tongue." "Thoughts unexpressed," Will Carleton once observed, "may sometimes fall back dead; But God himself can't kill them when they're said." Jeremy Bentham likewise reminds us that "the turn of a sentence has decided the fate of many a friendship and, for aught that we know, the fate of many a kingdom." No one could gauge the number of votes Thomas E. Dewey lost in Wisconsin when he delivered a speech from the steps of the State Capitol in Madison and inadvertently expressed his appreciation for the opportunity to speak "from the steps of your courthouse." And, no matter how hard Richard Nixon and President Eisenhower, tried, they could never quite escape the President's unfortunate reply to one question. When a reporter asked the President to mention some state decisions in which his Vice-President played a direct part, replied: "If you give me a week maybe I can think of one."

The Apt Quotation

Oral reading also furnishes the extemporaneous speaker with a more authoritative method of presenting short items, including statistical and factual data. The wise speaker, as we have indicated earlier, should fill his mind with the prose and poetry of the ages as well as with the works of modern authors. Such a practice will help the speaker enrich his own style and will also furnish him with the direct quotations, usually best read verbatim. Occasionally, a speaker will quote a point of view he opposes. Such quotations are better read than presented from memory. To read a quotation or to cite statistics directly insures accuracy and creates a favorable impression (not a false one we trust) of a speaker who has made every effort to present the exact position of a supporter or an opponent. Many listeners, perhaps to their own misfortune, are inclined to accept the published word as the authoritative word.

Lord Halifax, as British Ambassador to the United States, cleverly employed the technique of direct quotation to refute the Nazi point of view and establish his own.

I take at random a few examples from recent broadcasts. The German radio told you one evening:

"The British determine Washington's policy. Churchill requests, Roosevelt obeys."

But a week later the same radio was saying to us:

"The strategic directions are dictated solely by Washington; Washington orders, Churchill obeys."

Or there was this:

"It certainly never entered Churchill's calculations that old England would become a colony of the United States." But a little later Goebbels was saying to you:

"It must be frightful for Mr. Average American in these days not to be quite sure whether his own nationality is actually Yank or British."

Then you are told that:

"So long as the mothers of the United States are so willing, England will fight to the last drop of Iowa blood." And a few days later we are told:

"Churchill has not yet realized that the United States has resolved to fight to the last Tommy."

Well, if we are going to fight to the last drop of Iowa blood and you are going to fight to the last Tommy, it looks like being a hard war—for Hitler.[2]

DISADVANTAGES OF READING

The outstanding disadvantage of reading is that, without thorough preparation, the delivery is likely to lack spontaneity. Most persons have failed to develop the skills of oral reading. Even our own words, when we attempt to read them, sound dull and lifeless, as if they belonged to someone else. If a trained or untrained speaker is suddenly confronted with a deeply moving issue and rises in a public meeting to speak impromptu, his

[2] From an address delivered at a dinner under the auspices of the Association of the Chamber of Commerce, Baltimore, 1942.

words, unless he is overcome by stage fright, will probably sound natural and spontaneous. But, if you suddenly stopped the speaker and asked him to write out and read his message, the chances are that he will lose much of the color, vigor, and spontaneity that marked his impromptu effort. The difficulty, apart from his inability to write in oral style and his removal from the emotional situation, is his inability to read effectively his own or anyone else's prose.

The thinking of the oral reader often seems borrowed rather than an integral part of him, as it must become, if he is to read effectively. Thoughts and language, like clothes and speech, must match the personality of the speaker. Words and locutions appropriate to one speaker may not fit the person and style of another. One of the more ludicrous features of the declamation contest is the incongruity of the schoolboy reciting Patrick Henry's or Robert Ingersoll's oratory. Unfortunately, the reader cannot do very much about material not suited for him except to avoid it.

An extemporaneous speaker, unfettered by a manuscript, can modify his remarks when the audience response indicates the necessity. If, after presenting a point, the speaker receives unfavorable audience feedback, he can restate (using different phraseology) or amplify with an instance or an analogy. The reader enjoys less latitude.[3] If the words are another's, he is bound by the language and must continue regardless of the effect. He can only hope that the impression improves as he progresses. On the other hand an extemporaneous speaker, sensitive to the cues from his audience, can take direct action to correct an unfavorable impression.

Other factors being equal, the reader is usually less direct than the extemporaneous speaker. Too often the written material stands between the reader and his listeners. Notes may form a similar barrier for the speaker. Each time the reader or speaker refers to his material he risks a break in audience contact. But the good reader will make every effort to maintain or reestablish good listener relationships. At best, however, the written material constitutes a block he must somehow overcome if he is to communicate meanings to his listeners.

While reading, except for special occasions, may not constitute the best means of communication, it can be made effective if the reader is willing to master the techniques and minimize its inherent disadvantages. Fortunately, reading aloud is not without its virtues. We all derive much information and pleasure from manuscript public addresses, the reader's theater and the

---

[3] Excellent manuscript speakers often give themselves wide degrees of freedom and flexibility in departing from their manuscripts for impromptu remarks. Franklin D. Roosevelt, a masterful reader, could give a manuscript the informal flavor of a fireside chat, for which he was justly famous. One investigator concluded that Roosevelt made numerous changes in his manuscript during the actual delivery. See Earnest Brandenburg, "The Preparation of Franklin D. Roosevelt's Speeches," *The Quarterly Journal of Speech,* **35** (April 1949), 214–221.

artistic programs of talented interpreters of great poetry and prose. Indeed, most of us find ourselves in one or more of these situations from time to time. Our concern now is to make the most of these occasions, to communicate meanings, to express feelings, and to use the written page to full advantage.

HOW TO READ ALOUD

Basic Considerations

As we turn our attention to the techniques of oral reading, we need to recognize some fundamental principles underlying effective reading.

1. *Few persons have mastered the skills of oral reading.* Even persons in positions that call for extensive use of oral reading sometimes exhibit a frightful lack of skill. A few years ago Rudolph Flesch shocked the educational world by telling the experts *Why Johnny Can't Read.* Mortimer J. Adler of the University of Chicago had already discovered our deficiencies, pointing out that even college students and their teachers did not know how to read. His shocking conclusion was that adults read no better than youngsters just out of grammar school. If misery loves company, we can take some comfort in the thought that all of us seem to share the disability. With this awareness, we can at least strive to raise our oral reading level.

2. *Little correlation exists between skill (speed and comprehension) in silent reading and satisfactory achievement in oral reading.* For a number of years all students enrolled in oral interpretation classes at Oberlin took a silent reading test at the beginning of the semester. A comparison of their scores and their grades at the end of the semester revealed little apparent relationship between silent reading and skill in oral interpretation. While this cursory investigation could lay no claim to scientific accuracy, it may point to the fact that these two methods of reading demand widely different skills. Indeed, after we get past the initial reading stage, we are systematically discouraged from practicing any form of oral reading. Silent, rapid scanning with no perceptible movement of the lips or tongue is considered the ideal method of reading for the student who must cover vast reading assignments in short periods of time. Right though this method may be for silent reading, the result is a neglect of skills for oral reading.

3. *The material serves as the only authentic guide.* This is a cardinal principle for all oral reading. We cannot read a Shakespearian sonnet or, for that matter, a mountain ballad in the manner we might use for an after dinner speech.

4. *Effective reading, oral or silent, demands a complete understanding of the material.* Mere pronunciation of the words never represents reading. And just as we have all "read" several pages silently without comprehending a word, so oral readers sometimes "say" the words, but the essential meaning and feeling is neither understood by the readers nor communicated to the listeners.

5. *We read with our perceptions.* Unless our eyes behold the visual image and unless our bodies respond to the auditory, gustatory, motor, olfactory, and tactile sensations which envelop the written symbol, we have failed to catch the meaning or experience the emotion. While perhaps less true for highly objective material than for passages rich in feeling, we read all materials through our past perceptual experiences. A mathematical equation may leave some cold and others highly stimulated.

6. *Effective oral reading demands a total reaction, a complete response.* The reaction, as we indicated in (4) above must occur at the moment of utterance and requires the precise coordination of body and voice. Reading is an *active process,* demanding complete intellectual and emotional responses to the printed or memorized word.

7. *Oral reading demands the same skills in bodily action and voice as public speaking.* We do not imply that all written materials should be read in a conversational manner. Highly dramatic literature and poetry, for example, would probably sound ludicrous if so delivered. But in all situations involving oral communication, we employ the same basic skills of voice and bodily action. The reader, like the speaker, must achieve that high degree of *control, flexibility,* and *responsiveness* in which the audible and visible cues convey accurately the precise meaning and feeling contained in the selection.

8. *We are not here concerned with impersonation or acting.* Even though the stage calls for oral reading of memorized material, we are thinking primarily of the interpretative reader and the person who reads his message or incorporates memorized or manuscript materials in a speech.

Analysis of the Written Material

Obviously, the first step in achieving excellence as a reader is a complete understanding of the written material. With this comprehension should also come a wide discernment of differences, even within the same selection, making it virtually impossible to read all material in the same manner. Naturally, we would not expect to apply the same methods to the reading of prose as we would apply to poetry. And we would employ different techniques for the reading of one sonnet as compared with another. Although ballads have some common characteristics, no two are quite alike, each needing a particular interpretation. Probably the reading of a prose quotation from Winston Churchill would differ in some respects from one by Harry Truman or Dwight Eisenhower. Even in reading our own material, we must decide what kind of writing we have attempted—its meaning, purpose, and the occasion for which it is intended. Every selection then demands its own specialized analysis and treatment, requiring the reader to go beyond the form itself to an examination of the *logical* and *emotional* foundations.

The Logical Structure

Fundamental to our understanding of any selection is a complete comprehension of the logical structure and the author's motivations. While recognizing that logical and emotional meanings nearly always overlap, we need at the outset to discover the rationale for the material. We need to ask ourselves these questions:

1. *What was the author's purpose?* What was he trying to accomplish? The general purposes we discussed in our chapter on public speaking (see pages 279–287) furnish a good starting place. Did the author write because he wanted to entertain? If so, was he merely amusing or did he manage to get us so engrossed in the material that we forgot the physical world around us? Or perhaps he wanted to teach, either to impart information or to inspire and convince us to change our way of thinking or behaving.

2. *What were the author's motivations?* A writer never produces his work in a vacuum. He is often quite literally driven to the desk, drawing his substance from bitter or sweet life experiences, from the stress and pull of his environment. If we can discover the circumstances that motivated the writing, if we know the milieu and ferment, the mental and emotional struggle, we often gain a fresh view of the final literary product. For example, Edwin Arlington Robinson's poems assume new dimensions when we discover the hardship and suffering he endured during his productive years. Loneliness and agony marked his poetry and failure remained the basic theme of this man who could well understand how

> Miniver Cheevy, child of scorn,
>   Grew lean while he assailed the seasons;
> He wept that he was ever born,
>   And he had reasons[4]

---

[4] From "Miniver Cheevy" in *The Town Down the River,* by Edward Arlington Robinson. Reprinted by permission of Charles Scribner's Sons, New York.

or how even the rich, handsome, and superficially successful Richard Cory could go "home and put a bullet through his head."

Unless we understand the life-philosophy of the author, we are likely to miss the point of much that he has written. An outstanding example of a reformer whose writings we might misunderstand (and he has been misunderstood) is Jonathan Swift. He wrote his *Gulliver's Travels* to ridicule and reform British society of the eighteenth century, only to have his story become a children's classic. Swift wrote *A Modest Proposal* in an attempt to improve living conditions in Ireland. Unfortunately, many persons took him literally and thought Swift to be mad. Said Swift:

> I have been assured by a very knowing American of my acquaintance in London, that a young healthy child well nursed is at a year old, a most delicious, nourishing, and wholesome food, whether stewed, roasted, baked, or boiled; and I make no doubt that it will equally serve in a fricassee or a ragout.
>
> I grant this food will be somewhat dear, and therefore very proper for landlords, who, as they have already devoured most of the parents, seem to have the best title to the children.[5]

3. *What is the author's method?* Closely allied to the purpose and motivation is the method the author choses to achieve his goal. Is the approach intellectual or emotional? Does the writer appeal to reason or to feeling? In many instances the two elements are so intertwined they seem to defy separation. But if the main appeal is to reason, the writing should contain objective data, cause and effect thinking, and assertions supported by facts and inferences. If, on the other hand, the appeal is to feeling, the language should be rich in imagery, a factor we will discuss more fully in the section on the emotional structure.

4. *What are the word meanings?* Obviously, we can never judge the logical structure of a selection until we understand the meanings of all the words. The dictionary is helpful in giving us the denotative (literal) meanings, but in judging the logical structure, we may also need to understand these words in context and even sense their emotional connotations, and their affective meaning. We will discuss this element later in the chapter.

5. *What is the organizational pattern?* Constructing an outline of the selection often helps reveal the logical relationships. If you encounter difficulty, it may be that the author's logical thinking was faulty or you may have failed to analyze the selection properly.

6. *What is the basic theme?* The five preceding steps should help the reader understand the author's theme. One of the best methods for dis-

---

[5] Henry Craik (ed.), *Swift: Selections from his Works*, Vol. II, Oxford: Claredon, 1893, pp. 147–148.

covering the central message is to construct a *precis*, which we may define as a condensation of the original selection to as few words as possible. The *precis* usually runs about one-fourth to one-third the length of the original but still retains its style and organization. The *precis* is probably most useful with prose and less helpful with poetry.

In some writings the dominant theme is presented at the outset. The first sentence may state the theme, and the remainder of the writing may develop it. The passage below is an example of this kind of writing:

The United States is in sore need today of an aristocracy of intellect and service. Because such an aristocracy does not exist in the popular consciousness, we are bending the knee in worship to the golden calf of money. The form of monarchy and its pomp offer a valuable foil to the worship of money for its own sake. A democracy must provide itself with a foil of its own, and none is better or more effective than an aristocracy of intellect and service recruited from every part of our democratic life.[6]

Occasionally, a piece of writing seems to open with the essential thought of the selection. Actually, this may serve only as a transitional sentence leading to the dominant theme. Sometimes no one sentence states the major theme. The reader then must synthesize the theme from a number of related ideas found throughout the writing. The following selection from Benjamin Franklin illustrates this kind of writing:

There are two ways of being happy; we may either diminish our wants or augment our means. Either will do, the result is the same. And it is for each man to decide for himself, and do that which happens to be the easiest. If you are idle or sick or poor, however hard it may be for you to diminish your wants, it will be harder to augment your means. If you are active and prosperous or young or in good health, it may be easier for you to augment your means than to diminish your wants. But if you are wise, you will do both at the same time, young or old, rich or poor, sick or well. And if you are very wise, you will do both in such a way as to augment the general happiness of society.

Franklin seems to present the entire theme in the opening sentence, but does not. We might abstract the essential idea in the following statement: "We may be happy either by reducing our wants or increasing our ability to satisfy our wants. A wise man will do both. A very wise man, in doing both, will also try to make society happy."

The Emotional Structure

Few selections are totally devoid of feeling. Even the minutes of a meeting (wholly objective if they are properly written) carry emotional connotations for those who attended. Usually, the writer creates a mood, an atmosphere, an attitude or a feeling. In poetry and dramatic literature

---

[6] Nicholas Murray Butler, *True and False Democracy*, New York: Macmillan, 1907, pp. 14–15.

this is always true. It is likewise true for speeches to entertain, stimulate, and convince. Only a most objective, scientific report may lack an emotional appeal—unless it is described as "dreary" for the uninformed. And for those in the field, it may prove delightfully stimulating, even emotionally irritating.

Just as it was necessary to state the author's theme in as few words as possible for the logical analysis, so in our search for the emotional structure, it is important to translate the *dominant mood* into a word or a phrase. Possible terms might include *joy, sorrow, hate, eeriness, anger, reverence, righteous indignation, respect, trust, "other-worldliness," humility, awe,* and any other words that express an emotional state. Sometimes the author expresses the mood directly; for example, he may say, "It was an eerie night on the moor, a night fit for murder." More often the writer will describe, suggest, and add detail until we are overwhelmed with *terror* as we are when we read in Edgar Allen Poe's *The Tell-Tale Heart*:

No doubt I now grew very pale; but I talked more fluently and with a heightened voice. Yet the sound increased—and what could I do? It was a low, dull, quick sound—much such a sound as a watch makes when enveloped in cotton. I gasped for breath—yet the officers heard it not. I talked more quickly—more vehemently; but the noise steadily increased. I arose and argued about trifles, in a high key, and with violent gesticulations; but the noise increased.

In some selections the dominant mood is presented at the outset, while the theme is withheld until later. Such was the case when Harold Macmillan faced the television cameras immediately following the French veto of British entry into the Common Market. The prime minister immediately revealed his bitter disappointment and dismay over what he and many of his listeners considered the arbitrary and unfair action of General de Gaulle and the French government:

What has happened at Brussels yesterday was bad: bad for us, bad for Europe, bad for the whole free world. A great opportunity has been missed. Now, it is no good trying to disguise or minimize that fact. What we and our friends were trying to do at Brussels was something very creative and imaginative—dramatic. We were trying to stengthen the whole of Western Europe in a way which would spread all over the free world.[7]

Francis Thompson in his poem "In No Strange Land," establishes both the basic idea and the dominant mood in the opening stanza.

In No Strange Land

O world invisible, we view thee,
O world intangible, we touch thee,
O world unknowable, we know thee,
Inapprehensible, we clutch thee.

---

[7] *Vital Speeches* (March 15, 1963), p. 332.

Does the fish soar to find the ocean,
The eagle plunge to find the air—
That we ask of the stars in motion
If they have rumour of thee there?

Not where the wheeling systems darken,
And our benumbed conceiving soars!—
The drift of pinions, would we hearken,
Beats at our own clay-shuttered doors.

The angels keep their ancient places;—
Turn but a stone, and start a wing!
'Tis ye, 'tis your estrangèd faces,
That miss the many-splendored thing.

But (when so sad thou canst not sadder)
Cry;—and upon thy so sore loss
Shall shine the traffic of Jacob's ladder
Pitched betwixt Heaven and Charing Cross.

Yea, in the night, my Soul, my daughter,
Cry,—clinging Heaven by the hems;
And lo, Christ walking on the water
Not of Gennesareth, but Thames!

                              FRANCIS THOMPSON

MASTERING DETAILS

After reading a selection and analyzing the author's purpose, background, and method and becoming aware of the dominant theme and mood of the selection, we are ready for the next step—mastering the details.

Word Meanings and Sensory Images

We have already considered word meanings, at least those we can find in the dictionary. But the perceptive reader goes beyond the denotative definitions to look for shades of meanings, the subtleties, the implications, and the innuendoes. These submeanings are found not only in the connotations of the words, but in the relationship of word to word, phrase to phrase, and sentence to sentence. They are found in the sensory images these words invoke in the reader. Unless we understand the full meaning of the written words and respond to the imagery, we are bound to fall short of knowing the full meaning of what we have read, and, obviously, if we do not understand or sense what we have read, we cannot possibly communicate the meaning and sensation to others. The study of details, then, begins with a study of words and images.

We have already emphasized the necessity for consulting the dictionary for unfamiliar words. We may also need dictionary assistance when familiar words puzzle us by the context in which they are used. But some word meanings go beyond any dictionary. Take the word, "fire," for example. The dictionary lists some ten or twelve meanings, but it hardly hints at the terror this word inspires when shouted in a crowded theatre.

Affective Language

To some words we respond primarily with feeling rather than with thinking—if we can really separate the two responses. Further, we can speak almost any word in a way that makes its significance affective rather than intellectual. But with written language we must depend upon context and word selection to promote an emotional effect. Much of this sensation comes to us in that degree to which we are able to respond to the imagery the author's words are intended to produce.

Kinds of Images

Modern psychologists have isolated and added to the traditional five senses. For our purposes, however, if we add *motor* imagery to *sound, taste, smell, touch,* and *sight,* we can probably describe adequately most of the literary images. As you read the following selections, try to discover what sensations you experience. If you feel no sensation at the moment of reading, you are perhaps (1) merely pronouncing the words, (2) unaware of the meaning, (3) unfamiliar with the experience, (4) failing to *react* to the imagery.

Auditory Imagery.   Auditory images cover all the variations of sound, including pitch, quality, force, and duration, coupled with sweetest and sourest of musical notes or noises. Involved too are the onomatopoetic uses of words such as *hiss, buzz, whirr, whine, scratch, snarl, purr.* Reread the selection by Poe (page 368) and you will notice, in spite of the combination of images, a strong auditory impulse. Or listen to the "Ode for Music on St. Cecilia's Day," by Alexander Pope:

> In a sadly-pleasing strain
> Let the warbling lute complain:
>   Let the loud trumpet sound,
>   'Till the roofs all around
>   The shrill echoes rebound;
> While in more lengthened notes and slow
> The deep, majestic, solemn organs blow. . . .

Gustatory Imagery.   The taste buds are capable of strong reactions, and words themselves can set the salivary glands into action as they encounter the bitter, sweet, sour, or salty. The material following the first two lines in the stanza from John Keats' "The Eve of St. Agnes" are rich in gustatory imagery:

> And still she slept an azure-lidded sleep,
> In blanched linen, smooth, and lavender'd,
> While he from forth the closet brought a heap
> of candied apple, quince, and plum, and gourd;
> With jellies soother than the creamy curd,
> And lucent syrups, tinct with cinnamon;
> Manna and dates, in argosy transferr'd
> From Fez; and spiced dainties, every one,
> From silken Samarcand to cedar'd Lebanon.

Olfactory Imagery. Many consider the sense of smell one of the most powerful in moving the emotions, perhaps because it is linked to taste as well. In *A Christmas Carol,* Charles Dickens put together a mixture of smells, at least some of which the reader needed to experience to enjoy the description:

Hallo! A great deal of steam! The pudding was out of the copper. A smell like a washing day! That was the cloth. A smell like an eating-house and a pastry-cook's next door to each other, with a laundress's next door to that! That was the pudding!

Tactile Imagery. *Contact, pressure, intensity,* and, extent of *pressure, hardness, smoothness, roughness, softness, stickiness, sharpness, bluntness, claminess, wetness.* These and countless other words describe our reactions to touch. If as a reader you are responding to the images, you will feel something of the sensations H. G. Wells describes in *The Time Machine*:

While I stood in the dark, a hand touched mine, lank fingers came feeling over my face. . . . I felt the box of matches in my hand being gently disengaged, and other hands behind me plucking at my clothing.[8]

Visual Imagery. Probably the major element is color, but we also respond to brightness, shade and line as well. The imagery in the sonnet "Westminster Bridge" by William Wordsworth is mostly visual.

> Earth has not anything to show more fair.
> Dull would he be of soul who could pass by
> A sight so touching in its majesty:
> This City now doth, like a garment, wear
> The beauty of the morning; silent, bare,
> Ships, towers, domes, theatres, and temples lie
> Open unto the fields, and to the sky;
> All bright and glittering in the smokeless air.

[8] *Seven Science Fiction Novels of H. G. Wells.* New York: Dover, 1934, p. 46.

Never did sun more beautifully steep
In his first splendour, valley, rock, or hill;
Ne'er saw I, never felt, a calm so deep!
The river glideth at this own sweet will:
Dear God! the very houses seem asleep;
And all that mighty heart is lying still!

Motor Imagery. In "A Musical Instrument" by Elizabeth Barrett Browning appears a combination of auditory and motor images as the great God Pan "hack'd and hew'd as a great god can." The empathic muscle reactions we receive while watching an athletic contest shows the potency of this image. Amy Lowell in "A Winter Ride" catches the inspiration of motor impulses and if we are sensitive to the selection, we experience the muscle sensation too.

Who shall declare the joy of the running!
Who shall tell of the pleasures of flight!
Springing and spurning the tufts of wild heather,
Sweeping, wide-winged, through the blue dome of light.[9]

While reading any material, particularly poetry and drama, we must remain sensitive and alert to discover and to react to the images. Occasionally, we may respond to words affectively even though the writer intended them as essentially informative words. Our faulty response is probably a result of the prejudices and sterotypes which are a part of our upbringing. Scientific writing frequently contains words used informatively which most of us use only for affective purposes. If the reader analyzes his material and properly understands the method and purpose of the author, he will not confuse the affective word with the informative word merely because superficially they look alike.

PHRASING

The next basic step, closely related to determining word meaning and imagery, is the understanding of the phrasing. In written language, phrases are usually set off from one another by punctuation marks. But these marks are intended primarily for the silent reader, and the presence or absence of punctuation marks does not determine how we should read a sequence of words aloud. A phrase is a unit of thought. It may consist of a single word or of a group of words so related as to comprise a thought unit. Unless we have a thought unit, we have no true phrase. If conventional punctuation is misleading as to the thought units, then the reader must establish a "decent disrespect" for punctuation.

The oral reader faces three problems in phrasing:

1. He must determine the units of meaning.

---

[9] From *A Dome of Many-Coloured Glass* by Amy Lowell. Reprinted by permission of Houghton Mifflin Company, Boston.

2. He must decide how long a phrase he can legitimately expect his listeners to follow.

3. He must discover how long a phrase he is physically able to sustain.

The reader may occasionally find it necessary to break up a long phrase into two or more subphrases for the practical purpose of presenting the unit of words (thought) without labored breathing. From the point of view of oral language, then, *a phrase may be defined as a group of related words normally uttered without interruption for breath.*

Relationship of Ideas

Phrasing, however, includes more than the determination of thought units and appropriate length. The reader must also discern the relationship of unit to unit and to the material as a whole. At this point, then, the reader can decide how much emphasis each phrase should receive in terms of the whole selection. Of course, he must also analyze each phrase to determine which word presents the core-meaning. The reader must give special emphasis to the word or words that carry the heart of the message.

Clearly, the problem of phrasing is largely one of evaluation. The reader decides on the major units of meaning and the core of each unit. Having made these decisions, he next determines how he can communicate the related meanings to his listeners. Unfortunately, no absolute rules exist to guide the reader in his recognition of relative meanings, dominant thoughts, and subordinate thoughts. In general, however, the reader may assume that new ideas are more important than old ideas. A new idea when read aloud should, therefore, receive greater emphasis than an old idea. We may consider a "new idea" as one introduced for the first ·time; an "old idea" has already been presented in one form and is now being presented in a different or expanded form. This will become clear in an analysis of the following selection. The *"new ideas" are underlined;* the "old ideas" are printed without underlining.

When I Was One and Twenty[10]

When I was one-and-twenty
I heard a wise man say,
'Give crowns and pounds and guineas
But not your heart away;
Give pearls away and rubies
But keep your fancy free.'

---

[10] From "A Shropshire Lad"—Authorized Edition—from *Complete Poems* by A. E. Housman. Copyright © 1959 by Holt, Rinehart and Winston, Inc. Reprinted by permission of Holt, Rinehart and Winston, Inc., by The Society of Authors as the literary representatives of the Estate of the late A. E. Housman, and by Messrs. Jonathan Cape Ltd., London, publishers in England of A. E. Houseman's *Collected Poems.*

> But I was one-and-twenty,
>   No use to talk to me.
> When I was one-and-twenty
>   I heard him say again;
> 'The heart out of the bosom
>   Was never given in vain;
> 'Tis paid with sighs a-plenty
>   And sold for endless rue.'
> And I am two-and-twenty,
>   And, oh, 'tis true, 'tis true.

A. E. HOUSMAN

Suppose we examine Housman's poem for phrasing. The first phrase, we find, is the entire first line, "When I was one and twenty." In preparing to read this selection aloud we might mark off the phrases by placing, tentatively, a vertical mark (|) at the end of each phrase. As we read the selection, it becomes apparent rather quickly that all phrases are not of equal weight in their relationship to one another. Some phrases introduce "new ideas," others modify or expand "old ideas." Some phrases appear to be in direct contrast with others, their thoughts are not only "new" but different. In reading aloud to communicate thoughts to another, we may pause after each thought. In general, we pause longer when introducing a closely related idea. As a practical device we might add a second vertical line (||) to indicate a longer pause before the reading of a new or different thought; the single verticle line (|) may be used to separate phrases which are closely related in thought. The poem with phrase markings and "new thoughts" indicated might be arranged as follows:

> When I was one-and-twenty |
>   I heard a wise man say, |
> 'Give crowns and pounds and guineas ||
>   But not your heart away; ||
> Give pearls away and rubies ||
>   But keep your fancy free. ||
> But I was one-and-twenty, |
>   No use to talk to me. ||
> When I was one-and-twenty |
>   I heard him say again, ||
> 'The heart out of the bosom |
>   Was never given in vain |
> 'Tis paid with sighs a-plenty |
>   And sold for endless rue? ||
> And I am two-and-twenty ||
>   And oh, | 'tis true, | 'tis true. ||

We are now ready to reread the selection to determine which words carry the main meanings. As we indicated earlier, these are the basic or core words of the selection. We must emphasize these words so clearly and precisely that the listener will recognize at once the meaning, mood, and image the author of the selection had in mind. We might begin by asking ourselves, "What is the general theme of the poem? What, above all else, does the poet mean by his two stanzas?" The answer might be summed up in two sentences: "At twenty-one the poet was advised that it is easier and less expensive to give material things away than to give his heart away. At twenty-two the poet realizes that he should have followed the advice given him at twenty-one."

Which words present this dominant meaning and which words present the shades, implications, and modifications of the dominant meaning? The important words are those underlined once. These should be emphasized. The key or basic words are underlined twice. Those should be given even greater emphasis so that the listener cannot help but remember them.

TIIE TECHNIQUES OF READING ALOUD

Thus far in this chapter we have been chiefly concerned with how the reader can make certain that he gets the meaning of what he is reading. Unless the reader understands what he has read, unless he appreciates the thinking and feeling of the author, he has only a small chance of getting the thoughts and feelings across to his listeners. But to have good understanding of what is read is not enough! The effective reader-speaker must know how to communicate his knowledge to his listeners. He must know the techniques of translating written symbols into audible symbols so that his audience can share ideas with him.

Communicative Reading

Basic to all technique is the necessity for a clear, vivid portrayal of the author's intended meaning and mood to the listeners. This does not imply that the reader necessarily employ the "conversational mode," a "folksy literalness," or a highly "stylized" dramatic delivery. If the reader is delivering a speech, the chances are that he should try to keep his reading as close to excellent public speaking as possible. If his purpose in the speech is to entertain, he might assume a "folksy" manner of reading. The interpreter of Shakespeare will probably give the passage a decided dramatic flavor.

Communication is possible only if the reader is thoroughly familiar with his material. Indeed, he must so thoroughly master the word units and thought sequences that it will hardly matter if he loses his place on the written page. He can read from memory or substitute a word of his own for the word he can't find and still keep the proper ideas flowing. The reader can accomplish this feat only if he has become a creative as well as a re-creative artist. He has taken the work of another, and while remaining as true to the original as is humanly possible, he has, at the same time, read it with the only equipment at hand—his own experience, his own background —his own evaluations of another person's written words.

Mastery of Pronunciation

The reader not only should know what the words look like, but also should be certain of the sound of the words. All of us recognize at sight many words we have never attempted to pronounce. The first attempt at pronunciation should not take place before an audience interested in getting ideas. The one final way of preparing to read aloud is *to read aloud*. If doubt arises as to the pronunciation of a word, we should consult the dictionary and then say the word aloud several times in the context of the material. An incorrectly pronounced word will distract or confuse listeners and will probably cause them to lose confidence in the reader.

Audience Contact

Thorough familiarity with the written material makes it possible for the reader to keep in contact with his audience. The written page, we noted earlier, inevitably constitutes some degree of barrier between the speaker and his listeners. Each time the speaker takes his eyes away from his audience to look at the written material, direct eye contact with the audience is broken.[11] Contact may be maintained by the voice if the reader, knowing what comes next, continues to speak the phrase he remembers as next. Effective reading involves speaking what the eye has seen and the mind recalls. An effective reader has his eye a jump ahead of his voice. The word *jump* is intended literally, because good reading takes place in jumps or sweeps of the eye. A number of words are scanned, the eye pauses, the mind absorbs and translates written symbols into meanings, and the eyes move onto the next group of words. In oral reading we can train ourselves to take in long phrases quickly without losing the place on the page. In direct, expository material the reader should look directly at his audience as often as he can and for proportionately as long a period of time as possible. With practice, a courageous reader can learn to spend 75 to 80 per cent of his time in direct eye contact with his listeners, and 25

---

[11] We do not mean to imply here that every time the reader looks up from every kind of material, he must look directly into the eyes of some member of the audience. With highly introspective, emotional material, the speaker may even avoid eye contact, looking instead, like the actor, just over the heads of the audience.

per cent or less with the written page. But he can develop this skill only if he is familiar, almost to the point of having memorized his material.

Almost, but not quite to the point of memorization. Why not complete memorization? The answer is that complete memorization results in a loss of spontaneity. Memorized reading, to sound conversational and spontaneous, takes more time than most readers can afford. Effective memorized reading must *not sound memorized*. It must avoid sounding automatic and stilted. To sound spontaneous and conversational in reading from memory, the reader must memorize words and inflections and pauses as well as accompanying gestures. Even hesitations should be memorized so that the reading will not sound memorized. This becomes the job of the actor rather than that of the reader or speaker.

Vocal Variety

Good reading should be as close to good speaking as the situation permits. Good speaking calls for a speaker's voice that has variety. In an earlier chapter on the components of speech, we related voice variety to meaning and emphasis. This relationship is as important in reading as in public speaking or conversation. Pitch changes, for example, communicate both thought and feeling. In reading aloud, the range of pitch change is generally wider than in conversation. A large audience or a room separating the speaker from his listener calls for increases in any vocal changes the speaker employs.

Fundamentally, all vocal changes depend on the nature of the material and the meaning and mood of the selection. By way of review, we recall that high pitch and wide range is related to heightened emotion; low pitch and narrow range to depressive emotional states. Inflectional changes are used for intellectual implications and to indicate phrasing. A phrase which presents an incompleted thought will end with an upward, or rising, inflection; a phrase which presents a completed thought will end with a downward, or falling, inflection. Aside from phrasing, upward inflections imply doubt or uncertainty, deference, and occasionally weakness or cowardice. Downward inflections, on the other hand, imply completion, decision, certainty, and assurance. The following sentence illustrates the use of inflectional changes in phrasing.

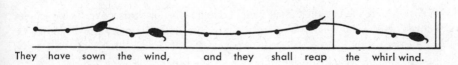

They have sown the wind,   and they shall reap   the whirl wind.

Of course, these principles are general and every reader must understand his material thoroughly, react totally and completely to the feeling and imagery. Without this total reaction any resort to planned vocal variety will probably produce merely a stilted and artificial sound.

Pitch Change

We may give ideas emphasis through the use of *pitch variation*. An important word in a phrase may be emphasized by raising the pitch level of that word above the level of the other words. Occasionally, we may emphasize a word by lowering rather than raising the pitch level. This kind of change is especially appropriate if the content is extremely serious or solemn. The essential point to remember is that change or variety attracts attention, and that which attracts attention will likely be remembered. Thus the job of the reader is to use vocal variety, in all its aspects, to emphasize the important content he wants his listener to remember. The example used above also illustrates the use of pitch change for emphasis.

Rate

The *rate of speech* in reading, especially of prose, is generally slower than that of conversation. This is especially true of material which is read during the course of a speech. The very fact that the speaker has chosen to read something rather than to present the material extemporaneously, implies that the material is important. Serious or profound matter calls for a slow rate of reading. Solemn content requires a very slow tempo. Content which is on the light side, the gay or trivial, calls for a comparatively rapid rate of reading. No selection of any length should be spoken at a uniform rate. If the general tempo of a selection is slow, the less important ideas will be spoken somewhat more rapidly that the more important ideas. Similarly, if a selection calls for a dominantly rapid rate, the words or phrases which are most significant should be spoken more slowly than the less significant words.

In reading prose or poetry we may vary the rate in two ways. The more usual way is through varying the duration of utterance of the individual speech sounds, especially of the vowels, diphthongs, and voiced consonants. Sentences such as those below from Lincoln's "A House Divided" should be uttered slowly. The underlined words should be spoken at an especially slow rate.

A <u>house</u> divided <u>against</u> itself cannot stand. I believe this <u>government</u> cannot <u>endure</u>, permanently <u>half slave</u> and <u>half free.</u> I do not <u>expect</u> the <u>Union</u> to be <u>dissolved</u>—I do not <u>expect</u> the <u>house</u> to <u>fall</u>—but I do expect it will <u>cease</u> to be <u>divided.</u> It will become <u>all one thing,</u> or <u>all</u> the <u>other.</u>

The second, and less usual, method of varying rate is through the *use of pause*. When we pause before a word we bring attention to the word that follows. In addition, a pause before a word produces a dramatic effect and creates a state of incompletion or suspense. The state of incompletion becomes satisfied by the word or phrase which follows the pause. In using pause for dramatic effect, the speaker should be certain that what he has to say is worthy of the preceding pause. To pause before the unimportant or the insignificant amounts to making too much out of too little. It reveals poor evaluation on the part of the reader and causes the listener to have a "let-down," disappointed feeling because he was led to expect more than he received.

To pause after a word or phrase is another method of creating emphasis. This device permits an idea to "sink in" into the listener's mind. Our minds tend to abhor emptiness. If, even for a moment, we hear nothing, we begin to recall the last item we heard. To pause after an item is equivalent to repeating the item, except that the listener rather than the speaker does the repeating.

In Shakespeare's *King Henry VIII* as Cardinal Wolsey sees the "frown" of the king, hears the taunts of his enemies, and recognizes the incontrovertible proof of his malfeasance in office, he realizes that his personal and political fortunes are at an end. In Wolsey's poignant soliloquy that follows, the symbol (||) will be inserted where such pauses may be effectively used. Again, we would caution that no two readers will read the same passage in precisely the same way and that no particular way is necessarily "correct."

> Farewell! (||) a long farewell, to all my greatness! (||)
> This is the state of man: (||) today he puts forth
> The tender leaves of hopes; tomorrow blossoms,
> And bears his blushing honors thick upon him; (||)
> The third day comes a frost, a killing frost,
> And, when he thinks, good easy man, full surely
> His greatness is a-ripening nips his root,
> And then he falls, as I do. (||) I have ventured
> Like little wanton boys that swim on bladders,
> This many summers in a sea of glory,
> But far beyond my depth: my high-blown pride
> At length broke under me and now has left me,
> Weary and old with service, to the mercy
> Of a rude stream, that must for ever hide me. (||)
> Vain pomp and glory of this world, I hate ye: (||)
> I feel my heart new open'd. O, how wretch'd
> Is that poor man that hangs on princes' favors! (||)

Force

Changing force or loudness is usually the least subtle way of using voice variety for emphasis. The naive speaker increases the volume of his voice for the important things he has to say and decreases the volume for the less important. If there is no need to be subtle, if a straight story is being read or a simple announcement being presented, emphasis through change in voice volume is in order.

Although we generally expect the emphasized idea to be spoken more loudly than the unimportant, there are exceptions to this rule. A marked decrease in volume will attract attention merely by the degree of change. If, for example, we read a sentence such as "Please dear, be still" with the last two words barely audible, the idea of stillness is impressed by the lack of force.

The well-trained speaker uses a change of force subtly and sophisticatedly. Deliberate, degree-by-degree change in volume, usually from low intensity to high intensity may produce a dramatic effect. It is important that the changes in volume are made smoothly, and that the material read is worthy of the technique employed. The effect of a gradual increase in loudness is to point to a climax. The material, therefore, should be such that the final idea at the height of the crescendo is climactic. We occasionally find this kind of material in impassioned prose; more often it is found in drama or poetry.

John Gillespie Magee, Jr., the young poet-flier who was killed in action three days after Pearl Harbor while on duty with the Royal Canadian Air Force gives us a poem rich in motor imagery. In "High Flight" the entire selection seems to build in intensity, requiring gradually increased vocal force until the reader reaches the last three lines.

High Flight[12]

Oh! I have slipped the surly bonds of Earth
  And danced the skies on laughter-silvered wings;
Sunward I've climbed, and joined the tumbling mirth
  Of sun-split clouds,—and done a hundred things
You have not dreamed of—wheeled and soared and swung
  High in the sunlit silence. Hov'ring there,
I've chased the shouting wind along, and flung
  My eager craft through footless halls of air. . . .

Up, up the long, delirious, burning blue
  I've topped the wind-swept heights with easy grace,
Where never lark, or even eagle flew—
  And, while with silent, lifting mind I've trod
  The high untrespassed sanctity of space,
Put out my hand and touched the face of God.

PILOT OFFICER JOHN GILLESPIE MAGEE, JR.

---

[12] In Hermann Hagedorn, *Sunward I've Climbed: The Story of John Magee, Poet and Soldier, 1922-1941.* New York: Macmillan, 1942, p. 7. Reprinted by permission of the poet's mother, Mrs. John G. Magee.

Quality

Emotional implications in reading, as in speaking, are projected through *changes in the tone quality* of the voice. The basic quality of the voice is subject to limited modification, and tone qualities are not readily taught. Like emotions, they are more easily caught. A specific tone quality such as we might associate with love, anger, fear, awe, or sorrow is attained through a combination of vocal factors. The combination includes muscle tension of the body as a whole and the vocal folds in particular, plus resonance and force. The vocal quality suggestive of fear can best be produced when the muscle tensions and "set" of the body are ones which are associated with a state of fear. The pitch will tend to be high, and the volume either very great or barely audible.

The use of tone quality as a special device for emphasizing emotional meanings will usually be reserved for artistic rather than informative reading. Such situations will include dramatic or imaginative prose or poetry and content in general having affective rather than informative language.

Action

Gesture and pantomime are added means of giving emphasis to thoughts when reading aloud to an audience. The speaker's inclination in reading, unless he has memorized his material, is to use less bodily movement than in extemporaneous speaking. The need, however, is for more rather than less movement. More visible action is needed in order for the speaker to gain a feeling of freedom which is restrained by the need to "stick to a set text." Written material, we recall, serves as a barrier between speaker and listener. The use of gesture and pantomine help to overcome the effects of the barrier.

The ability to execute an appropriate gesture or to use movements of the body as a whole (pantomime) becomes an effective test of the reader's capacity to understand what he has read. Actions are the outer manifestations of inner changes. If a reader knows his material thoroughly, he has experienced thoughts and feelings which have produced inner responses. These need to be translated to outer responses so that the observant listener can react to them and so get meanings out of what is being presented.

FINAL CONSIDERATIONS

Reading aloud, it begins to appear, is a more difficult method of public communication than is extemporaneous speaking. To read aloud well, especially when another person's material is being read, requires not less but more preparation than does speaking without manuscript. Despite the inherent disadvantages of the method, reading aloud is frequently a necessary mode of transmitting ideas and feelings. The techniques considered in this chapter need to be studied to insure effective communication.

A final word of caution is in order. The reader has an ethical obligation to an author, which is *never to modify intentionally* the context or manner of reading so that the reader's wishes rather than the writer's thoughts and feelings are presented. While it is true that we can read only in terms of our own experiences and our own backgrounds, we need to study the author's work until we can faithfully project the intended meaning. A reader may make an honest error of not understanding an author's meanings. That is unfortunate! But if a reader knowingly reads material in such a manner that the writer's meanings are perverted, the situation is considerably more that just unfortunate. In reading aloud, the reader-speaker is a translator of thought. His job is not to create new thoughts or feelings but to re-create those supplied to him by an author—the original creator. The reader's job is one of interpretation. His function is to transmit content with the least possible change. Effective use of the techniques of understanding written words and of presenting them to an audience help in accomplishing a safe and honest delivery.

Questions and Exercises

1. Select a famous American orator of the nineteenth century, e.g., Lincoln, Bryan, Ingersoll, Webster, Clay, or Calhoun, and write a five-minute radio speech on one phase of his speech-making. Prepare to read your speech to the class or if a tape-recorder is available, your speech may be recorded in advance and played back to the class.

2. Find two poems in which the basic mood of the one contrasts with the other. Prepare to read them in a manner designed to project the mood of each selection. Be ready to defend your method and explain to the class your techniques.

3. Select a short essay, requiring about five minutes for oral reading, and prepare ·to read it to the class. As a part of your preparation, prepare the following:

(a) a *precis,*

(b) a statement of the author's purpose in writing the essay,

(c) a list of words whose meanings (denotative) were unknown or not quite clear.

4. Find six selections in either prose or poetry to illustrate each of the kinds of imagery (motor, sound, taste, smell, touch, or sight) and prepare to read them to the class.

5. Cite three works of literature (prose or poetry) which could not be properly understood without a knowledge of the author's life. Prepare to read one of these selections aloud to the class.

6. Work out a short story in pantomime. Using no words, set up a short scene (two or three minutes) and try to convey the meaning solely through facial expression, gesture and bodily action. The class may attempt to discover what "idea" or "situation" you are portraying.

7. Write out and read to the class a description (with or without dialogue)

of the story or event you acted out in pantomime. How much of the physical activity of the pantomime carried over to the oral reading?

8. Watch a television news reporter read the news. Write a short critique including the following judgments:

(a) his freedom or lack of freedom from the manuscript,

(b) his use of phrasing,

(c) the transmission of meanings.

9. Analyze a selection of prose or poetry for the use of *affective language*. Compare the affective meaning the author has given the words with the literal meaning or meanings.

10. Prepare to read a literary essay from the works of a prominent nineteenth-century essayist. For your preparation, determine the author's purpose, his method, and the central theme of the essay. Write his theme in a brief sentence.

RECOMMENDED READINGS

Aggertt, Otis J., and Bowen, Elbert R. *Communicative Reading.* New York, Macmillan, 2nd ed., 1963.

Cobin, Martin. *Theory and Technique of Interpretation.* Englewood Cliffs, N. J.: Prentice-Hall, 1959.

Grimes, Wilma H., and Mattingly, Alethea S. *Interpretation.* San Francisco: Wadsworth, 1961, Chap. 4.

Lee, Charlotte I. *Oral Interpretation.* Boston: Houghton Mifflin, 1959, Chaps. 6, 7, and 8.

Lowrey, Sara, and Johnson, Gertrude. *Interpretative Reading.* New York: Appleton-Century-Crofts, 1953.

Parrish, Wayland Maxfield. *Reading Aloud.* New York: Ronald, 1953.

Woolbert, Charles H., and Nelson, Severina E. *The Art of Interpretative Speech.* New York: Appleton-Century-Crofts, 1956.

INDEX

[385]